THE SPY IN
THE TOWER

THE SPY IN THE TOWER

THE UNTOLD STORY OF JOSEF JAKOBS, THE LAST PERSON TO BE EXECUTED AT THE TOWER OF LONDON

GISELLE K. JAKOBS

For my Dad, Raymond,
who never knew what
happened to his father.
Until now.

Jacket Illustrations: *Front:* Josef Jakobs in April 1940. (Jakobs
family archives); *Back:* Chair in which Josef Jakobs was executed. Photo
taken circa 1970s. (*After the Battle* magazine – used with permission);
Author Photograph: Craig Fulker (c) 2019.

First published 2019

The History Press
The Mill, Brimscombe Port
Stroud, Gloucestershire, GL5 2QG
www.thehistorypress.co.uk

British Library Cataloguing in Publication Data.
A catalogue record for this book is available from the British Library.

ISBN 978 0 7509 8930 5

Typesetting and origination by The History Press
Printed and bound in Great Britain by TJ International Ltd

CONTENTS

AUTHOR'S NOTE

I began this journey over thirty years ago, seeking to answer the question: 'Who was my grandfather, Josef Jakobs?' The answer has been a long time coming. He was a rogue and a scoundrel. He was brave and courageous. He was a dentist and a criminal. He was a husband and a philanderer. He was a complex individual whose motivations were not always clear.

I can say this: Josef Jakobs loved his family above all else. It is a tragedy that his final letter, written on the night before his execution, was only handed to his two granddaughters in 1993, fifty-five years after his death. On the other hand, I am grateful that we received the letter and were able to give it to our father, Josef's youngest son. Thankfully, Josef's letter did not meet the same fate as the letters of the other spies – released to the National Archives in the late 1990s with their declassified MI5 files.

The process of uncovering Josef's story has involved many side excursions into the declassified files of the other spies sent to England by the German Abwehr. Sometimes, in genealogy, when one is stymied in a vertical direction, a breakthrough can happen by exploring laterally: siblings, aunts, uncles, etc. I experienced similar breakthroughs in researching Josef's case.

I must admit to being fascinated by the stories of the characters I discovered during my research, and their relationship to Josef. Connecting with their children and grandchildren has been very enriching. Thank you.

ABBREVIATIONS

English

AAG	Assistant Attorney General
AB	Alberta – Canadian province
AG	Attorney General
B1a	British Security Service (MI5) B Division – the section concerned with the double-cross system and run by Major T.A. Robertson. Originally B2a but was renamed B1a in mid 1941.
B1b	British Security Service (MI5) B Division – the section that analysed Abwehr decrypts and other intelligence related to the double-cross system. Originally B2c but was renamed B1b in mid 1941.
B1c	British Security Service (MI5) B Division – the section concerned with counter-sabotage. Originally B18, it was renamed B1c in mid 1941.
B1e	British Security Service (MI5) B Division at Latchmere House (also known as Ham or, later, Camp 020). Originally BL or B8a, it was renamed B1e in mid 1941.
BAOR	British Army of the Rhine (after the Second World War)
BBC	British Broadcasting Corporation
BC	British Columbia – Canadian province
CAB	Cabinet Office records at the National Archives

CMP	Corps of Military Police
CRIM	Central Criminal Court records at the National Archives
CSDIC	Combined Services Detailed Interrogation Centre
CT	Continental time
DB	Director B Division, British Security Service (MI5)
DDB	Deputy Director B Division, British Security Service (MI5)
DDG	Deputy Director General, British Security Service (MI5)
DG	Director General, British Security Service (MI5)
DPM	Deputy Provost Marshal
DPP	Director of Public Prosecutions
DPS	Director of Personal Services
DR	Defence (General) Regulations 1939
GCCS	Government Code & Cipher School
GIS	German Intelligence Service (see also GSS)
GOC	General Officer Commanding
GPO	General Post Office
GSS	German Secret Service (German Abwehr – Abteilung I – Espionage) (see also GIS)
HO	Home Office records at the National Archives
J	Supreme Court Judicature records at the National Archives
JAG	Judge Advocate General
KV	Security Service records at the National Archives
LCO	Lord Chancellor's records at the National Archives
LMA	London Metropolitan Archives
LRC	London Reception Centre (see also RVPS)
MEPO	Metropolitan Police records at the National Archives
MI5	Military Intelligence, Section 5 – British Security Service
MI6	Military Intelligence, Section 6 – British Secret Service or Secret Intelligence Service
Mk	Mark (German currency)
OSA	Official Secrets Act
PCOM	Prison Commission and Home Office records at the National Archives

POW	Prisoner of War
PREM	Prime Minister's Office records at the National Archives
PWIB	Prisoner of War Information Bureau
RAF	Royal Air Force
RAOC	Royal Army Ordnance Corps
RG	General Register Office records at the National Archives
RM	Reichsmark (German currency)
RSLO	Regional Security Liaison Officer, British Security Service (MI5)
RSM	Regimental Sergeant Major
RSS	Radio Security Service (MI8c, transferred to MI6 in mid 1941)
RVPS	Royal Victoria Patriotic Schools (see also LRC)
SIS	British Secret Intelligence Service (MI6)
SLB	British Security Service (MI5) – legal section concerned with prosecution of spies. Originally B13, but was renamed SLB in mid 1941.
SOE	Special Operations Executive
SS	British Security Service (MI5)
TNA	The National Archives
WEA	Western European Area
WO	War Office records at the National Archives
WORK	Office of Works records at the National Archives
XX	British Double-Cross System

German

ABT	Abteilung – German Abwehr Section
Abteilung I	Section I – Espionage/intelligence
Abteilung II	Section II – Sabotage
Abteilung III	Section III – Counter-intelligence
Abwehr	*Amtsgruppe Auslandsnachrichten und Abwehr* – essentially the German armed forces' Intelligence Service
AST	*Abwehrstelle* – Abwehr station in each military district within Germany

FHW	*Fremde Heere West* – Foreign Armies West – military intelligence under the Supreme High Command of the German army, received intelligence from the *Abwehr*
Gestapo	*Geheime Staatspolizei* (Secret State Police) under the RSHA
Nachrichtendienst	Intelligence Service – often used as a synonym for the Abwehr
OKW	*Oberkommando der Wehrmachts* – German Army High Command
Referat I Luft	subsection of Abteilung I concerned with gathering air intelligence
Referat I Marine	subsection of Abteilung I concerned with gathering naval intelligence
RSHA	*Reichssicherheitshauptamt* (Reich Main Security Office)
SD	*Sicherheitsdienst des Reichsführers-SS* (Security Service of the Reichsführers-SS) – intelligence agency of the SS (*Schutzstaffel*) and the Nazi Party in Nazi Germany – under the RSHA
SS	*Schutzstaffel* (paramilitary organisation of the Nazi Party)
X	Military District 10

ACKNOWLEDGEMENTS

I would not be sitting here today were it not for two men: Winston Ramsey (editor of *After the Battle* magazine) and Nigel West (well-known author and intelligence expert). They opened the door and revealed a treasure trove of information on my grandfather. Their support over the decades has been amazing.

I am indebted to a long list of the children and grandchildren of key characters in the Josef story. Thank you for sharing your stories with me: Sylvia Paskin (L. Knips), Kate Snell (W. Chidlow), Martyn Smith (H. Jaikens), Claire Robertson (H.C. Bäuerle), Richard Hall (W.E. Hinchley-Cooke), Adrian Birt (R.W.G. Stephens), Ted Watling (A. Watling), Martin Dearden (Dr H. Dearden), Pete Saul (H. Saul), Ramsey Hertzog (Dr W. Hertzog), Julia O'Grady (H. Coulson), Hannah Emmington-Thomas (C. Baldock), James Grew (B.D. Grew), Collinette (Gordon) Compton (C.V.T. Gordon), Melanie Veness (A. Haigh), Martha Fitzner (H. Fitzner), Guillermo Fitzner (H. Fitzner).

Special thanks to Kate Snell, Sylvia Paskin, Martyn Smith and Claire Robertson for graciously sharing photographs and allowing permission to publish them.

The National Archives provided the bulk of research material for this book. It was always a pleasure to visit the archives and dig into their files using their efficient system. All files in the National Archives are © Crown Copyright and are reproduced with permission under the terms of the Open Government Licence. Quotes from Hansard contain parliamentary information licensed under the Open Parliament Licence v3.0.

Other archives, museums, curators and researchers have also been most helpful: London Metropolitan Archives, Historic Royal Palaces,

Royal Armouries (Bridget Clifford), HM Prison Wandsworth (Stewart McLaughlin), Guards Museum (Andrew Wallis), Guards Archives (Leighton Platt), Ramsey Rural Museum (Martin Lovell), RHQ Royal Military Police (Richard Callaghan), Museum of Army Chaplaincy (David Blake), St Mary's Roman Catholic Cemetery, Kensal Green (Anna Humphrey), Military Provost Staff Association (Lester Pearse), King's College London (Joe Maiolo), Military Intelligence Museum (Alan Fred Judge) and Military Wireless Museum (Ben Nock).

Thanks are also extended to the following for their assistance in diverse ways: Mrs Enid Smith (Lord Chancellor's Office), Alan Fiddes (former Yeoman Warder, Tower of London), Jacqui Farnham (BBC), Father Rupert McHardy (Brompton Oratory), Nick Hinton (Gurkha Regiment), Traugott Vitz (author), Chris Bilham (author), Eckhard Froeb (Notar), A. Cebrian (pharmacist) and Stewart Jackson (Dovehouse Farm).

I am deeply grateful to Tony Kemp, Dr Paul L. Smith, David Auton, Rose M. Palfy and Lori J. McGinlay for reading various iterations of the manuscript. The feedback was always helpful and has guided me on this journey.

Many thanks to David Tremain (author) for breaking trail on the publishing front and answering my many questions. Your tips, advice and encouragement are much appreciated.

I would be remiss if I did not also acknowledge Starbucks® for providing me with writing space and wireless access.

Finally, this book would not have been possible without the staunch support of my family: Anne Taylor, Raymond Jakobs, Pamela Jakobs and Hildegard Jakobs. You believed, even when I sometimes lost hope, focus and umph!

DRAMATIS PERSONAE

Anderson, John — Secretary of State for the Home Department and Lord President of the Privy Council.

Baldock, Charles — Farm labourer who found Josef Jakobs near Ramsey, Huntingdonshire.

Bäuerle, Hedwig Clara — German cabaret singer and actress – mistress of Josef Jakobs.

Beier, Dr — Alias for Julius Jacob Boeckel.

BISCUIT — MI5 double agent, Sam McCarthy.

Boeckel, Julius Jacob — German Abwehr – Ast Hamburg – trained LENA agents – alias Dr Beier.

Brodersen, Knut — Norwegian – Abwehr agent, arrived in Scotland in early 1944.

Butler, Richard — MI5, SLB – involved in prosecution of spies.

Canaris, Wilhelm — Head of German Abwehr.

Caroli, Gösta — Swedish – Abwehr agent sent to England in September 1940 – double agent SUMMER.

Chidlow, William — Corps of Military Police – guarded Josef Jakobs from 23 July to 15 August.

Cornish, George Mervyn — Officer Commanding, Holding Battalion, Grenadier Guards.

Coulson, Harry — Farm labourer who found Josef Jakobs near Ramsey, Huntingdonshire.

Cowgill, Felix — MI6, Deputy Head of Section V.

Curedale, John	Ramsey Home Guard – involved in apprehension of Josef Jakobs.
Cussen, Edward James Patrick	MI5, SLB – involved in prosecution of spies.
De Deeker, Franciscus	Belgian – alias of Karl Theodore Druecke.
Dearden, Harold	MI5 – physician at Latchmere House.
DeGraaf, Johannes	Dutch-Canadian – Abwehr agent, arrived in England in late 1942.
Dierks, Hans	German Abwehr – Ast Hamburg.
Dixon, Cyril E.	MI5 – Regional Security Liaison Officer (RSLO) in Cambridge.
Dronkers, Johannes Marinus	Dutch – Abwehr agent, arrived in England in May 1942.
Druecke, Karl Theodore	German? – Abwehr agent, arrived in Scotland in September 1940.
Elkan, Abraham Wolfgang	German-Jewish stepfather of Josef Jakobs' wife.
Eriksen, Vera	Danish-Russian – alias of Vera von Wedel or Vera Schalburg, Abwehr agent who arrived in Scotland in September 1940.
Evans, Albert Daniel Meurig	MI5 – Latchmere House interrogator.
Frischmuth, Inspector	Alias for Walter Steffens.
Gerard, Charles Robert Tolver Michael	Deputy Provost Marshal, London District.
GANDER	MI5 double agent Kurt Karl Goose, aka Hans Reysen.
Glad, Tor	Norwegian – double agent JEFF.
Godfrey, James Harry	Ramsey Home Guard – involved in apprehension of Josef Jakobs near Ramsey, Huntingdonshire.
Goodacre, Edward Brereton	MI5 – Latchmere House interrogator.
Goose, Kurt Karl	German – aka Hans Reysen – double agent GANDER.
Grant, Douglas	Metropolitan Police, Special Branch.
Grew, Benjamin Dixon	HM Prison Wandsworth – Governor.
Hansen, Nikolai S.M.	Norwegian – Abwehr agent arrived in Scotland in September 1943.

Harker, Oswald Allen	Deputy Director General, MI5.
Heddy, William Reginald Huleatt	Coroner, East London District.
Hinchley-Cooke, William Edward	MI5, SLB – co-ordinated prosecution of spies.
Hippisley-Cox, Edward Geoffrey	Assistant Adjutant General, London District.
Jackson, Philip	Gunner with the Royal Artillery.
Jaikens, Horace	Huntingdonshire Constabulary, Ramsey Police – acting inspector.
Jakobs, Emma (née Lück)	Mother of Josef Jakobs, wife of Kaspar Jakobs.
Jakobs, Giselle	Daughter of Raymond Jakobs and granddaughter of Josef Jakobs.
Jakobs, Josef	German Abwehr agent.
Jakobs, Kaspar	Father of Josef Jakobs, former Catholic priest.
Jakobs, Margarete (née Knöffler)	Wife of Josef Jakobs.
Jakobs, Norbert	Eldest son of Josef Jakobs.
Jakobs, Pamela	Daughter of Raymond Jakobs and granddaughter of Josef Jakobs.
Jakobs, Raymond	Youngest son of Josef Jakobs.
Jakobs, Regine	Daughter of Josef Jakobs.
JEFF	MI5 double agent, Tor Glad.
JOHNNY	German Abwehr's code name for Arthur G. Owens (double agent SNOW to the British).
JULIUS	German Abwehr's code name for Josef Jakobs.
Kieboom, Charles Albert Van den	Dutch – one of the four spies who landed on the coast of Kent in September 1940.
Knips, Lily	German-Jewish – escaped from Berlin to London.
Knöffler, Alma Margarete	Wife of Josef Jakobs.
Lahousen, Erwin von	Head of Abteilung II, German Abwehr.
LEONHARDT	German Abwehr's code name for Wulf Schmidt (double agent TATE to the British).
Liddell, Guy	Director, MI5 B Division.

Lück, Emma	Wife of Kaspar Jakobs and mother of Josef Jakobs.
MacGeagh, Henry Davies Foster	Judge Advocate General.
Mackenzie, Eric Dighton	Officer Commanding, Holding Battalion, Scots Guards.
Malten, Major	Alias of Carl August Johannes Merker/ Merkel.
Margesson, David	Secretary of State for War.
Marlowe, Anthony Alfred Harmsworth	Lawyer for the prosecution at court martial of Josef Jakobs.
Marriott, John H.	MI5 – Secretary, Double-Cross Committee.
Masterman, John Cecil	MI5 – Chairman, Double-Cross Committee.
Maxwell, Alexander	Permanent Undersecretary of State, Home Office.
McCarthy, Sam	British – MI5 double agent BISCUIT.
Meier, Carl	Dutch-German – one of the four spies who landed on the coast of Kent in September 1940.
Merker/Merkel, Carl August Johannes	German Abwehr - Ast Netherlands - Referat I Luft - responsible for dispatching agents by air (alias Major Malten)
Mills, Thomas Oliver	Huntingdonshire Constabulary.
Milmo, Helenus Padraic Seosamh	MI5, Head of B1b – section that analysed Abwehr decrypts and other intelligence related to the double-cross system.
Moe, John Herbert Neal (Helge)	Norwegian-British – double agent MUTT.
MUTT	MI5 double agent, John Moe.
Neukermans, Pierre Richard Charles	Belgian – Abwehr agent, arrived in England in July 1943.
Newton, William Henry	Officer Commanding Ramsey Home Guard – involved in apprehension of Josef Jakobs.
O'Grady, Dorothy Pamela	British housewife on the Isle of Wight charged under the Treachery Act.

Owens, Arthur Graham	Welsh – double agent (SNOW to to the British and JOHNNY to the Germans)
Petrie, David	MI5, Director General.
Petter, Robert	possible real name of Werner Heinrich Walti.
Pons, Sjoerd	Swedish – one of the four spies who landed on the coast of Kent in September 1940.
Popov, Dusko	Yugoslavian – MI5 double agent TRICYCLE.
Pottle, Ernest	Ramsey Police – acting sergeant stationed in Bury.
Praetorius, Friedrich Karl	German Abwehr – Ast Hamburg.
Purchase, William Bentley	Coroner, North London District.
Rammrath, Egon	German – involved in black-market passport business with Josef Jakobs.
Rantzau, Dr	Alias for Nikolaus Ritter.
Reiwald, Herr and Frau	German Jews – Herr Reiwald was a former patient of Josef Jakobs and introduced him to Rammrath. Frau Reiwald introduced Lily Knips to Josef Jakobs.
Reysen, Hans	German – aka Kurt Karl Goose – double agent GANDER
Richter, Karel	Sudeten Czech – Abwehr sent to England May 1941.
Ritter, Nikolaus	German Abwehr – Ast Hamburg – alias Dr Rantzau.
Roberts, Owen	Dulwich Hospital physician in charge of care of Josef Jakobs.
Robertson, Thomas Argyll	MI5 – head of B1a, double-cross system.
ROBOTER	German Abwehr's code name for Karel Richter.
Rothschild, Victor	MI5 – head of B1c, counter-sabotage.
Rowe, Harold A.	Pharmacist who filled prescriptions for Rudolf Hess and Josef Jakobs.

Ryde, Michael	MI5 – Regional Security Liaison Officer (RSLO) in Reading.
Rymer, James	Alias for Josef Jakobs on his forged British National Identity Card.
Sampson, George Frederick	MI5 – Latchmere House interrogator.
Sauer, Lothar	German–Jewish – son of Lily Knips.
Saul, Henry	Corps of Military Police – guarded Josef Jakobs from 23 July to 15 August.
Schmidt, Wulf	Danish – double agent TATE.
Scholz	German Abwehr – alias of an officer from the Abwehr's Hamburg office.
Sergison-Brooke, Bertram Norman	General Officer Commanding, British Army – London District.
Sessler, George	German Abwehr – Ast Hamburg.
Short, Roland Alfred Frederick	MI5 – Latchmere House interrogator.
Sinclair	Alias for George Sessler.
Sinclair, D.H.	MI5, SLB – involved in prosecution of spies.
SNOW	MI5 double agent, Arthur Graham Owens.
Somervell, Donald Bradley	Attorney General.
Spilsbury, Bernard	Pathologist.
Steffens, Walter	German Abwehr – Bremen – alias Inspector Frischmuth.
Steiner, Florent	Dutch-Belgian – Abwehr agent, arrived in England in June 1941,
Stephens, Robin William George	MI5 – Latchmere House commandant and interrogator.
Stimson, Douglas Bernard	MI5 – Latchmere House administrator.
Stirling, Carl Ludwig	Deputy Judge Advocate General – served as Judge Advocate at court martial of Josef Jakobs.
SUMMER	MI5 double agent Gösta Caroli.
Swinton, Philip Cuncliffe-Lister	Chairman of the Home Defence (Security) Executive.
TATE	MI5 double agent Wulf Schmidt.
Taylor, R.W.	Medical officer at the Tower of London.
Timmerman, Alphons Louis Eugene	Belgian – Abwehr agent, arrived in Scotland in September 1941.

Tindal Atkinson, Edward Hale	Director of Public Prosecutions.
TRICYCLE	MI5 double agent Dusko Popov.
Van Hees	German – friend of Josef Jakobs.
Vivian, Sylvanus	Registrar General.
Waldberg, Jose	French? – one of the four spies who landed on the coast of Kent in September 1940 (in his appeal, he claimed that he was French and that his real name was Henri Lassudry).
Walti, Werner Heinrich	Swiss – aka Robert Petter – Abwehr agent, arrived in Scotland in September 1940.
Waters, Philip Duncan Joseph	Scots Guards (Holding Battalion) – officer in charge of execution of Josef Jakobs.
Watling, Alfred	Corps of Military Police – guarded Josef Jakobs from 23 July to 15 August.
White, Dick Goldsmith	Deputy Director, MI5 B Division.
White, Eric Vincent Ewart	Lawyer for the defence at court martial of Josef Jakobs.
Wichmann, Herbert	German Abwehr – Head of Ast Hamburg.
Wilford, Arthur	Scots Guards (Holding Battalion) – RSM in charge of execution.
Winn, Thomas Leith	MI5 – Latchmere House officer.
Winter, Franciscus Johannes	Belgian – Abwehr agent, arrived in Scotland in July 1942.
Ziebell, Jürgen	German lawyer involved in black-market passport business with Josef Jakobs.

FOREWORD
BY NIGEL WEST

In 1992, Prime Minister John Major appointed William Waldegrave, then Secretary of State for Health, as Chancellor of the Duchy of Lancaster; a Cabinet post without any specific portfolio. His assignment was to concentrate on science and ways of improving Whitehall administration. High on his list of goals was the Open Government policy, which was intended to reflect the conditions of the post-Cold War era when the United States was basking in what was then termed the 'peace dividend'. The Soviet bloc had collapsed, Russia had outlawed the Communist Party and Congress had embraced the principles of freedom of information.

In Great Britain, where Whitehall secrecy was an accepted part of the fabric of society, along with an unwritten constitution and the ubiquitous royal prerogative, any proposition to alter the thirty-year rule relating to the public disclosure of a limited class of government documents was regarded as iconoclastic and potentially dangerous. Nevertheless, the Waldegrave initiative took the opportunity to canvass all government departments in an effort to identify papers that could be safely declassified.

A surprising participant in this exercise was the Security Service, headed from October 1996 by Stephen Lander, a Cambridge history graduate who had joined the organization in 1975 from a history fellowship at Liverpool University. Although other branches of the British Intelligence community recoiled instinctively from the Open Government review, Lander, the director of H Branch (the relatively new corporate affairs division), embraced the concept and advocated greater engagement with the public. As a former director of T Branch, the counter-terrorism unit responsible for coordinating the defeat of the Provisional IRA, Lander's views were widely respected and held great weight. By the end of the decade, some 96,000 Whitehall files had been reviewed and released in an unprecedented process of declassification, a new work in the lexicon of Whitehall mandarins.

This was the cultural breakthrough, accompanied by the Freedom of Information Act 2000, which came into force in 2005, that allowed researchers to lift the lid on thousands of investigations conducted by the Security Service over the previous hundred years. Initially, MI5 lodged pre-war files, and then ventured into the archive of Second World War cases that might otherwise have been subjected to the time-honoured 'weeding' procedure and, most likely, been destroyed.

Happily, it has been this extraordinary reversal of political and administrative attitudes in Britain that has facilitated researchers such as Giselle Jakobs to search for her family's history and reconstruct the poignant story of her grandfather's role as an Abwehr spy, dispatched by a Luftwaffe parachute on a futile espionage mission to collect intelligence and, perhaps more importantly, to check up on Wulf Schmidt, a suspected double agent. At stake was the credibility of the now-celebrated Double Cross System, a sophisticated deception programme that was supervised by skilled MI5 case officers who sought to manipulate – and ultimately control – all the enemy's active spies.

If Josef Jakobs had succeeded in his mission, and confirmed what Schmidt's Hamburg controllers had already guessed, several other linked networks would have been compromised, thereby jeopardising the entire scheme. It is only now, with the benefit of access to the original MI5 dossier on Jakobs, that we can fully grasp the ironies and tragedy of how an unassuming Luxembourg-born dentist came to land to Huntingdonshire in 1941, to ultimately find himself facing a firing squad in the Tower of London.

Nigel West
Spring 2019
www.nigelwest.com

1

BROKEN FROM THE VIVID THREAD OF LIFE[1]

Josef leaned on his crutch at the window overlooking the concrete court-yard of Wandsworth Prison.[2] As the setting sun disappeared behind the rooftops, it set fire to the clouds overhead. He watched the sun gild the hairs on the back of his hand. He clenched his fist and tried to capture the light in his grasp. It was impossible, but his skin soaked up the sun's rays never-theless. He marvelled at the miracle of life – the ability to clench his fist and to open it, to feel each finger connected to the others through mus-cles, tendons and bones. The sunlight slipped from his hand and was gone. The light could not be captured and now the gathering darkness of night loomed before him. The sun had disappeared behind the buildings, but the gleam of its light lingered in the heavens, colouring the clouds an unearthly shade of orange and red. It was the last time he would witness a sunset.

The day had been filled with many last things – his last midday meal, his last supper, his last sunset, his last full day of life. He stared at his watch as it ticked away the seconds with unwavering precision. He could do nothing to stop time. He could only savour the small joys in each moment – swallows in flight, pink clouds in the sky, laughter that drifted over the prison walls. Too soon, it would all be gone.

The day of last things was coming to a close, but he had one last thing to do, something that he had prayed would not be necessary. He had hoped that a reprieve would arrive at the eleventh hour. There was none. The desk and chair in the corner of the cell waited for him. The paper and pen waited for him. He ignored their call, his eyes fixed on the view from the window. The gathering gloom dulled the colours outside. The glow from the departed sun had died. There was only twilight, that time when the world was caught between day and night, caught between light and dark, caught between life and death. He knew that place of twilight well, having lived in it for the previous eight months. As the light of day slipped towards the darkness of night, he knew that he needed to turn from life and face death.

One of his guards moved towards the window to draw the blackout curtains while the other stood ready to turn on the cell's lights. Josef asked for more time, just a bit more time. The guards glanced at each other and nodded their agreement. Silence settled over the room. Josef was alone with his thoughts.

The sky had darkened, and the first stars appeared, dotting the sky with points of light. He had gazed at these stars for months, his constant companions in this strange land. The stars appeared night after night and he knew that those same stars watched over his family almost 600 miles to the east. They had seen the same stars. They had seen the same sunset. The night sky was his connection to his wife and children. He wondered if they had gazed up at the stars and prayed for his safety. He had certainly prayed for theirs and he believed, with heartfelt conviction, that they were safe.

To the east, the horizon lightened slightly as the waning moon crept above the London skyline. Gazing at its scarred visage, he felt its connection with the departed sun. Even though the sun was gone, the lunar surface reflected the departed sun's light back at Josef, offering reassurance and hope. Soon enough, he too would be gone; his light would set and that would be the end. Or so it would seem. The moon told him differently. He believed with all his being that, even though the light of his spirit might disappear from the world, he would continue for eternity.

The wind shifted slightly and carried the faint tolling of Big Ben. He cocked his head, listened intently and counted the tolls. Another day had ended and a new one was in its infancy, scarcely a few seconds old. It was Friday, 15 August 1941, the Feast of the Assumption of Mary into Heaven or *Maria Himmelfahrt* in German. It was the last day of his life. It was his Good Friday. Today was the day of his suffering, his death and, he prayed, his entry into heaven. The hours slipped away so quickly and soon enough he would have to leave this place.

The changing of the day also signified the changing of his guard. With murmured apologies, one guard drew the blackout curtains. When they were tightly closed, the other guard turned on the lights. A knock at the door heralded the entrance of the new guards.

Josef was relieved. He knew these two well – Chidlow and Saul. There was a flurry of activity as the departing guards gathered up their kit, shook

Josef's hand and left the cell. Josef chatted briefly with Chidlow and Saul.[3] They asked him if he had written his letter and he shook his head. The two men offered him encouragement and then sat at a small table and gathered up a deck of cards. A quiet game of whist was in order. In the distance, Big Ben tolled a lone note. Josef sighed. It was time.

The wooden chair was hard. The desk was scarred and stained. He stared at the creamy blank sheets of paper embossed with the royal coat of arms. Squinting in the dim light, he could just make out the inscription beneath the rampant lion and unicorn: *Dieu et mon droit*. An ironic chuckle escaped him as his fingers caressed the coat of arms.

The inscription translated as 'God and my right'. The British monarch had exercised his right and denied Josef's request for mercy. For Josef, there was no way out; earthly judgement had been passed but it was not the only one he would endure. There was the eternal judgement and he knew that God would be his ultimate defender. He had done what he had to do, to the best of his ability, and he trusted God to take care of the rest; to take care of his family. Big Ben tolled twice … the hours passed so quickly.

He stared at the paper, blank and inviting, waiting for him to write the words of his heart on its surface. He picked up the pen, uncapped it, and began to write:

London, the 15th August 1941
On the Holy Feast of the Assumption of Mary

My dear, dear wife,

When you, my much beloved Gretchen, receive this letter, I will already be standing before the eternal Judge! For today is my last night on this earth, on the Sacred Feast of the Assumption of Mary, I hope to be well prepared to take the journey to eternity. In just 5 hours, I will be shot at the Tower of London, after I was brought before an English War Tribunal on August 5 on charges of espionage and condemned to death. I want to quickly tell you, how it came to that … [4]

He lifted the pen and looked up at the window. How could words written with pen and paper convey what was in his heart? Words were too fragile to carry the weight of his love; too weak to carry the depth of his compassion. He wished that he could speak to his loved ones. He wished that he had said more on that last night in Berlin. He wished that he had known how it would end. Had he known, he would have said it all. He would have said it many times, said it over and over again. Life would have been different; but there were no second chances in the game he had played. There was only a prison cell, a window, a desk, a chair, a pen and sheets of paper.

After a fitful start, the pen moved smoothly, and the words flowed effortlessly from its tip. He knew he had less than an hour for, at 3 a.m., Father Griffith would come to celebrate the last rites with him. His last confession. His last anointing. His last Holy Communion.

He sat back and put the pen down. He had said all that he could say using pen and paper. He was grateful that he would at least get a chance to say farewell to his family in the sure knowledge that the letter would eventually reach them.[5]

There was a knock at the door and Father Griffith entered the cell. Josef was grateful to this priest who had visited him every day since the court martial. He had listened to Josef, consoled him, guided his soul through the long days and prepared him for the final moment.

The guards stepped out of the room while Griffith prepared the small table by placing a white cloth on it. He reverently removed the Blessed Sacrament from his case and laid it on the table. Pulling a crucifix out of his bag, he gave it to Josef, who kissed it and placed it on the table. Josef bowed his head and uttered his last confession, receiving absolution with a sigh of relief. Josef closed his eyes while Griffith anointed his eyes, ears, nostrils, lips, hands and feet with the Oil of the Sick. Murmuring in Latin, Griffith recited the time-honoured phrase for extreme unction (last rites): 'By this holy anointing and by His most tender mercy may the Lord forgive you all the evil you have done through the power of ... (sight, hearing, smell, taste and speech, touch, ability to walk).'[6]

The Latin responses flowed from Josef's lips with ease and a grateful heart. It was the last time he would speak those words. The last time he would hear the Word of God. It comforted him in a way that it had not always comforted him. For many years he had been a lukewarm Catholic, living a life that was less than ideal. The trials and tribulations of the last few months, however, had sent him running back to the bosom of Mother Church, seeking solace and forgiveness. He had found it. Josef opened his mouth to receive Holy Communion. A last murmured prayer and the rituals were complete.

Big Ben tolled four times. Time had grown exceedingly short. Josef had written to his family. He had worshipped his God. He sat now with his friends – the priest and the guards. He had only known these men for a short time and yet they had become true friends. He had laughed with them, played games with them. He had told stories about his wife and children and heard stories about their families. Although they were enemies, they were soldiers, and their stories were more alike than different. Even to these men, however, whom he counted as dear friends, he had not shared his last secret. As he pulled on his jacket, his fingers found the spot along the bottom seam and he smiled to himself. The British had searched him on numerous occasions, had interrogated him for seven and a half months, and yet they had never found the tiny reminders of home. Two small photographs gave him comfort and strength to face the next few hours. His family would be with him in his final hour. They might not know it, but he knew it, and that was enough.

It was almost time. He limped to the mirror on the wall and combed his hair. He stared into the eyes that gazed back at him. He saw a lifetime of memories reflected there. A lifetime of joy and regrets. Soon those eyes would lose their light and the mouth its smile.

He turned from the mirror as another knock at the door heralded the arrival of Lieutenant Colonel Hinchley-Cooke, Cussen, Sergeant Watling and the Deputy Provost Marshal. Josef handed his letter to Hinchley-Cooke, who assured him that it would be delivered to his family at the end of the war. It was time to empty his pockets. He had no need for the comb, the lighter, or the handkerchiefs. He laid them all out on the desk for Cussen to gather up.

With one last glance around the room, Josef picked up his crutches and limped out of the door. His guards were a mere formality, for he could not have run from them even had he desired. The clicking of their heels echoed in the vaulted rotunda that formed the heart of the prison.

Josef paused at the top of the narrow spiral staircase and carefully set his foot on the first tread. Stairs were still an obstacle for him, but one that was not insurmountable. The procession paused as Josef methodically stepped down the stairs. Once again on level ground, the group picked up their pace and turned down one of the corridors radiating off of the rotunda. Ahead, a light shone from an office where Prison Governor Grew stood silhouetted in the doorway. The governor watched as the party approached him. Stepping to the side, Josef walked up to Grew, extended his hand and shook it. Josef thanked him for his courteous hospitality, clicked his heels and continued his journey.[7] The governor trailed behind the group as they exited the building and walked down the stairs into the forecourt where a pair of black cars with motorcycle outriders awaited them.[8]

The sky was shading slowly from black to grey. The sounds of London traffic drifted over the prison walls. Josef took a deep breath, and another. He savoured the beauty of breath, a thing he had once taken for granted but that had become an elixir to him. Tucked into one of the vehicles with Chidlow and Saul flanking him, Josef watched as the massive gates creaked open. His last journey had begun.

As the gates shut and cut off the view of the departing cavalcade, Hinchley-Cooke and Cussen took their leave of Grew, thanking him for his work. Years later, Grew would write, 'Of all the spies who faced execution I shall remember one [Josef Jakobs] for his soldierly manner, his courtesy and his quiet courage.'[9] Having watched Josef depart, Grew wrote, 'I remember I felt disinclined to return immediately to my office, and walked on for a short way still thinking of that firm handshake and the fast approaching end of a brave soldier.'[10]

Josef, the brave soldier, sat between Chidlow and Saul as the car wove through the streets of London. It was good to see the trees, to watch people going about their business. Soon enough, they passed over Tower Bridge and Josef saw the famous silhouette of the Tower of London, his final stop. He turned to Chidlow and offered him his reading glasses. He had no need of them anymore. It was small thanks for the many kindnesses shown to him by this military policeman, and Chidlow accepted them in the spirit with which they were offered.[11]

The car pulled up at the massive gates of the Tower and, after a brief consultation with the guard, the gates creaked open. A short drive, another guard, another gate. A sharp turn to the right and they were within the Tower. Josef and his entourage climbed out of the vehicles. Josef looked up at the massive walls that surrounded him on all sides. The first rays of the sun struck fire into the stones of the Tower. It was his last sunrise.

His guards escorted him into a room where he eased himself onto a chair with relief. Walking was painful and, even with his crutches, drained him of energy. An officer approached him with a medical bag clutched in his fist. Did Josef need anything to calm the nerves? Josef shook his head with a smile and sat in a bubble of peace as the others bustled around. He could hear the tramp of feet and the low murmur of voices outside. The firing squad was getting ready and so must he. A quick prayer, a caress of the photographs tucked in the seams of his coat.

His heart began to beat more quickly. Perhaps a sedative would be a good idea. The medical officer was summoned, and Josef swallowed the pill that was offered to him.[12] He thanked the officer and squared his shoulders. It was time.

A soldier opened the door. The end was coming. Josef stood and limped outside, accompanied by the priest and his guards. With halting steps, Josef navigated the cobblestones and stopped before a low wooden shed. He took one last look around him. The squad of soldiers stood nearby, waiting for him. There were eight of them. They looked very young. He turned his gaze upwards and stared at the sun. His parents had always told him not to look directly at the sun, that he would ruin his eyes, but now it mattered not at all. He looked and felt the full blast of the light in his eyes. Blinking back the tears, he allowed Chidlow and Saul to lead him into the dark interior of the shed.

A table with eight rifles was positioned across the width of the room near the doorway. A chair sat at the far end, tied to a wooden beam. A major appeared and led Josef and his entourage to the chair. With a nod from the major, the guards took the rope and tied Josef securely to the chair. A black mask was produced by the medical officer and Josef asked that he be allowed to face what was to come, but his request was denied.

The mask descended over his head and the light was gone. The priest murmured a last prayer and Josef felt his fingers make the sign of the cross on his forehead. He felt fumbling at his jacket as a target was pinned to his chest. Robbed of sight, Josef listened intently to the departing footsteps. A pause, and then the tramp of feet. The firing squad was getting into position. Silence surrounded Josef and then he heard the quiet click of eight safety catches being released. With a smile beneath his mask, Josef took one last breath and called out, 'Shoot straight, Tommies!'

They did not disappoint him. As the word 'Fire!' was shouted, a volley of bullets smashed into his chest.

2

SKELETONS IN THE CLOSET

I never knew my grandfather, Josef Jakobs. He died during the Second World War, decades before I was born. This is not unusual. Many people have fathers and grandfathers who died during the war. For many years I asked no questions about my paternal grandfather, in part, due to my father's own reticence. My father never spoke about his family, possibly because the last member died in 1971. He was the only survivor of the Jakobs family. There were no siblings, no cousins, no aunts or uncles. My father had left Germany in 1955 focused on creating a future in Canada, not bemoaning the past in Germany.

By my late teens, however, I had developed an interest in genealogy. I wanted to learn more about my German roots. One day, as my mother and I were sorting old family photographs, I asked her about my grandfather, Josef Jakobs. She told me that she didn't know all that much about him. She pulled a tattered orange paperback off my father's bookshelf – *Game of the Foxes* by Ladislas Farago. She flipped through the pages of the book, found a dog-eared page and pointed to one line, which read, 'Two of the seventeen spies sent to Britain in 1941 were tried *in camera* and paid the supreme forfeit. One was Josef Jakobs, a 43-year-old meteorologist from Luxembourg.'[1] That line sparked a decades-long quest to discover the truth about my grandfather, the spy.

In the mid 1980s, I went to Vancouver (BC) to study at the University of British Columbia. In the pre-internet era, finding information on a German spy, who had parachuted into England, in a Canadian library proved to be a challenge. With Ladislas Farago as a beacon, I found two key resources: Nigel West's book on the British Security Service, *MI5: British Security Operations 1909–1945* (1982)[2] and Winston Ramsey's magazine article 'German Spies in Britain' in *After the Battle*.[3] Both resources gave me enough information to confirm that my grandfather, Josef Jakobs, was indeed the German spy who had landed in Huntingdonshire on 31 January 1941 and was executed at the Tower of London on 15 August 1941. I also learned that Josef's court martial had taken place in camera, which meant that the file would not be released until 2041. I had visions of myself as a septuagenarian, travelling to London to track down information on my grandfather.

In 1990, I contacted *After the Battle* magazine, and in September 1991 travelled to London to meet the magazine's editor, Winston Ramsey. He had generously arranged to take me on a private tour of many of the sites associated with Josef's time in England: the wartime interrogation centre at Latchmere House, the Duke of York's headquarters where the court martial had taken place, the Tower of London where Josef had been executed and finally, St Mary's Roman Catholic Cemetery in Kensal Green where Josef was laid to rest in an unmarked grave. During our visit to the Tower of London, I met the author Nigel West, who was also a Member of Parliament.[4] Nigel said that secrecy around wartime affairs was easing and the government was planning to release declassified material to the National Archives. He asked me what our family thought about releasing the file on Josef Jakobs. If we had no objections, then perhaps my father could write a letter to Nigel giving our approval. I thought it was a splendid idea.

When I returned to Canada, I drafted a letter and sent it to my father to sign. I should mention that my parents had just gone through an acrimonious divorce. My father was living in Edmonton (AB), my sister and I were attending university in Vancouver and my mother was holding down the fort at home. Divorces often end up with one party being vilified and, in this case, it was my father. I went through a period where I wanted very little to do with him and this happened just as I was starting to delve more deeply into my grandfather's past.

I was like a bloodhound on the scent of a great discovery. The quest for more information on Josef satisfied the researcher within me. The more information I found, the more information I sought. It would take a few years but eventually my wishes would be fulfilled.

Our letter to Nigel West wound its way through a bureaucratic maze and in 1993 we received word that the court martial file was going to be released to the National Archives. As fortune would have it, my sister and

I were planning a trip to Europe in late August of that year. It didn't take much to rearrange our trip to include a visit to London.

On 14 September 1993, my sister and I visited the Lord Chancellor's Office in Trevelyan House, Great Saint Peter Street, London. We were greeted by Mrs E. Smith, who seated us at a small table and presented us with a photocopy of the court martial documents. She then brought out an envelope that had been found in another file. The envelope was addressed to our grandmother, Margarete Jakobs, 124 Rudolstädter Strasse in Berlin, and was to have been delivered at the end of the war. It contained the letter that Josef had written to his wife and family on the night before his execution.

We were stunned and received the letter with awe and disbelief. Mrs Smith told us that she had sent a letter in mid August letting us know about it but it had not reached us before our departure:

> A number of people in other government departments here know that we have been in correspondence about this case. As a result, I have been asked to ensure that you receive the farewell letter written in 1941 by your grandfather addressed to Margaret [*sic*] Jakobs. This letter was intended for delivery after the cessation of hostilities but has only just come to light, and in view of the interest taken by both you and your father in Josef's case, we should very much like you to have the letter now.
>
> The letter will, I am sure, be of very special family significance, and for this reason I do not want to entrust it to the post. I should prefer to hand it to you personally when you are in London, and can either meet you at Kew or here in my office whichever suits you best.[5]

I would like to be able to say that my sister and I took the letter to the Tower of London, opened it there and read it in the place where Josef had been executed. While that might make for a good vignette in a movie, the truth is more pedestrian. My sister and I only opened the letter once we were back in Canada and were immediately stymied. While my knowledge of German might have been enough to navigate a typewritten document, Josef's handwriting was indecipherable.

A few weeks later, my mother came to Vancouver for a visit. We sat and listened while she read the letter out loud. We cried. This letter, written from my grandfather's heart, to his mother, wife and children, had never reached them. They had died not knowing what had become of their son, husband or father. All except one. Josef's youngest son, my father, was still alive.

After transcribing and photocopying Josef's letter, I mailed the original to my father in Edmonton. He had been following my research with keen interest, and while I might be giving him the cold shoulder, he very much wanted a renewed relationship. Later, he told me that if Josef's letter had been handed to him, he would have destroyed it without reading it.

That is, I suppose, the danger of delving into genealogy and family history. What begins as a quest for information, for names, dates, places and cold, hard facts, can sometimes end up unearthing something deeper and closer to the heart. Josef's letter had a different impact on each of us. After listening to Josef speaking across the decades, my sister turned to me, put her hand on my arm and said, 'You need to write his story.' Me?

Who was I to write the story of my grandfather? I was a researcher and a scientist. I was comfortable in the realm of facts, less so in the realm of emotions, morals and motivations. I was a Canadian of German ancestry. I knew the history of Germany during the Second World War and it bothered me deeply that my grandfather was in any way associated with the Nazi regime. He was a German spy. Did that also mean he was a Nazi? I wasn't sure that I wanted to know.

We had the court martial file, but I only glanced at it. What I saw frightened me. Josef testified at his court martial and, from my brief glimpse of the material, I could already see that he was not a sterling character. I wasn't sure that I was ready to see my grandfather as anything other than a man of upstanding moral fibre. I had yet to learn that humans are complicated creatures, that good and bad can live within the same person, within the same spirit. So, I didn't read the court martial document. I put it in a drawer and let it sit there; my quest for Josef was on hiatus.

In 2001, Josef would come knocking on my psyche again when his declassified interrogation file was released to the National Archives. I travelled to London in 2003 and examined the file. There was a vast amount of information contained within hundreds of pages: reports, interrogations, memos, photographs and X-rays. It was all there. I paid the National Archives the princely sum of £1 per page (£800 in total) to copy everything and send it to me in Canada. At one point in time, I had craved information, and now I was buried in it.

Through it all, however, Josef's letter called to me. That, and the words of my sister – 'You need to write his story.' I shared the story of my grandfather with others and they told me the same thing.

Finally, in 2008, I picked up the gauntlet and began to write. Writing Josef's story was not a smooth flow; it came in fits and starts. I had so much information, but I didn't have enough historical context. Josef's story took me down avenues I never would have dreamed of. It forced me to face skeletons rattling around in long-forgotten documents. It brought my father and I closer together. It was a joy. It was a struggle. How does one tell such a tale? How does one stay true to the historical facts, while still revealing the humanity that colours them? How does one move through the fear of what will be uncovered: that he was a German spy, and that he was involved in the persecution of the Jews?

I read many books about espionage during the Second World War. The books were thick with historical facts and technical details about spies, double agents, security services and counter-espionage. I did not wish to write such a book for it would be impenetrable to the average reader. Neither did I wish to write a book that was disconnected from history or from the facts of Josef's life.

In the end, I came full circle. I decided to write this book for my father, who was only 9 years old when Josef disappeared. Early in my research, my father asked me, 'Do you think Josef had a fair trial?' At the time, I answered in the affirmative. How could it be otherwise? He had been tried by court martial in England, a land renowned for fair play and even-handed justice. It seemed pretty black and white. England and the Allies were the good guys; Nazi Germany and the Axis were the bad guys. Now, after years of research, my answer is far more nuanced.

There is no doubt that the Nazi regime was evil and committed despicable acts. At the same time, not every person, nor every group, within Germany was 'Nazi' or supported acts of evil. There is no doubt that the world is a better place thanks to the Allies emerging victorious at the end of the Second World War. At the same time, sacrifices had to be made, particularly in 1940 and 1941, when England was faced with the terrifying spectre of a German invasion. As one legal historian noted, 'War is a rough business; you cannot make omelettes without breaking eggs.'[6] Josef Jakobs was one of those broken eggs.

This book is not a technical espionage book. It is based on historical facts but necessarily includes inferences, deductions and educated guesswork. There are numerous books that provide the historical context to the times and circumstances surrounding espionage in the Second World War. They are a useful backdrop to the story of Josef and are referenced in the bibliography.

Before we get into Josef's story, some background details will help the reader to situate themselves and become familiar with key players, although much will be explained as the story progresses. For the moment, it is enough to know that Josef's life was sucked into a tug of war between two intelligence agencies.

In the autumn of 1940, Josef was recruited into the German Intelligence Service, commonly known as the Abwehr. The Abwehr was the intelligence arm of the German army and was not directly associated with the Nazi Party. In late January 1941, Josef parachuted into Huntingdonshire in England; his mission was to send weather reports back to Germany.

He was apprehended by the British Home Guard the next morning and handed over to the British Security Service, known as MI5 (Military Intelligence 5). MI5 was responsible for counter-intelligence within the borders of Great Britain and they interrogated Josef at length about his mission and his relationship with the Abwehr. Much of what is to come is based on the information gleaned from those interrogations, mixed in with family information and other research.

Josef was a complex individual, with character flaws, who also showed bravery in the face of brutal treatment and bad luck. He was caught in a web of deceit between the Abwehr and MI5. The Germans sacrificed Josef to the cause of misinforming the British by persuading them that invasion plans had not been shelved. This was done so ineffectively that, at the same time, it helped to undermine the Nazi regime. It will also become apparent that the British were intent on speeding up, if not perverting, the course of justice in order to make an example of Josef.

As with many historical events, the full truth about Josef Jakobs will never be known. Eyewitness accounts are necessarily filtered through the lens of the observer. The people involved are long dead. The records that survive are fragmentary. History is an imperfect science, but I hope that this story, incomplete though it may be, will shed light on the life and times of Josef Jakobs, the last person executed at the Tower of London.

3

INAUSPICIOUS BEGINNINGS

In 1862, in the ancient German city of Trier, a baby boy was born to linen weaver Franz and his wife Margarete.[1] As the eldest son, much was expected of Kaspar, but rather than take over the family business when he came of age, Kaspar chose a different path. After several years of study, on 18 March 1893, Kaspar was ordained a Roman Catholic priest in the Diocese of Trier.[2]

With the Oil of Chrism still wet on his forehead, the Reverend Kaspar Jakobs was sent to St Ludwig Parish in Saarlouis-Roden to serve as assistant pastor.[3] Just over a year later, in July 1894, Father Kaspar was abruptly transferred to Küs, a wine-making village nestled in the snug embrace of the Mosel River. Father Kaspar barely had time to settle into the community before he was once again transferred, in April 1895, this time to the coal-mining town of Kirchen.[4]

Twenty years earlier, in 1875, in the village of Sassenroth, near Kirchen, a baby girl named Emma was born to coal miner Wilhelm Lück and his wife Anna-Maria. Emma and her sister Lucia were raised in a staunchly Catholic family and Lucia would eventually go on to become a Catholic nun. Emma, on the other hand, chose a different path. In April 1895, Father Kaspar Jakobs arrived at St Michael's Parish in Kirchen as assistant pastor and Emma was entranced.

A handsome young priest and a smitten young woman – the future parents of Josef Jakobs. Rumours about Father Kaspar and his indiscretions reached the ears of Bishop Korum in Trier. On 1 May 1897, Father Kaspar was removed from Kirchen, hauled back to Trier, and given a stern reprimand and an episcopal lecture on the vow of chastity.[5] Father Kaspar promised to do better and was quietly reassigned as Pastor of St Pankratius Parish in the village of Ehlenz, near Prüm.[6]

Despite the 100 or so miles that separated Kirchen and Ehlenz, the transfer of Father Kaspar solved nothing. In the autumn of 1897 Emma was living in Bickendorf, a hamlet a few miles from Ehlenz. Did Emma follow Kaspar? Or did Kaspar bring Emma with him? History doesn't say. Whatever the case might be, in September 1897 Emma became pregnant. Rather than face the consternation of parishioners as the pregnancy became visible, Kaspar made arrangements for Emma to live in Luxembourg City, a comfortable 45 miles from Ehlenz. It was a different country and, most importantly, a different diocese. It would be much easier to hide the birth of an illegitimate child from the ecclesiastical authorities in the Diocese of Trier.

On 30 June 1898, a boy was born in Luxembourg City to Emma and his birth was duly registered under the name Josef Lück.[7] No father was listed on the birth certificate and Emma stated that she was a cook living in Bickendorf. Emma returned to Bickendorf with Josef in tow. Kaspar would visit Emma and his infant son – a son who would eventually bear the name Josef Jakobs.

As with any village, tongues began to wag, and word soon reached the sharp ears of Bishop Korum. On 17 October 1898 Father Kaspar was transferred again, this time to the village of Büdlich, in the hills east of Trier. The bishop gave the struggling priest another stern lecture but doubted the sincerity of his vow to do better.[8]

As we have seen, distance was no barrier to Emma and Kaspar. On 17 July 1899, Emma gave birth to Emma Maria Lück in Luxembourg City.[9] No father was listed, and Emma gave her address as Bickendorf. A year later, on 19 July 1900, Emma gave birth to another girl, Lucia Margaretha Lück, who passed away seven weeks later.[10] Shortly before Lucia's birth, on 1 July 1900, Father Kaspar was removed from the parish of Büdlich.[11] He would not be transferred to another parish – at least, not within the Diocese of Trier.

In 1901, Kaspar was transferred to the Diocese of Fulda where he apparently served in a pastoral role for several months.[12] A choice was placed before Kaspar. He could disown his two surviving children and renew his commitment to his priestly vows or he could acknowledge his children and leave the priesthood. After much discernment, Kaspar chose to leave the priesthood and began the process of laicisation.[13] His discernment may have been influenced by another encounter with Emma in late 1901. Nine months later, on 10 September 1902, Anna Lück was born in Cologne.[14]

While Kaspar was disentangling himself from the clerical ranks of the Catholic Church, Emma had moved to the village of Kommern, south-west of Cologne. By 1903, Josef was of school age and, according to his school records, attended the *Volksschule* (elementary school) in Kommern from 1903 to 1905.[15] While Emma and the three children languished in the rural backwater of Kommern, Kaspar made his way to Berlin intent on speeding up the laicisation process and beginning a new career as a teacher.

On 1 August 1905 at the age of 7, Josef arrived in Berlin with his mother and sisters. Berlin was a different world to the bemused youngster, a far cry from the village of Kommern. Upon arrival in Berlin, Emma and her children lived in Prenzlauer Berg, at a home for unemployed Catholic women run by the Grey Nuns from Sacred Heart Parish. Kaspar was living in Wilmersdorf, a suburb of Berlin, with the priests from St Ludwig's Parish. Finally, on 19 October 1905 Kaspar and Emma were married at St Ludwig's Parish.[16]

The family settled in Wilmersdorf and found an apartment on Güntzelstrasse, a few blocks from St Ludwig's Parish. Josef and his sisters attended the local *Volksschule* while Kaspar taught at a local school – but with his eye set on opening his own private school. Emma looked after the children and attended daily Mass at St Ludwig's. While she and Kaspar were officially married, Catholic guilt wrapped Emma in a dark cloud. In 1908, Kaspar and Emma travelled to Luxembourg City and Cologne so that Kaspar could officially claim the three children as his own. Long marginal notes were inscribed in the birth registers and all three children received birth certificates that listed their surname as Jakobs.[17]

Shortly after their return to Berlin, the family moved to Pfalzburger Strasse 72a, half a block from St Ludwig's Parish. A year later, in 1909, Kaspar opened his own private school. He taught foreign students, primarily Spanish-speakers from South America and Spain, some of whom even boarded with the family. Josef picked up some Spanish from his fellow students and developed deep and lasting friendships.

In April 1913, Josef was sent to the Dominican boarding school in Vechta, near Oldenburg. According to his Vechta school records, Josef was not an outstanding scholar, although he did get good marks in religion, suggesting that a career as a Catholic priest might have been an option. Unfortunately, his Latin marks were very poor. Josef earned fair marks in French, Greek, earth science, nature studies and writing/drawing. He was less accomplished in history, mathematics and German.

Had Josef owned a crystal ball in 1913, he might have chosen English as a course of study, one that would have proved to be far more vital in 1941 than Greek, Latin or French.[18]

In December 1913, eight months after enrolling in the Dominican school, Josef returned to Berlin. Perhaps he was too rambunctious for the monks or perhaps he continued his studies under his father's tutelage. His schooling would be disrupted again when, less than a year later, Germany was sucked into the war to end all wars. Josef was barely 16 years old when war broke out, but even though he was underage, he enlisted with the eager naivety of youth. He was assigned to the 2nd Foot Artillery Regiment[19] based in Swinemünde on the Baltic coast. After six months, Josef was discharged due to ill health and returned to Berlin to complete his education and pass his *Abitur* exam.[20]

The following year, on 16 October 1916, Josef re-enlisted, this time entering the Guard Rifle Battalion[21] in Potsdam as a *Fahnenjunker* (officer cadet). A month later, he was placed on active service and transferred to the 4th Foot Guards Regiment,[22] where he was trained in heavy machine guns. The 4th Foot Guards had suffered heavy losses during the Battle of the Somme (1 July to 18 November 1916) and replacement troops were desperately needed.

After brief training, Josef and his comrades were sent to the Western Front. It was their first experience of the horrors of trench warfare: the mud, the stench, the splintered remains of forests, the rotting corpses. Luckily for Josef and his comrades, both sides had suffered much during the Battle of the Somme and their job was simply to dig in for the winter and hold the line. Easier said than done – the real enemy for the men on both sides of the conflict was the bitterly cold winter. The frozen ground made digging impossible. It was a challenge to simply survive.

After the harsh Somme winter, Josef's regiment engaged with the enemy between April and June of 1917 in the region of Aisne, Argonne and Rheims.[23] In June 1917, Josef was sent to Berlin for an officer's training course. A month later, on 2 July, Josef's regiment was transferred to East Galicia.[24] The Russians had launched the Kerensky Offensive and gained some ground. They needed to be taught a lesson. Fortunately for the Germans, the Russian Army was demoralised, with revolutionary agitators spreading defeatist rumours. The German counter-attack was swift and decisive. The Russians retreated quickly with the Germans hot on their heels. Unfortunately, the lack of logistical support meant that the Germans could not fully capitalise on the collapse of the Russian lines.

Josef had rejoined his regiment in July or August and likely participated in the fighting in East Galicia. It was a far cry from the grim deadlock that gripped the Western Front. In the autumn of 1917, Josef claimed to have received his commission as a lieutenant and to have been awarded the Iron Cross Second Class.[25]

On 12 October 1917, the 4th Foot Guards were transferred back to France.[26] Not much had changed while they were gone. The land was still a desolation of mud and shell holes. Josef spent another winter in the frozen trenches of the Western Front. In late February, he likely received a letter from home informing him that his youngest sister, Anna, had passed away.[27] She was only 15 years old, too young to die, but within a few short weeks, Josef himself would narrowly escape death.

As winter eased its grip on the entrenched armies, the German commanders came up with a plan to break the deadlock. The 4th Foot Guards were slated to take part in the German Spring Offensive of 1918, the *Kaiserschlacht* (Kaiser's Battle). The Americans had entered the war and the Germans would be hard pressed to compete with their seemingly inexhaustible supply of men and equipment. After four long years of fighting and millions of casualties, Germany was waging a war against attrition. This attack would be their last chance at victory.

Launched from the Hindenburg Line near St Quentin (France), the goal of the offensive was to break through the Allied lines and end the war, once and for all. It was a grand plan that was doomed to failure. On 21 March 1918, using artillery and elite shock troops, the Germans advanced quickly, breaking through the Allied lines. Josef and his comrades came after the shock troops, dealing with pockets of resistance. During this period, Josef claimed that he was awarded the Iron Cross First Class.[28] Less than ten days later, the German advance stalled. It was extremely difficult to move through the wasteland of mud and shattered trees. The German troops had advanced too far, too quickly, and their supply lines could not keep pace.

This was the same problem that had beset the Germans in East Galicia; an inability to capitalise on battlefield victories. The Allies were also not hamstrung by revolutionary agitators and did not flee like the Russians. Allied reinforcements were brought up and the Australian units proved to be a formidable foe. In early April, the Germans made one last effort to seize Amiens, an important transportation hub.

On 4 April 1918, fifteen German divisions attacked seven Allied divisions near Villers-Bretonneux. The Germans sought to seize the high ground near the town, from which they could then bomb Amiens into submission. British and Australian troops held the line and after fierce fighting the German commanders called a halt to the offensive on 5 April.

Despite having claimed almost 40 miles of territory, the Germans had failed to seize key strategic points. In the process they had suffered heavy casualties, one of whom was Josef Jakobs. On 4 April 1918, Josef was wounded by a shot to the right side of his chest during the attack near Amiens. Although Josef later claimed that he was severely wounded, the German casualty list noted that he was '*leicht verwundet*' (lightly wounded).[29] The German military doctors quickly assessed soldiers as lightly wounded or severely wounded. The latter needed immediate medical attention in order to be saved. Treatment of the former could wait and, if their condition worsened, they could be upgraded to seriously wounded. This method of triage allowed doctors to determine the best allocation of their medical resources. Years later, the doctors at a London hospital, would note that Josef's X-rays showed evidence of an old area of injury to his right chest. Despite the fact that Josef claimed to have been commissioned as a lieutenant, the German casualty list did not record him as an officer. It is possible that the German military bureaucracy hadn't updated their lists, or that Josef simply exaggerated.

After being wounded and processed through the field medic stations, Josef was sent to Berlin, where he was still convalescent in early November 1918 as the war sputtered to an end. His regiment, stationed on the Western Front, had been decimated in the final months of fighting and mustered only 150 men (out of a possible 3,000).[30] It was clear that defeat was inevitable, but the German leaders were oblivious to ominous currents swirling through the nation.

Almost a year after the Russian Revolution, the German Empire found itself fighting internal enemies in the form of Spartacists (Marxists) and Communists (Socialists). The stirrings of revolution took Kaiser Wilhelm by surprise and on 9 November 1918 he abdicated and fled to the Netherlands. The political void left by his departure was filled with turmoil and the revolution raged for several months.

As for Josef, he claimed that he rejoined his regiment after his convalescence and helped to quell street fights. Given that soldiers of the 4th Foot Guards Regiment had been demobilised in December 1918 as part of the Armistice, it was more likely that Josef joined the Free Corps Reinhard.[31] This volunteer paramilitary regiment was formed by Colonel Wilhelm Reinhard, a senior officer with the 4th Foot Guards Regiment. Having returned from the Western Front in late November, he found Berlin torn by violent revolutionary demonstrations.

Reinhard formed the regiment with the blessing of Social Democrat politicians and in late December 1918 assumed the post of Commander of Berlin at the request of the German Defence Minister.[32] Communism was now the enemy and Reinhard sought to eradicate the red menace from the streets of Berlin. By the summer of 1919, after months of street fighting, the battle had been won and the Weimar Republic was born.

Josef re-entered civilian life, battered and scarred, but alive. He had survived the war to end all wars and the German Revolution. He had no idea that, twenty years later, he would fight in another war – in another land … in another way.

4

DENTIST AND FAMILY MAN

After Josef left the military, he claimed to have attended the University of Berlin and studied dentistry.[1] What moved him to enter this field of study is lost to history. Perhaps he had bad teeth, or perhaps he recognised a lucrative business opportunity given the number of First World War veterans who needed facial and dental reconstruction.[2] In 1921, after two years of study, Josef claimed to have passed the *Physikum*, an intermediate examination for the degree of Doctor of Dentistry.

The only relevant document in the possession of the Jakobs family was a report card issued by the Imperial German Association of Independent Higher Boy Schools and Preparation Institutes in late September 1921.[3] The report card was issued to Josef upon completion of a four-day written exam and a one-day oral exam. Josef was tested in German, French, Latin, history, earth science, mathematics and physics. Overall, his marks were either good or satisfactory, a definite improvement over his middle-school marks. The exams may have been a prerequisite to entering a post-secondary institution or a requirement for studying abroad. By 1921, Germany was sliding towards a financial abyss and Josef may have sought greener pastures.

Following the Treaty of Versailles in 1919, Germany was ordered to pay $31 billion in war reparations (an unimaginable sum, equivalent to $442 billion in 2015). Forced to make payments in gold (which it did not have) or foreign currency (which it also did not have), the German government simply printed more money with which it bought foreign currency to pay down the debt. This created a bigger problem: the rapid devaluation of the German mark (Mk). In 1919 the exchange rate between the German mark and the US dollar was 7 to 1. By early 1922, the exchange rate had fallen to 320 to 1 and by December 1922, 800 Mk were required to buy $1. A year later, in November 1923, $1 was worth 4.2 trillion Mk.

Germany teetered on the brink of economic collapse. Hyperinflation meant that prices for common goods increased so quickly that shops and restaurants could not keep pace. A loaf of bread that had cost 1 million Mk in the morning might cost 10 million Mk in the evening. Workers were paid by the hour, on the hour, and rushed to give their wages to their relatives before the money was worthless. By 1 November 1923, 1lb of bread cost 3 billion Mk, 1lb of meat cost 36 billion Mk and a glass of beer cost 4 billion Mk. Unfortunately, while prices rose exponentially, savings accounts did not. The end result was that the pensions and life savings of common folk were wiped out, including those of Kaspar Jakobs.

All the more interesting, then, to see that Josef claimed to have left Berlin for Buenos Aires in late 1921, after taking the exams in September. According to Josef, his father had hosted many South American students at his private boarding school and Josef had become interested in South American culture. Josef likely departed via Hamburg or Bremen and, after weeks at sea, arrived in Buenos Aires. His Spanish must have been passable, for he enrolled in the local university and studied dentistry. Josef claimed that he passed the State Examination for Dentistry in Buenos Aires and received the degree of Doctor of Dentistry.

Despite the fact that Josef was a qualified dentist, he didn't end up practising dentistry in Argentina. Instead, he spent two years on a farm near Buenos Aires as head steward, performing clerical duties. Josef earned 600 pesos per month (about 500 Mk), in addition to room and board.[4] Exactly what motivated him to turn his back on a lucrative dental career remains a mystery.

In 1924, Josef's parents asked him to return to Germany and, as he was their only son, he felt obliged to do so. By the time he arrived, Germany was well on the road to financial recovery. The Dawes Plan had reduced Germany's reparation payments to a manageable amount and a new German currency had been introduced. The golden age of the Weimar Republic had dawned, with Berlin its throbbing heart. Upon returning to Berlin, Josef again took the State Examination for Dentistry (June 1924), since foreign diplomas were not recognised in Germany. Having passed the examination, Josef settled down in his father's house as a dentist in April 1925. Finally, in October 1926, Josef was granted the title of Doctor of Dentistry.[5]

While no ship's passenger lists were found to confirm Josef's assertion that he travelled to Argentina, there was little reason for him to lie about the matter. Despite the lack of direct evidence to support his claim, the *Yearbook for Dentists: bound with the Address book of German Dentists, 1933–34*[6] included the following entry, 'Jakobs, José, W 15, Pfalzburger Str 13. G 98 N 27'.

The 'G 98' stood for the *Geburtsjahr* (year of birth), in this case 1898, which was the year Josef was born. The address, Pfalzburger Strasse 13, was the address at which Josef's parents resided and where he had set up his first dental practice. The 'N 27' stood for *Niederlassungsjahr*, the year in which the dentist established his business. The most interesting item was that Josef's first name was given as José, the Spanish variant of the name Josef. This would suggest that Josef spent time in a Spanish-speaking country and that his first dental degree was issued in Spanish. Josef could have spent time in Mexico or Spain, or any other Spanish-speaking country, but he repeatedly stated that he studied dentistry in Argentina. Further confirmation of Josef's career as a dentist came from the certificate that accompanied his First World War service medal (the Honour Cross of the World War 1914–1918).[7] The certificate was issued on 7 February 1936 to 'Dentist Josef Jakobs'.[8]

Josef was an accredited dentist with the potential for a solid income. It was time to start thinking about a family. On 27 May 1926, Josef married Alma Margarete Knöffler (whom he fondly called 'Grete' or 'Gretchen') at St Ludwig's Parish in Berlin.[9] The newly married couple lived with Josef's parents for several months before moving in with Margarete's mother and stepfather at Pfalzburger Strasse 34. The apartment was small, but Margarete got on better with her own mother than with Josef's mother. Truth be told, Josef and Margarete made an odd-looking couple. Josef was almost 6ft tall while Margarete barely brushed 5ft, but something had attracted these two people together.

Margarete was a beautiful young woman who, like Josef, had an unconventional past. Her mother, Therese, was the daughter of Albert Erwin Ludwig Knöffler, court hairdresser to Her Royal Highness Frau Princess Albrecht and Her Highness Princess Marie von Saxe-Meiningen.[10] In 1899, Therese married Adolf Hermann Georg Köhne, also a hairdresser, but their marriage was tragically brief and Georg passed away on 9 February 1901.[11] Just over a year later, on 17 February 1902, Therese gave birth to Margarete with no father listed on the birth certificate.[12] Based on family papers, the father was probably Johannes

Fitzner, a dashing young man from Upper Silesia who, perhaps upon learning of the unplanned pregnancy, emigrated to Mexico.[13] He settled in the province of Chiapas, married a local woman and fathered another eight children.[14] Therese was left to fend for herself and did so quite ably, raising her daughter on her own. On 6 March 1919, Therese married Abraham Wolfgang Elkan, a Jewish businessman.[15]

While Josef and Margarete lived on the same street, a few blocks from each other, they moved in different circles. Josef's family was Catholic while Margarete and her mother were staunch Protestants. However, Margarete had studied dentistry and it may have been that connection that brought her to Josef's attention. Whatever the means, despite their differences in religion and height, the two connected with each other and Margarete even converted to Catholicism prior to the wedding.

Once happily settled in Therese and Wolfgang's apartment, Josef and Margarete wasted no time in starting a family; but heartbreak soon followed. Their first child was stillborn in 1927[16] and their second child, Norbert, experienced a difficult birth in August 1928. The blood supply to Norbert's brain was interrupted during his delivery and he would suffer epileptic-like seizures for the rest of his life.[17]

As the young couple struggled to care for their ailing son, a pivotal event shook Josef's world on 13 June 1931, when his father died of a heart attack. Following the funeral at St Ludwig's Parish, Josef wrote a brief paragraph about his father in the Jakobs *Familienbuch* (Family Book):

Kaspar Jakobs; School Director; born on 4 August 1862 in Kürenz by Trier; died from a heart attack on June 13, 1931 in Berlin. Catholic. Prussian. He lived in Trier, Ehlenz; Müs by Fulda and since 1902 until his death in Berlin, Wilmersdorf, Pfalzburger Str. 13.[18]

Josef wrote little about his father, perhaps a reflection of his own lack of knowledge. Did Josef know that his father had been a Catholic priest? Josef must have wondered why his own birth was registered in Luxembourg seven years before his parents were married. Josef surely knew that he was illegitimate. Whether he knew the circumstances around that illegitimacy is a question that will never be answered.

Less than a week after Kaspar was laid to rest, Margarete gave birth to a daughter, Regine, followed a year later by another son, Raymond.

While Josef had taken the conventional road for starting a family, his sister Maria Jakobs had trodden a similar path to that of her parents.

In early 1925, Maria became pregnant and gave birth to a son, whom she named Balthazar Jakobs.[19] Balthazar and his younger cousins, Norbert, Regine and Raymond saw each other on occasion but Emma's disapproval of her daughter's illegitimate child was palpable. Over time, Maria and Balthazar were seen less and less by the Jakobs family, and by the time the war started, Maria and her son were living near Alexanderplatz in the centre of Berlin, far from Wilmersdorf.[20]

Josef's family was full of intrigues and illegitimate children, rife with faults and failings. They lived in challenging times and, with the addition of three mouths to feed, Josef and Margarete began to feel the financial pressure of providing for their growing family.

5

DESPERATE TIMES CALL FOR DESPERATE MEASURES

Since its inception in 1927, Josef's dental practice had been moderately successful.[1] He and Margarete had made a go of it and built up a significant client base. They had started a family and things were looking good for them – until 1931.

In 1927 and 1928 the German economy went into a steep decline as production decreased and unemployment rose. By 1929 the German government was again struggling to maintain war reparation payments and had accepted loans from the United States. The New York Stock Market crash of 1929 reverberated around the globe. The United States halted loans to Germany and requested repayment of the outstanding debts.

Faced with a stumbling economy and political unrest, the German government decided to increase taxes and reduce spending. The German economy took a nose dive and by 1931 unemployment had risen to 30 per cent. In mid 1931, after the failure of the Austrian bank, Credit-Anstalt, several German banks closed their doors. This precipitated a run on the remaining German banks. People wanted to withdraw their money but there wasn't enough cash on hand to satisfy everyone.

It's possible that Kaspar's heart attack was precipitated by the stress of this financial turmoil. Germany teetered on the brink of economic and political chaos. When the dust settled, almost two years later, the *Nationalsozialistische Deutsche Arbeiterpartei* (National Socialist German Workers' Party – the Nazi Party) would rule the country.

Josef's dentistry practice was a casualty of the crisis of 1931. Many of his clients were unable to pay their bills and he was forced to close his doors in April 1932. Josef said that his father had left him 100,000 Reichsmark (RM)[2] when he passed away in June 1931. That money might have survived the financial crisis of 1931–32, or it might have been swallowed up in the failure of the German banks. Whatever the case, Josef had three little children to feed and he became involved in a series of increasingly desperate business ventures.

Josef first took up a position as an independent book salesman for a Jewish publishing firm. He travelled to small towns, drumming up sales, on which he received a 25 per cent commission – but business was not brisk. A few months later, Josef joined Mercedes-Bureau-Maschinen GmbH (Mercedes Business Machines Company) as a salesman. Again, Josef spent a lot of time on the road, travelling to small towns around Berlin selling typewriters. He claimed that he made a net profit of 500–600 RM[3] per month, which was more than he had made as a dentist. If that was the case, his next career move was perplexing.

In early 1933, Josef left a profitable sales job for a dubious foray into foreign bonds and an import business. According to Josef, the key factor in this decision was the transformation of Germany's political climate. On 30 January 1933 Adolf Hitler was appointed Chancellor of Germany. The Nazis had gone from being a fringe party to ruling the country.

Josef's bank manager drew his attention to some Mexican government securities that had the potential to greatly increase in value. Josef liked the sound of easy money and got a permit from the German foreign exchange to purchase the securities. Josef then withdrew 40,000 RM from his bank account and borrowed another 10,000 RM[4] from a Jewish stockbroker. With permit and money in hand, Josef visited another Jewish broker and bought the Mexican securities. Given his annual typewriter sales income of 6,000 RM per year, 50,000 RM was a significant investment – eight years' worth of income. Perhaps Josef was trying to protect his money from the unstable German economy by dabbling in foreign investments. Or perhaps he was a victim of the classic line, 'I've got a hot investment tip for you.'

In February 1933, Josef travelled to Madrid to visit an old friend, Jesus Artigas, a former pupil of Kaspar Jakobs. Jesus' father, Ramon, was a director of the *Banco de Espana* (Bank of Spain)[5] and Josef may have picked up investing tips during their dinner conversations. Josef was apparently planning to move to Spain but, as with many of Josef's plans, greed got in the way. Josef learned that he could buy a shipload of tinned fruit in Spain for 20 pennies a tin.[6] Once he imported them into Germany, he would be able to sell them for 60 pennies a tin. Josef got stars in his eyes and asked Jesus to broker the deal for him.

When Josef returned to Germany, his plan ran afoul of the authorities. Josef tried to cash in some of the Mexican securities to pay for the tinned fruit, but the foreign exchange authorities took a rather dim view of his plan. They arrested Josef and confiscated the securities. The only thing that saved Josef from prosecution was the fact that he had bought the securities legally. As he would learn, buying securities legally was one thing, selling them was an entirely different thing. The foreign exchange authorities held onto the securities and sent Josef away empty handed. On top of that, the Nazis refused to issue an import permit because he was not an 'expert in the trade'.[7] Essentially, Josef was not a licensed importer/exporter but a rank amateur who got his fingers burned.

Within the space of a few years, Josef went from being a reputable dentist with a thriving practice to a moderately successful travelling salesman to an unlicensed importer who was arrested for foreign currency violations. While the latter could be ascribed to Josef's ignorance of the law, the same could not be said of his next, blatantly illegal, venture.

When the Nazis came to power in early 1933, they wasted no time in implementing Hitler's policies. Jews began to have their rights stripped away. Non-Nazi political parties were banned. Books were burned. Eugenic sterilisation was legalised.

In July 1933, the Law for the Prevention of Genetically Diseased Offspring[8] was enacted. This allowed a Hereditary Health Court[9] to order the sterilisation of citizens who suffered any one from a list of 'genetic disorders' – many of which were not genetic. One of the disorders was hereditary epilepsy. Josef's eldest son, Norbert, had developed seizures as a result of birth trauma. Such seizures could easily be mistaken for 'hereditary' epilepsy. In the world of the Nazis, even innocent children were at risk, particularly if they came to the attention of the Gestapo. Josef had had business dealings with Jews. He had worked for a Jewish publishing firm. The climate in Germany was changing and Josef turned to a questionable venture that got him out of the country.

Werner Goldstein, a Jewish friend of Josef's, was a chemist who had come up with a scheme to create a gold alloy that could be passed off as 14-karat gold. Werner took Josef into his confidence and the two men let greed get the better of them. Josef suggested that they take their gold counterfeiting enterprise to Switzerland where they could purchase second-hand gold more easily.

In April 1934, Josef and Werner smuggled 3,000 RM[10] into Switzerland and rented a flat in Zurich where they smelted their gold alloy. After cooking up their first batch of gold, they tried to sell it in Biel but were told that they needed a permit. Undeterred, the two schemers told the Swiss authorities that it was refugee gold and duly received a permit. Excited by their success, Josef and Werner quickly made up a second batch of gold, for which they also received a permit.

Josef and Werner had made a tidy profit from their first two transactions and decided to enjoy themselves. They travelled to Geneva, where they met Yvonne Sommerfeld, a Jewess from Nice, France. Yvonne and Werner became quite friendly and at one point were even thinking of marriage. Josef, uncharacteristically, wanted nothing to do with the seductive Yvonne, which was extremely fortunate because on 1 July 1934 Josef's wife came to visit him for two months.[11] Flush with cash from his gold ventures, Josef entertained Margarete lavishly. They spent time in Zurich, Geneva, Lucerne and even drove to Rome.[12] In photographs of the couple, Margarete looked youthful and full of life. In contrast, Josef, who was only four years older, looked gaunt and aged. In one photograph, Josef had his shirt unbuttoned and his ribs were visible in the middle of his chest. Josef was not a well man and his health would only deteriorate in the coming years.

In early August, Margarete visited the French Consulate in Zurich and received a French visa, but there is no evidence that she used it.[13] By 6 September Margarete was back in Berlin without Josef. Two days earlier, all of their plans had come to a crashing halt.

Even while Margarete was in Switzerland, Werner and Josef continued their business of smelting counterfeit gold. Unfortunately, when they went to sell their third batch of 'refugee' gold in late August, they were refused a permit. Despite this setback, they decided to remain in Zurich and concoct a different plan – but their time had run out. On 4 September 1934 Werner and Josef were arrested by the Swiss police. Apparently, their association with Yvonne Sommerfeld had raised red flags with the authorities.

While they were in custody, news of their fraudulent gold transactions surfaced when a Zurich jeweller received an assay report on a gold ingot sold to him by Werner and Josef.[14] Werner was tried before the Swiss high court and found guilty of fraud. Josef appealed his arrest and was tried before another court three weeks later, but the end result was the same. In early 1935, both men were sentenced to two years and three months' imprisonment. Josef had his first taste of incarceration – twenty-seven months in a foreign prison. He also had the unenviable task of letting his wife and family know that he would not be coming home, and he would not be sending money to support them.

Margarete still had 60,000 RM[15] from Josef's inheritance, but in all other things she was essentially alone. She had three young children to raise, one of whom suffered seizures and was already under the watchful eye of the Gestapo. Every knock at the door, every ring of the doorbell, would have been a test of her nerves. She only had to look around her neighbourhood, or read the local paper, to know that they lived in dangerous times.

The Nuremberg Laws of 5 September 1935 provided a legal definition of a Jew and limited the rights of German Jews even further. The Nazi definition of a Jew had nothing to do with religious beliefs or practices. A person who didn't practice Judaism and who was a Christian could still find themselves labelled a Jew if three or four of their grandparents had been Jews. A person with one or two Jewish grandparents was classified as a *Mischling* – a 'crossbreed' of mixed blood. The immediate effect of the Nuremberg Laws was to deprive German Jews of their citizenship and to prohibit the interracial marriage of Jews and Germans. Anyone with questionable ancestry was suspect, and Margarete, with no father listed on her birth certificate, would eventually need to hire a researcher to prove the purity of her paternal lineage.[16]

During 1935 Hitler also established the Luftwaffe (the German air force) and ordered the construction of a fleet of submarines, all in contravention of the Treaty of Versailles. At the same time, the Nazi government stipulated that only Aryans could serve in the *Wehrmacht* (German armed forces). Germany was rearming itself and many could see storm clouds gathering on the horizon.

During 1936, while Josef counted down the months until his release, Germany hosted the Winter Olympics in Garmisch-Partenkirchen and the Summer Olympics in Berlin. The Winter Games took place without any controversy in early February. Less than one month later, Germany violated the Treaty of Versailles by sending military troops into the Rhineland. Despite this blatant militaristic action, international reaction consisted of much hand wringing and little else. Hitler moved from triumph to triumph and the reaction in Germany was generally positive.

The next big coup for Hitler was the Summer Olympics. Speaking of the Games, Hitler said, 'The sportive, knightly battle awakens the best human characteristics. It doesn't separate, but unites the combatants in understanding and respect. It also helps to connect the countries in the spirit of peace. That's why the Olympic Flame should never die.'[17]

For Hitler, the Summer Games in Berlin were the stage upon which he could promote the Nazi ideals of racial supremacy. The official newspaper of the Nazi Party published an article that argued that Jews and 'black people' should be banned from participation in the games. Faced with a vocal backlash from other nations and the threat of a boycott, Hitler relented, and the anti-Jewish rhetoric was toned down.

Interestingly, Joseph Goebbels, Nazi Minister of Propaganda, hit upon the true goal of the Nazi promotion of the Olympics. 'German sport has only one task: to strengthen the character of the German people, imbuing it with the fighting spirit and steadfast camaraderie necessary in the struggle for its existence.'[18]

Berlin had hosted the Summer Olympics and been at the centre of the world stage. New sports venues had been constructed, international athletes had descended upon the city, and Josef had missed it all. Finally, on 20 June 1937, Josef was released from the Swiss prison and deported back to Germany. His accomplice, Werner Goldstein, had been released three weeks previously, but Josef never heard from him again.

Josef was embarrassed about his Swiss imprisonment and his reluctance to admit to it would cause problems for him in later years. Having returned to Berlin, Josef claimed that his wife still had 12,000 RM in cash and 50,000 RM[19] in bonds (the ones confiscated by the foreign exchange authorities). Josef always took pains to paint himself as a well-off gentleman who would never do anything simply for money. Although Josef was a free man, it was debatable whether he was a reformed one.

6

A DIFFERENT WORLD

Josef returned to Berlin, his apartment, his wife, his children and his family.[1] The lost son, brother, husband and father had returned and there was rejoicing for some and confusion for others. Josef's children had been 6, 3 and 2 years old when he departed for Switzerland. Upon his return, they were 9, 6 and 5 years old. Josef was a stranger to them, and they to him. They weren't used to having a father in the house and he wasn't used to having children underfoot.

Berlin was different too – there was a frisson of fear lurking in the cafés. People looked over their shoulders as they talked. Gestapo spies could be anywhere. One no longer knew who to trust. Margarete's Jewish stepfather, Wolfgang Elkan, told Josef horror stories about the methodical stripping away of rights from the Jews.

The writing was on the wall when, on 17 August 1938, the Nazis issued a decree that all Jews needed to take on an additional forename: Sarah for the women and Israel for the men. It was one more way in which the Jews were singled out and made more easily identifiable. Abraham Wolfgang Elkan would henceforth be known as Israel Abraham Wolfgang Elkan.[2] A businessman and restaurant owner, Wolfgang would eventually be forced to give up his business under another draconian piece of Nazi legislation.[3] Money was tight, and tensions ran high at Pfalzburger Strasse 34. Josef needed to find a new career, and quickly. As he picked up the threads of his life, Josef reconnected with an old friend.

In 1931, a former patient of Josef's had introduced him to *Oberleutnant* (First Lieutenant) Egon Rammrath, son of one of the richest and most prominent families in Wilmersdorf. Rammrath's father, Franz, was a builder, multimillionaire, philanthropist and a pillar of the community.

However, his son was cut from different cloth.[4] After Franz passed away, Rammrath lost much of the family's fortune during the hyperinflation of the early 1920s. In the late 1920s Rammrath dabbled in various ventures: a dealer in motor cars, a financier, a mortgage broker. He was granted a loan of 2.5 million Goldmark at the Bank für Deutsche Beamte, but lost it all through speculation, which, according to Josef, contributed to the bank's bankruptcy in 1929. Rammrath was prosecuted and sentenced to nine months in jail but fled to Switzerland in 1933 using a false passport. His freedom was short-lived and Rammrath was arrested by the Swiss police and deported to Germany, where he finally served his jail sentence.

This was the old friend with whom Josef reconnected in July 1937, shortly after returning from Switzerland. Rammrath brought Josef up to speed on the political situation in Germany. A growing wave of anti-Semitic hatred and violence meant that many Jews were desperate to leave Germany, but the process was not easy. In order to emigrate, Jews needed permission from the country they were trying to enter, generally in the form of a visa. Jews had to provide written testimonies from previous employers, or respected members of the community, attesting to their good conduct, as well as papers listing personal assets. Unfortunately, many countries had anti-immigration policies and the number of visas were limited. If a person was fortunate enough to acquire a foreign visa, the German authorities still had to give permission for the emigrant to leave.

Given the difficult and convoluted process in acquiring legitimate visas, it was no wonder that other options saw a surge in popularity. Rammrath told Josef that he was involved in a 'legitimate' venture with an Aryan lawyer, Dr Jürgen Ziebell, who helped German Jews acquire foreign passports. It was all very simple. The applicant submitted an account of his life, a medical certificate of health for himself and his family, a police certificate of good conduct, proof that he had not taken part in politics, four photographs and a detailed application. All of the documents were reviewed by the relevant authorities. If there were no objections, then the applicant would receive, from the Consul General of the country concerned or through a lawyer, a genuine passport and a document that proved the applicant had been naturalised. According to Rammrath, there were no problems with the German authorities, because Jews were strongly encouraged to emigrate, and German law permitted the acquisition of a second nationality. Jews with foreign nationality could remain in Germany for a year to settle their affairs and could often transfer their assets out of Germany under more favourable terms than German Jews.

Intrigued, Josef accompanied Rammrath to the posh offices of Ziebell in the Kurfürstendamm. Ziebell, who had been a public prosecutor for many years, confirmed Rammrath's story and told Josef that he had taken over the business from a Jewish lawyer, Dr Hans Blum.[5] Ziebell knew a man named Emil Dochnal who had contacts in various countries, through whom he could obtain passports for Finland, Cuba, Sweden, Uruguay, Ireland, France and Chile. Ziebell also said that he could quickly and easily get South American visas for Jews if they already had a German passport. Ziebell also told Josef that he helped with the Aryanisation of Jewish businesses. Under Nazi rule, Jews were forced to register all of their assets (domestic and foreign) and, up until 1938, were strongly encouraged to 'voluntarily' sell their businesses to Aryans. Ziebell would take over a Jewish business and then sell it to an Aryan German firm. Ziebell was able to get an applicant's capital transferred at a rate of 20 per cent (i.e. they would get 20 per cent of their money in the end). This was to the advantage of the Jews and was done by bribing German officials. Ziebell also told Josef that he could get Jews out of concentration camps. They had to have their relatives send an application for naturalisation beforehand, because the Jews had to pledge to leave Germany three days after their release – the fee for this was 30,000 RM.[6]

Ziebell and Rammrath told Josef that he could claim a finder's fee for every rich Jew he introduced to Ziebell. He would be able to earn a significant amount of money, but they made it clear that he would be working on his own account. Ziebell had a set fee for the services he offered and Josef would have to negotiate a higher amount with clients so that he could claim the difference. For example, Ziebell generally charged 22,000 RM[7] for a foreign naturalisation – 12,000 RM[8] went to Ziebell and 10,000 RM[9] covered various expenses (e.g. bribery). When negotiating with a client, Josef could claim that foreign naturalisation cost 30,000 RM.[10] He could then pocket the 8,000 RM[11] difference. For visa applications (Chile, Uruguay, Cuba and Argentina), Josef could earn 3,000 RM[12] per visa. Ziebell claimed to have made a fortune through this business and Josef could well believe it.

To Josef, this sounded like easy money, but he was also a cautious man and consulted his stepfather-in-law, Wolfgang Elkan. To Josef's astonishment, he learned that Wolfgang already had connections through a former Jewish banker and that he was negotiating for Yugoslavian naturalisation. Convinced of the legality of the business and eager to recoup his lost fortunes, Josef jumped into the passport business with both feet.

In the fourteen months during which Josef was actively soliciting clients for Ziebell, he introduced forty or fifty Jews to him. Most of the deals involved emigration, naturalisation and visas, although Josef did help with the Aryanisation of one business. During that time, Josef figured that he earned, after expenses, about 150,000 RM.[13] He had made back his father's inheritance and then some, but money was not everything. Money had long since started to corrupt Josef. He might have gained wealth, but at what cost?

7

A JEW ESCAPES TO ALBION

Of all the Jews Josef introduced to Ziebell, one would play a pivotal role in his mission to England – Frau Lily Knips.[1] Lily was born on 20 July 1891 in Hannover, the youngest daughter of German-Jewish parents, Jacob Katz and Jenny Goldschmidt. Jacob was a successful businessman who founded the Germania Brewery and, later, the Heuweg-Werke (Hannoversche Eishaus und Waren-Einkaufs-Gesellschaft), a clear-ice manufacturing plant. Jacob was a wealthy man and his two daughters, Elsa and Lily, had a comfortable childhood.

In 1913, Lily married Ludwig Sauer, a German-Jewish lawyer from Hannover. Their only child, Lothar Sauer was born on 12 August 1914 in Hannover. Unfortunately, the marriage was not a happy one and in 1920 Lily divorced Ludwig. While Ludwig ended up in Brussels, Lily made her way to Berlin where, in 1926, she married Franz Knips, a German Catholic. Franz was the director of the Niederlausitzer Kohlwerke AG (a coal company) and a wealthy man. He had one daughter from a previous marriage, Hildegard Maronn (née Knips), but she had already left home by the time Lily married Franz. Lily thoroughly enjoyed life in cosmopolitan Berlin and Franz doted on his stepson, Lothar. Their house, at Freiherr-vom-Stein Strasse 8, faced Stadtpark Schöneberg (now Rudolph-Wilde Park) and was located in a much sought-after area of Berlin.

On 6 January 1934, at the age of 19, Lily's son Lothar left Germany to study at the London School of Economics, the Institute of Actuaries and Pitman's College. Lothar returned to Germany for short holiday visits and was undoubtedly disturbed to witness the changes in his home country. On 11 June 1936, Lothar wrote to the British Home Office requesting an extension of his landing permit so that he could take up employment in an insurance office. His permit was granted and on 1 September 1936 Lothar took a job at E.B. Nathans.[2]

A year earlier, in 1935, Lily's second husband, Franz Knips passed away in Berlin. He left Lily a small fortune and she continued to live at their home at Freiherr-vom-Stein Strasse for another six months. She then lived in a hotel for two years and, in 1937, took a flat in Wielandstrasse 30, not far from where Josef lived.

The deteriorating situation in Germany caused Lily deep anxiety. Her non-Jewish husband had died and the Nazi vice-grip was slowly strangling the life out of German Jews. Lily was desperate to get out of Germany.

In the spring of 1938, Lily was having coffee with Jewish friends at a public tennis court near her flat. One of the ladies, Frau Reiwald, spotted Josef and waved him over. Josef was well known at the tennis club and was affectionately called '*Länglich*' ('Stretch' or 'Lanky') by the regulars. Frau Reiwald introduced Lily to Josef and told her that Herr Jakobs was a clever man who could help Lily get a passport to leave Germany and assist her with financial matters.

A few days later, Josef visited Lily at her flat to discuss business. Lily told Josef that she was anxious to leave Germany and was making preparations to join her son in London.[3] She knew that she wouldn't be allowed to work in England but had plans to open a boarding house. Josef told Lily that he could get her a foreign passport (French, Finnish or Irish) and that with an Irish passport, Lily would be able to work in England. Normally, such a passport would cost 40,000 RM[4] but, as a special favour to Lily, Josef was willing to lower the price to 25,000 RM.[5]

Lily was not a fool and thought that such an arrangement didn't sound legal. She wanted to leave Germany legally for the sake of her 83-year-old father, who would be left behind in Hannover. Josef assured her that the whole thing was very legal and invited her to come with him to visit Ziebell. Lily was slightly reassured to learn that that Josef had helped arrange a foreign passport for a friend of hers, Fraulein Schachtel, for 80,000–120,000 RM.[6] In light of that astronomical sum, 25,000 RM didn't sound so bad and Lily agreed to meet with Ziebell.

A week later, Lily accompanied Josef to Ziebell's office, where she also met Rammrath. Ziebell told her that the passport mentioned by Josef could easily be obtained for 25,000 RM. Lily again asked about the legality of the arrangement since she did not want to get into trouble with the authorities in Germany or any other country. She stressed that she would be leaving her aged father behind and did not want her actions to cause trouble for him. She found Ziebell to be evasive and Rammrath told her that she was wasting the lawyer's time. Lily did not get a good feeling from Rammrath and suspected he was a Gestapo official.[7] After leaving Ziebell's office, Josef told Lily that he and Rammrath brought clients to Ziebell, who made all the necessary arrangements for procuring legal passports. Lily told Josef that she was not at all satisfied with what she had heard and wanted nothing more to do with the scheme. She and Josef continued to see each other socially and remained on friendly terms.

In August 1938, along with every other female Jew, Lily was forced to add 'Sarah' to her name. Her stress level went up and her desperation increased. When Josef saw her a few days later at the tennis club, he noted her signs of tension and told her that he had come up with another scheme to assist her. As a Jew, Lily would not be able to take much of her capital wealth with her, since most of it would be confiscated by the Nazis, but Josef had a solution. He knew a Swiss national, Herr Seiler, who had a great deal of capital in Switzerland. He had taken over a large Jewish clothing factory in Berlin and needed working capital. He didn't want to invest his Swiss capital into the business but instead was looking for German capital. Josef told Lily that if she put all of her money in Seiler's Berlin bank account then Seiler would transfer a matching amount from his Swiss bank account to her son's account in England.

Josef was a persuasive salesman and brought Seiler to Lily's flat a few days later to discuss the deal. They ended up agreeing that Lily would deposit 30,000 RM[8] to Seiler's account in Berlin. Seiler, in turn, would deposit £27,000 (£900 = 1,000 RM)[9] into her son's British bank account. Seiler told Lily that he had the permission of the German *Devisenstelle* (currency control) to buy Jewish capital, which reassured Lily that the whole deal was legitimate. After additional meetings to hammer out the details, Lily liquidated some of her assets and placed 30,000 RM into a joint account at the Deutsche Bank. Seiler supposedly travelled to London to place a deposit at a bank that consisted of securities, not cash.

In early September 1938, Lily travelled to England on a temporary passport to visit her son for two weeks. Lothar, worried about his mother, wrote to the Home Office on 2 September 1938 and requested a visa for her so that she could move to the United Kingdom. Lothar said that he would fully support his mother and even arranged a tenancy agreement for her at 9 Compayne Gardens, London. A week later, Lothar was pleased to hear that the conditions under which he had landed in the United Kingdom were cancelled. There was no longer a time limit on his stay in

Britain and Lothar quickly applied for naturalisation as that would make it much easier to bring his mother to England.

While celebrating Lothar's good fortune, Lily was distracted by the financial deal with Seiler. Josef had telephoned her three times in London and asked her to come back to Germany and free up the money for Seiler. Lily may have shared the details of the deal with her son and told him that Seiler had even deposited securities at a British bank in Lothar's name. As an accountant, Lothar could sniff out a rat and the whole thing smelled suspicious. He likely urged her to look into the matter in more detail when she returned to Germany.

When Lily got back to Berlin in mid September, she consulted her bank director about the situation. Alarmed at what he heard, the bank director told Lily to consult her lawyer, who wrote to the German currency control offices on her behalf. Lily learned that Seiler had no permission to purchase Jewish capital and that none would be granted. It was all a scam.

Lily confronted Josef with righteous anger. She told him that she thought the whole scheme suspicious. Faced with her steely gaze, Josef admitted that he had met Seiler in a Swiss prison where he was serving a sentence for fraudulent bankruptcy. Relieved that she had skirted the edge of disaster, Lily visited her solicitor and agreed to pay Seiler 600 RM[10] for his expenses and washed her hands of the whole affair. The remainder of her money was transferred to her own bank account. She was back where she had started.

In the aftermath of the failed deal with Josef and Seiler, Lily was fearful that Josef would get her into trouble with the authorities. In order not to offend him, she continued to see him from time to time. Josef, on the other hand, was anxious to arrange another financial deal for her: mortgages, marriage to foreigners, etc. Lily fended him off as much as possible but did sell him her Chrysler car at a reduced price.[11]

In late September 1938, worn down by his persistent harping on about mortgages, Lily told Josef that he should discuss it with her father, who understood such matters. Josef and Lily drove to Hannover, where Lily's father listened to Josef's proposals with a keen ear. Although he was 83 years old, Jacob was still a sharp businessman. Jacob pulled Lily aside and told her in no uncertain terms that she should have nothing to do with Josef. The man was a scam artist of the highest order.

Despite this exhortation from her father, Lily continued to meet Josef socially. They lived in the same neighbourhood and frequented the same cafés and clubs. She told Josef about her new address in England,

9 Compayne Gardens, a fact that would come back to haunt her three years later.

In early October 1938, Josef came to Lily's flat and told her that Ziebell, Rammrath and Martin Goldstein (no connection to Josef's friend, the gold counterfeiter, Werner Goldstein) had all been arrested and imprisoned. Lily never saw Josef again and, in early December of that same year, she learned from Josef's wife that he had been arrested by the Gestapo after visiting the flat of one of his incarcerated associates. If she was going to get out of Germany, it was not going to be with the assistance of Herr Jakobs. The Nazi dragnet was tightening around German Jews and their associates.

On the evening of 9 November 1938 the terror of Kristallnacht echoed through Germany and Austria. The pogrom was ostensibly carried out by 'outraged citizens' in retaliation for the assassination of a German diplomat in Paris by a Jew. Orchestrated by the Nazis, the frenzy of violence destroyed or damaged thousands of Jewish businesses, schools, hospitals and synagogues. Tens of thousands of Jews were arrested and sent to concentration camps. Lily was spared, but the events of Kristallnacht haunted her. The nervous tension of living in constant fear for her life was wearing her thin.

In January 1939, Lily's British solicitors wrote a letter to the Home Office requesting a decision on her visa application since she was suffering from 'severe nervous strain on account of the present situation in Germany as regards Jews'.[12] Finally, in April 1939, Lily was granted a British visa and arrived in the United Kingdom on 24 April. She was safe. The only cloud in her sky was the fate of her elderly father in Hannover and her sister in Berlin. Rumour had it that the Nazis were not targeting elderly Jews, so she prayed that her father would be spared. Lily had escaped the clutches of the Nazis.

As for Josef, his downfall began in late September 1938 in Hamburg. An Aryan lawyer was arrested by the Gestapo for 'immoral conduct', a charge that could include homosexuality, loitering, refusal to work or venereal disease. His house was searched, and the police discovered the addresses of Berlin Jews, including that of Dr Hans Blum, the Jewish lawyer who had started the passport business. Blum was arrested by the Gestapo in early October and quickly gave away the name of Rammrath, who then exposed the entire business.[13]

Around the same time, on 5 October 1938, the Nazis decreed that the passports of all German Jews were invalid. All Jews who wanted to use their passport for emigration purposes needed to have it validated by having it stamped with a large red 'J' (for Jew). The avenues for Jewish emigration were slowly being squeezed shut, including Ziebell's business.

On 10 October 1938, Josef was arrested by the Gestapo. Sixty other people were arrested around the same time, including four Aryan lawyers and ten Jewish lawyers. Josef claimed that they were arrested under suspicion of political intrigue and high treason, but that was likely not the case. As it turned out, Ziebell did not have a permit for the emigration business and, as an Aryan, was prohibited from looking after Jewish interests. Josef claimed that many other people were engaged in the same business and that it was entirely legitimate. As proof, Josef said that the Gestapo did not confiscate any of his money (200,000 RM).[14] Upon his arrest, Josef said that the Nazis itemised various points that had brought him under suspicion: (1) Josef and his parents were active members of the 'Central Party',[15] (2) Josef and his wife gave their youngest son an English Christian name (Raymond) and would not change it, despite repeated summons, (3) Josef had enrolled his children in Catholic schools and, (4) Josef had refused to become a member of any Nazi organisation.

Josef languished in Moabit prison for over six months awaiting trial. On 24 July 1939 the *Generalstaatsanwalt* (Attorney General) drew up a prosecution document for those individuals involved in the passport business, including Ziebell, Rammrath, Dochnal, Goldstein and Josef. All five were charged with black-market activities and the document noted that Josef had previously been punished for domestic fraud (possibly a reference to the Spanish imports and/or Mexican securities fiasco).[16]

Despite their protestations of innocence, Josef and his associates were found guilty and sent to Sachsenhausen concentration camp just north of Berlin.[17] Sachsenhausen was built in the summer of 1936 and the first prisoners were mostly political opponents of the Nazi regime and real or perceived criminals. Later, increasing numbers of people from so-called racially or biologically inferior groups were sent there. By 1939, large numbers of citizens from the occupied European states arrived. Tens of thousands of people died of starvation, disease, forced labour and mistreatment, or were victims of the systematic extermination operations of the Nazi *Schutzstaffel* (SS).

Josef arrived at Sachsenhausen in the autumn of 1939. As he walked through the camp gate, he crossed a frontier from which few returned. The words *Arbeit Macht Frei* (Work Makes Free) mocked him and all who passed through the gates of concentration camps. There was no freedom within the walls of the camp. Newly arrived prisoners were clubbed and made to stand in rows for roll call. Beatings and whippings were common. Some prisoners laboured in the brickworks outside the prison walls. Others worked in a counterfeit currency factory where British bank notes were cranked out by the thousands.

The most unfortunate prisoners worked in the *Schuhläuferkommando* (Shoe Walking Commando), a shoe testing track. Prisoners were forced to test shoes and boots by walking 20 miles a day around a circular track composed of cement, cinders, broken stone, gravel and sand. They might march for days. Those who fell were beaten; those who did not get up were sent to the punishment block. Prisoners who questioned guards or who did not work fast or hard enough were also sent to the punishment block.

Josef claimed to have been sent to the punishment block, where he was placed in a tiny, solitary cell with no bed and no chair. Unable to sit or lie down, Josef remained standing for three weeks. Later, he was hung from a tree branch with his arms tied behind his back in a torture known as *strappado*. He suffered that punishment three times in total, with each session lasting thirty minutes.

While thousands of people died in Sachsenhausen, Josef was one of the lucky ones. On 22 March 1940, Good Friday, Josef walked out of the gates.

8

A NEW WORLD

Josef came out of the concentration camp into a different world and a very different country. The changes had begun months before his arrest when Germany annexed Austria in March 1938 and occupied the Sudetenland in October of that same year. Nazi Germany flexed her muscles and greedily snatched *Lebensraum* (living space) for the German race.

Other nations bent over backwards to appease Hitler, desperate to maintain peace at any cost, but 1939 would be different. The German war machine continued to grow as ships, aeroplanes and tanks poured out of German factories. On 1 September 1939, Hitler threw down another gauntlet and ordered German troops to invade Poland. The allies of Poland – France and the United Kingdom – picked up the gauntlet and war once again enveloped Europe.

The next six months were known as the Phoney War, for Hitler was focused on the Eastern Front and there was little conflict on the Western Front. It was only on 10 May 1940 that Hitler turned his attention to the west. The Phoney War ended quickly as Germany headed rapidly for France, invading Belgium, Luxembourg and the Netherlands in the process. Allied forces hunkered down behind their fortified lines in France and Belgium but were caught by surprise when the Germans outflanked them by pushing through the thick forests of the Ardennes.

By late May, the Allies were trapped along the French coast near Dunkirk. It looked as if all would be finished, but just when victory was within reach, the German army halted its advance. That was a mistake. Over the next week, hundreds of thousands of Allied troops were evacuated from Dunkirk by civilian and military ships of every size and shape.

The evacuation was a miracle but still a bitter defeat for the Allies, particularly the British.

Prime Minister Neville Chamberlain had resigned in mid May 1940 in the aftermath of Hitler's invasion of the Low Countries. Chamberlain wanted peace at any cost and was not a suitable leader for a nation at war. After a hurried consultation with government leaders, King George VI appointed Winston Churchill prime minister. It was the right decision for a country at war; Churchill rallied the British people and in light of the Dunkirk evacuation, said:

> We shall fight in France, we shall fight on the seas and oceans, we shall fight with growing confidence and growing strength in the air, we shall defend our island, whatever the cost may be, we shall fight on the beaches, we shall fight on the landing grounds, we shall fight in the fields and in the streets, we shall fight in the hills; we shall never surrender.[1]

By mid July 1940 most of Europe had surrendered, capitulated or been defeated, with the exception of Britain. Hitler made an offer of peace that was flatly rejected. Churchill would not bow to Hitler's demands as Chamberlain had done. Angered at Britain's rejection of his bloodstained olive branch, Hitler gathered his generals in Berlin and outlined his next great plan, Operation SEALION – the invasion of England.

As outlined in Hitler's *Führer Directive 16*, the implementation of Operation SEALION would depend on a number of key factors. The German army let Hitler know, in no uncertain terms, that an invasion of England could only succeed if the Royal Air Force was destroyed. Germany needed to rule the skies before it could ever hope to cross the waters of the English Channel. A second key part of the invasion plan was the need for a host of German spies who could report on weather conditions in England and guide the German troops inland when the invasion began. After much discussion and consideration, the invasion of England was set for September 1940. The German generals dispersed to begin preparations.

Admiral Canaris, head of the Abwehr, the German military intelligence agency, had an unenviable task. He needed to insert a multitude of German spies into England, and quickly, in an undertaking that was codenamed Operation LENA.[2] He delegated the task to the Abwehr office in Hamburg (Referat I Luft), which was responsible for air intelligence in the United Kingdom and the United States. The Abwehr handlers in

Hamburg flipped through their little black books and stared glumly at the meagre lists. During the mid 1930s, several German spies had been arrested in England and convicted of espionage. Such publicity was not good for public relations and Hitler had forbade further espionage attempts in the United Kingdom.[3] He did not want to antagonise a nation with whom Germany had historically (and royally) had such close ties. He thought that peace with England was possible. He was wrong – and now the Abwehr was paying the price for Hitler's hesitancy.

The Abwehr handlers were also depressed by the general unavailability of potential spy candidates in England. With the declaration of war in September 1939, England had moved quickly to intern suspicious foreigners and political agitators. The pool of possible spies was extremely shallow, but not entirely empty. Nikolaus Ritter, one of the Abwehr handlers, had one agent who he had been cultivating for several years. Agent JOHNNY was a Welshman named Arthur G. Owens who had a grudge against England. He had approached the Germans in 1936 and offered to spy on the hated English. Germany had one agent they could trust – but more were needed, many more.

Ritter and the other Abwehr handlers in Hamburg beat the bushes seeking young men to send to England. They put ads in newspapers; they trawled the prisons. They weren't looking for long-term professional spies; they were looking for men who could live off the land for a few weeks after being despatched to England.[4] The invasion would follow hot on their heels. As a result, the qualifications for the job were different from those one would expect of a spy – but even Abwehr handlers such as Ritter had questionable qualifications.

Born on 8 January 1899 in Rheydt, Rhineland,[5] Ritter joined the Imperial German Army in 1917.[6] He was assigned to the 162nd Infantry Regiment, wounded twice and promoted to lieutenant in June 1918.[7] After the war, Ritter trained as a textile engineer[8] and in late 1923, boarded a boat for the United States, the land of opportunity.[9]

Ritter found a job working for the Mallinson Silk Company in New York,[10] but he didn't stay there long and worked a series of odd jobs.[11] In the summer of 1924, Ritter took an English course at Columbia University and met Mary Aurora Evans, an Irish-American school teacher from Alabama.[12] Two years later, the couple married and settled down in New York.[13] During their first year of marriage, Ritter cycled through twenty-two different jobs while Aurora supported the couple with her teaching.[14] In the mid 1930s, Ritter took Aurora and their two young children back to Germany to visit his ailing father.[15] After several months, Ritter returned to America to earn money to bring his wife and children back to the United States.[16] Unable to find employment, Ritter liquidated his wife's assets and returned to Germany in 1936.[17] He was greeted with open arms by the German Abwehr. His on-the-ground knowledge of the United States, coupled with his near-perfect American English ensured that he was a rising star in the Abwehr, despite the fact that he had no concrete espionage experience.

In early September 1940, four Abwehr spies were set adrift off the coast of Kent in a pair of rowing boats. The two groups landed a few miles apart, but the three Dutchmen and one German were captured within forty-eight hours. Only one could speak English fluently but even he was completely unaware of British customs and stood out like a sore thumb. It was not simply that the would-be spies were inept and poorly trained; they had landed in a country that was on high alert. Every British citizen was on the lookout for suspicious characters who might be foreign invaders or spies.

Less than a week after the Kent spies had been scooped up, two spies landed by parachute within a few days of each other: Gösta Caroli (Swedish) and Wulf Schmidt (Danish). The two men had trained together and were friends and ardent Nazis. After landing in England, the two spies made wireless contact with Germany, where Nikolaus Ritter raised his hands in jubilation. He had three operational spies in England, men who might even end up being long-term spies!

In truth, Ritter and the German Abwehr had none. Schmidt, Caroli and Owens were all double agents under the control of MI5, the British security service. Wulf Schmidt (LEONHARDT to the Germans) was known as TATE to the British. Gösta Caroli (Nilberg to the Germans) had become agent SUMMER for the British. As for Ritter's prized agent, JOHNNY, he had fed the German Abwehr information that looked genuine but was ultimately intended to deceive, for he was double agent SNOW to the British.

In the autumn of 1940, one of SNOW's subagents, Sam McCarthy (BISCUIT), met with Ritter in Spain and handed over a British National Identity Card and ration book that had subtle errors courtesy of MI5.[18] The Germans happily reproduced the papers, including the errors, and used them for future spies, unwittingly marking their agents as clearly as if they had been branded on the forehead. Operation LENA was not off to a great start and Josef would soon become a pawn in a high-stakes game.

9

SOLDIER OR SPY

In March 1940 Josef was released from Sachsenhausen concentration camp.[1] His incarceration had played havoc with his health. He languished in bed for days, weak and worn down. His nerves were on edge and the squabbling children exhausted his already limited patience.[2]

Between March and September 1940 Josef applied to the Abwehr. His motivations were multifaceted and complex. The core motivation would seem to be that Abwehr agents were protected from the Gestapo.[3] On top of that, civilians could serve their military duty in the Abwehr.[4] Chief of the Abwehr, Admiral Canaris, and many of his subordinates were secret anti-Nazis and many Jews found refuge within its ranks.

Safety from the Gestapo appealed to Josef, who was often in trouble with the authorities. The life of a spy also sounded romantic – parachute into England, sit in London cafés, meet other agents and send back wireless reports. On the other hand, Josef was clearly not ideal spy material. He was not a young, ardent Nazi who spoke perfect English, but the Germans were desperate for agents to throw at England in the name of Operation LENA. At that point, they were prepared to recruit any person for a mission that some already called *Himmelfahrt* (journey to heaven), a euphemism for a suicide mission.[5]

In the middle of August, Josef's application was forwarded to the Abwehr offices in Bremen and then on to Hamburg. It wasn't until 20 September 1940 that Josef heard back from them. His application had obviously not been a high priority but, at that point the focus of the Abwehr had altered. The Germans were no longer looking for invasion agents; they were looking for disposable agents.

From 24 August to 4 September the German Luftwaffe bombed Royal Air Force installations with merciless precision. Day after day, aeroplanes were destroyed, personnel were killed, and airfields were damaged. The RAF suffered seemingly unsustainable losses, but the Luftwaffe only saw that it kept flying and seemed as strong as ever. In truth, the RAF was on the verge of collapse, but it was saved from annihilation when the Luftwaffe shifted its focus from bombing the RAF airfields to attacking civilian cities. Hitler ordered the shift in retaliation for the 25 August Allied bombing of Berlin.

The RAF was bruised and battered but not destroyed and Operation SEALION was essentially cancelled. Hitler, however, wanted Britain to think that the invasion had only been postponed.[6] The Abwehr still needed to send agents to the United Kingdom, and any warm body would do.

On 22 September, Josef caught a train from Berlin to Hamburg. The trip took him the better part of a day and upon arrival in Hamburg, he checked into the Reichshof Hotel across the street from the *Hauptbahnhof* (main train station).

The Reichshof Hotel had opened its doors in 1910 to much fanfare. At the time it was the largest hotel in Germany and featured a lift, electric lights, running water and a telephone in every room. The years had been kind to the hotel and it still oozed opulence in 1940. Once Josef was checked in, he picked up the telephone in his room and dialled the number he had been given by the Abwehr. He asked to speak with 'Herr Schneider' (a code name) and was put through to a man who called himself Dr Beier.

Dr Beier was the alias of Captain Julius Jacob Boeckel, born on 8 December 1894 in Mittelbergheim, south-west of Strasbourg.[7] After completing his schooling, Boeckel worked for an import–export firm in Strasbourg. He served in the heavy artillery during the First World War and finished the war as a commissioned officer.[8] In 1937, Boeckel attended a training camp for reserve officers of the Luftwaffe (he had learned to fly privately in 1932) and was remobilised in 1939. On 15 June 1940 Boeckel was recruited into the Abwehr by Nikolaus Ritter, who had risen to lead the air intelligence section of the Hamburg Abwehr office (Referat I Luft).

Boeckel had no espionage experience, but since he was a businessman who had travelled extensively, Ritter thought he might be useful.[9] The principal task of Ritter's section was to supply information on the air force and aeroplane industries of Great Britain and the United States. Three sources of information were used to obtain information: espionage agents, the interrogation of travelling businessmen and the study of newspapers and technical journals.

Boeckel started his espionage career by studying reports from other branches of the Abwehr and extracting items of interest to Referat I Luft. Ritter also put him to work editing reports from agents in Britain. Although Boeckel received no formal training in his duties, he was given the task of instructing Operation LENA agents in espionage tactics.

Josef, a novice spy, found himself under instruction from Boeckel, a novice spymaster. The foundation of a successful espionage career was riven with cracks, but Josef was oblivious. Boeckel told Josef that, as a member of the Abwehr, he could not be transferred to any other service (e.g. military) or be harassed by the Gestapo. Josef definitely liked the sound of that and, after negotiation, reached an agreement with Boeckel. During his training Josef would be on the Abwehr payroll. After he departed on his mission, his wife would receive 200 RM[10] per month.[11] When Josef returned from his mission, his Mexican securities, still held by the foreign exchange authorities, would be returned to him. Finally, Josef received permission to travel home to Berlin every weekend to visit his wife and children. Both men signed the contract, and with that, Josef was formally an agent of the Abwehr.

Over the next few weeks, Boeckel showed Josef messages that had come via wireless transmitter from spies in England. Josef needed to learn how the Abwehr wanted messages sent. One message gave a description of industrial buildings and factories in Coventry before the heavy air raid of 14 November 1940. Another message was partly written in Swedish and described a newly constructed factory. Other messages described road barricades, gave advice not to use a specific aerodrome (as it was laid with traps) and gave the names of ships in dry dock.[12] Boeckel said that Hamburg was pleased with the information and even one useful message was worth the high expenditures associated with each agent.

Under Boeckel's instruction Josef learned map reading, an indispensable skill in England where all directional signs had been removed to confound potential invaders. If he was to be a useful agent, Josef would need to know how to connect lines on a map to the streams, roads and railways around him. Josef was also taught how to make a rudimentary secret ink using Pyramidon, a headache remedy readily available in German pharmacies, and presumably British ones as well. Boeckel stressed that secret ink should only be used if all other avenues of communication failed. While it was relatively easy to obtain, a secret ink made from Pyramidon was also easy to detect.

Boeckel ensured that Josef received training in the basics of weather reporting – wind speed and direction, cloud height and type, air temperature and pressure. Boeckel told Josef that he would receive more intense training in weather reporting later. Finally, Josef was taken to several aerodromes around Hamburg and instructed in technical aeronautical matters. He learned to identify British aeroplanes and anti-aircraft guns. Boeckel encouraged Josef to enroll in English classes at the Berlitz school in Hamburg.

Interestingly, the Abwehr did not see fluency in the English language as an integral requirement of their LENA training programme. After the war Boeckel admitted to MI5 that, while none of the agents spoke perfect English, 'Berlin insisted that they be despatched as rapidly as possible.'[13] The agents were told that their strong accents would attract little attention in Britain due to the high number of German-Jewish refugees who were an accepted part of British society. Nothing could have been further from the truth.

During most of his training, Josef never encountered any other espionage trainees but on one occasion, during an outing to an aerodrome with Boeckel, Josef met fellow agent Karel Richard Richter. A Czechoslovakian of German descent, Richter had been born in 1912 in Kraslice, Sudetenland.[14] After working at his father's metalwork business, Richter became a machinist on ships that served the Hamburg–New York route. In 1938 Richter automatically became a German citizen when Germany annexed Sudetenland.

The ramifications of that event had little impact on Richter until the autumn of 1939 when war was declared. Afraid that he might be drafted into the German navy, Richter deserted his ship and returned home. After bidding farewell to his parents, Richter travelled to Sweden, intent on finding a way to return to America, where he had a girlfriend and a young son. He was arrested by the Swedish police for not having the proper documentation and imprisoned for several months. In July 1940, Richter was deported to Sassnitz in Germany, where he was promptly arrested by the Gestapo and imprisoned in Fuhlsbüttel concentration camp near Hamburg. It was here that he was recruited by the Abwehr as a spy. Josef later learned that Richter wasn't the best espionage trainee, having been reprimanded for his excessive drinking, fighting and tardiness.

Josef did not find espionage training all that strenuous and thoroughly enjoyed his time in Hamburg. He was safe from the Gestapo, he was drawing a pay cheque and his evenings were his own. After four weeks at the Reichshof Hotel, Josef moved into the Hotel Sorgenfrei, also in the vicinity of the *Hauptbahnhof*. Josef's love of music drew him to the Café Dreyer, near the train station, where orchestras and singers were always on the programme. As it turned out, Richter also enjoyed the big-band style of American dance music and frequented the café. Both men agreed that the Bernard Ette Orchestra (or Ette Orchestra) was excellent but differed in their opinion of one of the female singers. Richter thought that she was tall and ugly, but Josef was entranced by the deep-voiced Clara.

Hedwig Clara Bäuerle,[15] born on 27 August 1905 in Ulm, Baden-Württemberg,[16] first appeared on the German artistic scene in the early 1930s when she landed a small part in the motion picture musical *Die Blume von Hawaii*.[17] A few years later, she played a young lady at the ball in the film *Bal Paré*.[18] Clara's sultry voice piqued the interest of a recording studio. In September 1940 she was featured on recordings by the Tempo record label and appeared with the Ette Orchestra.

Clara was flattered by the attention of the lean and handsome Josef. He had an air of mystery about him and she gracefully accepted the drinks that he bought her. She was less impressed with the taciturn scowls of Richter.

In October 1940, having played at the Café Dreyer for several weeks, the Ette Orchestra (and Clara) left on a tour that took them to Leipzig, Dresden, Forst, East Prussia and Berlin. Josef was disappointed to see Clara depart, as their relationship had become more intimate and she had moved into his rooms at the Hotel Sorgenfrei. On the other hand, Josef was able to devote more attention to his espionage training, which had moved into the realm of wireless transmission.

A non-commissioned officer named Peterson, the Abwehr's chief wireless instructor, was in charge of Josef's wireless training. The first step was for Josef to become proficient in transmitting and deciphering Morse code. Josef brought his Morse sender back to Berlin at the weekends and tried to increase his transmission speed.[19] Peterson told him speed was of the essence; once he was in England and began a transmission, the British would hear his signal and try to triangulate his position. It was extremely important that Josef keep his time on the air as short as possible to avoid detection. Peterson also probably trained Josef in the use of a disc code with which he could encode his transmissions using a simple transposition code.

Josef's wireless transmitter/receiver was an impressive feat of German engineering and miniaturisation. The transmitter, once a relatively bulky instrument, had been redesigned to fit into an attaché case. Josef, dressed in business clothes and carrying such a nondescript case, would pass unnoticed through the London crowds.

Josef was told that every person had a unique way of sending a Morse code message; something called their 'fist', which an expert could recognise easily. Peterson told Josef that they would make recordings of his 'fist' and share them with the wireless operators listening for his signal.[20] If he was captured and the British tried to use Josef's transmitter, pretending to be him, the German wireless operators would immediately recognise the impersonation.

During one of his sessions with Boeckel, Josef asked what he should do if his wireless set failed. Boeckel said that if his wireless set malfunctioned, or if he thought that he was being watched by the British Security Service (MI5), he should send a message to that effect and wait. He would be told how to get in touch with another agent and how to transmit under cover of that agent. Boeckel assured Josef that the safety of the agents was paramount and the most dangerous aspect of his mission would be discovery by MI5.

Hamburg often didn't expect to receive a message from a newly inserted agent for four to six weeks. They knew that the agent had to find a place to stay and a safe place from which to transmit, which could take time. Sometimes Hamburg would wait as long as six months, listening every day for a transmission from the agent. One of the agents who had parachuted into England in September had hurt his ankle upon landing (Schmidt/ TATE) and it had taken a while before Hamburg had heard back from him. That admission prompted Josef to ask if he could make a couple of practice parachute jumps. Boeckel waved Josef's concerns aside and told him that it would be better to avoid practice jumps. The first jump was often lucky, and people were often much more nervous when jumping for the second time.

The reality of his upcoming mission did not distract Josef from enjoying the finer things in life. On 7 November 1940 Josef phoned Clara Bäuerle in Forst and set up a meeting in Berlin. The Ette Orchestra was scheduled to play at the Neue Welt in Hasenheide, Berlin, from 23–24 November. It just so happened that this was a weekend and it dovetailed perfectly with Josef's weekly visit to his family. Josef was enamoured with Clara and would do anything to see her. Josef's wife knew that he loved big-band music and it didn't take much for him to talk her into an evening out in Hasenheide to listen to the Ette Orchestra. The children could be left in the care of their grandmother and it would be an evening just for the two of them, or so she thought. The Ette Orchestra was lovely, but Margarete was a shrewd woman and when Josef introduced her to Clara, she could smell a rat. She saw the way they looked at each other, the familiarity with which they laughed and chatted. Margarete was not a happy woman, but Josef was leaving for Hamburg the next day and she held her tongue.

On 25 November, Josef and Clara returned to Hamburg and settled into his rooms at the Hotel Sorgenfrei. Josef resumed his English lessons at the Berlitz school and this time Clara joined him. Clara enjoyed singing with the Ette Orchestra but told Josef that the pay was not great. Josef had already taken Clara into his confidence about working for the Abwehr. The two of them put their heads together and, soon enough, Josef introduced Clara to Boeckel. Perhaps Boeckel could get Clara a gig singing for the troops? Richter saw Josef and Clara around town and shook his head. Josef was more interested in his affairs with women than he was in espionage, but events would soon push him over the edge.

On his weekend trips to Berlin, Josef often got together with old friends. One of them was a man named Van Hees, a veteran of the First World War, who lived in Berlin-Halensee.[21] Van Hees was a wealthy man who owned several houses in Cologne, living off of the rental income. Josef and Van Hees had met years ago at the Bridge Club of the Lessing High School and continued to meet regularly at the iconic Café Trumpf on Kurfürstendamm. The two men shared other things in common, for Van Hees had served two years in prison in the early 1930s for a foreign exchange violation. He continually grumbled to Josef that he was harassed by the Nazis and even admitted that he listened to English radio transmissions, an offence punishable with imprisonment. Van Hees had also spent ten years in London and that was enough for Josef to reveal his secret plan.

Josef told Van Hees that he had no intention of sending information to the Abwehr from England. He intended to contact the British Security Service and/or continue onwards to the United States. He had negotiated a deal with the Abwehr and expected to receive £2,000[22] of his own money (from the Mexican securities) and a Swiss passport. With these in hand, Josef told Van Hees that this was his big chance to get out of Germany and away from the watchful eye of the Gestapo. Van Hees gave Josef his word of honour that he would keep silent. Josef assumed that Van Hees was trustworthy, but he was mistaken.

In late December Josef travelled home to Berlin to celebrate Christmas with his family. It was a less than idyllic visit. Margarete was unhappy about his affair with Clara and voiced her displeasure. Josef flatly denied any wrongdoing and tried to sweet-talk his wife.

The New Year did little to ease the tension. On 3 January 1941, Josef received a phone call from Boeckel, who ordered him to return to Hamburg as soon as possible.[23] On 5 January Margarete and Josef bid each other a stiff goodbye; neither knew that it would be their final adieu. Once back in Hamburg, Josef was hauled into the office of the head of the Hamburg Abwehr and told that the Gestapo in Berlin had issued a warrant for his arrest for treason. Josef was shown a written denunciation given to the Gestapo by none other than Van Hees, a Gestapo informant.

Josef tried to cover his tracks and told the Abwehr officers that he had only said those things to Van Hees to see if he was loyal. It was the word of Van Hees against the word of Josef. After hours of questioning, two German officers vouched for Josef and said that he was a good German, his training was complete, and his departure was imminent. The Abwehr took a dim view of the Van Hees denunciation but decided to send Josef to England nonetheless. They were desperately short of agents and, after all, they had his wife and children as hostages. If word reached Germany that Josef had done anything traitorous, the Gestapo could take their revenge on his family. As a consequence, however, Josef was not allowed to take any of his own money and only received an identity card instead of the Swiss passport.

After his questioning by the Abwehr, Josef was transferred to The Hague on 7 or 8 January 1941. He stayed at the Zeben Hotel in Molenstraat and was placed under the command of Major Malten of Referat I Luft in The Hague.[24] Malten arranged a ration book for Josef and ensured that he received a salary of 12 RM per day.[25]

While in The Hague, Josef received intense instruction in weather reporting, wireless transmission and coding messages using the disc code. Every day he was picked up at his hotel and driven to 131 Vondelstraat. There, in a nondescript flat, Josef was grilled on wireless transmission by a man named Schulz while Malten's second in command, an officer named Hiller, pointed out Josef's transmission errors. Sometimes, Josef was driven to Wassenaar, a suburb of The Hague, where he would send messages back to the Vondelstraat address, where they were taken down by another espionage trainee. Josef claimed that he never met any other agents while he was at the Vondelstraat address, although he did bump into Richter at the Hotel Central.

One evening, as a big-band orchestra played, Richter told Josef that he was being trained to build a wireless set from scratch. With a smug grin,

Richter bragged that he had found all the pieces for a set in Hamburg, quite a feat during wartime. Richter was confident that once he landed in England, he would be able to scrounge all the necessary parts and be able to communicate with Germany. On top of that, Richter claimed that he had memorised the secret code. Josef listened with disbelief and challenged Richter on the last claim. It was impossible to memorise the code because it changed daily, but Richter insisted that he had a special system whereby he could always remember the code.

Josef went back to his instructor, Schulz, and asked him if he could also be trained in wireless construction, a process that took four to five months. Schulz assured Josef that his transmitter would be fine and that he should not listen to Richter, who was considered irresponsible.

As the date for Josef's departure drew ever nearer, his nervousness increased. He and Richter had both been assured that their accent would cause little difficulty and that they could easily learn English within two weeks. According to his Abwehr handlers, it was very simple. Once Josef landed, he would bury his parachute gear and make his way to the nearest village where he would buy a third-class ticket to London. Once in London, he would find a flat, set up his wireless transmitter and begin sending weather reports at the scheduled times. It sounded easy in theory, but Josef had his doubts.

Schulz tried to allay his fears by telling him that important agents could be brought back to Germany by aeroplane or boat. If Josef wished to return to Germany at any time, all he had to do was send a message to Hamburg and an aeroplane or a boat would be sent to fetch him. If he ran out of funds, the Russian or Japanese embassies could provide him with money. The Abwehr had thought of everything and numerous agents had already succeeded in their missions. However, despite these assurances, Josef had concerns.

In January, Josef wrote several letters to his wife and sent her a dried rose.[26] He apologised for his failures, professed his love for her and swore that he had never had an affair with Clara.[27] One could wonder at the sincerity of his protestations, for he also wrote letters to Hamburg begging Clara to come and visit him.

Alas, on 21 January 1941 Josef received word that Clara was ill in hospital. Wracked by worry, Josef was unable to rush to Clara's bedside. His departure was imminent, and he needed to remain in The Hague. The days dragged as Josef waited for favourable weather conditions. Every day, between 5 and 6 p.m., Major Malten received the weather reports. Every day, Josef sat in his hotel room between those hours, packed and ready to leave on his mission. Josef had been told that he couldn't bring any personal items with him, but he had tucked two small photographs into the seam of his jacket. Every day, for weeks, Major Malten had telephoned Josef at 6 p.m. and told him that the weather conditions were not favourable and that he was free for the evening.

On the evening of 31 January, Josef picked up the telephone receiver and heard Malten's voice tell him that the weather conditions were favourable. The mission was a go.

10

A LEAP INTO THE UNKNOWN

Malten drove to Josef's hotel and went to his room, where he found Josef hurriedly putting on layer after layer of extra clothing.[1] He could bring no suitcase with him, so he was trying to wear as much as possible. The rest of his belongings remained in the suitcase, which Malten said would be sent to Boeckel in Hamburg.

A short while later, Malten and Josef sat in the back of the car as it wove through the streets of The Hague – destination Schiphol Aerodrome outside Amsterdam. Upon arrival at Schiphol, Josef was introduced to his flight crew: *Oberleutnant* (First Lieutenant or Flying Officer) Marke,[2] *Leutnant* (Second Lieutenant or Pilot Officer) Mueller and a *Feldwebel* (sergeant) whose name Josef didn't catch.

As the flight crew made their preparations, Malten handed Josef two identity cards, one blank and one in the name of James Rymer, which he was told to sign. Malten also handed him a ration book and £500 cash.[3] Marke then sat down with Josef, pulled out a map, and showed him where they planned to drop him by drawing a triangle between the cities of Peterborough, Cambridge and Bedford. Marke made two other marks on the map, but in the hustle of preparations Josef wasn't clear about their significance.[4]

The three men helped Josef pull on the flight suit and found a helmet that fitted him. His pockets were stuffed with the identity cards, the map, wallets and the cash. Other pockets held a folding knife, food, a pistol, spare ammunition, cigarettes and a lighter. Josef climbed into the parachute harness, which was pulled tight by the air crew. Finally, the attaché case containing the wireless set was strapped to his chest. He was ready.

With growing trepidation, Josef joined the crew as they walked out to the aeroplane in the gathering gloom. Malten wished him luck, privately musing that he would need it. The aeroplane, painted black, was hard to see and Marke told Josef that it had been modified so that the bomb hatch was a trapdoor through which parachutists could drop.[5] Marke noted that there was always a chance that, upon arrival over England, weather conditions might have deteriorated, so the jump was not a sure thing, but at this point, everything looked good. Marke claimed to have dropped two or three other agents and had sometimes had to abort the drops three times because of unfavourable conditions.

Josef and the aircrew climbed into the belly of the beast. Marke and Mueller went up front to prepare the aeroplane for take-off. The *Feldwebel* showed Josef where to sit along the side of the fuselage and how to strap himself into a safety harness. He said that after take-off they would climb quickly to 10,000m, so Josef would need to use the oxygen supply that hung nearby. When they reached the correct position, they would cut the engines and glide down to 3,000m, at which point Josef would jump through the narrow trapdoor.

The engines started with sputtering coughs but soon found their rhythm and as the aeroplane bumped along the taxiway, Josef looked at his watch – 8 p.m. Less than three hours had passed since Malten had telephoned him with the news that the weather conditions were favourable. For better or for worse, Josef was on his way to England. The engines changed their pitch, their muted rumble becoming a bellow, and with increasing acceleration the aeroplane thundered along the runway. One last jolt of the tyres and they were airborne, climbing steeply over the North Sea.

After several minutes, the *Feldwebel* stuck his head around the corner and motioned that it was time to use the oxygen supply. After a bit of fumbling, Josef inhaled deeply and almost gagged from the smell of synthetic rubber. The drone of the engines was mindnumbing and it was hard to concentrate. On top of that, the temperature in the aeroplane had plummeted. Uncomfortable, Josef squirmed to find a better position, but it was hopeless. Major Malten had given him a choice of coming by aeroplane, boat or submarine, and he had thought that the aeroplane sounded more adventurous. Perhaps it was too adventurous. Certainly it was cold, uncomfortable, cramped, noisy and smelly. At 10,000m, the aeroplane levelled off – they were flying high above the North Sea, further and further away from his family and his mistress.

Less than an hour later, the roar of the engines eased, and the aeroplane began to glide down above Huntingdonshire. As they descended, the *Feldwebel* removed his oxygen mask, stood up and opened the trapdoor. As the icy night air whistled through the opening, the *Feldwebel* helped Josef to stand. His right leg was numb with cold and Josef struggled to maintain his balance as the *Feldwebel* grabbed a strap attached to the frame near the opening and clipped it to the release cord on Josef's parachute. The *Feldwebel* leaned towards Josef and shouted over the wind, 'You will sit on the edge of the opening here, facing backwards. You'll hang on to this bar here, and when I tell you, you will put your legs through the opening, then your body, and then you will let go of the bar. Your parachute will release automatically. Understand?' Josef swallowed dryly and nodded. Gingerly, he approached the edge of the hole, which showed unrelieved darkness.

Encumbered by the attaché case and the parachute, Josef edged closer to the opening and tentatively placed his legs into the gaping hole. The wind seized them, and he quickly pulled them up again. The *Feldwebel* nudged him and assured him that he would be fine. Once again, he braced himself and put his right leg through the opening, thinking that he would have better control over one leg than over two. His leg was snatched by the turbulence and thrown against the side of the opening. Piercing pain shot through his leg and he cried out. The *Feldwebel* looked at him quizzically. Josef knew that he could let the crew know that he was injured but he was committed. There was no going back.

Josef pulled his right leg up again and then put both legs through the opening trying to control them as the turbulence tugged them to and fro. Grasping the bar, he slid his body into the opening, but the parachute and attaché case were wedged against the metal. He was stuck. The wind was doing no favours to his right leg and he winced with every gust. The *Feldwebel*, seeing his predicament, pushed on the attaché case and the parachute, until finally he was free. For a brief moment he hung onto the bar and then his hands slipped, and he was whipped away into the darkness.

Turning and tumbling, Josef could barely breathe; the speed of his fall sucked the air from his mouth. The silence was numbing after the roar inside the aeroplane but then suddenly Josef heard the flutter of fabric unfurling and his fall was arrested as the parachute opened fully. His lower right leg was throbbing horribly, and every little gust of wind that pulled at him sent another stab of pain through his body. He knew that he still had a landing to endure. He hoped that his leg was simply sprained; he couldn't tell and would have to wait until he landed on the earth. The *Leutnant* had told him that if he exited at 3,000m, he would have less than five minutes of descent time. How much time had already lapsed? He tried to remember what Major Malten had said about parachute landings. It was like jumping off of a 6ft high wall. Unfortunately, descending through the night sky, Josef had no idea where he would be landing. It could be fields or woods, or a pond. Another stab of pain from his right leg and he wondered if he should try to land on his left leg alone.

It happened quickly. One moment he was drifting through the darkness and the next moment he made violent contact with the earth. In an instant, he lay in a crumpled heap on the ground. Pain seared through his lower right leg, far worse than in the aeroplane. He lay gasping, clawing the soft earth with his hands. A frigid drizzle caressed his face. He pushed himself up with his hands and tried to move his right leg, which was trapped awkwardly under his left. Moaning with pain, he pulled on the trouser leg, lifting up his left leg until the right one was free. Collapsing onto his back, Josef muttered a prayer. It couldn't be that bad. It was just a sprain.

Sitting up again, he felt down his right leg. His thigh was OK, his knee felt fine. His shin and lower leg were not fine. His searching fingers felt the jagged sharpness of bone pressed against skin. Beyond that, his foot was bent in a way that no foot should ever bend. He fell back to the ground. He knew he had hurt his leg in the aeroplane, but the landing had made everything much worse. He sat up again and tried to roll over. His right leg would not follow. The pain was unbearable. Every little movement sent a sharp stab of pain up his leg. There was no escape. He could not walk; he could not crawl. He was well and truly stuck ... stuck on that soft patch of earth.

Darkness all around him. The soughing of the wind in the dead grass. Far away, the bark of a dog. Josef unzipped his flying suit with shaking fingers and fumbled in a pocket for his lighter. By the light of its flickering flame, he saw that it was 9.30 p.m. Continental time (CT), or 7.30 p.m. British time.[6] He was cold and the drizzle was making him wet. Reaching into another pocket, Josef pulled out the pocket knife, opened up the blade and reached back over his shoulders to cut the parachute cords. He pulled the parachute towards him; it wasn't much, but it would offer some protection from the weather. Reaching down, he wrapped part of the parachute around his legs, and then tucked it around his upper body. The helmet was heavy on his head and he unbuckled the strap and pushed it to the side. Reaching into one of the flying suit pockets, he pulled out a slightly battered trilby hat. It would offer a bit of protection from the drizzle.

The attaché case was digging into his chest and stomach, so with stiff fingers he undid the straps. The wireless set was useless to him, worse than useless, for it incriminated him as a spy more surely than anything else. Digging into another pocket, he pulled out his cigarette case and lit one from the lighter. He inhaled deeply and let the smoke trickle out through his nostrils. The minutes slipped by and he was aware that he needed to answer the call of nature. He was pinned to the ground as surely as if a stake were driven through his lower right leg. There was nothing he could do but wet himself and release his bowels. This was not how he had pictured the life of a spy. No one had mentioned that one could break a leg and soil oneself, waiting in the dark and cold to be found by the enemy.

Josef toyed with the idea of firing shots into the air from his pistol, but it was night-time. Even if someone heard the shots and opened their door to investigate, they would have no idea in which direction to look, for sound played tricks in the dark. He had no idea how far away he was from civilisation, from a village or farmhouse. The hours passed with excruciating slowness. He shivered in the chill night breeze. Sleep was impossible. The pain in his leg ensured that he would have no rest that night. He lit another cigarette.

Time after time he checked his watch with the lighter as he lit another cigarette, grateful for the light and warmth that the small flame afforded him. A few hours later, even that comfort abandoned him when the lighter simply sputtered and went out. He shook it and tried again, it was empty.

Ever so slowly the sky shaded from unrelieved black through shades of grey. He looked at his watch and saw that it was 9 a.m. CT (7 a.m. British time). It was Saturday, 1 February. His children were already at school for their half a day of instruction. His wife was at home. What would she think once his last letter came and none followed? Would the Abwehr tell her that he had left on his mission? Even the Abwehr wouldn't know what had happened to him. It would be as if he had simply vanished, sucked into the darkness of the British skies, never to be seen again.

As it grew lighter, Josef propped himself up and looked around. Fields all around him, farmhouses in the distance and, further still, a church steeple. He could hear the crowing of roosters and the barking of dogs. Someone would surely come past soon and find him – which gave him pause. There he lay, covered by a camouflaged parachute, with a German helmet, an incriminating attaché case and a flying suit over the top of a civilian suit. Most likely it would be uneducated farm labourers who found him and, dullwitted folk that they were, think 'Nazi spy' and mistreat him. The attaché case needed to be hidden. With a groan of pain, Josef sat up and used the collapsible shovel to dig a shallow hole behind and beneath him. He placed the case in the hole, pulled the soil over the top and sat on it.

He lay back again to rest. The minutes passed, and he looked about again. There was no one in sight. The minutes ticked away and then suddenly, faintly, he heard the rumble of male voices. Looking up he saw two men walking through the fields. Josef fumbled for the pistol and his fingers brushed against cardboard. The code. The damned, incriminating code! He pulled out the disc code and tore the cardboard to shreds and threw the pieces away from him.[7] Then he pulled out the pistol and prepared to meet the British.

11

SPY CATCHERS

It was the morning of 1 February 1941 and the mist clung to the damp ploughed earth south-east of the sleepy village of Ramsey in Huntingdonshire. Two smallholders, Charles Baldock and Harry Coulson, ambled across Dovehouse Farm on their way to work from the neighbouring village of Warboys.

At 8.20 a.m., Josef raised the loaded Mauser pistol into the air and fired three shots. He craned his head and saw the men pause and look around. Josef waved an arm over his head, but the men continued walking. Josef fired four more shots into the air. The men stopped again as Josef waved frantically, but he was too low to the ground, and they were still at a distance. As they resumed walking, Josef fired two more shots into the air.[1] His ammunition was limited, and this was his best hope at rescue. The farmers stopped again. The two shots had sounded very close and suddenly they saw Josef lying in a potato field about 150 yards from where they stood.[2]

Both men held up their hands and Baldock shouted, 'Don't shoot!'[3] Josef put up his hands in return and Baldock approached him cautiously. As Baldock drew near, Josef threw his pistol into the helmet. Baldock saw that Josef was covered with a camouflage parachute, which explained why he had been so hard to spot. Coulson stayed on the path along the dyke and only came near when he saw that Josef had given up the pistol.[4]

Baldock picked up the pistol and asked Josef, 'What are you up to?' Josef understood the gist of the English – the farmer wanted to know what he was doing there. That would have needed a long answer and it suddenly dawned on Josef that he was defenceless before these men, one of whom now held the pistol. There was nothing to stop them from shooting him.

Who would cry over a dead spy in a farmer's field? He needed to say something, but in his weakened state, his English was almost non-existent. He stumbled over the words and muttered something about, 'Solo flying'. Baldock asked him where he was from, and that too was complicated. Josef needed to communicate to them that he was no threat and so he said, 'Hamburg – I am in no war.' He opened his flying suit and pointed to his civilian clothes, then touched his leg and said, 'Broken.' That statement resulted in action. Baldock knew that he and Coulson could not handle the spy on their own and he sent Coulson to nearby Wistow Fen Farm for assistance. As Coulson left, Josef realised that he was now alone with one man, who still carried the pistol. Hoping to garner sympathy, Josef told the farmers that he was a Frenchman who had been sent from Hamburg.[5]

Coulson hurried into the yard at Wistow Fen Farm at about 8.45 a.m. and found farm labourer Harry Godfrey, who was also a Home Guard volunteer. Breathlessly, Coulson told Godfrey that he and Baldock had found a German parachutist in a nearby field. Godfrey's ears perked with interest. Months ago, all of the Home Guard had received a lecture on what to do with enemy parachutists. Godfrey knew the routine and went inside to telephone Ramsey Police Station while Coulson headed back to Baldock. Godfrey asked to be put through to Acting Inspector Horace Jaikens and then briskly reported the news of a suspected enemy parachut-ist. Godfrey told Jaikens that the man had been disarmed and was under the supervision of two members of the Home Guard. Hanging up the phone, Godfrey hurried off to join the growing crowd of farm labourers standing in the distance.

A few miles away, Jaikens picked up the telephone and informed Acting Police Sergeant Pottle, in the nearby village of Bury, that Godfrey of Wistow Fen Farm had called to report a parachutist. After notify-ing Pottle, Jaikens telephoned Captain William H. Newton, Officer Commanding the Ramsey Company, Home Guard, and told him that a German parachutist had been discovered by Home Guard volunteers near Dovehouse Farm. Jaikens presumed that the Home Guard would like to have the honour of apprehending the parachutist and transfer-ring him to the police station. Jaikens then called Detective Sergeant Thomas Oliver Mills (Huntingdonshire Constabulary) in Huntingdon and advised him of the news.

Meanwhile, Godfrey joined the group around Josef and asked him what he was doing. Josef again replied, 'Me solo flying'. Godfrey looked around incredulously and asked Josef what he had done with his aeroplane, to which Josef could make no reply. Godfrey asked him if he was hurt and Josef gratefully acknowledged that his leg was broken. Godfrey lifted the parachute off Josef and eyed the mess of his right leg. Removing a scarf from around his neck, Godfrey gently straightened Josef's legs and tied them together to stabilise the broken one. As he worked, Godfrey looked up and asked Josef where he was from and Josef said, 'Me not in this war, from Luxembourg, made to come.'[6]

Back in Ramsey, Captain Newton telephoned Platoon Commander Lieutenant John Curedale[7] of the Home Guard and officiously told him that they had urgent business in connection with their Home Guard duties. Curedale put on his uniform and drove to Newton's house, where he learned that a suspected enemy agent had landed near Ramsey. The two officers set off for Ramsey Hollow and Wistow Fen Farm.[8]

At about 9.20 a.m., Newton and Curedale, both dressed in their Home Guard uniforms, arrived at the potato field[9] and found Josef on the ground surrounded by Godfrey, Baldock, Coulson and several curious farm labourers. The two officers noted that Josef was wearing civilian clothes under a brown overall with zip fasteners. Baldock handed Newton the pistol and a box of ammunition. Newton asked Josef if there was anyone else with him and received an answer in the negative. He asked Josef who he was, and Josef replied, 'I am a Frenchman.' As he listened to the exchange, Curedale would later note that, based on Josef's answers and the shape of his helmet, he thought that the man was a foreigner and probably an enemy agent.[10]

For Josef, the pain in his leg was overwhelming. He knew that the British were allied with the French and that Luxembourg, his birthplace, was a neutral country. He knew that to speak the truth, to say that he was a German, might not bode well for him. He knew that if the Nazis were to find a wounded British parachutist in a German field, dressed in civilian clothing, especially one who could not walk, they might be tempted to despatch him right away. The men before him appeared to be soldiers and were unlikely to view any German as a friend. He may have stretched the truth, but the language barrier was also a source of misunderstanding.

Newton turned to Godfrey and asked him if he had searched Josef and Godfrey admitted that he had not. The two men performed a cursory search of Josef and his clothing, seeking to remove anything that he might try to destroy. Newton found a large bundle of £1 notes in Josef's pockets. They also found a leather note case with more money, a leather wallet with identity papers as well as a packet of sandwiches and a small bottle of alcohol.[11]

A number of pieces of torn brown cardboard were scattered on the ground around Josef (from the disc code) and under Newton's orders, these were carefully collected by Baldock and the others. Curedale was ordered to take charge of the confiscated articles and placed them in a sack.[12]

Newton commandeered a horse and cart from a nearby farm but as the group prepared to lift Josef into the cart, one of the men kicked the attaché case that had been buried in the ground beneath Josef. The men placed Josef in the horse cart as gently as possible, but it still caused him excruciating pain. His harness, parachute and attaché case were also placed in the cart.

Accompanied by another Home Guard volunteer,[13] Godfrey climbed into the cart, picked up the reins and started the slow procession to Ramsey Police Station. Newton and Curedale turned their attention to the cluster of curious farm labourers and shooed them away with strict orders to avoid the potato field.

Satisfied that they had done all that they could, Newton and Curedale returned to their vehicle and drove off in the direction of Ramsey. Coulson and Baldock wandered off with the other farm labourers, who peppered them with questions. What had happened? Who was the parachutist? Both men were late for work but revelled in the attention and shared details with the news-hungry group. Behind them, the field lay empty. The soft ploughed earth held the impression left by Josef's body. Water pooled in the hollow. Soon the hollow would be gone, and nothing would remain to mark the location of the drama that had unfolded that morning.

The cart ride, across open fields and rutted farm lanes was unbearable for Josef – every rut, every bump, sent arrows of pain through his leg. He tried to brace himself against the sides of the cart, but it was hopeless. The grey skies had lightened considerably since dawn, but the air still had a damp chill that gnawed at his bones. He was cold and tired. He was hungry and thirsty. He was in pain and far from home. He was humiliated by his incontinence and being carried to an unknown fate. He knew that he needed to keep his wits about him, but it was hard to concentrate. It was hard to know what to say. He knew that if they had no use for him, he would end up on the gallows. He needed to make them believe that he was more useful alive than dead.

The cart lurched off the muddy rural lane onto the cobblestone streets of Ramsey. They passed the local church and Josef offered up a prayer for strength and good fortune. Along the High Street, people paused to turn and stare – women wearing little hats; soldiers in uniform; farmers with haycarts; delivery men with wagons of beer; the postman with his bag. After watching the cart pass, people turned to each other and began to whisper and wonder, 'Who is the man in the back of the horse cart?'

The cart turned to the right, off High Street onto Blenheim Road. A short distance up the road was a low whitewashed building with a police globe lamp hanging in front. The cart made the turn into the rear court-yard of the police station and several officers came out to greet them.

12

AN ENGLISH GAOL

Half an hour earlier, Newton and Curedale had arrived at Ramsey Police Station with the sack of confiscated articles. Inspector Jaikens made a detailed list of the items: £497 in £1 bank notes, one Mauser pistol (two live rounds), seven rounds of ammunition in a cardboard box and a metal helmet. A brown leather wallet contained a ration book; an identity card marked 656/301/29 with the name of James Rymer, London, 33 Abbotsford Gardens, Woodford Green, dated 4 June 1940; a blank identity card; and a picture postcard of a woman on which was written in English, 'My dear, I love you forever, yours, Clara, Landau, July 1940.'[1] There was also a packet of minced meat sandwiches, a portion of brown sausage and a small bottle of spirits.[2]

While Jaikens was cataloguing the items, the door opened to reveal Detective Sergeant Mills from Huntingdon. Jaikens brought Mills up to speed and pointed out the registration number on the identity card. Both men agreed that it was an obvious forgery: the registration number had three numbers instead of the four-letter prefix and the address was written in Continental fashion, with the city before the street address.[3] Jaikens suggested that the pink traveller's ration book was also suspicious as it was brand new and none of the particulars had been completed. Mills held up several bank notes and thought that some might be forgeries. Their conversation was interrupted by a constable, who announced the arrival of the cart.

Mills, Jaikens, Newton and Curedale went out to greet the prisoner. After a quick look at Josef's leg, Jaikens returned to the office and telephoned Dr Wilhelm Hertzog (a native of South Africa).[4] By the time the doctor arrived, Josef had been brought into the police station on a stretcher. After a brief conversation with Jaikens, Hertzog gently examined Josef's right leg. He confirmed what everyone already knew; Josef had a severely broken right ankle. Hertzog applied a splint to the leg but told Jaikens that the leg needed advanced medical attention, and quickly. Hertzog then wrote a certificate that stated Josef was fit to be transported to London.

With Josef's injury stabilised, Jaikens asked him basic questions: name, age, place of birth, occupation and the circumstances surrounding his arrival.[5] Josef's poor English made communication difficult but Jaikens may have drawn on his rusty German picked up during the Great War. (In September 1916, while serving in France with the Royal Warwickshire Regiment, Jaikens had been captured by the Germans and sent to the Giessen prisoner-of-war camp, where he spent the last two years of the war.) Jaikens noted that Josef Jakobs had been born in Luxembourg and was 42 years old. He had worked as a dental mechanic but claimed to be a soldier. Josef said that the German authorities had supplied him with his clothing, money and other equipment. He left Holland at around 8 p.m. (CT) on 31 January 1941, in a German aeroplane[6] which flew to England.[7] He jumped out of the aeroplane at about 9 p.m. (CT) at 3,000 feet [*sic*].[8] He had been instructed to report on the weather and to contact a woman in London, but no one in Huntingdonshire.[9]

Mills knew even less German than Jaikens and tried to speak slowly using simple English words. He wanted to know if any other agents had been dropped the previous evening, but Josef said he was the only one. In spite of these assurances, Mills ordered the surrounding countryside be searched.

Jaikens and Mills then subjected Josef to a more thorough examination, turning out all of his pockets. They discovered: five £1 bank notes, a map of Great Britain, a cigarette lighter, a propelling pencil, a packet of twenty Cordon Rouge cigarettes,[10] a pair of reading glasses in a blue leather case marked 'Optiker-Ruhnke', two packets of Dutch chocolate,[11] a small tube of capsules, a Roman Catholic badge, a wristwatch on a black leather strap,[12] a leather cigarette case marked 'Zeka Wettig Geder', a brown leather purse with zip fastener, a blue leather note case with chain guard attached, a pocket knife marked 'Swing', a comb in a case, a pair of scissors and a nail file in a leather case,[13] a blue German–English dictionary marked *Metoula Sprachführer* (a German–English phrasebook), a 2½ cent piece, a new pair of grey socks, a pair of ear pads, two keys, a new coloured handkerchief, an electric torch and a cigarette holder. Josef used the keys to open the attaché case, which contained a wireless set.[14]

During the search, a peeved Acting Sergeant Pottle burst into the police station. Having received the call from Jaikens at 9.10 a.m., Pottle had driven to Wistow Fen Farm, only to be told that the parachutist had been found at Dovehouse Farm. Upon arrival at Dovehouse Farm, farm labourers told him that the parachutist had been taken to the police station. Pottle was miffed at having missed out on all the excitement.

After the examination, Josef told the officers that a small spade had been left in the field and Jaikens ordered Pottle and Police Constable Creamer to retrieve it. The two men found the spot where Josef had landed and Pottle discovered the hand spade partially buried in the soil. There were also torn pieces of cardboard (from Josef's disc code) lying on the ground about 4 yards from the spade. Pottle and Creamer gathered up the pieces of cardboard and returned to the police station.

While Mills examined the items found in Josef's pockets, Jaikens wrote a physical description of the man before him: about 5ft 9in tall, brown hair turning grey, brown eyes, pale complexion, clean shaven, hollow cheeks, full set of dentures with three good teeth in the lower jaw, no visible marks or scars, and a slight build. Jaikens also noted that underneath the light brown parachute suit, Josef was wearing a light grey herringbone overcoat, a blue trilby hat, black shoes, grey spats with zip fasteners, a grey-striped lounge suit, three woollen pullovers, one top shirt with a semi-stiff collar and tie, two undervests, blue woollen socks and two woollen scarves.[15]

In reviewing the items found on Josef, Mills made particular note of several items. The map had pencil markings and, when questioned, Josef said that these marked the area in which he was to work. Mills noted that Josef's clothing had a Continental cut and that all of his property had tabs or markings that indicated they had been made in Germany or in a German-occupied country.[16] The complete inventory of items, combined with the wireless transmitter and Josef's broken English, led Mills to conclude that Josef was a foreign agent.

Mills telephoned Major Cyril Egerton Dixon,[17] the MI5 Regional Security Liaison Officer (RSLO) in Cambridge, and informed him that the Ramsey Home Guard had captured a suspected spy. Dixon dropped everything and drove north towards Ramsey, arriving around noon. After a series of phone calls to London, it was decided that Dixon and Mills would take charge of the prisoner and his property and transport him to London.[18] At around 2.30 p.m. Josef was loaded into a vehicle for the next leg of his journey.

Once Josef was gone, the work of the local officers was not complete. Jaikens ordered that all persons who were likely to give useful information be interviewed.[19] Over the next two days, Pottle took statements from Baldock, Coulson, Godfrey and Newton, while Jaikens took statements from Curedale and Pottle. Jaikens submitted his report to Superintendent Afford in Huntingdon on 4 February, while Mills submitted his report on 3 February. Meanwhile, in London, preparations were underway to welcome the newly arrived spy and to possibly add him to MI5's stable of double agents.

13

PREPARATIONS TO RECEIVE A SPY

The war was less than two years old, but the British had a well-organised system for dealing with spies. MI5 had initiated an elaborate double-cross system and each new arrival was assessed for their suitability as a double agent using three criteria: the personal character of the agent, the circumstances surrounding their arrival and capture and the political climate at the time. In all of this, speed and secrecy were of the essence. In an ideal situation, the agent was captured quickly and quietly without a lot of fanfare; the agent was co-operative and turned without much fuss, 'convinced that he could save his life by working for [MI5]'.[1]

On the morning of 1 February, the wheels of the Security Service began to turn and Josef became grist for the mill.

The double-cross system was run by Major Thomas Argyll Robertson, affectionately known as TAR by his MI5 colleagues. Born in 1909 in Sumatra, the son of Scottish expats, Robertson attended boarding school in the United Kingdom. In the late 1920s, Robertson joined the Royal Military College at Sandhurst and received a commission with the Seaforth Highlanders. As a young officer during peacetime, Robertson lived the good life and soon found himself in debt. After complaints from his father, who had to foot the bill, Robertson resigned his commission in December 1930.

A few years later, he was approached by an old school chum, John Kell, and introduced to John's father, Vernon Kell, the founding director of MI5. Kell ran MI5 like a personal fiefdom and hired officers based on personal connection. He liked the look of his son's friend, as well as his pedigree, and with that, Robertson was an MI5 officer.

He made an easy transition into the ranks of MI5. The secretaries of the typing pool found him dashingly handsome and unfailingly polite and good-natured. He did have a tendency to wear the tartan trews (trousers) of the Seaforth Highlanders around the office, which earned him the nickname 'passion pants' among the secretaries.

With the declaration of war, Robertson found himself dealing with the imminent threat of German spies. He was assigned as case officer for Arthur G. Owens, England's first double agent, known to the British as SNOW and to the Germans as JOHNNY. The idea of using double agents to bamboozle the Germans was a tempting idea and Robertson was one of the original architects of the double-cross system during the Second World War.

In June 1940, turmoil struck MI5 when Vernon Kell was dismissed by Prime Minister Winston Churchill. Kell's second in command, Brigadier Oswald Allen Harker temporarily picked up the reins of MI5 but, in the end, the directorship of MI5 would go to Sir David Petrie. It was a tortuous time for MI5 and morale was low.

After the dust settled, Robertson became head of the double-cross system under the umbrella of Guy Liddell's B Division (counter-espionage).[2]

In early September 1940, the first four German spies landed on the shores of Kent and Robertson was tasked with assessing their suitability as double agents. The four were not considered prime material, but in mid September, Wulf Schmidt and Gösta Caroli arrived within a week of each other, equipped with wireless sets. Both men were quickly turned, and Robertson began to populate his stable of double agents.

In late January 1941, MI5 recognised that if their double-cross system was to flourish and thrive, it needed the co-operation of other military agencies. MI5 was using the double agents to feed false information to the Germans mixed in with the chickenfeed of relatively unimportant truths and half-truths. In order to co-ordinate the flow of information, the Double-Cross Committee was formed, often referred to as the XX Committee or the Twenty Committee (XX is, of course, twenty in Roman numerals). Robertson was a member of the committee, which met every week and handled the overarching logistics of running a functional double-cross system. The chair of the Twenty Committee, Oxford don, John Cecil Masterman, later said that while Robertson was 'no intellectual', he was a 'born leader gifted with independent judgement' and 'an extraordinary flair in all the intricate operations of his profession'.[3]

This, then, was the man who, on the morning of 1 February 1941, received a phone call from Dixon with the news that the Ramsey Home Guard had captured a suspected enemy parachutist. Dixon told Robertson that he and Mills, along with the prisoner, expected to arrive at Cannon Row Police Station at around 6 p.m.[4]

Normally this would have been a relatively routine procedure. The prisoner would have been transported to London, undergone a preliminary assessment at Cannon Row Police Station by Robertson, and then been sent off to Latchmere House, MI5's secret interrogation centre, for further questioning. In Josef's case, the sequence of events was not routine.

Dixon informed Robertson that Josef had a broken ankle that needed urgent medical treatment. While arrangements had been made for Dixon to bring Josef to Cannon Row for a preliminary assessment, the final leg of the journey to Latchmere House would not be possible. Josef's leg would need to be examined by a medical officer and set in a cast.

Armed with this information, Robertson telephoned Inspector Tensley at Special Branch (Metropolitan Police Force) and asked him to inform Cannon Row Police Station that an injured parachutist would be arriving that afternoon and a police surgeon would be required.[5] Robertson then telephoned the Ministry of Information and requested a stop notice in the press. Dixon's office, at Robertson's request, had already warned the Ministry of Information representatives in Cambridge to keep an eye on the local press. Unfortunately, the local press would turn out to be the least of their worries.

Robertson and his colleague, John H. Marriott (secretary of the Twenty Committee), arrived at the police station at 6.20 p.m. on 1 February.[6] Cannon Row was conveniently located between Whitehall and Victoria Embankment, around the corner from the Houses of Parliament. About half an hour later, the car carrying Dixon, Mills and Josef arrived at the police station and Josef was transferred onto a stretcher and carried into the forbidding stone building.

Awaiting Josef were Robertson and Marriott, as well as Police Sergeant Grey and Police Constable Templeman of Special Branch.[7] After being carried into an interrogation room, Josef was attended by Dr Marran, the Police Divisional Surgeon, at around 7.30 p.m. Marran noted that Josef's right ankle was badly broken and that he needed to be taken to a hospital, where he would have to remain for at least a week.[8] Since it was clear that Josef would not be transferred to Latchmere House that evening, Robertson arranged for him to be admitted to the infirmary at Brixton Prison.[9]

Prior to his transfer, Josef asked if he could make a voluntary statement, for which the surgeon considered him fit enough. Robertson, with the assistance of Constable Templeman, who spoke German, cautioned Josef that anything he said would be taken down in writing and might be given in evidence against him. Josef said that he still wished to make a voluntary statement, which was translated by Templeman and written down in English by Robertson.[10] Josef's statement read:

I am Josef Jakobs, a German subject born 30 June 1898 in Luxembourg and lived there for the first five years of my life, when I went to Germany and lived in Berlin. From 1920 to 1923 I lived in Buenos Aires and learned dentistry. I returned to Germany in June 1923 where I practised as a dentist in Berlin until 1933 with my wife, who is also a dentist. After this I was unemployed for two years. For one year I was engaged in selling typewriters. In 1937 I was selling books. I then went into business as a money changer for the Jews leaving Germany. On 10 October 1938, I was put out of business by the Gestapo for dealing with Jews and put into a concentration camp, where I remained until March 1940. I then joined the German Air Force and was in the *Wetternachrichtung* [weather intelligence], *Abteilung* 5 [Section 5], General, Hamburg.[11] I was an *unteroffizier* [non-commissioned officer]. My principal was *Hauptmann* [Captain] Dr Beier [alias of Boeckel], but I do not believe this is his right name.

I left Hamburg on 8 January 1941 and I went to The Hague. I left Schiphol Aerodrome at 8 p.m. on 31 January 1941 in a Junkers two-engine machine with three other people.[12] At 9 p.m. I was ordered to jump from 3,000 metres. This was my first jump by parachute and the first time I had flown in an aeroplane. I knew that I was flying over England. I broke my ankle on landing and spent the night covered by my parachute. At 9.30 a.m. this morning I fired eight rounds from my pistol to attract attention. Half an hour later, I fired six more rounds, when two men came and found me.[13] I asked them for help.

The only person I know in England is [Frau Lily Knips], 9 Compayne Gardens, N.W. 7. I have one son and two daughters living with my wife in Berlin at 124 Rudolstädter Strasse. I was a member of the German Catholic Party and an anti-Nazi. I was ordered to go over to England with a wireless set and transmitter and send weather messages back to

Germany by wireless. I considered this a means of getting out of the country and intended making my way to my aunt in America.[14]

The physical and mental state of Josef, as he gave this statement, can only be imagined. He had broken his ankle almost twenty-four hours previously, lain awake in the cold and damp for twelve hours and endured several trips during the next twelve hours. Was he competent to give a voluntary statement to the police? Was the interpreter up to snuff?

Josef did not have one son and two daughters but two sons and one daughter. In the statement, he acknowledged that he had been ordered to send weather reports back to Germany but his intention had been to escape Germany and make his way to his aunt in America. Less than twenty-four hours after landing, Josef stated *his* intention in coming to England – not the intention of the German Abwehr, but the intention of Josef Jakobs. His intention in coming would become the key issue during his court martial, a bone of contention between the prosecution and the defence that would ultimately make or break the case against him.

At around 10.30 p.m. Josef was transferred to Brixton Prison in an ambulance from Millbank Hospital, under escort by Police Sergeant Grey.[15] Upon arrival at Brixton, Josef was tucked into a white-sheeted infirmary bed in a private ward.[16] Relieved of his pain by injections, Josef may even have slept.

The morning of 2 February began early for Robertson and involved copious amounts of paperwork. Concerned that other German agents might have landed via parachute on the night of 31 January, Robertson had a conversation with the Air Ministry. They identified four areas where other German aeroplanes had been tracked on that night.[17] A memo was sent to the local police and Home Guard of those areas to be on the look-out, but with the understanding that the information should absolutely not be made public.[18]

Robertson next wrote a report to his superiors that outlined the circumstances surrounding Josef's capture and included a copy of the voluntary statement and a list of Josef's possessions.[19] All of the items,[20] with the exception of the clothes that Josef was wearing, had been handed over to Richard Butler of MI5 (SLB)[21] for safekeeping. Robertson ruefully noted that a great number of people knew about Josef's arrival.[22] While the press could be controlled, silencing the flapping lips of civilians and Home Guard volunteers was more of a challenge. At that point, Josef's best chance for life depended upon his suitability as a double agent. Yet the vital components of speed and secrecy were already compromised by a broken ankle and a relatively public capture.

Robertson then wrote a receipt for Josef's body and possessions to Dixon and asked him to thank the Huntingdonshire Constabulary for their work. Robertson sent a copy of Josef's voluntary statement and the list of possessions to Major Robin W.G. Stephens,[23] the commandant of Latchmere House, informing him that Josef was being held at Brixton Prison infirmary. A badly broken ankle was not enough to deter Stephens, who told Robertson that he intended to conduct a preliminary interrogation of Josef that afternoon.[24]

14

ABANDON HOPE ALL YE WHO ENTER

While Robertson was working on the paper trail precipitated by Josef's arrival, Josef himself awoke in Brixton Prison infirmary. After an examination by the physician, who re-bandaged the ankle as best he could, Josef was once again bundled onto a stretcher for another ambulance trip, this one to MI5's secret interrogation centre at Latchmere House.

Latchmere House was constructed in the early 1800s as a private dwelling on Ham Common, an area of common land within the Borough of Richmond. During the First World War, Latchmere House was leased to the government as a hospital for shell-shocked officers. When the Second World War erupted the dilapidated buildings were spruced up and the site was repurposed as an interrogation centre. The facility did not appear on Red Cross lists and the British did not consider the inmates to be prisoners of war.[1] Therefore, Geneva Convention did not apply and, to all intents and purposes, any prisoner who entered the gates of Latchmere House simply disappeared off the face of the earth.

As the ambulance pulled up before the doors of Latchmere House, Josef was met by physician and psychiatrist, Dr Harold Dearden. Born in 1892 in Bolton, Lancashire, the son of a wealthy cotton manufacturer, Dearden was uninterested in taking over the family business. Dearden studied medicine at Cambridge and was certified as a physician in 1911. With the outbreak of war in 1914, Dearden joined the Royal Army Medical Corps and served in France with the Grenadier Guards. The war was to have a profound impact on Dearden, who wrote about his experiences in his memoirs. He noted that patching up wounded soldiers to send them back into the fray simply turned an 'illogical business into an insane one'.[2] Yet, he also noted that the war was a 'fantastic business'[3] that served him magnificently. After the cessation of hostilities, Dearden took up psychiatry and also turned his hand to writing. With the outbreak of the Second World War, Dearden was called into action once again and ended up serving at Latchmere House.

After supervising Josef's transfer inside, Dearden took note of his personal particulars while Lieutenant Thomas Leith Winn, a dentist in civilian life, examined Josef's teeth.[4] According to Dearden, Josef was a tall (5ft 10.25in),[5] slender man who weighed 133lb. He had a narrow head with a thin, almost emaciated face. His brown, grey-tinged hair framed a sallow face. He had large brown eyes and a large mouth with creases that extended from nostril to lip corners. He had a normal chin with a small dimple. His left ear stood away from his head while his right ear was more or less normal. Josef's hands were well shaped, with long palms and narrow fingers. Winn offered the opinion that none of Josef's teeth contained a reservoir of secret writing materials.

At this point, the newly arrived prisoner would normally have had two natural photographs taken. Dressed in normal clothes, the prisoner's photograph could then be presented to other individuals, with no indication that the person was a prisoner. Josef's first photographs were different. His hair was unkempt. His chin was unshaven. His cheekbones were gaunt. His eyes were haunted. Josef stared at the camera with desperation. In most photographs, including another set taken at Latchmere House in late July 1941, Josef's eyes were hooded and veiled. The soul of the man was hidden from view. Such was not the case with the photographs taken by Dearden. Josef's soul gazed out of the photographs with penetrating intensity. They were the most honest photographs of Josef.

Following the rather gentle reception given by Dearden and Winn, Josef's stretcher was carried into another room, where he was confronted by Lieutenant George F. Sampson, Lieutenant Albert D.M. Evans and Major Robin W.G. Stephens. With a monocle wedged in front of his right eye, Stephens had earned the nick-name of 'Tin-Eye', and was renowned for his fierce temper and his extraordinary ability to break stubborn spies.

Stephens was born in Alexandria, Egypt in 1900, the son of British expats William H. Stephens and his wife Julia E. Howell.[6] Although William was a teacher, both Stephens and his older brother, Howell, were sent to school in England. In 1914, with the outbreak of war, the two boys were eager to serve their country. Howell, older by two years, enlisted with the Worcestershire Regiment and was killed near Ypres in

July 1917. Stephens joined the army as an officer cadet in 1918 but missed the fighting in Europe.

Eager to see action, Stephens transferred to the Indian Army, where he joined the Gurkhas, an elite regiment of Nepalese troops.[7] The Gurkha motto, 'Better to die than to be a coward', would colour Stephens' life view for years to come. Stephens saw active service with the Gurkhas and even received a Mention in Despatches for Distinguished Service during the Mahbar Rebellion in Waziristan.

In 1931, after serving as Deputy Assistant Judge Advocate General in India, Stephens resigned his commission and set sail for England with Gwendlen, his wife of four years. Life in England was not easy, and Stephens quickly found himself declaring bankruptcy and filing for divorce. He bumped through a series of odd jobs as a journalist, physical fitness instructor and budding author.[8]

In September 1939, with the declaration of war, Stephens' fortunes changed when he was recruited by MI5 on the recommendation of a former commander. Stephens was a polyglot who could speak French, German, Italian and Urdu, as well as a smattering of Somali and Amharic.[9] Although he had seen much of the world, Stephens was a self-acknowledged xenophobe, having little patience for Jews, Poles, Belgians, Italians and other racial groups. He reserved his fiercest hatred for Germans, particularly German spies who were 'the rabble of the universe, their treachery not matched by their courage'.[10] Stephens fancied himself as an amateur psychologist and sometimes found himself at odds with Dearden.

Normally, a prisoner would be led into the room to face a panel of officers chaired by the immaculately dressed Stephens. Armed with his knowledge of languages and a loud voice, Stephens dominated the interrogation. He discouraged familiarity or words of comfort and the prisoners were kept standing at attention throughout. They were made to feel that their actions were indefensibly wrong and hopelessly compromised, and that their interrogators were motivated by 'an implacable hatred of the enemy'.[11] No chivalry, no gossip, no cigarettes. Questions were rapid, sometimes shouted, but there was no physical violence. According to Stephens, most people would talk under torture, but they would only tell you what they thought you wanted to hear. A good interrogator should seek truth, not humiliation.[12] The point of this style of interrogation was to, figuratively, keep the prisoner at the 'point of a bayonet'.[13] Stephens would fire questions at the unsuspecting victim in such rapid succession that answers were virtually impossible. Stephens' intent was to break his victim as quickly as possible.

In Josef's case, the interrogation was conducted while he lay on a stretcher, but other than that, it took the form described above. While the first questions were thrown at Josef in English, it soon became clear that Stephens would have to switch to German. In Stephens' opinion, Josef's standard of English was 'incredibly low', although he suspected that Josef's knowledge of English was better than he made it out to be, and he was acting. It was simply unfathomable to Stephens that the Germans would have sent such a poorly qualified agent to spy in England.[14] During the two-hour interrogation (4.45 p.m. to 6.45 p.m.) Stephens learned much about the man before him.

He learned that Josef had a family back in Germany, a mother, sister, wife and three children. Stephens made careful note of this valuable information. He knew very well that while an agent might not break under personal threat, they would often crack if their family was threatened.[15]

Stephens made another note when Josef stated that, while he himself was not a Jew,[16] he had helped Jews to escape Germany. Josef's interactions with Lily Knips, and the revelation that she was living in London, stirred Stephens' ire. A German-Jewish refugee associated with a spy was never a good thing.

After hearing Josef's sad tale of the concentration camp, Stephens made a note that the story rang true but wondered if Josef would remain loyal to his country or if his treatment in Sachsenhausen would 'overcome his very proper hereditary scruples'.[17]

Stephens perked up his ears when Josef described his Abwehr training in Hamburg. Some of the names sounded familiar, in particular, Petersen, the wireless instructor, and Dr Beier (Boeckel).[18] Other names, like that of Major Malten, were new to Stephens, but he knew that he could always run the names past other spies interned at Latchmere House. It might jog their memories and loosen their tongues.

At one point, Stephens thrust the picture postcard in front of Josef and demanded to know the identity of the woman and whether or not she had ever been to England, because the inscription on the back looked suspiciously like London. Josef, however, denied that the woman, German cabaret singer Clara Bäuerle, had ever been to England. When pressed by Stephens, Josef admitted that she was his mistress.[19] Stephens had another potential lever to use against Josef.

Stephens knew that knowledge was power, and each piece of information that Josef revealed was a victory. One of the questions dealt with the amount of money found on Josef. The previous spies had been equipped with £100[20] or £200, while Josef arrived with £500 tucked away in various pockets.[21] Why? Was Josef a particularly important agent? Did he have orders to give the money to another agent? Stephens pressed his questions on Josef and learned that the money had been given to him shortly before his departure. The Germans had decided that the previous allowance of £200 was insufficient. Josef denied that he was a courier and said that the money was expected to last him until June 1941, by which time England would have been occupied by the Germans. Despite Josef's assurances, Stephens wasn't buying any of it. 'I am still quite convinced that this is a man of importance for he held comparatively, a large sum of money. A simple interpretation may be that he had brought over money for a contact in this country.'[22]

Time was short, and it was clear that Josef's ankle was affecting his ability to provide coherent answers. Stephens needed to zero in on the most important questions. Stephens presented Josef with the fragments of the torn disc code and referred to the codes of previous agents. In the face of Stephens' overarching knowledge, Josef revealed his call sign,[23] his transmission frequencies and his transmission times. Stephens also knew that agents often had a second emergency code and it didn't take much persuasion before Josef revealed his emergency code, which was based on the words *Marinesoldat* (marine soldier or marine) and *Winterhilfswerk* (winter relief work).[24] During Josef's demonstration of the emergency code, Stephens obtained the key to it and a specimen message.[25] Stephens also knew that enemy agents could be equipped with secret writing material and a cover address to which they could send letters. Josef, however, denied that he had been given a cover address and insisted that the tablets found in his possession were strictly medicinal (codeine, 'aceticone'[26] and Pervitin).

As for Josef's mission, he claimed that while he had been instructed to transmit weather reports after buying a thermometer and barometer in England, he had had no intention of carrying out his mission. He had hoped to travel to London and, with the assistance of Lily Knips, make his way to America where he had an aunt. Stephens didn't buy the aunt story and made a note that Lily's name sounded 'unsavoury'.[27]

Stephens and his crew had gleaned a lot of information from Josef during the two-hour interrogation. Later that evening, Stephens wrote a report summarising the results of their questioning. Stephens gleefully noted that Josef had 'sustained a fracture to a bone in his ankle, a happy incident which has put an end to his nefarious activities'.[28]

That injury, however, meant that Stephens had only been able to arrange for the temporary transfer of Josef from Brixton Prison to Latchmere House. The interrogation was necessarily short, given that Josef was injured, but was not difficult, for Josef responded to the 'calculated atmosphere' that Stephens and his team created during the interrogation.[29] According to Stephens:

> No promise whatever has been made to him by me but the lever may be described as his affection for his wife and three tolerably young children at present resident in Berlin. In crude language, Jakobs is under the impression that we can liquidate these persons if he fails to do what we require.[30]

Faced with such a threat, Josef agreed to 'work as the servant of his captors'.[31] The question Stephens asked was, would Josef remain loyal to Germany, or would he turn on the Nazis who had incarcerated and abused him in a concentration camp?

Stephens believed that Josef, if properly handled, would prove to be a useful double-cross agent. Stephens thought it would be a mistake to reject Josef 'merely because of his apparently despicable character'.[32] The fact that Josef had responded to 'threat in a comparatively short period of time' was promising.[33] The fact that Josef carried so much money, and was the 'highest paid agent' to come into British custody,[34] indicated to Stephens that the German Secret Service[35] valued Josef. Stephens strongly recommended that contact between Josef and the German Abwehr be established quickly. If properly handled, Josef could end up being a much more amenable agent than some of the others. Further interrogations of Josef were necessary, and Stephens' final recommendation was that Josef's 'small injury' should be X-rayed and put into plaster of Paris so that he could return to Latchmere House.[36]

The word 'interrogation' brings to mind different images, gleaned from our media-saturated culture. Those images might include a small windowless room with a bare lightbulb dangling from the ceiling. The prisoner might be seated on a hard wooden chair or even tied to the chair. Two or more men (or women) alternately play 'good cop' and 'bad cop'. There might even be violence in the interrogation. In extreme cases, as when we think of what happened in Abu Ghraib or Guantanamo Bay, there might even be torture.

Latchmere House was an interrogation camp, but what interrogation methods were used there? The British had a reputation for being polite and yet they could be ruthless in their own way. In 2005, the news was full of stories about newly released documents that outlined the brutal tactics used on Nazi officers at a wartime interrogation centre simply called the London Cage.[37] Had the same thing happened at Latchmere House?

Although Stephens was unmoved by the plight of enemy agents who passed through Latchmere House, he was also an avid armchair psychiatrist. He firmly believed that torture and physical coercion produced information of dubious quality, 'Violence is taboo, for not only does it produce answers to please, but it lowers the standard of information.'[38] Stephens wrote, 'Never strike a man. In the first place, it is an act of cowardice. In the second place, it is not intelligent. A prisoner will lie to avoid further punishment and everything he says thereafter will be based on a false premise.'[39] On one occasion, Colonel Scotland, Commandant of the London Cage, visited Latchmere House and struck Wulf Schmidt during an interrogation. Stephens immediately evicted Scotland from the interrogation room and banned him from participating in any further interrogations there.[40]

While physical coercion might be taboo, psychological intimidation was honed to a fine art at Latchmere House, thanks to Stephens and Dearden. Agents were threatened with execution. They were told that their families could be murdered. The calculated atmosphere in the interrogation room was designed to demonstrate to the hapless agent that the British Security Service was omnipotent and already knew what the agent was hiding. Cells were bugged, stool pigeons were used, and agents were played against each other. Inmates were housed in solitary silence and sometimes threatened with an isolation room opposite the old mortuary. In some cases, recalcitrant prisoners were forced to stand naked before the interrogation panel and an unimpressed female stenographer. Food rations might be bland and virtually inedible and sleep deprivation was a common tactic.[41]

Stephens created a 'calculated atmosphere' in which to interrogate Josef, an atmosphere designed to create co-operation as quickly as possible.[42] Josef had had one night of rest in Brixton Prison. He was still in pain and easy prey for Stephens. In two hours the interrogators learned much about him. They learned that he had been incarcerated in a Nazi concentration camp. They learned that he was afraid of the Nazis and never planned to carry out his mission. They learned that he had a family back home. It was this last piece of information that proved critical. As interrogators, they were looking for something that would help them to break Josef. Something that would loosen his lips and make him share everything that he knew. Something that would convince him to work for the British.

They had found it. Josef had a wife and family – a family that he loved. Stephens and the interrogators immediately used that information as leverage against Josef. Rather than just threaten him with physical harm or death, they threatened his family. They told him that they could liquidate his family in Berlin.

Josef knew that the Nazis were keeping an eye on his family. He had been in a concentration camp and was already under suspicion. He had taken on the mission to go to England and spy for Germany. Now he was captured. If he shared what he knew with the British, what would happen if, or when, the Gestapo found out? They would most assuredly exact their revenge on his family. His only hope in the face of the Nazi threat was to remain loyal to Germany to protect his family, but the British placed him in a different dilemma. They told him that unless he co-operated with them and turned against Germany, his family was in danger. Faced with an awful dilemma, Josef promised to work for the British, to keep his family safe from Stephens' threat of liquidation.

Josef shared the story of his life with the officers and while Stephens believed that Josef had been incarcerated in a concentration camp, he did not believe Josef's story that he had no intention of carrying out his mission. Stephens made his judgement call as to what was truth and what was fiction in Josef's account of his life. Perhaps Josef was telling the truth. Perhaps he and Margarete had concocted a wild plan for their future. Josef would take the money and flee to England. He would contact Lily Knips and find a way to America. From America he would arrange for his family to be brought over to freedom. It was a crazy idea, and if true, it would have relied on many things going according to plan. It required a successful parachute landing and journey to London. It required a co-operative Lily Knips. It required a passport to travel to America. There were so many ways for the plan to fall apart, which was exactly what had happened.

As he faced the officers, Josef knew the penalty for being caught as a spy in England – it was death. He also knew the penalty for turning against the Germans and becoming a double agent – also death. Death was hounding him at every turn and, ultimately, it would find him.

15

MEDICAL RESPITE

While Josef was being interrogated at Latchmere House, discussions were taking place elsewhere regarding his health and immediate future. The medical officer at Brixton Prison told Dick White (Liddell's deputy)[1] that if Josef's leg was to be saved, he would need to be transferred to Dulwich Hospital for an operation.[2]

Brixton Prison was a secure facility, whereas Dulwich Hospital was not, and that raised a whole host of concerns. Liddell's office made arrangements so that Josef, during his stay at Dulwich, would be kept closely guarded and isolated from others as much as possible.[3] Those arrangements took time and it was only on the following day that Josef was transferred from Brixton Prison to Dulwich Hospital.

A technicality was also cleared up when, after checking with Sir Alexander Maxwell, Permanent Undersecretary of the Home Office, it was accepted that Josef, as a German national, could be held under the royal prerogative and needn't be immediately charged with an offence.[4]

Josef arrived at Dulwich Hospital at 4 p.m. on 3 February, along with a slim file of medical records.[5] The admission form noted that Josef was very thin and dirty and looked quite ill. One doctor suspected Josef might have a carcinoma.[6] Shortly afterwards, Josef's leg and chest were X-rayed.[7] The need for a leg X-ray would have been obvious, but the reasons for a chest X-ray were more nebulous. Josef may have developed a lingering cough after his overnight exposure, or perhaps his emaciated state had doctors suspecting tuberculosis or lung cancer.

The X-ray report for Josef's leg showed that he had a 'comminuted fracture of lower end of shaft of tibia & fibula with overlapping of tibia fragments and forward displacement of upper tibial fragments'.[8] In other words, the lower bones of his right leg were shattered. The chest X-ray revealed 'very slight infiltration of right upper zone which is apparently old and no sign of local infiltration and left lung is clear'.[9] Josef had an old area of injury in his right lung, likely from his First World War wound. Josef was immediately prepped for the operating theatre, so the doctors could realign his leg and set it in a cast.[10]

Several days later Robertson visited the hospital to get an update from Dr Owen William Roberts, the surgeon in charge of Josef's care.[11] After closing the door to his office, the doctor told Robertson that Josef's injuries were 'very severe' and clipped the most recent X-rays to the light box. It was obvious that Josef was completely immobilised by his injury and both Dr Roberts and Robertson agreed that the Special Branch agent who had been watching Josef could be released from his duty.[12]

After a moment of consideration, Robertson decided to take Dr Roberts into his confidence, at least as much as was possible. He let the doctor know that Josef was an important prisoner. It was therefore vital that no one should be allowed to visit him, even if that person had a pass, unless MI5 had cleared them and advised the hospital in advance that someone was coming. If anyone else came to see Josef, they were to be told that he was too ill. The hospital staff should then encourage the visitor to leave their address and phone number on the pretext that they would be notified as soon as Josef was well enough to receive guests. If Josef tried to send out a note via any nurse or employee, that note should be confiscated and handed over to MI5.[13]

With both men satisfied that the parameters for Josef's secure confinement had been set in place, Dr Roberts took Robertson to Josef's ward, which contained about thirty beds.[14] Josef's bed was in a corner behind screens, which was not ideal from a security point of view. Dr Roberts reassured Robertson that Josef would be moved to a smaller ward with more privacy the following week. Robertson peeked behind the screens, but Josef was in no state to speak to anyone.

Robertson and the doctor stepped out into the hallway, where they had a whispered conversation. Dr Roberts admitted that Josef appeared to be getting worse and suspected that he had contracted pneumonia as a result of his exposure. Based on his dealings with Josef, Dr Roberts was under the impression that he was an educated and intellectual man who understood a great deal of English, although he feigned incomprehension.[15] The general opinion among patients and staff was that Josef was a German airman who had bailed out of his aeroplane and had a hard landing.[16] Robertson liked the sound of that rumour and saw no harm in letting that story circulate.[17] As Robertson took his leave, Dr Roberts assured him that he would notify MI5 as soon as Josef was fit to be moved.[18]

Alas, several days later, the story of the German airman created a problem for Robertson. The Prisoner of War Information Bureau (PWIB) received a casualty chit from the clerical staff at Dulwich Hospital that stated Josef Jakobs had bailed out of a German aeroplane on 31 January and been injured. Normally, upon receipt of such a chit, the PWIB would have sent forms back to the hospital requesting personal particulars. The hospital staff would have completed the forms to the best of their ability and returned them to the PWIB. A copy of the forms would have been sent to the International Red Cross in Geneva, and on to Germany. Had this happened, the Germans would have learned that Josef was being treated as a prisoner of war (POW).

Luckily, Robertson's office was notified of the disaster in the making and Robertson had an urgent conversation with the PWIB.[19] Josef's casualty chit was quickly pulled out of the regular pile and his information was recorded in a secret register at the PWIB.[20] Robertson heaved a sigh of relief. It had been a near miss for the double-cross system and MI5. Had Josef been registered as a POW, he would have been transferred to a regular POW camp, along with his knowledge of Latchmere House and some of the personalities in MI5. Prisoner-of-war camps were notoriously leaky when it came to the flow of information and word would have made its way back to Germany. It didn't bear thinking about.

Nearly two weeks after Josef's admission to Dulwich Hospital, there was still no word as to when he would be released. At Latchmere House, Stephens was getting impatient. He knew that time was of the essence and wanted to interrogate Josef more thoroughly. Rather than phoning Dr Roberts himself, Stephens asked Dr Dearden to do the honours, perhaps reckoning that a physician might be privy to more medical information than an intelligence officer.

On 14 February, Dearden telephoned Dr Roberts and enquired about Josef's condition. Roberts pulled Josef's chart and told Dearden that Josef had developed a raging fever (102°F) and showed signs of developing a patch of pneumonia in his right lung.[21] Dearden and Roberts discussed the possibility of transferring Josef to Latchmere House, where Dearden and nursing orderlies could take over his medical care. Roberts listened to Dearden's description of the medical facilities at Latchmere House but felt that they were inadequate given Josef's complicated condition. He did agree to let Dearden know when he felt that Josef was in a fit condition to be transferred to Latchmere House. After getting off the phone with Roberts, Dearden wrote a memo to Stephens in which he summarised Josef's condition. Stephens was less than pleased with the delay but admitted that, as much as he wanted Josef at Latchmere House as soon as possible, he would 'have to be patient'.[22]

Ten days later, on 24 February, Dearden telephoned Roberts again and learned that Josef was recovering from a nasty case of bronchopneumonia.[23] Roberts felt that Josef's leg was healing nicely and that the plaster cast could be removed at the end of March.[24] If Josef's convalescence progressed favourably, Roberts felt that he could be transferred to Latchmere House within seven to ten days, provided, of course, that Latchmere House had a trained nursing orderly who could attend to him.[25] After getting off the phone, Dearden warily wrote another memo to inform Stephens of the ongoing delay. The two men didn't get along and Dearden suspected that he might be berated for being the bearer of bad news. In his memo, Dearden expressed his opinion that Josef's injury was likely sustained by direct impact with the ground upon landing.[26]

As Dearden had suspected, Stephens was even less pleased with the second memo. Stephens expressed his displeasure in a memo to Dick White, noting that while he was most anxious to have Josef return from hospital, he was 'check-mated by the humanitarian motives of the Medical Profession'.[27] Stephens admitted that, from the professional point of view, the course the doctors were adopting was the 'correct one', but from the war and intelligence point of view, the delay was 'indefensible' and he was trying to shorten it as much as possible.[28]

With Stephens breathing down his neck, Dearden telephoned Roberts on the morning of 27 February for a status report. The news was not good. Josef had developed an acute septic condition at the site of the fracture, likely due to his broncho-pneumonia. Given Josef's poor state of health, Roberts was adamant that it would be very dangerous to transfer him. Roberts was preparing to perform an operation on Josef's leg and suggested that Dearden telephone him again on Monday morning to hear his report. Dearden explained that Latchmere House now had a qualified nursing orderly who could care for Josef. It was of the utmost importance that Josef be transferred to Latchmere House at the earliest possible moment. Roberts acknowledged the news and then excused himself to begin the operation.

Dearden put the phone down and, with a reluctant sigh, composed another memo to Stephens. He had evidently heard about the 'humanitarian motives of the Medical Profession' comment, perhaps from Stephens himself. Dearden took the opportunity to shoot barbs of his own. In his report, Dearden said that he concurred with Roberts' decision, which he felt had nothing to do with humanitarian considerations. Josef's general state of health meant that it was inadvisable to transfer him as it might jeopardise his survival and thus destroy his usefulness for intelligence purposes.[29] Stephens probably read Dearden's memo with irritation and threw up his hands in disgust at yet another delay.[30]

While Roberts and Dearden played their game of tug of war, Josef was engaged in a desperate fight for his life. Although penicillin had been discovered in 1928, it wasn't used widely until the mid 1940s. Josef's bacterial infections were probably treated with sulfa drugs that, while dramatically reducing the likelihood of death, were not 100 per cent effective. Prior to the widespread use of antibiotics, pneumonia was often a death sentence, but Josef was a fighter and he survived.

Unfortunately, while Josef's prolonged convalescence in hospital had improved his physical health, it ultimately shortened his life. The extended delay in his thorough interrogation meant that, with each passing day, his potential career as a double agent slipped further from his grasp. In the weeks since his capture, news of his arrival had spread far and wide.

16

THE COST OF LOOSE LIPS AND TITTLE-TATTLE

One of the key requirements for an enemy spy to be turned into a double agent was absolute secrecy. There could be no word of the agent's capture. It couldn't be in the newspaper. It couldn't be the topic of village gossip. Secrecy was of the utmost importance during the war. Enemy informants could be anywhere. Letters were screened by the Ministry of Information and sometimes censored or even confiscated. Too much information was not a good thing, and the British were diligent in keeping their secrets to themselves.

Robertson had noted on 1 February that 'unfortunately it appears that a great number of people already know about [Josef's arrival and capture]'.[1] Almost a dozen people in Ramsey had been directly involved in apprehending Josef: the farmers, the Home Guard, the doctor, the police. It is a well-known fact that the more people who know something, the higher is the likelihood that information will leak out. That was exactly what happened with Josef, in so many different ways. It wasn't malicious. It wasn't designed to hamper the war effort. It was gossip, and it was deadly.

In Blackburn, Lancashire, 200 miles north-west of Ramsey, lived Mrs Greenwood of 5 Crosshill Road. Her husband, Alan C. Greenwood, was a Royal Air Force (RAF) officer who had been visiting Ramsey during the week of 1 February. Mrs Greenwood's husband wrote her a letter telling her that on the night of 31 January he had heard an aeroplane and on the following morning a farm labourer had come in and told them that he had caught a German spy with a broken ankle. The spy wore civilian clothing and carried a ration book, identity card, English money and a portable transmitting set.

Mrs Greenwood shared this fascinating news with her friends, who then told their husbands. On 8 February, Mrs Greenwood received a polite visit from the Blackburn Police. At first, she may have thought the worst, that her husband had been injured or killed in action. After reassuring the nervous housewife, the policeman said he had heard about her husband's letter. Mrs Greenwood was surprised to learn that her letter had come to the attention of the police. She retrieved the letter and read out some of the information to the police officer. She admitted that she hadn't thought it was a big secret, since the spy had been captured and her husband hadn't told her to keep it under her hat.[2]

The Blackburn Police report was forwarded to Major H.J. Baxter, MI5's RSLO in Manchester, who passed it along to Dick White in London. Baxter wasn't sure if it was worthwhile to try to prevent such information leaks, but if so, then secrecy in all the services (RAF, Home Guard, etc.) needed to be thoroughly emphasised.[3]

Elsewhere, a mere 9 miles south-east of Ramsey, in Chatteris, lived a woman nicknamed Queenie who, on 2 February, posted a rambling nine-page letter to Mr Horace Porter, of 2902 Halldale Avenue, Los Angeles, California. While Horace had been born in Chatteris, his wife had been born in Germany.[4] Queenie, possibly one of Horace's sisters, shared bits and pieces of news about bombings, the war, rationing and the hope that the Americans would soon join in the war effort. On the third page of her letter, Queenie noted:

A German landed by Parachute in the Acre Fen. He fired his gun to attract attention as his ankle was broken (it's a pity it wasn't his neck says I!). He was equipped with 500 English £1 notes, a transmitting wireless set, ration and identity card, and attired as a civilian and spoke fluent English. Six more came down near Warboys but were captured same time as we are warned to expect Invasion at any hour.[5]

Queenie's letter never made it to Horace, being intercepted by the Ministry of Information on 8 February.[6] Queenie's letter did, however, make it onto the desks of the MI5 officers, who were upset, and understandably so. At Robertson's request, Marriott wrote to Dixon and expressed concern that Queenie had such alarmingly accurate information about Josef. He wondered if it would be possible to determine how she got this knowledge but acknowledged that it might be difficult as there was no surname and no return address on the letter. Dixon wearily replied that the details mentioned in Queenie's letter were known to a large number of people around Ramsey and Chatteris on 'account of the inability of the Home Guard to keep their mouths shut'.[7] Dixon had asked the Home Guard to keep all the details to themselves but, clearly, they had not done so. As it would turn out, it wasn't just villagers and farm labourers who liked to gossip about a captured spy.

In Cambridge,[8] 20 miles south-east of Ramsey, lived a boarder with the nickname of Poll.[9] On 16 February, Poll sent a sixteen-page letter to Miss E. Boyd, Box 486, Oyster Bay, Long Island, New York. The letter included a passage that read, 'Did I tell you in the last letter that two parachutis [*sic*] had been caught near Huntington and another one after that with over 500 pounds on him. So you see they can't help an odd one getting through …'[10] This letter also never reached its intended recipient; it was intercepted by the Ministry of Information on 22 February and retained by Robertson.[11] He could have wallpapered his office with such letters.

In Huntingdon, 10 miles south of Ramsey, lived the 9th Earl of Sandwich, George Charles Montagu, the Lord Lieutenant of Huntingdonshire. The earl gave an elegant cocktail party in early February that was attended by a large number of people from diverse backgrounds. It was at this cocktail party that the Home Guard Battalion Commander of the region, perhaps after too much sherry, loudly 'gave out all the details [of Josef's capture]'.[12] Word of this indiscretion reached Dixon, who planned to gather evidence against the Home Guard Commander and 'have a major row with him'.[13]

A few days later, in Peterborough, 8 miles north-west of Ramsey, a businessman visiting the city, Mr Gordon Sinclair of Tithebarnes House, Ripley, Surrey, was told about an enemy parachutist by a colonel of the Home Guard. The colonel told Sinclair that, a night or two previously, the Home Guard had been called out to investigate the reason for shots being fired. They found that the shots were fired by a man lying in a field who was suffering from broken legs [*sic*]. He was dressed in a blue suit, spoke English with a slight accent, had £5,000 [*sic*] in English money, a portable wireless transmitting set, a German–English dictionary in which were added notes of the vernacular commonly used in connection with various coins, and a map of the district that indicated the position of woods, thickets, etc. The colonel said that the man had landed by parachute from an enemy aeroplane. Mr Sinclair was surprised at this upfront revelation and several weeks later, on 20 February, shared the story with a senior staff officer of the Air Ministry and three others.[14]

There was consternation in MI5 regarding the colonel of the Home Guard and memos flew back and forth about what to do with him. Group Captain D.L. Blackford of the Air Ministry (Deputy Director of Intelligence) heard of the encounter and suggested that Mr Sinclair should receive a mild reproof and that the colonel should be traced and suitably admonished. Blackford said they had taken extensive steps to try and prevent the leakage of this information that, while somewhat exaggerated in the report, had some foundation in fact. Attempts to trace the colonel of the Home Guard were unsuccessful as the investigating officers did not know his name.[15]

In Huntingdon lived a woman named Grace. On 5 March, Grace sent a four-page letter to Mrs Clara N. Stizza of 162 Main Street, W. Orange, New Jersey. In her letter, Grace mentioned:

> [Two] parachutists were caught the other week in Ramsey, a few miles from here close to the Aerodrome, one had his ankles broken. If they came down near us when George was home I'm sure he would shoot them on the way down. We have two sporting guns in the house.[16]

Grace would have been pleased to learn that one didn't need to shoot spies in order to kill them – writing letters and spreading gossip was equally efficient.

On 3 March, Dick White admitted that there had been wide publicity about Josef and MI5 had decided that they would not be using him as a double agent. As a result, they were no longer overly concerned with the ongoing leakage of information.[17] Whether it was Queenie, or Poll, or the colonel of the Home Guard, it all boiled down to one thing – people loved to share information. 'It's just gossip. It's just a titbit of news. Everybody knows about it. What can it hurt?' No wonder England was covered with posters urging people to speak with caution. Enemy agents and spies could be anywhere. Catchy phrases like 'loose lips sink ships', 'careless talk costs lives' and 'tittle-tattle lost the battle' warned Britons that sharing seemingly immaterial gossip could cost British lives.

One couldn't blame Mrs Greenwood, Queenie, Poll or Grace. They were civilians sharing the horror of war. They heard about the parachutist, and the news was different from the regular bombing reports. It demonstrated the imminent threat of invasion. There was a plea for America to join the fight. They were passing along second-hand information, sometimes accurate, sometimes not. Someone else had told them about it and so they thought they could share it. The longer the gossip trail grew, the more they thought it didn't matter who they told. On the other hand, the colonel of the Home Guard, the Home Guard battalion commander and the RAF officer should have known better.

Finally, there were the farmers who went out into the fields day after day and who served as Home Guard volunteers. Every day was the same, except on the morning of 1 February. They caught a German spy! They shared the news. They went to the pub and spread the word. They told the barman. They told RAF officers. They stuck out their chests and bragged, 'Caught a German spy, I did. What do you think of that?' It's human nature. They wanted to be respected. They wanted to be important. They might not wear an RAF uniform, but they had contributed to the war effort and captured a German spy. Little did they know that keeping their mouths shut also contributed to the war effort. MI5 was using the double-cross agents to save British lives by passing along subtle misinformation to the Germans, but the British public were not aware of that. Their gossip destroyed Josef's chances of becoming an anti-German weapon in the arsenal of MI5's double-cross system. A titbit of gossip, a morsel of news, and Josef's fate was sealed. The more the news spread, the more tenuous his chances for life became.

As it would turn out, however, the decision to erase Josef's name from the double agent list was made several weeks earlier. On 14 February, double agent SNOW travelled to Lisbon to meet his German spymaster, Nikolaus Ritter. During their conversation, Ritter expressed frustration with the parachute method of inserting spies into England. He acknowledged that the Abwehr had 'lost many men by parachute'[18] and his suspicions were aroused. 'We've sent a lot of men over and nothing's happened. They've gone wrong. There's something wrong somewhere.'[19] Ritter suspected that one agent had landed in a canal and drowned but wondered what had become of the others. SNOW then told Ritter about 'the man who came down near Newbury,[20] who broke his ankle and who shot off his revolver [*sic*] for help'.[21] SNOW had been primed by MI5 to pass along that titbit of information to the Germans. It was something that bolstered SNOW's credibility with them, but it would all be for naught. Upon his return to England, MI5 decided that SNOW was playing a nasty triple-cross game. He was imprisoned for the remainder of the war.

On 17 February 1941, a few days after SNOW had left for Lisbon, Dick White wrote a memo, which summarised the situation, 'Obviously we can do nothing with Jakobs as the news of his arrest is now far and wide.

This is a point we must always bear in mind when a parachutist is captured and we think of using him.'[22]

After an initial favourable impression, Josef had been sacrificed to maintain the integrity of the double-cross system. The fact that Josef didn't meet the criteria for double agents didn't, however, mean that he was useless. There was still a lot of information that MI5 wanted to squeeze out of him, information that had to wait until he was released from hospital. In the meantime, MI5 turned their attention to his possessions.

Josef's possessions passed through several sets of hands and although each person made a list of the items, none of these matched.[23] The Huntingdonshire Constabulary had a list, Robertson had a list, Butler had a list, Latchmere House had a list. They were all different. Some only recorded the most important items from an espionage point of view. Others listed every single item in his possession.[24] From the MI5 point of view, only a few items were of burning interest: wireless set, disc code, identity cards, ration book, tablets and, surprisingly, his cigarette lighter.

17

CLANDESTINE COMMUNICATION

It was all well and good for Germany to send spies over to England but that was only the first step. The spies needed to be able to send reports back to Germany and receive instructions from their spy handlers. In the era before emails and text messages, there were three primary methods of communicating at a distance: telephone/telegram, letters and wireless transmission. The telephone and telegram were out of the question since too many ears and eyes could eavesdrop. Letter writing was also a tricky business, particularly during wartime – an agent couldn't simply write a letter to the German Intelligence Service saying that he had visited certain airfields and here was a list of their defences.

The British Ministry of Information had a list of known cover addresses for the German Intelligence Service and kept a watchful eye on outgoing mail. Any letters sent to the cover addresses, often in neutral countries, were automatically opened and scrutinised with care.

Writing in code was also fraught with difficulties. An obviously encoded letter, which would look like gibberish, was guaranteed to arouse suspicion. An agent could use prearranged code language, for example, 'I saw twenty dolphins, two sharks and one whale in Portsmouth Harbour' could be interpreted by the Germans to mean, 'I saw twenty cruisers, two destroyers and one battleship in Portsmouth Harbour.' Such letters, however, could easily arouse the suspicions of an eagle-eyed censor.

An agent could also write an innocuous, chatty letter, but then write a second message on the same piece of paper using invisible ink. Unfortunately, the Ministry of Information had a standard series of tests to reveal invisible ink in suspect letters.

Finally, there was the relatively new technology of the microdot. A piece of paper with text could be photographed and reduced to the size of a typewritten full stop and inserted into a regular letter, although this too could be identified with practice.

That left wireless transmitters, but, up until the late 1930s, most were far too bulky to be used by the average parachute spy. By 1940, however, the Germans had developed one that could fit in a small suitcase. The wireless transmitter was the ideal communication tool, particularly if it was of a type that could both send and receive. Spies could send reports to Germany and receive instructions in return.

There were, however, several caveats with the transmitters. The agent needed to find a place where the long aerials could be stretched out – often a tricky undertaking, particularly in a small flat in the city. Poor placement of the aerials often meant that signals could not be sent or received. Once the aerials were well placed, the agent would send a message using Morse code, a signal that any wireless operator in England could pick up, including the Radio Security Service (RSS). Using a process of triangulation from receiving stations, the location of the transmitter could be determined, particularly if the agent remained on the air for any length of time.

Finally, sending a message *en claire* was obviously not ideal, so most spies were given a method for encoding a message (e.g. disc code, code word, grid code, etc.). Instead of sending 'ARRIVED CAMBRIDGE', the transmission might look like 'WERF DTLG WOFC MHET'.

No system was foolproof, however, and the wireless transmitters depended on their quartz crystals and batteries. The failure of either one of these components meant that the agent would be mute and therefore useless to Germany.

When Josef was captured, the British were interested in his communication tools. Josef's attaché case, which complemented his business suit, contained a wireless set that could both send and receive. In mid February, the wireless set was examined by Leonard William Humphreys of the RSS.[1] Humphreys had examined the wireless sets of other spies and determined that Josef's set and aerials were similar to their models.[2] The attaché case also contained a spare valve, spare quartz crystal and several aerial wires. Humphreys did note that the spare crystal had been placed in the key socket and, had the set been turned on, the crystal would have fractured. Other than that, the set worked fine and picked up good, steady signals.

Josef's attaché case contained a typical spy wireless set and, in late February, Richard Butler (SLB) loaned it and other items found in Josef's possession to Major Michael Ryde, MI5's RSLO in Reading.[3] With strict instructions not to tamper with the set in any way, Ryde used the set and other items in a meeting with the local police. Ryde returned the set to Butler in early March with a note of thanks. Given that the wireless set and other items would be used as evidence against Josef, one naturally wonders at the integrity of the chain of custody for such key evidence.

When Josef was discovered in the farm field near Ramsey, several torn pieces of cardboard were found near him. These were dutifully gathered up by the Home Guard and Ramsey Police and sent off to London. After Stephens used the fragments in his interrogation of Josef, they were returned to Robertson, who then forwarded them on to Felix Cowgill, head of MI6's counter-espionage section, for reconstruction.[4] The fragments were partially reassembled by staff at the Government Code and Cipher School (GCCS) at Bletchley Park and were revealed to be part of a disc code, 'the same as the others but with a different inner disc'.[5]

Josef's disc code was labelled #9, which suggested that eight discs had already been issued to other German spies. Disc codes #6 and #7 had been found in the possession of agents captured by MI5 in the autumn of 1940.[6] Disc code #8, however, had not been found. It might have been assigned to Engelbertus Fukken (aka Jan Willem Ter Braak), a Dutch national who parachuted into England in early November 1940. He evaded capture for several months but ran out of money in March 1941. Fukken killed himself in an air raid shelter near Cambridge at the end of March 1941.

Josef was also given two words *Marinesoldat* (marine soldier or marine) and *Winterhilfswerk* (winter relief work) that could be used to create a grid code for use in emergencies. MI5 was less interested in the emergency code words since they were easily broken, although Stephens did extract a sample message from Josef on 2 February.

Finally, although Josef denied having any invisible ink material, he did have suspicious tablets in his pockets that he claimed were medicinal: Pervitin (to help one stay awake), codeine and 'aceticone' (both cough cures).[7] In early February, Butler sent the tablets to Lord Victor Rothschild (MI5 – B1c), who passed them along to the National Institute for Medical Research in Hampstead, London.[8] Were they medicinal, or could they be used for secret writing? The lab in Hampstead conducted exhaustive tests on the tablets using mice as test subjects.[9]

The first set of tablets were identified as a cerebral stimulant similar to Benzedrine, likely N-methylbenzendrine.[10] Josef had said that one set of tablets was Pervitin (Methedrine), which helped one stay awake. Both Benzedrine and Methedrine are amphetamines. In low doses, Methedrine increases self-confidence, concentration and the willingness to take risks, while at the same time reducing sensitivity to pain, hunger, thirst and reducing the need for sleep.[11]

The second set of tablets contained codeine phosphate, a mild painkiller that could also be used as a cough suppressant and to treat diarrhoea.[12]

The third set of tablets contained ammonium chloride, French chalk and probably a liquorice extract.[13] Josef had said that the third group of pills were 'aceticone' – possibly a mispronunciation of Acedicone, the trade name of the drug Thebacon. Acedicone is a hydrochloride salt, often flavoured with liquorice, and used as a cough suppressant.

The final report from Hampstead concluded that none of the tablets contained a secret writing compound. While the tablets did contain starch, which could have made a very simple ink, starch was also a perfectly normal binding agent.[14]

The Hampstead report was quite clear, but in late April, Helenus P. Milmo (MI5 – Section B1b) sent the pills to H.L. Smith, of the Scientific Section of the General Post Office, for a second analysis.[15] Milmo asked Smith to examine the tablets, keeping in mind that the pills and wrappers would need to be produced as exhibits in court.[16]

In his 25 April report, Smith said that none of the tablets would be useful for secret writing as they all contained too much sugar and starch. The first set of tablets were mostly sugar but contained a non-alkaloid substance such as strychnine. There was nothing in them that would be useful for keeping one awake. This contradicted the first analysis, which concluded that the tablets were similar to Benzedrine. The second set of tablets contained a small amount of codeine phosphate. The third set of tablets contained sugar, ammonium chloride and a vegetable extract (perhaps liquorice) which would be useful in case of a cough. In Smith's opinion, Josef appeared 'to be carrying genuine medicine which would not be used for secret writing'.[17]

Josef had a wireless transmitter, a disc code and an emergency code. He was well equipped to send signals to Germany, but in order to accomplish his mission he would have needed to present himself as an Englishman, or at the very least a legitimate refugee, complete with the proper identity papers.

18

A NEW IDENTITY

On 3 September 1939, Britain declared war against Germany. Two days later, Parliament, with royal assent, passed a National Registration system. With war declared, evacuations looming and the last census eight years old, the government wanted to know who lived in the United Kingdom. On the evening of 29 September 1939, under the supervision of Sir Sylvanus Vivian, the Registrar General, a national registration took place of all people in the country.

The National Identity Card issued as a result of the registration was paired with a ration book, which was introduced in early 1940. In order to receive rationed goods (e.g. bacon, butter, eggs, sugar), everyone needed a ration book and an identity card. People were required to carry their identification papers at all times and to present them for inspection when requested. The identity card was not a complicated document. It had no photograph and simply listed the person's name and registration number. Later, in May 1940, people were told to add their address and sign and date the card.

The registration numbers were basic: a four-letter prefix, followed by two numbers. The four-letter prefix was a district code, similar to an enumeration district. The first number was a household number. The second number was the person's position within the household. So, DBEV/35/2 would mean district code DBEV, household 35 and person 2 in the household.

It was a simple system, but it worked – for MI5, it worked even better. In July 1940 BISCUIT, one of SNOW's subagents, took an identity card and a ration book (a pink traveller's version) to Spain and presented them to Nikolaus Ritter of the Hamburg Abwehr. The Germans wanted to reproduce the identity card and ration book as faithfully as possible for the LENA spies. Unbeknownst to Ritter, the documents brought by BISCUIT had been subtly altered by MI5. Genuine cards were folded by hand, whereas the forged ones were machine folded. German forgeries of these papers would be easily identifiable. In addition, the German forgeries had a number of other issues:

1) In a genuine card, the surname should have appeared before and above the Christian name:
   RYMER
        James
   The Germans invariably wrote the name simply as:
        James Rymer
2) In a genuine card, the registration number and name were written by the registration authorities. The address was only filled in later by the individuals themselves. Thus, the two sections should have had different handwriting. The Germans used the same handwriting for both sections.
3) In a genuine card, the date would not have been earlier than 20 May 1940. On some forged identity cards, the date was prior to 20 May 1940.
4) A genuine card generally had a rubber stamp from the issuing authority. The forged cards had no stamp.[1]

The Abwehr office in Hamburg also asked SNOW for specimen names and registration numbers for the forged identity cards. MI5 promptly came up with a dozen examples, eight of which were genuine and four of which were fictitious. When the first wave of agents landed between September and November 1940, MI5 found that their identity cards used the names and registration numbers supplied by SNOW. Most were swiftly captured by MI5 and several were turned into double agents. The Germans had taken the bait.

In November 1940 the Germans asked TATE how his identity card had worked as they needed to know for future agents. TATE said that it worked well, although the ration card was not so good. Later that same month, Hamburg asked SNOW for another four names and numbers to use on identity cards, but this time they requested addresses that had been bombed out. MI5 dug up the information and cheerfully sent it over via SNOW on 12 December – they could expect a fresh wave of spies.[2]

Josef was the first agent of 1941 and MI5 was intrigued to see which of the false identities he had been assigned. Robertson was the first MI5 officer to write a report about Josef's identity card. On 2 February, he noted that the card was made out in the name of James Rymer, London, Woodford Green, 33 Abbotsford Gardens. The name and address were genuine, and the address had been bombed out, one of the requests from the Germans, but that was where routine ended and strangeness began.

The registration number that SNOW had sent over to the Germans to accompany the James Rymer information was ARAJ/301/29. The registration number on Josef's card was 656/301/29. The Germans had replaced the four-letter prefix with a three-digit number. The registration number on Josef's identity card was not valid and would have been immediately recognised as such by anyone who inspected the card. The substitution was most perplexing and Liddell (Director of B Division), mused at length about Josef's identity card:

> The parachutist is at Brixton hospital. He says his name is Josef Jakobs. He says that he was in a concentration camp at Oranienburg. This may be true but it is a story that we have heard before. He had with him £500. This is more than any of the other agents have brought. He had one address on him, that of Mrs Lily Knips, 9 Compayne Gardens, NW 7, reputedly a Jewess with whom Jakobs intended to communicate. Jakobs said that it was eventually his intention to go to America where he had an aunt.
>
> It is difficult not to be sceptical about these people. Firstly, it seems almost incredible that if Jakobs' story is true the Germans could imagine that he was going to be of any real value to them. Secondly, why did they give him a registration card with no letter prefix? Incidentally it was one of those about which SNOW sent numbers. If they had wished to alter the letters or the numbers, that would have been different, but to rule out the prefix and put in numbers instead would seem to be rather more than a clerical error. Did they intend that Jakobs would be captured, on the assumption that they know that these [double-cross] agents send weather reports and other information which though limited is at least accurate. If he had a number and name submitted by SNOW and SNOW was not trusted, they might have sent him over to test SNOW in some way although it is difficult to see exactly how, since SNOW could perfectly well say that he had been captured owing to the blunder about his registration card. A better test would seem to have been to try and place him in direct touch with SNOW. Another point which occurs to me is that the Germans must now be wise to the game of collaring an agent and forcing him to use his wireless set in our interests. There is in fact evidence that they are doing it themselves. Surely therefore they would have some

arrangement, for example the dropping of the first letter of the prefix by which the agent could indicate that he was not acting under compulsion. We know that in some ways the Germans are extremely crude and sketchy in their methods and this may of course be the explanation but I find it difficult to believe. Jakobs has already agreed to assist us to make use of his wireless set.[3]

A few days later, Robertson sent the two identity cards[4] and ration book to Sylvanus Vivian, the Registrar General. In his memo to Vivian, Robertson admitted to being perplexed by Josef's identity card and wondered why the Germans would have seen fit to alter the registration number.[5] He did note that, other than the substitution of numbers for letters, the quality of the fake identity card was a great improvement on previous efforts by the Germans.[6] Vivian said that normally a ration book would be expected to contain forged entries and food stamps, but this had not been done. It might be that the Germans did not feel comfortable forging the particulars that were added to a ration book when it was issued. Anyone found with such a ration book in their possession would probably have been arrested on the spot under suspicion that they had stolen an official blank from a Food Office. Vivian also pointed out that the print was 'completely out of date'.[7] Josef's ration book was a good forgery, except for the fact that it lacked entries, food stamps and was out of date.

There was no further discussion regarding the mysterious registration number on Josef's identity card, at least none that survived declassification of the MI5 file. Given that the Germans had already used the registration numbers provided by SNOW, without a hint of alteration, for other agents, one is left wondering what went wrong with Josef's identity card. Was the technical section of the German Abwehr that inefficient? Even Liddell did not believe that was the case. This leaves the possibility that the Germans deliberately altered the registration number on Josef's identity card. To what purpose? Surely, they would have known that even a cursory examination of his papers by the sleepiest bobby would have resulted in Josef's immediate arrest. Josef's ration card was so crisp and new that it too would have resulted in his immediate arrest. Why would the Germans have gone to all the trouble and expense to send over a well-paid agent to England in the full knowledge that the British would snap him up instantly? This question vexed the officers of MI5 in early February. Josef was an unknown factor and was becoming less suitable as a double agent by the day.

19

DRESSING THE PART

From Josef's perspective, he had been given a British National Identity Card in the name of James Rymer, but the papers were only part of his act. Josef needed to look like an Englishman, someone who could blend into the streets of London and not merit a second glance. Josef was operating with one major handicap when he leapt from the aeroplane; he couldn't bring a suitcase. Everything that he needed, he had to tuck away into the pockets of his trousers, jacket, coat or flying suit. Plus, the Abwehr had a few must-haves that took up space in his pockets: a pocket knife to cut away his parachute, a folding spade to bury his parachute gear and a torch to signal aeroplanes.

Josef knew that he might need to live rough for several days, so he had also brought a packet of minced beef sandwiches, a brown sausage, Dutch chocolate and a small bottle of spirits. These food supplies were hardly enough to sustain him for very long. Most tellingly, Josef carried no water. In September 1940 it was thirst that drove one of the first four German spies out of hiding and into a pub, where he promptly drew attention to himself by asking for a glass of cider at the wrong time of day. Other spies gave themselves away by entering restaurants and trying to use their ration books to pay for meals. Food and drink were of critical importance to a newly arrived spy, but for Josef both would prove to be a moot point. His broken ankle meant that he had little appetite for either.

He did, however, derive much comfort, during that long night, from smoking a series of cigarettes. When the British found him, he had a pack of twenty cigarettes,[1] a leather cigarette case with one cigarette, a cigarette holder and a lighter. Harry Godfrey, the Home Guard volunteer called to the landing site by one of the farmers, noted that Josef was surrounded by cigarette butts. Josef likely would have smoked his remaining cigarettes except that his lighter had run out of fuel.[2]

That same lighter caused a stir at MI5. Every object found on a spy was suspect and the MI5 officers sometimes expended a great deal of effort trying to decipher the hidden meaning of innocuous items. Josef's lighter had 'KW' engraved on the bottom, which gave rise to much speculation. One MI5 officer suggested that KW could refer to Kurt Wenkel, a German agent who had gone to Bulgaria. The information was dutifully passed along to Cowgill (MI6), who dismissed the Wenkel theory but thought that the initials reflected Josef's real name. Stephens, from Latchmere House, noted that, while he had yet to see the lighter, several officers at Latchmere House had lighters bearing those initials and thus he thought that KW was simply a trademark. Had the MI5 officers had access to the internet, a quick search would have revealed that Stephens was correct. Karl Wieden was the name of a Solingen-based company who manufactured lighters from 1905 to 1980. The trademark initials of the company were KW and there was nothing suspicious about Josef's lighter.

The MI5 officers were less interested in Josef's other smoking paraphernalia. Josef had a cigarette holder, but there was no mention of its size or composition. Cigarette holders were a fashion accessory in the early to mid 1900s. They were considered an essential part of lady's fashion, although men used them as well (e.g. Noel Coward, Franklin D. Roosevelt). The holder could be made of silver, jade or even Bakelite, and came in a variety of lengths: opera, theatre, dinner and cocktail. There was a proper cigarette holder for every occasion. Cigarette holders were also practically useful. In the days before cigarettes contained built-in filters (pre-1960s), the cigarette holder contained a filter that helped to prevent nicotine staining on the fingers and reduced the amount of toxins being inhaled.

Josef also had a leather cigarette case marked 'Zeka Wettig Geder', a Dutch company. Cigarette cases were extremely popular in the 1900s, particularly with soldiers. Cigarettes were sold in cardboard packages that did not afford much protection, so most cigarette cases were metal, although some were made of leather or even precious metals. During the two world wars, some cigarette cases even saved the lives of soldiers by stopping bullets.[3]

Josef would have looked elegant sitting in a London café smoking his cigarettes with a cigarette holder. Naturally, he would also need to look well groomed. It wouldn't do to have clean fingers but dirty fingernails and unkempt hair. Tucked away in his pockets was a pair of nail scissors, a nail file and a comb. His dapper look would have been topped off with a wristwatch and a pair of reading glasses in a blue leather case, tellingly marked 'Optiker-Ruhnke' (a German company).

Were anyone to give Josef a casual glance, they would have seen a British businessman or a refugee from the Continent. From head to toe, Josef presented a picture of respectability. He was dressed in a grey-striped lounge suit, under which he wore a top shirt with a semi-stiff collar and tie. Over his suit, he wore a light grey herringbone overcoat. His feet were clad in blue[4] woollen socks, over which he wore black shoes with brown laces. The incongruence of blue socks, black shoes and brown laces would not have been noticeable as they were covered by grey spats with zip fasteners. To top off the whole ensemble, Josef had a blue silk scarf and a blue trilby hat.

Unfortunately, Josef did not have much of a chance to blend into the London scene. Even if he had landed safely, his dapper clothes with their Continental style would have marked him as a stranger in Ramsey. His elegant appearance would also have been marred by the fact that under his overcoat, Josef was also wearing three woollen pullovers, two undervests and two woollen scarves. His pockets would have bulged with a map of Britain, a dictionary, 497 £1 bank notes, and several wallets.[5]

Josef set off from Schiphol well dressed but not well equipped. His mission could have ended differently had he been provided with proper paratrooper boots that would have protected his ankles far better than dress shoes. During his hospitalisation, the cause of Josef's injury was a topic of hot discussion at MI5 headquarters and elsewhere. Did Josef injure himself leaving the aeroplane or upon landing?

By late February, it was clear that Josef would not be leaving the hospital in the near future. Some Air Ministry officers were anxious to question him about his injury. Given Josef's extended convalescence, Stephens suggested that Robertson and Wing Commander Samuel D. Felkin visit him at the hospital. On 12 March, Wing Commander Felkin and Lieutenant Sampson from Latchmere House visited Dulwich Hospital and questioned Josef, despite his septic ankle.[6]

Josef again told the story of his flight from Holland to England. He explained that he had been dropped through a narrow trapdoor. His right side had been very cold and when he placed his right leg through the opening, as he faced aft, it smashed against the fuselage.[7] It was a simple explanation, but was it true?

Felkin and Sampson had a short discussion outside the hospital, during which Felkin admitted that he doubted that Josef's injury could have been sustained in the way that he described. Felkin promised to send a report to MI5 and the two men parted ways. Sampson returned to Latchmere House, reported to Stephens and told him the result of their questioning. Stephens sent a memo to Robertson, who mused over the conclusion for long minutes. Josef had said that he injured his ankle leaving the aeroplane. Felkin thought that this was unlikely. Who was right? What actually happened? It was too bad that the German air crew couldn't break the deadlock, although in actuality, they had already offered their opinion, and MI5 knew about it.

On 3 February double agent SNOW received a wireless message from his German handler that stated: 'Dropped man 31st [of January], 30 miles south of Peterborough. Was badly hurt leaving [aeroplane]. Perhaps dead. If you hear anything please let me know.'[8] The reason for the Air Ministry's interest in Josef's injury was clear. They wanted to know if Josef was the man referred to in the SNOW message or if a second agent had been dropped on the evening of 31 January. Josef landed 10 miles south-east of Peterborough, not 30 miles south of the city. Was there another agent who had injured himself badly leaving the aeroplane? As it would turn out, there was no other agent and the message did indeed refer to Josef. In the inky night-time darkness of 31 January, the German pilots had got their distances confused and thought they had dropped Josef further south than they had.

The British had independent proof that Josef was telling the truth. He had hurt his ankle leaving the aeroplane. He would tell the same story during his defence at his court martial. He jumped knowing that he was injured. He could have told the crew he was hurt and they would have flown him back to Holland. Instead, he chose to drop out into the English night, desperate to escape from the Nazis. While Felkin did not believe Josef's story, Stephens noted in a report on 24 April that Josef 'was suffering from an ankle broken while leaving the German aeroplane'.[9]

Naturally, MI5 never told Josef, or his defence lawyer, about the SNOW message. They couldn't reveal the source of their information without exposing the entire double-cross system. Would it have made a difference at Josef's trial? Perhaps not, but it would have attested to his credibility and veracity. For that was always the question with Josef, at least in the eyes of MI5. Was he telling the truth?

However, there was at least one person in England who could testify to part of Josef's story: the German-Jewish refugee, Lily Knips.

20

AN UNSAVOURY NAME

During his first two interrogations, on 1 February at Cannon Row Police Station and on 2 February at Latchmere House, Josef told the MI5 officers that he had planned to contact Frau Lily Knips at 9 Compayne Gardens. He had hoped that she would help him in his bid to reach America. Any person associated with a spy was highly suspect and Stephens made a note that Lily's name was 'unsavoury'. In naming Lily, Josef immediately placed her within the crosshairs of MI5, a dangerous position even for the innocent and particularly for a German-Jewish refugee.

The MI5 officers did a background check on the unfortunate Lily, requesting information from the Traffic Index (United Kingdom arrivals and departures), Central Aliens Register and Home Office files. The Traffic Index came up as 'no trace' but the other two registries were useful. The officers learned that Lily was, as Josef had said, a Jewish refugee who had moved to England in April 1939. Lily had been granted exemption from internment on 21 December 1939 and was not perceived as a threat to national security. Appearances could be deceiving, however, and the officers had learned to be suspicious of everyone. On 13 February MI5 widened its dragnet and requested a background check on Lily's son, Lothar Sauer. Lothar, too, seemed an innocent character. He had come to England in 1934 to study and was naturalised. In the summer of 1939 he married Hermine Apfel (an Austrian Jew), who also wished to become naturalised.

The declaration of war in September 1939 put a different spin on things. Foreigners and refugees were viewed with suspicion by the authorities. Many refugees would find the welcome mat pulled out from under their feet; they might be part of a Fifth Column, ready to leap up during an invasion and sabotage the British war effort. In June 1940, in a bid to demonstrate his loyalty to his new country, Lothar valiantly offered to join the Pioneer Corps, a British unit that accepted enemy aliens. Most Pioneer volunteers were German refugees, either Jews or political opponents of the Nazi regime, and the unit was dubbed 'The King's Most Loyal Enemy Aliens'. Some members of the Pioneer Corps joined fighting units while others were recruited by the Special Operations Executive (SOE) and parachuted behind enemy lines as secret agents. Joining the Pioneer Corps was hazardous for German nationals. If they were captured by the Germans, they would be executed as traitors. Lothar's noble gesture never came to fruition for on 21 June 1940 he was interned under the Enemy Aliens Act. He was released in August for medical reasons and was not seen as a threat to national security.[1]

Having researched Lily and her son, MI5 belatedly added her address to the postal censorship list on 26 February 1941. Unbeknownst to Lily, postal censors would open and inspect every piece of mail that originated from, or was destined for, her address. They would even test her letters for secret ink. If she had even a passing connection with the German Abwehr, MI5 wanted to know about it.

In the meantime, Dick White consulted with Stephens and Special Branch and arranged to have Lily interrogated at her home. On 28 February, MI5 officers Lieutenant Roland A.F. Short and Captain Edward B. Goodacre, along with Sergeant Louis V. Gale of Special Branch, gathered outside the entrance of 9 Compayne Gardens. Neighbours probably peered through their windows with undisguised curiosity.

The men pressed the buzzer and the door was opened by Lily.[2] Her shock must have been palpable. She had lived through the Nazi terror and the sight of three male officials outside her door would have triggered many memories, none of them pleasant. The men were polite, but Lily must have led them into her sitting room with fear and trembling. Gale told Lily that they wanted to ask her some questions. They began gently enough, asking her questions about her immigration and financial situation. Her fear probably escalated. Had she done something wrong? Were they going to send her back to Germany? At an opportune moment, Short produced the photograph of Josef taken at Latchmere House on 2 February.[3] Lily was visibly distraught at Josef's dishevelled appearance and her hands flew to her mouth. She named him as Herr Jakobs without hesitation and told the officers the circumstances surrounding her acquaintance with him in Berlin.

Lily said that while she had heard nothing from Josef since his arrest in October 1938, she had received two mysterious letters since her arrival in England. The first was addressed to 19 or 29 Compayne Gardens and arrived in the summer of 1940 with a postmark from Holland or Denmark.[4] The letter, in poorly written German, asked her to pay 40,000 RM[5] to an American bank into the account of a woman whose name Lily did not recognise and had since forgotten. The letter exhorted Lily to travel to Switzerland and visit the writer, but the signature was illegible. Lily gave the letter back to the postman and told him that it must have been intended for some other person. The second letter was addressed to 9 Compayne Gardens and arrived shortly after Christmas 1940 with a Shanghai postmark. It was signed by a Frau Goldstein, who said that she had been informed by Herr Jakobs that he had given Lily 40,000 RM on Frau Goldstein's behalf. Lily was told to send that amount to Frau Goldstein's bank in Shanghai. Goldstein mentioned that Herr Jakobs had already written to Lily concerning the matter, at which point Lily recalled the earlier letter and thought that it might have come from Herr Jakobs. Goldstein wrote that Lily had met her husband (Martin Goldstein) with Herr Jakobs in Berlin and that both men had been released from prison at Easter, 1940.[6] Lily destroyed that letter.

Short then showed Lily a picture of Clara Bäuerle, but Lily did not recognise the face nor the name. Lily seemed to be a dead end but the officers searched her flat and found a quantity of correspondence, documents and an address book, all of which were confiscated for further inspection. Short thought it unusual that Lily's flat had no photographs, but Lily told him that her only interest in life was her son. According to Short, Lily's closest living relatives were her father in Hannover, from whom she had received a letter the previous month, and her stepdaughter in Berlin, with whom she had had no contact since 1936.[7]

The officers thanked Lily for her co-operation and left her flat. Lily leaned against the door in shock. She was a sensitive and highly strung woman and it was all too much. The photograph of an unkempt Herr Jakobs. The questioning by the officers. The confiscation of her belongings. She had left Germany to escape danger, but it seemed that danger could be found even in England.

Fortunately for Lily, both MI5 and Special Branch concluded that she was not a threat to national security. Short was left with the impression that Josef and his associates had made a considerable fortune 'browbeating and, to some extent, assisting Jewish people desirous of leaving the country'.[8]

He thought that Josef had likely pestered Lily in Berlin and suggested various illegal ways by which she could get her money out of Germany. Lily claimed that she had seen through his schemes, but out of fear of him, continued in friendly relations with him until his arrest. While Lily insisted that their relationship was of a businesslike and friendly character, Short sensed a 'close intimacy' between the two.

Gale thought that her assertion that she wanted all their dealings to be perfectly legal was not entirely credible. Gale suspected that Lily was aware of Josef's convictions from the start but that she was prepared to conspire with him and his associates to get herself and her money out of Germany, legally or otherwise.

Both officers agreed that the two letters were suspicious, and Gale doubted that Lily had told them the complete truth. She appeared to be a shrewd woman and it was unlikely that she would have failed to recognise the implications of the first letter and conclude that it was not intended for her. She may indeed have been involved in financial deals with Josef, Goldstein and others, and the letters may have reflected demands for money that the writers felt were due to them. The writers may also have been trying to blackmail her in connection with their former activities. Short leaned towards the idea that the letters reflected an attempt by the Nazis to blackmail refugees into supplying their agents in England with money.[9] There was a great deal missing from her explanation, but it probably had no bearing from a security viewpoint. It would, however, explain her anxiety to get rid of the letters and conveniently forget the details.[10]

MI5 did a thorough background check on the individuals mentioned by Lily and on the names found in her papers.[11] Lily had suggested that a certain Clara Gronau, a German-Jewish refugee living in London, could provide useful information since she had been friendly with Frau Reiwald in Berlin.[12] In due course, Clara received a visit from MI5 and Special Branch but she did not recognise Josef's picture nor his name. She told the officers that there had been a lot of gossip amongst the Berlin Jews about finances and passports, but she could not recall individual cases. Clara was cleared of suspicion, as were Lily's other contacts and, on 19 March, she was reunited with her confiscated papers.[13] MI5 also attempted to trace the first letter that Lily had received but nothing further was heard from the Postal Service.[14] However, thanks to Lily Knips, MI5 had background information on Josef against which they could compare his statements.[15]

On 26 March, Josef was released from Dulwich Hospital and transferred to the Latchmere House infirmary.[16] Stephens finally had Josef within his grasp, but his glee was short-lived; two days later Josef developed a temperature and had a relapse. Stephens wearily agreed that Josef could be transferred to Brixton Prison infirmary for additional medical care.[17] Finally, on 15 April, Josef was transferred from Brixton Prison to Latchmere House. He had recovered sufficiently from his pneumonia and septic broken ankle and was now fair game for the Latchmere House interrogators.

21

ONCE MORE UNTO THE BREACH

Josef had first been brought to Latchmere House on 2 February for a brief interrogation by Stephens, Sampson and Evans. It was an unsatisfactory interrogation for both parties. Josef had been in extreme pain from his broken ankle and Stephens had been unable to use his full arsenal of interrogation techniques. Despite those challenges, Stephens had triumphantly reported that the interrogation of Josef was not 'a difficult matter'.[1] The 'calculated atmosphere' that Stephens and his men created had worked its magic and Josef had quickly accepted Stephens' demand that he work as a 'servant of his captors'.[2] At the time Stephens felt that Josef, if properly handled, would be a useful double-cross agent. Liddell (Director of B Division) noted in his diary entry for 2 February, 'Jakobs has already agreed to assist us to make use of his wireless set.'[3]

As we have seen, however, much had altered over the intervening weeks. Josef's second visit to Latchmere House was very different from his first. The welcome mat, such as it was, had been withdrawn. Josef was no longer a player in the double-cross game, he was simply a source of information. He would be squeezed dry and then discarded, destined either for imprisonment or execution. Josef, however, was still under the impression that he had an agreement with MI5 – work for the British and he could save the life of his family and better his own position.

After arriving at Latchmere House on the morning of 15 April, Josef was escorted to a cell by Sampson, the officer in charge of Josef's case. Sampson pointed to the typewriter and paper already placed within the cell and ordered Josef to write the story of his life. Josef complied and over the next three days painstakingly pecked out three statements.[4] The first, written on 15 April, gave an account of his life. The second, written on 16 April, articulated how he had not come to England as an enemy. The third, written on 17 April, gave the reason for his journey to England. The statements were translated from German into English and provided Sampson and Stephens with a wealth of information. When Josef handed in his third statement, Stephens felt obliged to record his own thoughts on the encounter:

> Administratively, I do not know whether it was the intention of Jakobs, in appearing before me ex hospital naked in a blanket, to emulate the frolics of Cleopatra when she appeared before Caesar in a carpet. I do know, however, that Captain Stimson [Latchmere House administrator] expressly visited Kingston and purchased a brand new outfit for this scrofulous Nazi, so that the least said about the penultimate paragraph of Jakobs' statement of 17.4.41 the less danger will there be of plagiarism when Captain Stimson deals with this case himself.[5]

The paragraph in Josef's statement that caused Stephens to sputter with such indignation simply stated:

> Finally, permit me to express a wish. I should be most grateful if, until you finally decide upon my employment, you would allow me to spend out of my own money the sum of about £3 on things which I am in urgent need. Since my release from the Dulwich Hospital, I have not been able to clean my teeth, because I have neither tooth brush nor paste. I have no comb, mirror or shaving tackle, and have no change of underclothing – in short I have nothing. I feel so dirty that it is extremely unpleasant for me. I have no shoes either, mine have vanished and nobody seems to know where they are. And then if it is at all possible, I should like to supplement the food here, for I am suffering here from hunger. On account of my long illness at the hospital, when for many days I was unable to eat anything, I lost a great deal of weight, my body now demands to make up for this. I should also like to buy my own smoking materials as I am a heavy smoker and naturally find it impossible to manage on 10 cigarettes. I take it for granted that you will understand that tobacco helps one through many a difficult hour caused by imprisonment and uncertainty regarding one's fate. I trust that my requests will be taken into consideration and granted.[6]

While Stephens mocked Josef's request, it did produce action. On 29 April, Stimson sent a letter to Butler (SLB) requesting Josef's personal property since the items were of no operational value. The requested items were: lighter, pencil, cigarettes along with case and holder, watch, Catholic badge, wallet containing comb, scissors and nail file, dictionary, socks and handkerchief.[7] Alas, Josef had not travelled with spare underclothing, although perhaps the officers relented and provided him with some. The next day Butler sent the items to Latchmere House, noting that the Catholic badge had disappeared but he included the silk tie even though it had not been requested.[8] Clearly, the MI5 officers were not concerned that Josef might use the tie to hang himself. (A few months later, another suspected spy, Olaf Saetrang, would choose that method of escape to avoid interrogation.[9] After that incident, scarves and silk ties were forbidden to the inmates of Latchmere House.)

It took Sampson a couple of days to review Josef's statements and draw up a list of additional questions. On 20 April, Stephens called Sampson into his office and informed him that they had a bigger issue on their hands: double agent TATE.

Since his arrival in England in September 1940, TATE had proved to be an outstanding double agent. The information that he sent back to Germany via wireless was a mixture of trivial chickenfeed, a few nuggets of tarnished truth and a fair amount of blatant misdirection (all vetted by the Twenty Committee). The Germans gobbled it up and considered TATE to be a pearl beyond price.[10]

On 14 January 1941, TATE, who had landed with only £200,[11] told the Germans that he had run low on funds and needed an immediate injection of cash. His case officers in Hamburg assured him that they would send him more money. Although Josef denied that he had been sent with funds for another agent, it is perhaps too much of a coincidence that he arrived with a significant amount of money shortly after TATE's request. If the Germans were using Josef as a courier, the fact that they knew that he had been badly injured leaving the aeroplane meant that they quickly decided that other arrangements needed to be made for TATE. On 4 February, the Germans told him that a friend would send money via the post and, true to their word, on 11 February (before his Lisbon trip) double agent SNOW sent £100 to TATE.

All was well, or so it seemed at the time. By late March, SNOW was considered a triple agent, which meant that he was blown, possibly along with any agent with whom he had had been in contact. SNOW had sent money to TATE, so was TATE also blown?

The British decided to test the Germans and on 24 March 1941 TATE requested several hundred pounds. Almost a month later, after asking TATE to be patient, the Germans told him that a friend from the Phoenix Hotel in Hamburg would arrive at the end of April with £300 and a new crystal for TATE's wireless transmitter. The man was tall, blond-haired and blue-eyed, with a wart over his right eye. In bemusement, TATE wrote back that he could not remember anyone of that description. No problem, said the Germans, the man would recognise TATE. Stephens was excited by the news. This new agent had trained in Hamburg and might even know Josef.

Stephens and Sampson called in the rest of the interrogation team, briefed them on the latest developments and devised a series of questions for Josef centred on his Abwehr training in Hamburg. On 21–22 April, those questions were presented to Josef during several interrogation sessions. Josef told them about his handler, Dr Beier (Boeckel), but flatly denied that he had met any other spies in Hamburg or The Hague. The officers moved on to other topics, but always circled back to his time in Hamburg. Who had he met at the Phoenix Hotel? Josef denied ever meeting anyone at the Phoenix Hotel and likely denied that he had even been there. Finally, at the end of one interrogation, a frustrated Sampson told Josef that 'his story was so unconvincing and he had told so many lies, that he could only help himself by telling the whole truth'.[12]

On 29 April, after a few days alone with his thoughts, and Sampson's admonition ringing in his ears, Josef requested an interview. Josef began by telling Sampson that he 'would willingly give all the information in his possession if he could be satisfied that this information would not fall into the hands of the Nazis'.[13] Sampson told him that they expected him to give full information and that he 'need have no fear of the Nazis'.[14] With that shaky reassurance, Josef admitted that he remembered a man from Hamburg who might be identical with the man from the Phoenix Hotel. Josef said that he first encountered the man while he was being driven around by Dr Beier (Boeckel). While they hadn't spoken to each other on that occasion, they bumped into each other later at the Café Dreyer. The man was about 24–28 years old and said that his name was Richter. He was taller than Josef, with straw-coloured hair, blue eyes and a round, clean-shaven face. Josef had only met Richter a few times and hadn't noticed a wart over his right eye. Sampson strongly encouraged Josef to write another statement about his time in Hamburg and anything else that he might have forgotten.

Sampson reported back to Stephens, who passed the word up the MI5 ladder. The officers of MI5 rubbed their hands with glee. Another German agent was about to parachute into their laps. Even better, Josef and Richter knew each other, a prime opportunity to play the two men off of each other.

While Stephens sharpened the figurative knives of his interrogation tactics in preparation for Richter's arrival, Sampson was tasked with sorting the wheat from the chaff in Josef's typewritten statements. There was so much seemingly unimportant information and not a few discrepancies, the worst of which surrounded Josef's recruitment into the German Intelligence Service and his reason for coming to England.

22

OH, WHAT A TANGLED WEB

During his first two interrogations, on 1 and 2 February, Josef told a simple story to his interrogators. In both statements, Josef said that he was released from Sachsenhausen concentration camp on 22 March 1940 and that he joined the German air force as an *unteroffizier* (non-commissioned officer) in the weather department, Section 5, Hamburg. His commanding officer was Captain Dr Beier (Boeckel). Josef had been sent to England to send weather reports back to Germany, but he had had no intention of doing so. He considered his mission to England a means of getting out of Germany. Upon his arrival, he had intended to contact Lily Knips and ask for her help in emigrating to America, where he had an aunt.

By the time Josef was released from hospital in mid April, he had fleshed out his story, but were the additions fact or fiction? In the latest version, Josef was released from Sachsenhausen on 22 March 1940 after signing a statement in which he promised to never disclose information about the camp. Josef then resumed his former occupation as a travelling salesman with limited success. He was unable to practice as a dentist because he would have needed a permit from the Gestapo and none would have been granted given his incarceration in Switzerland and Sachsenhausen.

A couple of months later, in June 1940, Josef was called up for military service as an officer and sent to Spandau, where a new regiment was being formed to look after prisoners of war. He told the commanding officer about his Swiss conviction in the hopes of being released as 'unsuitable for military service'. His hopes were realised when, after three days, he was released until the situation around his Swiss conviction could be clarified.

A few weeks later, he met a Jewish friend who suggested that he apply to the German Intelligence Service (Abwehr). At this point, Josef added a whole other layer of complexity to his story. During his time in Sachsenhausen Josef claimed to have learned about the existence of a secret anti-Nazi organisation named *Die Zentrale*. After his release from the camp, Josef joined the organisation, which had about 60,000–70,000 members throughout Germany. Josef approached his contact in the organisation, a mysterious Dr Bergas, with the idea of joining the Abwehr. Dr Bergas approved the idea and said that Josef could, once in England, drum up financial and political support for the anti-Nazi organisation.

Josef had hoped to bring £2,000[1] of his own money to England. He would then use £400 for his own expenses and, with the remaining £1,600, buy German bank notes from Jewish refugees. The rate in Britain would be 100 RM to the £1, while in Germany the rate was 9 RM to the £1.[2] The anti-Nazi organisation figured that with £1,600 he could get 100,000–150,000 RM. He had also hoped to get donations from refugees in Britain who still had relatives in Germany. Once he had the German money in hand, he planned to travel to Lisbon and hand the money over to a courier, a woman named Frau Doktor Scholte, who also belonged to the anti-Nazi organisation. Everything depended on whether or not Josef could enlist the support of the British Secret Service as he would need their assistance to travel from Britain to Lisbon.[3]

Josef went to great lengths to convince his interrogators that he was no friend of the Nazis. He had been imprisoned in a concentration camp and suffered at the hands of the Nazis. He was a good Catholic who had watched the Nazis interfere in the Catholic education of his children. He attempted to convince the British that the Nazis were the enemies, not only of Britain, but of Germany as well:

> Free speech in Germany is virtually impossible because Gestapo spies are everywhere. People are no longer masters of their time or their personal wishes, but are slaves of the Nazis, under the control of Gestapo agents. As a travelling salesman, I came into contact with various classes of people in all parts of Germany and I know how the majority felt about the Nazis. Most of Germany is anything but pro-Nazi, but the Nazis remain in power because people are afraid of the Gestapo. I was greatly surprised to read statements in the English newspapers that Hitler is the most popular man in Germany; this is absolute nonsense. The crowds that gather to hear Hitler are employees, workers and their children who are forced to attend, or end up in a concentration camp. Only the rich and powerful, those who hold high positions, are Nazis.[4]

In Josef's opinion, Britain would never win the war against Germany, not even with the help of the United States. There was no foothold in Europe from which the Allies could launch an attack and there was no way that Britain would be able to starve Germany into submission. The only way in which Hitler and the Nazis could be beaten would be by a revolution within Germany. Josef said that he had come to Britain in the hope of enlisting the assistance of the British for his anti-Nazi organisation.

The officers of MI5 read Josef's statements, each more convoluted than the last, and probably had a variety of reactions. Some may have shaken their heads in disbelief and confusion as they tried to sift out nuggets of useful information from all the verbiage. Others may have burst out laughing at the outrageousness of Josef's story. Some may have simply let their foreheads thud onto their desks, exhausted by their attempts to untangle Josef's intricate web. A web of truth or a web of deceit? Or a combination of both?

In his early statements, Josef claimed that he was trying to get to his aunt in America. There was no evidence that MI5 tried to expand on that titbit of information. At no point in the declassified MI5 file does anyone attempt to extract the name of this mysterious aunt from Josef. In all likelihood, the MI5 officers had heard this type of story often enough and simply dismissed it as a fiction. As it turned out, Josef did indeed have an aunt in America.

Josef's mother, Emma Lück, had a younger sister named Lucia Lück, born on 11 May 1881 in Sassenroth. While Emma dallied with a Roman Catholic priest, Lucia entered the Sisters of St Francis of Perpetual Adoration on 5 July 1905. A month later, Lucia left Germany on the SS *Barbarossa* with several dozen other postulants; their destination was St Francis Convent in Lafayette, Indiana, United States of America. Nine years later, on 29 June 1914, Lucia made her final profession of vows and took the religious name Sister M. Columbana. For the next thirty-two years she worked as a nurse at St Francis Hospital in Chicago, a facility run by the Sisters of St Francis.[5]

Josef had told the truth, at least part of it. He did have an aunt in America, but did he join the Abwehr in order to escape Germany and travel to America? He left behind a wife, three young children, a mother, a sister and a nephew, all of whom were virtual hostages in the hands of the Gestapo. Josef would have needed to be an exceedingly callous and self-centred individual to abandon his entire family in order to save his own skin.

When Stephens first interrogated Josef on 2 February, he placed a choice before Josef – co-operate or we'll liquidate your family. Josef chose to co-operate and, in mid April, restated his desire to co-operate but begged that news of his co-operation would never make its way back to the Nazis. In many ways, Josef was caught in a catch-22. He could co-operate with the British in the hope of saving his family but incur the fury of Nazis and put his family at risk. Or, he could refuse to co-operate, thereby saving his family from the wrath of the Nazis but risking their lives at the hands of the British, who told him that they could liquidate them at will.

Josef was very aware of his predicament and his story became more complex as he tried to give more information to the British, but nothing that would compromise his family in the eyes of the Nazis. Josef even tried to use Lily Knips as a witness to the veracity of his story. She could vouch that he was not a friend of the Nazis. She could confirm that he was a man of means and hadn't taken the mission to England for financial gain. If Lily didn't confirm his story, Josef wanted to confront her so that he could prove the truth of his statements.[6]

At the end of the day, Stephens and his officers waded through Josef's story about *Die Zentrale* and discarded it as improbable. They did believe his account of the Jewish passport business, as it tallied with what Lily had told them. They also accepted Josef's story that he had been imprisoned in a concentration camp. They were perplexed about Van Hees' denunciation and wondered how the Abwehr could have used Josef as a spy if they had any doubts about his loyalty. The truth was, the British had had questions about their star double agent SNOW for months and yet repeatedly sent him off to meet with the German spymaster, Nikolaus Ritter. The same could be said of the Abwehr. They were desperate to have agents in England, and they knew that they had Josef in a tight spot.

Overall, Josef did not make a great impression on the MI5 officers. On 30 April 1941 Stephens wrote a report in which he dismissed Josef's story and, ultimately, his life:

> I have not the slightest doubt that Jakobs came over here as an active and willing spy for the Germans. His talk of Nazi oppression is in my opinion 'cover', so that too much attention should not be paid to his 'Anti-Nazi organisation'. Information, howsoever, in regard to persons such as Richter is important, because I think it is true and in particular dictated by the necessity to build up Jakobs' defence in this country. It may be that he thinks he is gaining our confidence, and so long as

he remains under that preposterous illusion we are likely to get further information from him from time to time. I do not, however, think it is a case which should be unduly postponed in so far as action under the Treachery Act is concerned.[7]

Within two weeks, however, even the irascible Stephens would change his tune and state that Josef was more useful alive than dead. Josef's case took another twist when fellow agent Karel Richter parachuted out of the sky near London Colney on 12 May. He was expected, but he was late.

23

STUBBORN CZECH

In late April, MI5 had made hasty preparations to snap up Richter when he met TATE at one of several pre-arranged venues in London.[1] But 30 April came and went with no sign of Richter. Finally, on 5 May, TATE received a message from Germany stating that his Phoenix friend's departure had been delayed due to bad weather. TATE reiterated his dire financial circumstances and demanded an immediate solution.

On 14 May Hamburg happily reported that the friend had left several days earlier, and TATE could expect him at one of the rendezvous points the following day. TATE eagerly attended the rendezvous locations at the appointed times, but no one approached him with a smile of recognition and the passphrase, 'Hello George, how are you?'[2] TATE became testy with his handlers and, in his characteristically blunt style, sent an unencoded message to Hamburg, 'I shit on Germany and its whole fucking secret service.'[3] TATE would finally get his money on 29 May after a clandestine meeting on a London bus with a Japanese naval attaché, but what had happened to Richter?

On the evening of 14 May, a lorry driver stopped to ask directions from a gentleman walking along the side of the road near London Colney. The man muttered a few words and continued walking. The driver and his assistant looked at each other and shrugged but when, a few hundred yards further along, they came across a War Reserve Constable, they shared the story of the surly man. After giving the men directions, Constable Alec Scott cycled off and found the man standing in a phone box. The stranger explained in broken English that he had come from Ipswich and was on his way to Cambridge but felt sick and needed to go to a hospital.

Scott phoned the police station and spoke with Sergeant Palmer, who told Scott to detain the stranger until he arrived.

Palmer drove to the phone box and asked the stranger for his identity papers. The man produced an expired Czech passport in the name of Karel Richter and a British National Identity Card in the name of Fred Snyder. The identity card sealed Richter's fate, because its registration number was VXAQ 195/1. That particular number had been sent to the Germans by the British through SNOW but was a dud, because none of the registration numbers began with the letter 'V'. In addition to that red flag, the identity card had other errors that branded it a forgery: the address was written in Continental fashion, the date should not have been earlier than 20 May 1940 (Richter's card was dated 23 February 1940) and the Alien Particulars section had not been filled out. The identity card was all Palmer needed to detain Richter, bundle him into the police car and take him to St Albans County Police Station. A search of his person yielded £552,[4] US$1,400,[5] and a few Dutch notes along with a German-made knife, a map of East Anglia, two packets of Dutch tobacco, a blank pink traveller's ration book and a compass.

Richter was transferred to the Hertfordshire Constabulary Headquarters in nearby Hatfield and a call was placed to Major Dixon, the Cambridge RSLO. While waiting for Dixon to arrive, the police superintendent questioned Richter in more detail. The superintendent stated that he questioned Richter 'in accordance with the terms of the Home Office letter dated 7 March 1941, number Gen.212/1/31 and G.700550/7'. Nowhere in his report does he mention that he cautioned Richter that anything he said could be used against him at a later date.[6]

Richter claimed that he was a refugee who had landed by motorboat on 10 May near Cromer, Norfolk. He emphatically denied that he had arrived by parachute or that he had brought any wireless equipment. He said that his father had given the money to him and that he had hoped to use it to buy passage to America, where he had a fiancée and an illegitimate son.[7] He claimed to have bought the identity card and ration book in Holland.

Upon Dixon's arrival, Richter repeated his story and said that he had been sleeping in fields since his arrival as all of the hotels were full. Richter was held overnight in Hatfield and the following morning Dixon informed Robertson that another agent had been captured, most likely the one eagerly awaited by TATE. Later that morning, Richter was bundled into a car and taken directly to Latchmere House, arriving in the early afternoon. It would appear that whatever information Richter possessed, Stephens wanted to extract it as quickly as possible. The traditional official statement made to Robertson at Cannon Row Police Station, under caution, would have to wait.[8]

Richter went through the usual welcome at Latchmere House. He was strip-searched, subjected to a physical exam and photographed. After these preliminaries, Richter was escorted into the interrogation room, where he stood facing Stephens, Sampson, Short and Dearden. It was 3.55 p.m. and Richter stuck by his story. He was a refugee who had sailed from Holland hoping to use his own money to get to America. He had not come down by parachute. He did not have any wireless equipment. Stephens and Short probably tried a technique that Stephens called 'blow hot – blow cold'. Stephens came across as the 'heavy' and Short, 'a rotund, owlish figure who was as cheery as his boss was menacing',[9] stepped in to offer a sympathetic ear. Nothing worked. No matter what tack the officers took, Richter stuck by his story.

Breaking an agent quickly was of paramount importance, but Richter was a tough nut. Luckily Stephens had an ace up his sleeve. Richter was shown photographs of TATE and Josef, but he claimed to recognise neither of them. At that moment, a carefully prepared Josef was brought into the room. Josef stated that he recognised Richter from an encounter at the Phoenix Hotel in October. Even in the face of Josef's denunciation, Richter claimed that he had never seen Josef before.

In the end, however, Richter broke and gave up information about his mission to England. The interview ended at 7.30 p.m., with Richter still insisting that he had come by boat without a wireless set. He did admit that he was supposed to meet a man at the Regent Palace Hotel and deliver £450, but he had no idea as to the identity of the man. The rest of the money was his and he had planned to skip the rendezvous and escape to America.

Richter was a challenge, and in his 16 May report Stephens noted:

Richter was one of the more difficult types in interrogation. He was stubborn and relied upon long silences, contradictions and occasional tears to gain sympathy. He was quite determined to tell the well-rehearsed tale of a refugee from Nazi oppression who had accepted an innocent mission with the ultimate object of an escape to America. Each time he was prevented from telling his threadbare fable he relapsed into a mournful silence. In due course of time the truth has, in my opinion emerged.[10]

Stephens concluded his report with the following:

> My last observation in this case concerns proceedings under the Treachery Act. From a public policy point of view, I quite appreciate that proceedings must be taken from time to time. From an Intelligence point of view however I still belong to the 'human reference library' school of thought. Apart from information supplied by [Robertson] through Source TATE, Richter was technically 'broken' owing (a) to information elicited from Jakobs under report from [Latchmere House] of 30.4.41 [in which Josef gave a description of Richter and their time together], (b) identification by Jakobs and (c) confrontation by Jakobs.
>
> Without Jakobs I am doubtful whether the case of Richter would have been cleared and yet Jakobs is on the selected list for trial under the Treachery Act in the near future. Jakobs was so selected because he was considered comparatively unimportant and also because he was not a member of an espionage conspiracy, but I do venture to suggest that Jakobs is an outstanding case where early prosecution would have been detrimental to MI5 interests.[11]

In a later report, on 28 June 1941, which summarised the Richter case, Short would similarly note:

> Richter proved one of the most obstinate persons under interrogation that we have so far dealt with at Latchmere House. He was a truculent and stubborn trained agent. The fact, however that we had obtained previous information from Jakobs shook his confidence, and when finally he was confronted by Jakobs – who had been carefully trained for the part – this resulted in a 'break'.[12]

Breaking Richter happened piecemeal. Josef helped to crack the fortress wall and thereafter Stephens and his men enlarged the opening. On 18 May, Richter finally admitted that he had landed by parachute near London Colney. With growing excitement, the officers organised an excursion and, after picking up Superintendent Albert Foster of Special Branch,[13] pulled into a side road outside London Colney. Stephens, Sampson,

Dearden, Short, Goodacre, Foster, Richter and a guard from Latchmere House climbed out of the vehicles. After a moment, Richter got his bearings and led the party along the edge of a farm field. A short distance away, a family was having a picnic. A curious little girl asked her mother, 'What are the soldiers doing?' and was told, 'Never you mind dearie. You never know what the military are up to next.'[14] Leaving the picnic party behind, Richter led the officers to a hedgerow, where they found his parachute and harness, overalls, steel helmet, empty knife sheath, packet of food and a hand trowel. A second hedgerow in another field yielded a torch, an automatic pistol and two camera cases containing wireless parts.[15]

Back at Latchmere House, Stephens and Sampson slowly teased fragments of the truth from Richter. It was painstaking work and took a great deal of time. Richter was terrified of the Gestapo and avoided making any statement in his own handwriting. During Richter's interrogations the MI5 officers promised to protect his family if he would co-operate with them. This was simply a mirror image of the threat made to Josef – 'co-operate or we will liquidate your family'. Richter was more frightened of the Gestapo and their concentration camps than the idea of being hanged or shot by the British. Richter was told many times by the interrogators that his story was 'impossible', but he insisted on the truth of it.

The fact that Josef and Richter had trained together in Hamburg and The Hague, however, gave Stephens another tool in his interrogation arsenal – the cross-ruff, a delicate game in which two agents were played off against each other. In some cases, the agents were placed in a room together where, inevitably, they began to talk; a conversation that was recorded via hidden microphones. One, or both of them, might have been primed beforehand to steer the conversation in a certain direction. Sometimes the cross-ruff was as simple as interrogating one agent about the other and then using those answers against the second agent.

From Josef, Stephens learned that Richter had not been completely truthful about his employment with the Abwehr. Richter claimed that his only contact with the Abwehr had been a man named Scholz (likely an alias) from the Hamburg Abwehr's naval office (Referat I Marine).[16] Josef, however, claimed that Richter had first been employed by Dr Beier (Boeckel) of the Hamburg Abwehr's air intelligence office (Referat I Luft) before being taken on by Scholz. With Josef's answers in hand, Stephens set up a scenario to intimidate the truth out of Richter.

Richter was sitting in his cell, possibly mulling over more ways in which he could dance around the truth, when Short stormed through the door.

With barely concealed indignation, Short told Richter that he had gotten Short into serious trouble with the commandant. Stephens was 'extremely angry' and dissatisfied with the previous day's interrogation because he knew for a fact that Richter had been employed by the Abwehr not only under Scholz but also under Beier (Boeckel). In the face of his obvious lies, Short told Richter that he was being transferred to Cell 14.

While there was nothing particularly ominous about Cell 14, the isolation cell, its reputation among the prisoners was ominous. Located opposite the old mortuary, it was said to be haunted and rumour had it that people went mad in the cell. It was talked about in hushed tones by interrogators and prisoners alike and was widely seen as a place of no hope, for the next stop would be the gallows or the firing squad.

Cell 14 worked its dark magic on Richter and a few hours later he requested an interview. Sampson, Short and Winn brought Richter into the interrogation room and began to extract titbits of truth from him. At one point, Stephens burst into the room, in a high state of displeasure, and tore a strip off of Richter. This too was part of his plan to intimidate Richter and, in Stephens' own words, 'it worked admirably'.[17]

Richter claimed that he had been recruited from Fuhlsbüttel concentration camp in early November 1940. He had been employed by Beier (Boeckel), taught wireless by Petersen, and finally handed over to Scholz. In early May the Abwehr made several attempts to land Richter on the English coast via boat but the weather had not co-operated. Finally, on 12 May at 3 a.m., Richter parachuted into England. Upon landing, he was to make his way to London and hand over £400 and a spare wireless crystal to a man (TATE) at the Regent Palace Hotel on 15 May (or 20 or 25). Scholz had told another Abwehr officer that the man Richter was to meet 'will be surprised when he gets money from two or three quarters at once'.[18] Richter was to use his wireless equipment to send messages back to Germany by transposition code, as he had no disc code (reserved for spies of Abwehr Referat I Luft). In addition to reporting on the weather, Richter had been taught how to identify British aeroplanes and anti-aircraft guns.

At one point, Richter begged his interrogators to let him to send a message to his contact in Sweden telling him that he had broken his leg and hadn't been able to make the rendezvous at the Regent Palace Hotel. He wanted to protect his family from the Germans who, prior to his departure, had reminded him that he needed to remember his relatives. His request was denied, and Richter told Stephens that he wanted to die.

Stephens, in typical acerbic fashion, said Richter's death would be at MI5's convenience and perhaps they would simply send him back to Germany with a note saying that he had told MI5 everything.

Stephens telephoned news of the break in the Richter case to Robertson and Liddell on the afternoon of 20 May. Both Robertson and Liddell were still considering using Richter as a double agent but, by the next day, had decided that he was unsuitable. At the end of a report on 21 May, Stephens wearily noted, 'Richter has lied to such an extent that modifications in reports are necessary from day to day.'[19] When asked why he had lied so much, Richter readily replied that:

> He had done this to avoid telling the truth, and in particular so that he would not be required to make a statement denouncing persons connected with, or supplying information about, the German Secret Service, which might implicate him when the Nazis invaded England in July or August. He felt absolutely convinced that this invasion would take place, and he remembered what had happened in Poland when the Nazis took over the Polish prisons, and had obtained access to the files.[20]

Richter was terrified of the retribution of the Nazis – but what about the British? His fate hung in the balance, was it to be prison or the gallows? Was he, like Josef, a candidate for prosecution under the Treachery Act?

24

TREACHERY ACT (1940)

We need to retrace our steps, for at the same time that Josef was helping Stephens break Richter, Stephens was recommending that Josef be prosecuted under the Treachery Act. Recall that on 30 April 1941 (two weeks before Richter's arrival), Stephens had written a report in which he stated, 'I do not, however, think [Josef's case] should be unduly postponed in so far as action under the Treachery Act is concerned.'[1] That report set a ball in motion that would not be deflected from its course. Josef was about to run afoul of the Treachery Act (1940), a draconian piece of legislation that was rushed through Parliament in May 1940. To understand its birth, we must go back even further.

In August 1939, with war looming on the horizon, Britain passed the Emergency Powers (Defence) Act, which allowed it to implement the Defence (General) Regulations (DR). The government was given far-reaching powers to do whatever it felt was necessary to pursue the war effort effectively on the Home Front. If the government needed to commandeer houses, cars or petrol, then it had the power to do so. If someone tried to undermine the war effort 'with intent to assist the enemy' then the government had the power to imprison them but, in a strange loophole, the government could not impose the death penalty. At the time, it was thought that spies or saboteurs could be dealt with under the Treason Act (1351) or the Official Secrets Act (1911).

Less than a week after Britain declared war on Germany, the Director of Public Prosecutions (DPP), Edward H. Tindal Atkinson, questioned the wisdom of using the Treason Act to prosecute enemy agents. The Treason Act was a tangled mess of overlapping statutes and, given the fact that enemy aliens had no allegiance to the British monarch, Atkinson thought it unlikely that they could be tried for treason.[2] Atkinson even went so far as to state that the Treason Act was so cumbersome and archaic 'it would seriously embarrass [me] if the only way of getting a spy put to death was by proceeding against him for treason'.[3]

The issue of how to deal with enemy agents proved to be contentious. Should suspected spies be tried by court martial or by civil trial? Should they be shot or hanged? It was agreed that general courts martial were far speedier, less prone to information leaks and far less complicated than civil trials. If the War Office had had its way, every suspected spy would have been hauled before a court martial.

On the other hand, the Home Office argued that spies from neutral territories, as well as British citizens, had the right to be tried by a jury of their peers. At the same time, suspected spies who were members of the armed forces (whether British, neutral or enemy) needed to be shot (honourable death) and not hanged, otherwise it could lead to reprisals by the enemy.[4]

An early draft of the nascent Treachery Act was distributed for review in late October 1939. It stated that after a civil trial, the Secretary of State could decide if the convicted person was to be shot. This draft provoked the wrath of the Judge Advocate General (JAG) of His Majesty's Forces who wanted to know, 'Who is to do the shooting? Is it to be the Public Hangman armed with a humane killer, or are the Navy, Army or Air Force to be the "executioner" of a sentence with which, in other respects, the Service Authorities have been in no way concerned?'[5] He went on to note, 'If this abnormal and unpleasant duty is to be imposed upon the Services, I take it that the Service Authorities have been or will be consulted before this Bill in its present form is introduced.'[6]

Executing individuals condemned to death by a military court was one thing, but executing individuals sentenced to death by a civil court was a completely different matter. The military lawyers were not happy. The Treachery Act was sent back to the drawing board, while the Home Office grumbled at the squeamishness of the military. In early January 1940, Sir Alexander Maxwell (Home Office) wrote:

We have noted the War Office objection to asking soldiers to act as executioners for civil courts, and I and my colleagues have done our best to try and find a way round the difficulty ... but is the difficulty of asking soldiers to act as executioners really a serious one? Everyone will recognise that the duty of a shooting party is a most unpleasant one and that it should not be imposed on any soldiers if it could be avoided, but if it is recognised that it is the duty of soldiers to shoot a spy or enemy agent who has been tried by a court-martial, I find it extremely difficult to see what greater objection there is to asking soldiers to shoot a spy or enemy agent who has been convicted by a civil court when the Home Secretary after consultation with the War Office has decided that as a member of the enemy's armed forces he is entitled to a soldier's death.[7]

The Home Office didn't get the point that the Judge Advocate General had been trying to make – the military had no problem shooting people as long as it had had a hand in condemning them.

The Home Office and the Secretary of State looked back in history to the spies who had been executed during the First World War. There was one burning question: why were two of the spies (Breeckow and Muller) tried civilly and shot, whereas another (Rosenthal) was tried by court martial and hanged? It made no sense. The War Office consulted their files and H.T. Allen reported that Breeckow and Muller had been tried civilly because they were charged jointly with British civilians. Under the Defence of the Realm Act, the civil court had ordered that the sentence of death was to be carried out by shooting. As for Rosenthal, Allen noted that there were two stories as to why he was hanged and not shot. One story suggested 'that the Court considered a bullet too good for Rosenthal on account of his extremely cowardly behaviour during the trial'.[8] Another story suggested that due to the circumstances surrounding the military occupation of the Tower of London, the authorities decided that Rosenthal should be hanged and not shot.[9]

After much discussion and countless memos, it was decided that courts martial would be reserved for members of the British armed forces, members of enemy armed forces (as long as they were not charged jointly with a civilian) and some civilian enemy aliens. British subjects would be entitled to a civilian trial, as would citizens of neutral countries. In cases where there was doubt as to the nationality of the accused, they would have to be given the benefit of the doubt and allowed to go to civil trial.[10]

The Home Office, War Office, Attorney General (AG), Lord Chancellor and Secretary of State passed drafts of the Treachery Act back and forth for several months while they debated the merits of key points. Their debate ceased in May 1940, when Britain was faced with a terrifying spectre – the imminent invasion of Britain by the Third Reich.

The date of 10 May 1940 was marked by two momentous events. The German army, battle-hardened and confident after the successful invasion of Poland, began its lightning-fast advance into France and the Low Countries. In London, Prime Minister Neville Chamberlain, who had pursued a path of appeasement with Hitler, was replaced by Winston Churchill. This passing of the baton represented a quantum shift in Britain's position. Appeasement was replaced by resolution. 'Peace for our time' was replaced by 'We shall never surrender'.

In the short term, however, nothing changed. The German army swept through the Low Countries and France, pushing the Allied forces backwards with startling ease. Dismayed by the speed with which the Germans moved through Belgium, Luxembourg and the Netherlands, many British politicians speculated that an active fifth column facilitated the German invasion. If a fifth column was active in those countries, then there might be such a group in Britain.

Faced with the possibility of a German invasion of Britain, the government tidied up the loose ends of the proposed Treachery Act. On 22 May 1940, the draft bill sped through the House of Commons, going through all readings and being passed on to the House of Lords. On 23 May, the Upper House passed the Act within minutes and the king granted royal assent that same evening. At the time, one scholar noted that the Treachery Act 'was the creation of the Parliament of a free nation superbly determined, in an extremity of circumstances, to defend its liberties and its life'.[11]

The gist of the Treachery Act was simple:

> If, with intent to help the enemy, any person does, or attempts or conspires with any other person to do, any act which is designed or likely to give assistance to the naval, military or air operations of the enemy, to impede such operations of His Majesty's forces, or to endanger life, he shall be guilty of felony and shall on conviction suffer death.[12]

Prosecution of the Act could happen through civil trial or court martial. A court martial could be used for members of the military or a civilian enemy alien, a person who was a citizen of a country at war with Britain.[13] If found guilty of the offence, the sentence was death. Generally, the method of execution was hanging, but if the Secretary of State decided that, at the time of the offence, the person had been a member of the military (of the Crown or of any other foreign power, including the enemy), then death could be by firing squad.

For the previous 125 years, Britain had been moving toward the abolition of the death penalty. In 1808 Samuel Romilly (the former Solicitor General) introduced reforms to reduce the number of offences (220 at its height) for which the death penalty could be imposed. No longer could one be sentenced to death for pickpocketing or for fraternising with gypsies. In 1823, Parliament abolished the death penalty for letter-stealing and sacrilege. Judges were also given the authority to commute the death penalty for all offences except murder and treason. In 1861, the list of capital crimes was reduced to murder, treason, espionage, arson in His/Her Majesty's Dockyards and piracy with violence. The mandatory punishment for murder was death by hanging, although the Home Secretary could commute the sentence to one of life imprisonment. In 1938, the House of Commons held a vote that called for legislation to abolish hanging in peacetime for a five-year experiment. When war broke out in 1939, the experiment was postponed.

When the House of Commons was presented with the Treachery Act on 22 May 1940 it generated discussion. While the vast majority of MPs supported the Act, there were some who had concerns and raised their voices in protest.[14] Miss Eleanor Rathbone (MP for Combined English Universities)[15] questioned the mandatory death sentence. She wanted to know what would happen if the prisoner was found guilty of a lesser offence. Would the prisoner be sentenced to death or would they be acquitted because there was no possibility of a lesser penalty?[16]

Sir John Anderson (Secretary of State for the Home Department) replied that, in order to be charged under the Treachery Act, the offence would have to be of a 'grievous description', including 'grievous cases of sabotage'.[17] He also noted that under the Defence Regulations, there was provision, which they did not propose to abrogate, in Regulations 2A and 2B, for dealing with acts done with intent to assist the enemy and with acts of sabotage. According to Anderson, it would be possible for the court to charge the person jointly under the Defence Regulations and the Treachery Act. The court might then come to the conclusion that only a lesser case of treachery applied, as contemplated by Defence Regulations 2A and 2B, and therefore impose the penalty provided under those regulations. The maximum penalty under 2A[18] was imprisonment up to penal servitude for life and a fine. Under Defence Regulation 2B (sabotage), the penalty was penal servitude for a period not exceeding fourteen years and/or a fine not exceeding £500.[19]

Mr George Benson (MP for Chesterfield) stated, 'The death penalty is morally repugnant to a very large number of people, of whom I am one, and I do not feel I can allow the Bill to go through without making a protest.'[20] He made the point that one could not measure what someone deserved in terms of a penalty. A century previously, a man was considered to deserve death if he stole a sheep. In Benson's opinion, just deserts were not inherent in the offender or the offence but were subjective judgements. Benson went on to say, 'I feel passionately that the death penalty is beneath the honour and dignity of a great and civilised community, and it is for that reason, and that reason alone, that I oppose the Bill.'[21]

Mr James Barr (MP for Coatbridge) had sat on the Select Committee on Capital Punishment in 1930 that considered the question of capital punishment in cases tried by civil courts in times of peace.[22] They concluded that the death penalty was not a deterrent. If that was the case in peacetime, then it could not be a deterrent in wartime.

Mr Thomas Edmund Harvey (MP for Combined English Universities) also opposed the death penalty and asked the House to consider not merely the question of principle but the question of expediency.[23] Executing enemy aliens could lead to hard feelings between the two countries at a later date. The second problem with the death penalty was its irrevocability. According to the Treachery Act, the intention of the offender was of primary importance. How could any court make a perfect judgement as to intention? In most cases, intention could only be inferred by a process of reasoning deduced from acts. Mistakes could be made that might only come to light afterwards. If the death penalty was inflicted, there was no possibility of redress. Harvey agreed that severe measures should be taken, but suggested that the Treachery Act be amended to include a clause that would allow the court to impose a long sentence of imprisonment. He didn't like the idea of charging a person jointly under the Defence Regulations and Treachery Act but much preferred giving an option to the court in the Act itself.

In response to Harvey, Major James Milner (Deputy Speaker) noted that it was not essential in every case, after a verdict of guilty, that the death penalty should necessarily be inflicted. Milner also noted:

I am aware that this is the law at present in regard to murder, and indeed in regard to treason and one or two other offences, but the Home Secretary pointed out that it would be competent for the Attorney General so to conduct a prosecution as to join other and lesser offences with those constituting the charge under the Bill. In that way, a loophole would be found whereby, in less serious cases of offences coming under the Bill, it would be possible for the court to award a less [*sic*] penalty than death.[24]

Mr Samuel Silverman (MP for Nelson and Colne) had his doubts about the wording 'with intent to help the enemy'. That would be the first thing that the prosecution would have to prove, and the onus would lie upon the prosecution. He wondered if there was not a legal rule that the court might infer intention, in which case all the prosecution would have to say would be:

> I cannot prove any actual intention positively, but I can and I do prove that it is a reasonable consequence of this act that it will have this effect; as every man is presumed to intend reasonable consequences I have proved reasonable consequences, and I have therefore proved the intent.[25]

Silverman was right to question the wording of the Treachery Act, for proving intent was often a matter of inference on the part of the prosecution, as we shall see with Josef's case. The AG, however, did not think that there was any such danger and the burden was on the prosecution to convince the jury.

Lieutenant Colonel Sir William Allen (MP for Armagh) had a question regarding the use of the court martial since he had seen courts martial in which not a single person had any knowledge of the law. The JAG might be neither a judge, nor an advocate, nor a general. He requested that at least one person on the court martial panel should have some knowledge of the law.[26]

After the second reading of the Treachery Act, Mr Thomas Harvey (MP for Combined English Universities) moved that the following clause be added to the penalty of death: '... or imprisonment for a period not exceeding twenty years'.[27] This would give the court an option for punishment. Otherwise, if the prisoner was not charged jointly under the Defence Regulations and the Treachery Act, but only under the Treachery Act, the penalty would be death. Mr Cecil Wilson (MP for Sheffield, Attercliffe) and Mr George Muff (MP for Hull, East) supported the amendment.

Mr Osbert Peake (Undersecretary of State for the Home Department) did not advise the House of Commons to accept the amendment.

The Treachery Act was designed to deal only with the 'most serious cases of the base crime of treachery'.[28] Less serious cases of sabotage or espionage, or acts done with intent to assist the enemy, could be dealt with under the Defence Regulations (2A and 2B). The Treachery Act was only ever intended to deal with cases of the most serious character. Unless there was the clearest possible evidence of all the most serious elements of the charge, undoubtedly the prosecution would join the more serious charge with lesser charges under the Defence Regulations. For him, the real argument against accepting the amendment was that it would be contrary to British judicial procedure and tradition to give any alternative to the death penalty and to place a judge in the position of having to choose which punishment to administer. There was, of course, always the prerogative of mercy that could be exercised by the Crown.

After a vote, the proposed amendment was rejected.

From the above discussion, it is clear that the Treachery Act was meant to be applied in 'the most serious cases of the base crime of treachery'.[29] Less serious cases could be prosecuted under the Defence Regulations. Thus, instead of giving the judge a choice between death and imprisonment, the choice was simply passed up the line to Tindal Atkinson, the DPP. He would decide whether a person was charged jointly under the Treachery Act and the Defence Regulations, allowing the possibility of a lesser sentence of imprisonment, or solely under the Treachery Act, with death being the only option upon conviction. As one author noted in 1992, 'by the end of June [1940], Britain had become, in the name of liberty, a totalitarian state' but that seemed 'to have been more or less what most people wanted'.[30]

Interestingly enough, only a few months previously, during the numerous revisions of the proposed Treachery Act, a memo had noted, 'The Home Office made it quite clear that, in practice, charges under [Section 1 of the Treachery Act] would *always* [emphasis added] be joined … with charges under the appropriate Defence Regulation.'[31] By the time the Bill was presented to Parliament, however, it was clear that people charged with 'the most serious cases of the base crime of treachery'[32] would be charged solely under the Treachery Act. For some, there would be no loophole, there would be no choice between imprisonment and death; there would be only death.

Several MPs had questioned the language of the Act and its use of the word 'intent', and with good reason. The intent of a person was virtually impossible to discern with any certainty. As Mr Silverman noted, it might be tempting for the prosecution to infer intention:

> I cannot prove any actual intention positively, but I can and I do prove that it is a reasonable consequence of this act that it will have this effect; as every man is presumed to intend reasonable consequences I have proved reasonable consequences, and I have therefore proved the intent.[33]

How would the implementation of the Treachery Act play out in real life?

25

LIFE OR DEATH

Prior to Josef's arrival, several spies were charged under the Treachery Act. The majority of them were found guilty and executed, while a few escaped with their lives. Were the concerns of the Members of Parliament valid?

On 7 September 1940, four German spies landed in pairs from two rowing boats along the coast of Kent. Each pair of men had a wireless transmitter (but no receiver) and food to last a week. Only one could speak English. That strip of coast was one of the most heavily fortified places in the country and one of the most restricted. Within twenty-four hours, all four spies had been captured. They were taken to Latchmere House, interrogated and charged under the Treachery Act. They were not charged jointly under the Defence Regulations (2A or 2B) and death would be the only punishment meted out. In November 1940 they were tried in civil court.

Jose Waldberg (German)[1] had set up his transmitter and sent a message back to Germany. Upon the advice of his lawyer, he pleaded guilty to the charges, under the impression that the penalty would be imprisonment. He was hanged in early December 1940. Carl Meier and Charles Van den Kieboom (both Dutch) had hidden their wireless transmitter but committed no overt act of espionage or sabotage. Both were found guilty and hanged in early December 1940, despite the fact that Kieboom pleaded coercion by the Gestapo. Sjoerd Pons (Dutch) did not hide his transmitter and, at his trial, claimed that the Gestapo had threatened to harm his father if he did not take on the mission. The jury was sympathetic towards Pons and acquitted him, much to the chagrin of MI5. He was interned for the duration of the war under Defence Regulation 18B.

All four men were charged with intent to assist the enemy on two counts under the Treachery Act: (a) conspiring to transmit information about His Majesty's forces and (b) landing in the United Kingdom.[2] One wonders how the second count qualified as a 'grievous case of espionage'[3] as opposed to simple 'espionage'. A 'grievous case of espionage' merited death under the Treachery Act whereas simple 'espionage' merited imprisonment under the Defence Regulations. The intent of Waldberg could be deduced with a fair degree of certainty. He had sent information back to the Germans. As for the others, their intentions were less clear, particularly those of Kieboom and Pons. Both men claimed coercion by the Gestapo but only one escaped with his life.

On 4 September 1940, a few days before the four hapless spies landed on the coast of Kent, a German agent parachuted out of the sky near Denton, Northamptonshire. Gösta Caroli (Swedish), an ardent Nazi, had a wireless transmitter/receiver strapped to his chest. As he landed, the wireless case struck him on the chin, rendering him unconscious. A few hours later he awoke and dragged himself underneath a hedge, where he passed out. A farmer found him the next morning and Caroli was bundled off to Latchmere House.

He was not the most co-operative prisoner, but Stephens learned that Caroli had become friends with another spy who was due to arrive any day. While Caroli appeared to have no concern for his own life, Stephens correctly deduced that Caroli would co-operate in order to save the life of his friend. Caroli was told that, if he co-operated, his friend Wulf Schmidt would not be executed. Caroli agreed and became double agent SUMMER. Caroli was sequestered in an MI5 safe house from which he sent doctored wireless reports back to Germany. Alas, his career as a double agent didn't agree with his psyche and he became depressed and suicidal. In early January 1941, he overcame his guard and tried to escape on a motorcycle with a canoe strapped to his back. He didn't make it far and was recaptured and interned for the duration of the war.[4] His career as a double agent had been brief, but he escaped with his life.

Wulf Schmidt (Danish) arrived on the evening of 19 September and he too had a rough descent, hurting his hand while exiting the aeroplane, getting caught in telephone wires on the way down and spraining his right ankle upon landing. The following morning, Schmidt hid his equipment and wandered into the nearby village of Willingham, Cambridgeshire, where he purchased a new watch, since his had been broken leaving the aeroplane. Schmidt had spent several years in Cameroon and spoke good

English, albeit with a foreign accent. He washed his ankle at the village water pump, an act that aroused suspicion. He was asked for his identity card, which had the usual errors. Schmidt was detained by the local Home Guard and sent to Latchmere House. Schmidt was another ardent Nazi who refused to co-operate with Stephens until he learned of Caroli's betrayal, at which point he bared his soul. MI5 had their next double agent, TATE.

On 5 October 1940 Kurt Karl Goose (aka Hans Reysen), a soldier in the Abwehr's elite commando unit, the Brandenburg Lehr Regiment, landed by parachute near Wellingborough, Northamptonshire, equipped with a wireless transmitter (but no receiver).[5] He was quickly captured and sent to Latchmere House. He claimed that he was not a Nazi and only wanted to make his way back to America, where he had been a geology student. He too agreed to work as a double agent, codenamed GANDER, but wireless contact with Germany could not be established. He was interned for the duration of the war after he was caught trying to bribe a guard to send a letter to the German Embassy in Dublin. He too escaped with his life.

None of these men would be charged under the Treachery Act, despite the fact that Caroli and Goose both committed acts that could have assisted the enemy (escape and attempting to contact the Germans). It would appear that, having made an agreement with the men, MI5 would stick by it. Caroli and Goose would only be imprisoned for their treacherous acts, not executed.

A few days before Goose landed via parachute, three spies disembarked from a German flying boat off the coast of Banffshire and rowed ashore in a dinghy. Werner Walti, Vera Eriksen and Karl Druecke[6] had planned to cycle to London but their bicycles had been swept overboard in the choppy seas. Eriksen and Druecke walked to Port Gordon train station, where their salt-soaked shoes and trouser cuffs aroused the suspicion of the station master. Walti walked to the nearby village of Buckie and caught a train to Edinburgh, where he was arrested shortly after his arrival. All three were sent to Latchmere House, where Walti and Druecke proved impossible to crack.

Staunchly loyal to Nazi Germany to the last, they were charged, under the Treachery Act, with landing in the United Kingdom and conspiring with intent to help the enemy. The two men were found guilty at a civil trial in mid June 1941 and hanged at Wandsworth Prison in early August 1941. They were not charged jointly under the Defence Regulations.

As for Eriksen, she was a mysterious woman about whom many rumours have circulated throughout the decades. She did not become a double agent, nor was she executed. Vera was interned for the duration of the war, much to the detriment of her mental and physical well-being.

Finally, we have the sad case of Dorothy Pamela O'Grady, a bored British housewife on the Isle of Wight whose husband was stationed in London, training firefighters. In the summer of 1940, the Isle of Wight was high on the list of possible invasion targets. Defences had been strengthened, soldiers swarmed the island and the shoreline was a prohibited area.

Dorothy knew all this but was a stubborn woman. Her black retriever loved to swim in the ocean and Dorothy did not let a few strands of barbed wire and 'No Trespassing' signs stop her. She was found on prohibited beaches by different patrols and each time, was given words of warning and sent home. Finally, on 9 August 1940, one patrol had had enough, and Dorothy was arrested under Defence Regulation 16A (being in a prohibited area) and released on bail. She was scheduled to appear before the magistrates on 27 August and would probably have received a stern warning and a slap on the wrist. However, Dorothy did not appear. The police were sent to find her, but she was not at home. She had disappeared into thin air. A few weeks later, she was found in a guesthouse on the other side of the island, living under an assumed name. Things got exponentially worse for the eccentric housewife. Dorothy was remanded into custody until 1 October and sent to Holloway Prison on the mainland, where she was interrogated by MI5 officers. On 16 December she appeared in court charged with offences under the Treachery Act, the Defence Regulations and the Official Secrets Act. One day later, on 17 December 1940, British housewife Dorothy P. O'Grady was sentenced to death under the Treachery Act.

What grievous offence had this British housewife committed? Besides entering the prohibited foreshore with her dog, Dorothy was an artist who had drawn wonderfully accurate sketches of the shoreline that, unfortunately, included the coastal fortifications. She was also found with a pair of nail scissors on her person and gleefully confessed to having cut some telegraph wires, although no one saw her commit the treacherous act. Although there was no evidence that Dorothy had had any contact with the Germans, she was still prosecuted to the full extent of the law.

Despite having been charged jointly under the Defence Regulations and the Official Secrets Act, both of which carried non-lethal penalties, the jury found Dorothy guilty under the Treachery Act and the penalty was death. Members of Parliament had been assured that the Treachery Act would only be applied to the most serious and grievous cases of espionage and sabotage. Did Dorothy's case fit the bill?

Luckily for Dorothy, the judge in her case had made a technical error while instructing the jury and in February 1941 her lawyers successfully appealed her conviction under the Treachery Act. Her sentence was reduced to fourteen years' imprisonment, of which she served nine.

Was Dorothy a spy? Unlikely. Liddell himself noted, 'Personally I doubt whether she is guilty of anything more than collecting information. She probably pictured herself as a master spy, and cannot bring herself to say that there was really nothing behind it all.'[7] Medical records from Holloway Prison indicate that she was mentally disturbed and displayed a range of masochistic behaviours. By her own admission, Dorothy said it was all a 'huge joke'[8] and that the most thrilling moment in her life was when the judge sentenced her to death. Her biggest disappointment was when she was told that she would not be shot facing the firing squad with her eyes wide open, but rather hanged with a hood on her head.

26

INTELLIGENCE VS PROSECUTION

By 5 October 1940 ten spies had been apprehended in England: nine foreign agents who arrived by parachute or boat and one British housewife.[1] At the same time, not a single spy had yet been tried or executed and Churchill was, once again, getting impatient with MI5. In June 1940, a month after taking office, Churchill had fired Vernon Kell, the founder of MI5. Unhappy with the direction in which the organisation had been heading, Churchill appointed Lord Swinton as head of the newly formed Home Defence (Security) Executive. From June 1940 to January 1941, MI5 was in a state of upheaval. Between the ineffective temporary leadership of Harker, the meddling of the Swinton Committee (as it was unofficially known), and the huge influx of work, the officers of MI5 were being worn thin.

The arrival of the first four spies along the coast of Kent had also given MI5 some ethical, legal and procedural problems. Under the Treachery Act, the spies were liable to the death penalty, but MI5 was keen to use suitable spies as double agents. Executing German spies was a short-term solution that demonstrated to the public (and the politicians) that MI5 was doing its job and keeping England safe. Turning the spies into double agents and using them for intelligence purposes was a long-term plan whose benefits might not be seen for years.

On 10 September 1940 the issue of how to handle newly arrived spies was discussed at the Security Intelligence Centre. Swinton and the DPP proposed that when a spy was captured, MI5 would be notified, and they would decide if the spy was to be invited to make a statement to the police under caution or if he was to be interrogated by MI5. If interrogation was decided upon, then 'the prisoner was to be given an opportunity later to make a statement under caution for use as evidence in prosecution, and it was essential that no form of inducement should be held out to him'.[2] After discussion it was decided that captured spies should always be interrogated and Swinton 'confirmed that it was completely within the discretion of the Services [MI5 and MI6] whether they would forego prosecution and use the agent in any particular case for their own purposes'.[3]

In light of this clear statement, MI5 assumed that it could disregard the rule against offering inducements in suitable cases, as with Gösta Caroli and Kurt Karl Goose. In return for their co-operation, Caroli and Goose had been promised their lives. No matter what they did afterwards, MI5 was bound by its agreement with the two men. They would not be executed.

By early October, MI5 had recruited three double agents and were looking forward to adding more to their stable, but it was not quite so simple. On 7 October 1940 Lord Swinton appeared in the offices of Liddell (Director of B Division) to review the recent spy cases. According to Swinton, Churchill was asking why the captured spies had not been shot as had happened in the First World War. Liddell told Swinton that he thought that MI5 had been given 'a more or less free hand to promise a man his life if we thought we were going to get information'[4] and that information was the most important matter to be considered.

Swinton disagreed. He quoted the minutes of a meeting that said MI5 had absolutely no authority to grant a man his life and decreed that in future no man should be offered his life without Swinton's express authority. Liddell privately voiced the opinion that Swinton seemed to 'think that he is head of MI5 and to some extent even of MI6'.[5] Later, after looking up the minute to which Swinton had referred, Liddell found that it was irrelevant. It 'merely referred to the DPP's attitude in these cases, which was that if we [MI5] wished to prosecute we should not offer a man any inducement to talk'.[6] What Liddell called irrelevant however, would prove highly relevant in the cases of Josef Jakobs and Karel Richter. For them, it was a matter of life and death.

Lord Swinton made it quite clear to Liddell that, if spies were to be prosecuted, then they should not be offered inducements to talk. Inducements in this case could be promises or threats. Gösta Caroli had been promised his life and the life of his friend if he would co-operate. Goose too, had been promised his life if he co-operated. This was standard procedure, according to Masterman, who later said that the captured spy was turned into a double agent, 'convinced that he could save his life by working for [MI5]'.[7]

Despite the fact that Caroli later tried to escape and Goose had tried to smuggle a letter out to the Germans, Swinton, MI5, the DPP and the AG decided in November 1941 that prosecution of former double agents was not in Britain's best interests. They agreed that prosecution was not an option 'if MI5 had used an agent or given him a promise: the risk that the agent's double-cross work would be revealed in court had to be considered; and a promise once given had to be honoured'.[8] While the promises given to Caroli and Goose had been clearly phrased, some were less clear.

On 2 February, Stephens had his first shot at Josef Jakobs. Josef was suffering from a broken ankle and Stephens went in for the kill. In his report that evening, Stephens noted, 'To cut a long story short I obtained the key to the emergency code, a specimen message and an acceptance of my demand that this man should work as the servant of his captors.'[9] Stephens noted that Josef 'responded to threat'[10] but also claimed that he was abiding by Swinton's directive:

No promise whatever has been made to [Jakobs] by me, but the lever may be described as his affection for his wife and three tolerably young children at present resident in Berlin. In crude language, Jakobs is under the impression that we can liquidate these persons if he fails to do what we require.[11]

Stephens had threatened the lives of Josef's wife and children unless he co-operated with MI5. There were two implicit promises contained within this threat: (1) Do what we want, and we promise not to liquidate your family, and (2) Don't do what we want and we promise that we will liquidate your family. A threat is an inducement, a promise of violence unless the person co-operates. Stephens seemed to dance his way around Swinton's directive; after all, he hadn't promised Josef his life in return for information, had he?

On 3 February, the day after Josef agreed to work as the 'servant of his captors', Liddell visited Latchmere House and had dinner with Stephens. After discussing the issue of enemy agents, they agreed that Liddell and Valentine Vivian (MI6) would try to convince Lord Swinton that 'bumping off' enemy agents should be the exception rather than the rule. 'We all felt that it was far preferable to keep these people as reference books since we never knew when they might be useful or when some further piece of information might turn up which would render interrogation desirable.'[12] A week later, Liddell brought up the issue with Swinton, who suggested that Vivian and Liddell should make a case for it, which they presumably did.

If MI5 was expecting to get a favourable response from Swinton, they were sadly mistaken. In a memorandum to MI5 in March 1941, Swinton let them have it with both barrels. According to Swinton, Churchill had 'laid it down as a matter of policy that in all suitable cases spies should be brought to trial'.[13] Swinton said, 'Nothing should be done or omitted which could in any way jeopardise a successful prosecution.'[14] Human reference libraries were out and prosecutions were in. Inducements, of any sort, could jeopardise a successful prosecution, which leads us back to the case of Josef Jakobs.

The verbatim transcripts of Josef's interrogations have been, for the most part, weeded from the MI5 file, and what we are left with are summary reports from the MI5 officers. Yet even there, we begin to find hints of further inducements made to Josef. On 21 April, Stephens happily reported that Sampson had taken over the case and 'induced Jakobs to make three written statements'.[15] Whether this was simply a poor choice of words by Stephens or not, it does make one wonder as to what methods Sampson used to 'induce' Josef to make his three statements.

Over the next week, the interrogators made it clear to Josef that if he wanted to save his life then he needed to tell them everything. The wording of their statements implied that Josef did have a chance of saving his life and working for the British. During one of the April interrogations, Sampson lost his patience with Josef and told him that 'his story was unconvincing and he had told so many lies, that he could only *help himself* [emphasis added] by telling the whole truth'.[16] Always there was the implication that if Josef told them the whole truth then he could save his life or help himself. At one point, Josef was told:

> If he did not answer this and all other questions he must accept the consequences. Jakobs then asked if he had a chance of working for the English here. The interrogating officer told him that he had a chance, but that he also [had] an equal chance of being executed as a German spy. Eventually he said that he would reply to all questions.[17]

At other times, Josef was fearful of the Nazis and said:

> He would willingly give all the information in his possession if he could be satisfied that this information would not fall into the hands of the

Nazis. He was told that we expected him in any case to give full information, but that he need have no fear of the Nazis.[18]

In that regard, Sampson was completely accurate; Josef had little to fear from the Nazis, and everything to fear from the British. By 30 April 1941 Stephens noted that Josef may think 'he is gaining our confidence, and so long as he remains under that preposterous illusion, we are likely to get further information from him from time to time'.[19]

A month later, on 6 June, Stephens noted, 'Jakobs is a slippery customer and is certainly anxious to save his neck. It is, therefore, difficult to tell whether he is telling the truth or whether he is romancing in order to curry favour.'[20]

The officers at Latchmere House were playing with Josef. He believed that he would be working for them as a double agent. They continued to let him believe that story months after they had dismissed him as suitable for such a role. He believed that he could save his life if he gave the MI5 officers what they wanted. With the arrival of Karel Richter, the Latchmere House officers began to pump both men for more and more information.

27

THE TRUTH WILL OUT

As Josef and Richter were played off of each other in the dangerous cross-ruff game, each man fought to gain points with their interrogators. Both men believed that if they could only provide enough information, they could save themselves. The Latchmere House officers gleefully noted that neither man trusted the other. Josef repeatedly told Richter that the MI5 officers knew everything and that he should work for them, as Josef himself was doing.[1] Richter felt that he had been betrayed by Josef and was understandably leery of such advice.

Over the course of several weeks, MI5 coaxed Josef and Richter into talking about their training in Hamburg and The Hague, a topic near and dear to the hearts of the MI5 officers. Who had Josef and Richter met? Who else was being trained to come to England? Eventually, the two spies admitted that they had seen another agent receiving training at the Vondelstraat flat in The Hague. The man, called Gaston by his handlers, spoke English and was apparently being trained for England. Upon hearing this news, Short grumbled that it was unfortunate that an Abwehr agent named Günther Schütz was in the hands of the Irish Free State.[2] Schütz had arrived in Hamburg in late 1940 for training[3] and Short thought that he might be the mysterious Gaston.

During another conversation, Josef revealed that he had been instructed to sign his transmissions with JULIUS. Richter admitted that his code name was ROBOTER. His name was taken from a novel of that name by Karel Capek. Richter said there must be a reason why the Germans chose JULIUS for Josef, but Josef said that the name had been given to him by Petersen in Hamburg. Petersen had told Jakobs that it was customary to preserve the initial letter in the surname:

Jakobs @ JULIUS,
Richter @ ROBOTER
Boeckel @ BEIER or BRUHNS
Ritter @ RANTZAU
Sessler @ SINCLAIR
Merker/Merkel @ MALTEN[4]

The MI5 officers thought that Josef's code name of JULIUS or JULIE may have originated from a novel by J.J. Rousseau called *Julie, ou la nouvelle Héloïse*. The connection would have been Josef Jakobs' initials. A more likely scenario, but one that is only available with hindsight, is the link between Josef's name and that of his spy handler, Julius Jacob Boeckel. Josef never knew Boeckel's real name but some Abwehr officers may have thought that Julius Jacob and Josef Jakobs was too good a play on words to pass up.

Back and forth it went, with Josef and Richter being played against each other and revealing more information as each one upped the stakes. Stephens noted that while both men were in terror of being hanged, their attitudes were different. Stephens, Sampson and Short all agreed that although Richter gave information reluctantly, the officers were inclined to believe that it was true. Josef, on the other hand, was 'so anxious to please that he draws upon his imagination' and the officers felt that most of what he shared was false, although there were occasional grains of truth.[5]

It would seem that Stephens' admonition against physical violence could be extended to threats of violence or death as well. 'Violence is taboo, for not only does it produce answers to please, but it lowers the standard of information.'[6] Josef had been threatened so much that he was simply producing answers to please.

By the end of June 1941, Stephens and his crew thought that they had finally extracted the truth about Karel Richter. After being deported to Germany from Sweden, Richter had been arrested by the Gestapo and sent to Fuhlsbüttel concentration camp. It was there that he had been approached by Boeckel and recruited for the Abwehr. Boeckel had him sign a form promising to work faithfully for Germany. The form also contained a clause that stated Richter's 'betrayal of Germany would result in reprisals being taken against his family in Sudetenland'.[7] While Josef had denied receiving any training in secret writing, Richter had been trained to make a rudimentary secret ink by dissolving tablets (redacted – probably Pyramidon or Aspirin) in alcohol.

Richter proved to be a poor student at Morse code, however – slow to learn and slow to transmit. Boeckel eventually told Richter that his services were no longer required but he was quickly snatched up by Dr Scholz, another member of the Hamburg Abwehr. In January 1941, Richter was transferred to The Hague, where he practised wireless transmission at the Vondelstraat address. Richter was told by Major Malten that his position should be regularised during his stay in Holland. He was given a certificate that described him as an *Angestellter* (employee) attached to Feldpost 34290 (military field post office), which was a *Dienststelle* (military office) at The Hague.[8]

In March 1941, Richter was arrested for buying black-market food cards and spent several weeks in prison. During that time, Scholz visited him and suggested that he undertake a mission to Britain. Richter was to meet another agent (TATE) at the Regent Palace Hotel and hand over a spare crystal and money (£400). Afterwards, he would report on the weather using a simple transposition code.

It sounded like a straightforward story, but on 5 July Richter overturned Stephens' applecart when he requested a meeting with Short.[9] Before beginning, Richter asked for assurances that the information he was about to divulge would not impair his own case with the British authorities. Short gave him the standard line that 'any information he was in a position to furnish, provided it were truthful and accurate, would be given favourable consideration, and that in any case, he could not make his case worse'.[10] With that shaky promise in his back pocket, Richter stated that his journey to Britain had been twofold: (1) to bring TATE money and (2) to ascertain if TATE was double-crossing Germany.[11]

Richter was to get friendly with him and discover whether he was under control or whether the messages he was sending were authentic. According to Scholz, TATE was a pearl 'and if this one were false, the entire string would be equally false'.[12] Richter was to tell the agent that he was supposed to obtain full details of the grid system of electrical supply and take that information back to Germany personally. After enlisting the agent's help in getting a boat, Richter would sail back to Germany and report to Scholz on the agent's clothing, mannerisms and peculiarities.

Short was stunned and delivered the results of the interrogation to Stephens. The next day, Stephens interviewed Richter and heard the same story. Consternation reigned in the corridors of the double-cross system. Robertson was already concerned that TATE was under suspicion given his tangential relationship with double agent SNOW. If SNOW was blown, as MI5 suspected, then the Germans must necessarily suspect TATE. With a few words, Richter had confirmed their worst fears.

After careful consideration, however, Short became suspicious of Richter's claims. A great deal of careful preparation had gone into Richter's mission but the details of his return to Germany (via boat) were haphazard, to say the least. Short's conclusion was that 'until further evidence is made available the greatest care should be exercised in utilising TATE on our behalf, especially since Richter states that upon his non-arrival back in Germany by Saturday, July 12th, [TATE] would automatically be considered by the German [Intelligence Service] as unreliable'.[13]

MI5's double-cross system hung in the balance, along with Richter's life. Did the Abwehr really expect Richter to sail back to Germany? Such an operation seemed doomed to failure, but Richter swore that it was true.

The Abwehr officers had told him to go to a small English harbour and either buy or rent a motorboat, but to avoid dealing with fishermen. On the night of his departure, he was to transmit a message to the Abwehr as to his location, course and approximate port of arrival.[14] Such an operation, even in the best of circumstances would have been complex and dangerous. Trying to escape 'Fortress Britain' in the summer of 1941 would have been virtually impossible. The coastal areas of Britain were heavily fortified in addition to being restricted areas. Had Richter reached the coast, he would, as a foreigner, have immediately raised suspicion in attempting to rent or buy a motorboat. Even if he had stolen a boat, he would likely have been blown up by the minefields strategically laid along the coastline.

Not for the first time, the officers of MI5 mused on the state of the German Abwehr, which seemed an oxymoron. The Germans were normally extremely efficient and organised, yet the Abwehr seemed to be the complete opposite.

28

OPERATION LENA: THE MISSION TO HEAVEN

Having met some of the Abwehr's espionage agents, one could wonder at the training that these men received. They were not first-class spy material to begin with and their training seems to have been inadequate in the extreme. MI5, too, scratched their heads at some of the spies that were sent to Britain, but over time, they began to build a comprehensive picture of the methods used by the Abwehr to recruit and train agents.

The two Abwehr locations involved in inserting agents into England via Operation LENA were Hamburg and its satellite office in Bremen. Each office had a *Forscher*, a recruiter. The *Forscher* knew the strategic picture and what type of men were required.[1] It was his job to recruit agents, leaving the Abwehr officers free to focus on intelligence work. Reporting to the *Forscher* was a network of talent spotters; men who would pass along the names of suitable candidates. Talent spotters might be employed by the police, immigration officers, employment agencies, shipping agencies or other government organisations. They often looked for men who had had a brush with the law, men who were desperate and who could be coerced into working for the Abwehr.[2] Smugglers and black marketeers were a favourite target of Abwehr talent spotters. Several spies said that Abwehr recruiters visited concentration camps enlisting men as spies. Other spies said that they had been promised protection from the Gestapo, some because they were half-Jewish.

The *Forscher* would meet with the candidate and form an opinion of the man. If it was a favourable one, he would send details back to Hamburg or Bremen. If the officer in charge agreed that the prospect had potential, a local officer was sent out to form a second opinion. The candidate's information was then sent to Berlin and, if approved, the man was sent to Bremen or Hamburg for training.[3]

Once the trainee arrived in Hamburg, they were subtly groomed by the Abwehr officers. A psychological officer would make constant reference to the ease with which an agent's mission could be carried out: 'England is devastated by bombing, security is minimal and the entire country is in chaos. Several spies have already left for England and have encountered no difficulty in landing or in sending messages.' The Abwehr officers would retell tales of the heroic exploits of some of Germany's most trusted agents[4] – 'Spying in England is a walk in the park! If you need to return to Germany, it is a simple matter to go down to the coast, buy a boat and set sail for the Continent. If, perchance, you are captured by the English they will treat you as a prisoner of war. In any event, you will not be imprisoned for long, for our invasion will commence within a few weeks.' These particular lies were told to various spies in late 1940 and early 1941.[5]

The LENA agents then received training in wireless transmission, Morse code, cryptography, secret writing, map reading and aeroplane identification. Few of the agents received any training in parachute jumps. Caroli, as with Josef, had never practised a parachute jump.[6] On the other hand, a later parachutist, Nikolai Hansen, made several practise jumps from two tables stacked on top of each other.[7] Perhaps the Abwehr finally realised that first jumps were far from lucky, and more often unlucky.

Once the agents started their training, the cold, hard reality of the endeavour sank in. Several men (including Caroli) got cold feet, but were warned that withdrawal from the programme could have fatal consequences.[8] Even though the Abwehr recognised that fear and coercion were not great motivators, they often had the agent sign a contract with an oath of allegiance, 'I bind myself to fulfill the commands of the [German] Intelligence Service and am fully aware of the consequences if I do not fulfil them.'[9] No one needed to expand on the type of consequences. Agents were reminded that they would be leaving family members behind and that wartime Germany could be a dangerous place. Some contracts promised to give the agent or their family members a monetary reimbursement for their service to the Fatherland.[10] Other contracts made the agent promise not to divulge the names and addresses of the people met in connection with the German intelligence service.

Of course, the best agents were the ones motivated by conviction rather than coercion, men like Caroli, Druecke and Walti.[11] Such men were extremely difficult to break, and MI5 struggled with those three in particular. Caroli laughed at the idea of execution for himself but broke when promised the life of his friend and fellow spy, Wulf Schmidt. Druecke was paired with Vera Eriksen and wavered in the face of her pleas but ultimately held firm. Walti never did break and went to his death stubbornly mute.

Some spies were convinced that the German invasion was imminent and were terrified of revealing anything to the British for fear of Teutonic vengeance. Kieboom had been 'frightened by the Germans to such an extent that he is still afraid to tell us anything because of what the Germans will do to him after they have conquered England'.[12] And so the terrified spies lied to the MI5 officers in their initial interviews but as the weeks and months passed without a German invasion, they began to crack.

MI5 learned that it was relatively easy to convince the hapless spy that he had been made a fool of by the Abwehr and sent on a hopeless mission, poorly trained and poorly equipped, into a country that was not beaten or broken.[13] The overall sense of MI5 was that the directors of the German Intelligence Service were often 'entirely indifferent' to the fate of some of their spies.[14] Within the Hamburg Abwehrstelle sceptics believed that the LENA spies were being sent on a *Himmelfahrt* mission, a journey to heaven.[15] Most of the sacrificial spies were men, but the Abwehr was not above sending women on a fool's errand (e.g. Vera Eriksen).

29

ACTRESS, SINGER, MISTRESS, SPY

Richter's revelation in early July about the Abwehr's suspicions of double agent TATE cast long shadows across the double-cross system. At around the same time, Josef cracked and revealed a secret of his own.

Josef had been found with a picture postcard of a woman in his wallet. During his first interrogation at Latchmere House, on 2 February, Josef said that the woman was Clara Bäuerle, a singer with the Ette Orchestra. He reluctantly acknowledged that Clara was his mistress and that he had first met her in Hamburg in September 1940. The location on the back of the photograph looked suspiciously like London to the officers, but Josef said that Clara had never been to England and that the location was Landau, a town south of Mannheim, Germany.[1] Josef said that Clara did not speak English, but when the interrogators pointed out that the inscription on the back of the postcard was written in English, Josef admitted that she had learned some English at the Berlitz school in Hamburg. Being caught in a contradiction by the MI5 officers was never a good thing. Stephens called Josef a liar and wasn't at all satisfied with the information that he had gleaned during that first, imperfect interrogation. He suspected that Josef was playing for time, particularly with regard to questions around Clara.[2] During Josef's hospitalisation, MI5 searched diligently for information on Clara.

MI5 asked MI6 for information, but they could find nothing, although they concluded that the postcard had been printed in Germany, the address was Landau, and the handwriting was that of a German. The Ette Orchestra was well known and MI6 suggested that enquiries be made with individuals in theatrical ventures, none of which yielded any useful information.[3] Finally, in April 1941, a Home Office report revealed that a

Klara Sofie Bäuerle, a German born on 29 June 1906, arrived in Britain on 10 October 1930 and left Warwickshire for Germany on an unknown date.[4] The Central Register of Aliens had been notified of her departure on 21 June 1932.[5] There was no evidence that this particular Klara had ever visited Britain again, or even that she was Josef's Clara.

When Josef returned to Latchmere House in April, Clara was on the minds of the MI5 officers and they squeezed him for information. If Josef had only met Clara in September 1940 in Hamburg, why was the photograph dated July 1940 in Landau? Josef said that Clara was a capricious woman who was always handing out postcards of herself with various dates.[6] Josef had first met her at the Café Dreyer in Hamburg in September and she had moved into his rooms at the Hotel Sorgenfrei in early November. Josef told Clara about his work with the German Intelligence Service and even introduced her to Boeckel, who got her an engagement entertaining the troops. She didn't earn all that much with the Ette Orchestra and Josef said that she much preferred working for Boeckel.[7] In December, both Clara and Josef enrolled in English lessons at the Berlitz school in Hamburg.[8] After he was sent to The Hague, Josef said that he never saw Clara again and heard that she was ill in hospital. It was a neat story, but Josef had left out one detail.

In early July 1941 Josef was having another recorded conversation with Richter. They were discussing their time in The Hague and Josef casually mentioned that 'Major Malten told me that Clara would be coming over to join me.'[9] The MI5 officers pounced on the revelation and dragged Josef back into the interrogation room. Was Clara a spy? Was she coming to Britain? Josef admitted that Clara, in addition to taking a few English classes at the Berlitz school, had also received wireless training in Hamburg. She had introduced Josef to an Abwehr officer named Sinclair (likely George Sessler, Ritter's assistant[10]) who had once replaced Boeckel and driven Clara and Josef to the Air Defence Base in Hamburg. In early January, when Josef had been abruptly called back to Hamburg due to the denunciation by Van Hees, Clara was one of his main defenders. She said that although Josef was not a Nazi, he was reliable, and she was prepared to work with him in England. In January, while Josef was in The Hague, Clara had sent him a letter telling him that once the Abwehr received news from him in England, she would be sent over to join him. Major Malten confirmed this when he told Josef, 'Now you work hard, because Klara [*sic*] is coming soon and I have heard that you will have an important job of work to do together.'[11] Since the Abwehr had received no news of him, however, Josef rather doubted she would be sent to Britain.[12]

That assertion did little to assuage the concerns of the MI5 officers and Stephens noted in one report that the information gleaned from Josef justified 'the inclusion of KLARCHEN [Clara Bäuerle] in our list of prospective enemy agents to this country'.[13] According to Josef, Clara was about his height (i.e. around 6ft tall) with dark blonde hair, brown eyes and a wide nose. She had a deep voice and was a contralto singer. Not content to trust Josef's description of the woman, MI5 officers asked Richter about Clara. Richter admitted that he had only met her twice but confirmed that she was tall.

Clara Bäuerle's name went onto MI5's 'most wanted if she ever arrives' list. As the months and years passed, however, there was not a flicker of Clara's name on the double-cross airwaves. No tall, deep-voiced female parachutist landed in the fields of England or struggled ashore from an inflatable dinghy, or tried to sneak past the immigration authorities as a refugee. If Clara Bäuerle had ever been destined for a mission in Britain, the Abwehr officers must have changed their minds. Back in Germany, Clara continued to appear on recordings with the Ette Orchestra, but the recordings ceased after 1941. Decades later, Clara's name would be dragged from the archives of history and linked with an enduring British mystery.

On 18 April 1943 near Stourbridge, West Midlands, four boys found a skull in a hollow wych elm in Hagley Wood. The Worcestershire County Police recovered a skeleton from the trunk along with clothing fragments. The pathologist concluded that the remains belonged to a woman who had been placed into the tree about eighteen months previously (October 1941) while still warm. She had likely been asphyxiated and was thought to be 35–40 years old. She was about 5ft tall, with mousy brown hair and a deformed lower jaw. She wore a cheap gold wedding ring, no more than four years old, and had given birth at least once. Despite an extensive police investigation, the woman's identity remained a mystery. Six months later, graffiti asking, 'Who put Bella down the Wych Elm' appeared in the region. Did someone know something? If so, no one was talking.

The woman had seemingly come from nowhere and was missed by no one. Some speculated that the woman had been the victim of an occult ceremony. Others thought that she might be a Roma who had run afoul of her community. Still others thought she might be a refugee or a spy.

In 1968, Donald McCormick wrote a book (*Murder by Witchcraft*) in which he claimed that Bella had been a Nazi spy named Clarabella, recruited by the Abwehr and given the code name Clara. McCormick claimed to have seen Abwehr records that suggested Clara had parachuted into the West Midlands in 1941 but had failed to make contact. This theory was revived in March 2013 when *The Independent* newspaper, after blending McCormick's poorly researched speculations with fragments of information from Josef's MI5 file, suggested that Bella was none other than Clara Bäuerle.

There is, however, compelling evidence that Clara Bäuerle, the mistress of Josef, did not end up stuffed into a hollow tree in the West Midlands. The pathologist stated that Bella was 5ft tall, but both Josef and Richter affirmed that Clara Bäuerle was a tall woman, approaching 6ft. Clara Bäuerle's mysterious disappearance from the music scene in Germany in 1942 can be explained by the simple fact that she died in Berlin on 16 December 1942[14] of veronal poisoning.[15]

Clara was never sent over to Britain, and so, in many respects, she was one of the lucky ones. Her career as a spy fizzled out. Her career as a singer was short-lived, but in a strange way, she lives on, her voice immortalised in recordings.[16] Her deep contralto voice croons, 'The men are worth the love … there is no substitute for a real man.' Was Josef that 'real man'? If his mission to Britain had been successful and Clara had joined Josef, would they have attempted to escape to America together?

The question was a moot point. Several weeks before Richter and Josef revealed their respective secrets, Josef's fate had already been sealed.

30

CASE FOR LIQUIDATION

When Josef left for Britain on the evening of 31 January 1941, he entered a minefield of danger and potential death. Three precarious paths lay before him. The first was that of a successful, undetected spy. The first step on that path required an uneventful landing in England and an unremarkable journey to London. The moment he leapt from the aeroplane with his injured ankle, that first path vanished.

The second path was that of a double agent, an option dependent on several key factors. His capture needed to be kept quiet. He needed to be broken quickly by the MI5 officers. He needed to be co-operative. That path began to fade the moment he injured his ankle. It vanished completely as word of his capture spread like wildfire.

That left the third path, his only chance at life. He could become a valuable source of information for MI5. He could prove his usefulness by sharing everything he knew about the Abwehr and other agents bound for Britain. That option required Josef to be honest and up-front with the MI5 officers. It was not to be.

Stephens noted marked inconsistencies and discrepancies between Josef's February and April statements. His story about what happened after he was recruited by the Abwehr did not add up. At one point he said that he was paid by Boeckel but then claimed that he refused to accept money from the Abwehr. Stephens noted that the MI5 officers 'who have had the misfortune to contact this very odious personality Jakobs' could only smile at his story.[1]

It didn't end there. In February, Josef said that he came to Britain to get to America. In April, he said that he came to Britain to work for the anti-Nazi organisation. When Stephens pressed Josef against the jagged edges of his inconsistencies, Josef's explanations were weak and unconvincing. Stephens didn't buy any of it. He had 'not the slightest doubt that Jakobs came over here as an active and willing spy for the Germans'.[2] He thought the talk of Nazi oppression was a cover, and 'too much attention should not be paid to his "anti-Nazi organisation"'.[3] Josef might think that 'he is gaining our confidence, and so long as he remains under that preposterous illusion we are likely to get further information from him from time to time'.[4] Stephens' overall sense was that Josef was 'endeavouring to please' and that any information gleaned from him would be suspect until it could be confirmed.[5]

The MI5 officers repeatedly warned Josef of his 'precarious position' and advised him to give as much information as possible.[6] Stephens said Josef was 'a slippery customer and certainly anxious to save his neck'.[7] Unfortunately, it was hard to tell whether Josef was telling the truth or whether he was 'romancing in order to curry favour'.[8] Sampson, too, believed that Josef was an 'unprincipled blackguard with a criminal background'[9] who was trying to gain favour by showing a willingness to help them. He also believed that Josef actually knew very little about the Abwehr or other spies and was drawing upon his imagination to try to 'better his case', telling them what he thought they wanted to hear.[10] Sampson, too, could see that the threats and promises they had thrown at Josef, in a bid for more information, were simply muddying the waters. In Sampson's opinion, Josef was 'an unprincipled scoundrel with a good deal of low cunning' and all of his statements needed to be taken with the 'utmost reserve', although some grains of truth might be extracted.[11] In Sampson's opinion, the only tangible information Josef had provided was on Karel Richter, but only after he realised that MI5 already had a description of the agent. Sampson believed that Josef would have carried out his mission if he had been given the opportunity and that there were 'no extenuating circumstances in his case'.[12] This naturally stands in stark contrast to Stephens' statement of 16 May 1941 in which he admitted, 'Without Jakobs I am doubtful whether the case of Richter would have been cleared.'[13]

The MI5 officers described Josef as a 'very odious personality', a 'scrofulous Nazi', a 'prize liar' and a 'slippery customer'.[14] One could be forgiven for thinking that Stephens and his men held Josef in utter contempt. Stephens had a reputation for being flamboyant and dramatic in his reports on individual spies and his reports on Josef were no exception. Whether or not that was how he actually saw Josef was a different matter entirely.

In 1948, Stephens wrote a history of Latchmere House in which he sum-marised the spy cases that had passed through its gates. Stephens said that the patriots in the ranks of the spies were few, and the brave were fewer still. In his opinion, Josef was one of the few; a courageous man who did not bend to the will of his interrogators.[15] He only gave them as much information as he sensed they already had. Disgusted as Stephens was that Josef would not reveal more information, there was a grudging respect for him and an acknowledgement of his bravery. Whether Josef was protect-ing his country or his family was up for discussion. When it counted, Josef stood by his integrity and did what he thought was the right thing, but it didn't mean that his life would be smooth, or long.

In mid May the officers of MI5 turned their eyes towards prosecuting Josef under the Treachery Act. In light of the fact that he was an enemy alien, a person who was a citizen of a country with whom Britain was at war, MI5 wanted to prosecute him via a court martial. On 15 May Stephens drafted a summary of Josef's story and highlighted the case that they had against him. Josef had been trained in Morse code and weather reporting. He had parachuted into Britain with numerous incriminating articles in his possession.

In his 1 February statement to Robertson, Josef admitted that he had been sent to Britain in order to transmit weather reports to the German Intelligence Service. According to Stephens, there was no question that Josef's statement from 1 February would be admissible as evidence, but it remained to be decided whether that statement or a new one would be more satisfactory. Given the list of items found on Jakobs and the statement taken from him, it appeared that it was sufficient for prosecution under the Treachery Act. In addition, Josef was not a member of a conspiracy and real evidence was available in his case.[16] Stephens said that the considerable intelligence information obtained at Latchmere House would not need to be produced at all.[17]

In so far as the defence was concerned, Josef would probably say that it was never his intention to carry out his orders but he had merely used his mission as an opportunity to escape Germany and make his way to an aunt living in the United States.[18] Stephens said the following circum-stances were not in Josef's favour:

1) He tried to destroy the disc code – such an action was hardly in accordance with the desire of a refugee from Nazi oppression to assist the British authorities.

2) While in Dulwich Hospital, Josef explained how he broke his ankle, but Wing Commander Felkin had not accepted his explanation. Stephens suggested Felkin be called as a witness.

3) Josef said he was an anti-Nazi and, as proof, cited the Jewish emigration business and his internment in Sachsenhausen concentration camp. He claimed to have helped Lily Knips and to be on friendly terms with her. Lily had been interviewed and she said that Josef pestered her frequently regarding her financial affairs and that she was afraid of him. Given that Josef said he earned 150,000 Marks [sic] doing this business, it could be inferred that he entered this business as an Aryan determined to make his fortune indirectly from the persecution of the Jews.

4) In his statement to Robertson on 1 February, Josef said that he joined the Wetternachrichtung Abteilung[19] in Hamburg after being released from the concentration camp. This account, in which he was a member of this unit as far back as March 1940 and was sent to England to report on the weather, did not really fit in with his story that he wished to 'take in England en passant on his way to America'.[20]

Stephens' report landed on the desk of Brigadier Harker, Deputy Director General of MI5. Harker put out feelers about the possibility of trying an enemy agent by court martial. Given that Josef was the only foreign or alien agent tried by court martial during the Second World War (within the borders of Britain), Harker's letter to Dick White in mid May 1941 explained the logic involved in MI5's decision to pursue the course:

> The question has been raised as to whether it would not be more satisfactory to arrange that enemy agents who are under arrest and awaiting disposal in this country should not be tried by Court-martial instead of being handed over to the civil authorities. Under Section [redacted] of the Treachery Act, the AG may order an <u>enemy</u> alien to be tried by Court-martial instead of by the civil power. From the Security Service point of view there appear to be certain advantages for this procedure which roughly fall under the following heads:
>
> (i)   In view of congestion of criminal cases at the Old Bailey [civil court] and the fact that it will not be possible to hold a session at all until the 15th June, it would help to accelerate matters.
>
> (ii) It is impossible always to forecast how a jury may react and we have had two unfortunate instances recently where either

sentiment or stupidity has produced an acquittal.[21] Regarding the facts, both the Law Officers of the Crown and the Director of Public Prosecutions are satisfied that there was no question. I feel that with a military court such miscarriages of justice would be impossible.

(iii) There is always the possibility that in some of these cases there may be repercussions regarding the work of [Major Robertson and the double-cross system], and I should feel very much happier as regards secrecy, which in this respect is of the greatest importance, were the case tried by Court-martial rather than by the civil power with the attendant risk of leakage – particularly through jurymen.

I have discussed this matter unofficially with the DPP who has consulted with the Parliamentary draftsman regarding the intentions lying behind the Treachery Act and while nothing appears to have been said when the Treachery Bill was before the House, it was at that time the intention of the Attorney General to limit the use of his power to handing over for trial by Court-martial such enemy aliens as were in the military service of their country.

The DPP, however, tells me that he is perfectly prepared to take this matter up with the AG and further considers that it might be as well to have a suitable case to give him to consider.

Colonel Hinchley-Cooke, on my instructions has also unofficially discussed this with the JAG's office, and I understand from him that in any ordinary case the JAG would probably be able to put the case through and get it finally disposed of in two to three weeks.

The question, therefore, for first consideration is which case we should put before the AG. I understand that Josef JAKOBS is the case that you are ready to release, and on the papers that have been put to me by Major Stephens I think this is a good one with which to make a start.

Before, however, I submit this to the [Director General of MI5], I would like from you a list of such individuals as you consider you would like to have put up before a Court-martial, and further whether you are now perfectly happy about JAKOBS being handed over.

Before submitting your views would you please discuss this with Captain Liddell?[22]

It all sounded straightforward, and the next day, presumably having discussed things with Liddell, Dick White sent a handwritten note to Lieutenant Colonel William E. Hinchley-Cooke:

You will no doubt want to proceed with this case on the lines of the [Deputy Director General's] arrangements at an early date. Stephens' memorandum may supply you with a general picture from which to work. I presume you will now wish to transfer Jakobs to a Prison and have all exhibits turned over to you.[23]

This smooth plan for a rapid court martial was derailed, however, by Richter's arrival at Latchmere House. Josef's prosecution was put on hold while they induced him to challenge Richter. Even so, in a few weeks, MI5 would pick up the court martial baton and see it through to its inevitable conclusion. As Stephens stepped into the wings, a new player would step onto the stage, the implacable Lieutenant Colonel William Edward Hinchley-Cooke.

Hinchley-Cooke[24] was born on 31 January 1894 in Dresden, Germany, to a British father (William Thomas Cooke) and a German mother (Angeline Elizabeth Jordan).[25] In early 1914, after studying science at Leipzig University, Hinchley-Cooke found a job as a clerk at the British Legation in Dresden.[26] With the outbreak of the First World War on 28 July 1914, he and the rest of the legation were expelled from Germany and sent back to Britain.

Hinchley-Cooke was only 20 years old when he arrived in England, but his fluent German made him a tempting recruit for the nascent Security Service (MI5). His former boss, Minister Resident at the Court of Saxony, Arthur Grant Duff, recommended Hinchley-Cooke to Vernon Kell (Head of the Security Service) with the comment, 'He is entirely British in sentiment and the fact that he speaks English with a foreign accent must not be allowed to militate against him.'[27] Kell was impressed and on 21 August 1914 Hinchley-Cooke joined the Security Service. Given Hinchley-Cooke's foreign accent, Kell had the foresight to write a note on his War Office Pass that certified, 'He is an Englishman'.[28]

Hinchley-Cooke's first assignment was as liaison between the Security Service and Scotland Yard. Hinchley-Cooke examined the papers of suspected enemy agents, on the lookout for incriminating information. He was skilled at deciphering cryptic allusions in letters and had a knack for picking out letters with secret ink. In Kell's opinion, Hinchley-Cooke was responsible for the arrest of several German spies.

On 8 May 1915, Hinchley-Cooke was transferred to the British Ports, where he questioned foreign arrivals, often posing as a German, Wilhelm Eduard Koch, which threw travellers into confusion. 'A German working for the British? What has the world come to?' There is evidence that he posed as a German prisoner of war and worked as a stool pigeon in several POW camps in Britain.[29]

After the war, Hinchley-Cooke remained attached to the Security Service and, in 1933, he testified at the trial of Norman Baillie Stewart, a British Army officer who sold secrets to the Germans. A couple of years later, in the autumn of 1935, Hinchley-Cooke played a role in the apprehension of German agent Dr Hermann Goertz. While 1936 and 1937 were slow spy years, the following year made up for it. Hinchley-Cooke was involved in the arrest of two dangerous spies: hairdresser Jessie Jordan from Dundee, Scotland, and racing journalist Donald Adams.

On 1 September 1939, with war looming on the horizon, Hinchley-Cooke was assigned to the War Office with the rank of lieutenant colonel. Although he was attached to the Territorial Army Reserve (Royal Artillery, 55th Anti-Aircraft Brigade), the Germans could never find his name in the British Army List and thought he was a policeman. The Germans described Hinchley-Cooke thus: 'He wears glasses, is strong and has a fresh complexion. He has a friendly nature and speaks German fluently with a mixture of a Hamburg and Saxon accent.'[30]

In the autumn of 1940, Hinchley-Cooke interrogated the first German agents to arrive in England: Jose Waldberg, Carl Meier, Sjoerd Pons and Charles Van den Kieboom. Hinchley-Cooke, known as Cookie to his colleagues,[31] was far more than a simple MI5 interrogator, he was one of Britain's top military intelligence legal experts. He was kept busy during the war, evaluating spy cases and recommending who would be charged and who would be spared. This was the man who replaced Stephens as the most important MI5 contact in Josef's life from mid June to mid August 1941. For the first time in many months, Josef was able to converse with an MI5 officer whose mother tongue was German. It would do little to help him.

31

A FALSE SENSE OF SECURITY

By mid June 1941, Josef had helped to break Richter by way of cross-ruffs with his fellow spy, encounters that had helped to expand MI5's knowledge of Abwehr operations in Hamburg and The Hague. There was no doubt that Josef had co-operated with the MI5 officers. Whether he had given them all of the information he possessed was another matter. In his mind at least, Josef believed that his co-operation was earning him a reprieve from the hangman's gallows. He had been told that if he co-operated, he could 'help himself' and have a chance at life. Josef, in his turn, had told Richter the same thing.

Unbeknownst to Josef, MI5 had a different point of view and, in mid June, the liquidation report on Josef had been taken off the backburner and was once again front and centre. On 16 June, Edward J.P. Cussen,[1] a barrister and MI5 officer who worked with Hinchley-Cooke in the prosecution of suspected spies, prepared a brief on the case of *Rex vs Josef Jakobs*.[2]

Cussen drew up a five-page report in which he summarised the events of Josef's landing, apprehension and transfer to London.[3] He listed the items found in Josef's possession that would be pertinent to the case. Cussen also provided copies of the witness statements obtained by the Huntingdonshire Constabulary in early February. Interestingly, the statements all had handwritten marginal notes that added to, removed from or modified the originals.[4]

Two days later, Cussen's report was laid on the desk of Hinchley-Cooke. After reading the report Hinchley-Cooke telephoned Latchmere House and asked Stephens if Josef could be made available later that day (18 June), so that he could be brought to New Scotland Yard.[5] Stephens said that Josef would be available but added that it would be most helpful if Hinchley-Cooke could avoid letting Josef know that he would shortly be placed on trial. Josef was, to put it delicately, being used as an associate in collecting information from other detainees at Latchmere House (e.g. Richter).[6]

Stephens assured Hinchley-Cooke that no promises had been made to Josef with regards to the work that he was doing at Latchmere House.[7] One could naturally wonder if Josef would have agreed with that statement. Stephens' insistence that Josef be kept in the dark about his impending trial indicates that Josef still believed he was holding up his end of the bargain agreed on 2 February. Had Josef known that he was going to be prosecuted, he would have realised that the deal was off; the threats, promises and inducements made by Stephens would only lead to one outcome.

On the afternoon of 18 June, Josef was driven to New Scotland Yard, housed in the same complex as Cannon Row Police Station. In many ways, Josef had come full circle from his first statement to Robertson at Cannon Row on 1 February. Four and a half months later, Josef would make another statement to a different MI5 officer, but under very different circumstances. No longer wracked by pain from his broken ankle, Josef was able to think clearly and answer coherently. Fresh from two months of interrogation by the officers at Latchmere House, Josef may even have been lulled into a false sense of security. He did not understand the importance of this encounter with Hinchley-Cooke. In his mind, he was co-operating with MI5 and securing his own life, and that of his family.

Upon being escorted into the interrogation room by Detective Inspector Douglas Grant (Special Branch), Josef was met by three men: Hinchley-Cooke, Detective Sergeant Smith and Detective Constable Wills (both of Special Branch).[8] Josef took a seat at the table and, after introducing himself, Hinchley-Cooke asked if he could speak English. Josef said that he could speak very little English but understood Hinchley-Cooke if he spoke slowly.[9] It soon became clear that the conversation would need to take place in German. Hinchley-Cooke's initial set of questions covered Josef's background: name, date and place of birth, citizenship, parents and military service in the First World War. Naturally, Hinchley-Cooke asked about his recruitment into the Abwehr. This time, Josef said that he had been called up in June 1940. He was discharged after three days due to questions surrounding his Swiss prison sentence. According to Josef, the Germans wanted to clear up his civil status before they reinstated him as an officer. Josef claimed that when he landed in Britain he was actively serving in the Intelligence Service of the German General Staff (5th Section).[10]

At that point, Hinchley-Cooke paused and told Josef, 'It is my duty to warn you that you need not answer any further questions but whatever you do say will be taken down in writing by this Police Officer and may be used in evidence at a later stage.'[11] Josef acknowledged his understanding of the caution and continued to answer the questions put to him. He had already answered similar questions at Latchmere House and he likely thought nothing in answering them again. Josef told the story of how he had parachuted into England from a German aeroplane. He acknowledged that he had been equipped with a transmitter in order to report on weather conditions in England. He repeated the story of how he had broken his ankle leaving the aeroplane and fired his pistol the following morning to attract attention.

Satisfied with the answers, Hinchley-Cooke and the group dispersed, only to reconvene the following day after the shorthand notes had been transcribed.[12] Hinchley-Cooke and Josef reviewed the statement together and Josef suggested three additions and corrections. Once both men were satisfied that the transcript was accurate, Josef and Hinchley-Cooke signed the document, and that was that. Josef returned to Latchmere House and, over the next few weeks, continued to be interrogated and played against Richter. In the eyes of Josef, little had changed in his life. Behind the scenes however, outside of his view, the wheels were turning with vigour.

While Hinchley-Cooke was taking Josef's statement, Cussen was marshalling other resources. Cussen asked Dixon, the RSLO in Cambridge, to contact the Chief Constable of Huntingdonshire and see if the individuals present at Josef's capture and arrest were available to serve as trial witnesses: Mills, Jaikens, Pottle, Newton, Curedale, Godfrey, Baldock and Coulson.[13] A week later, Dixon confirmed that all of the witnesses were available except for Trooper John Curedale, who was currently serving with the Royal Armoured Corps in Hampshire.[14]

The officers of MI5 had all of their ducks in a row for Josef's court martial. Hinchley-Cooke, Dick White and Guy Liddell drafted an application to the AG asking that Josef be tried by court martial under Section 2(1)(b) of the Treachery Act.[15] The application was extremely brief. It included a one-page summary in which the MI5 officers took pains to point out that Josef, based on his own testimony, was a German subject (enemy alien) and a member of the German armed forces – either one of which was a key requirement for a court martial. In addition to the one-page summary, the application included Josef's statement to Hinchley-Cooke and a list of his possessions. The application was submitted to the DPP, Tindal Atkinson, at Devonshire House in Piccadilly on 23 June.

Tindal Atkinson was no stranger to spy trials. He had been appointed Director of Public Prosecutions in 1930 and had overseen the interwar espionage cases. At the start of the Second World War he helped to prepare the Defence Regulations and the Treachery Act, and he was naturally involved in the prosecution of all of the wartime espionage cases. He had been forewarned of MI5's intentions regarding Josef's case, so the arrival of the application to the AG did not come as a surprise. After reviewing the submission, Tindal Atkinson wrote a cover letter to the AG on 24 June and noted that 'as far as I am aware, this is the first case in which such a direction [to proceed by court martial] has been sought'[16] and, as a result, he included three arguments in support of the request:

1) The trial could take place very quickly – within two weeks – far more quickly than a civil trial.
2) There was less likelihood of information leaking out from a court martial than from a civil trial. (A recent spy case was under investigation due to a leak.)[17]
3) Finally, it appeared beyond doubt that Josef was an enemy alien.[18]

Tindal Atkinson's letter, accompanied by MI5's application was hand-delivered to the Royal Courts of Justice, a massive Victorian Gothic complex on the Strand near Aldwych. After wending its way through the maze of corridors and offices, the application was laid on the desk of the Attorney General, Donald Bradley Somervell. A barrister and Member of Parliament for the Conservative Party, Somervell was appointed AG in 1933. Over the next nine years, he oversaw such crises as the abdication of King Edward VIII and the declaration of war. Having dealt with many thorny issues during his illustrious career, Somervell didn't take long to evaluate MI5's application. On 25 June, the AG's fiat was sent back to the DPP:

> In the Matter of the Treachery Act, 1940.
> In the Matter of Josef Jakobs.
> Pursuant to my powers under section 2(1)(b) of the above-named Act, I HEREBY DIRECT that JOSEF JAKOBS, who is alleged to have committed an offence or offences against the above-named Act, shall be prosecuted before a Court-martial.[19]

On the same day, Tindal Atkinson (DPP) notified the JAG, Sir Henry Davies Foster MacGeagh, that the proceedings for Josef's court martial were now in his hands.[20]

A barrister who saw active military service during the First World War, MacGeagh was appointed JAG in 1934. For the next twenty years, MacGeagh would oversee military justice and the post-war trials of German war criminals. In May 1940, during the parliamentary debate on the Treachery Act, Lieutenant Colonel Sir William Allen (MP for Armagh) had grumbled that the JAG might be neither a judge, nor an advocate, nor a general. In his opinion, at least one person at a court martial should have some knowledge of the law.

This gloomy vision of British military justice wasn't entirely accurate. In Britain the JAG was a law officer of the Crown appointed by the king, on the recommendation of the Lord Chancellor. He was an independent member of the judiciary and always a civilian, although he might have served in the armed forces. The JAG was not a general of the army; the word 'general' basically meant broad oversight, similar to Attorney General. It was the JAG who would now oversee Josef's prosecution by court martial.

32

FIRST ESPIONAGE COURT MARTIAL

While the officers at Latchmere House were wrapping up Josef's case, Hinchley-Cooke met with officers from the JAG's office and the London District Adjutant General's office to arrange for Josef's incarceration, court martial and possible execution. It wasn't a simple matter.

MI5 had thought that once the JAG's office was ready to take the Summary of Evidence (in preparation for the court martial), Josef could be taken from Latchmere House and held at Wandsworth Prison. Several other spies had already been transferred to Wandsworth and hanged, so the prison governor, Benjamin D. Grew, was well versed in the care of high-security cases. Sir Alexander Maxwell (Home Office) had no objections to that course of action but thought that the Army Act might interfere with their plan.

Given that Josef was being tried by court martial, he was subject to the terms of the Army Act and needed to be held in military custody. Hinchley-Cooke, his colleague Cussen, Colonel Henry Shapcott from the JAG's office and Colonel Geoffrey Hippisley-Cox from the London District Adjutant General's office sat down and considered the various military premises that might be suitable for Josef's custody.[1] Various factors needed to be taken into account: location, distance to London, security, detention facilities and medical support. Finding an option that satisfied all of those criteria was a challenge.

The first option was the Tower of London. It ticked many of the boxes, but Hippisley-Cox's enquiry revealed that the only suitable quarters in which Josef could be held were occupied by the Major of the Tower. The second option was the military police detention cells at Great Scotland Yard, but after further enquiry, they concluded that general arrangements at the Yard were 'unsuitable'.[2]

The only other option within the London area was Latchmere House. Perhaps Josef could simply remain at Latchmere House and be held there during his court martial. If he was found guilty, it would be a relatively short trip to the Tower of London for his execution. Hinchley-Cooke spoke to Stephens, who was less than thrilled with the idea. Stephens allowed that he would be willing to accommodate Josef if it was absolutely necessary, but news would spread quickly amongst the detainees. If the other prisoners learned of Josef's trial, the outcome would be 'undesirable'.[3]

The officers looked further afield and briefly considered holding Josef at Cockfosters Internment Camp, north of London. The camp housed captured German officers and, as was the case with Latchmere House, it was undesirable that they should learn of Josef's court martial.

An obvious choice, at least from the military perspective, was the Military Detention Barracks at Aldershot, west of London. Commonly known as the Glasshouse because of its glass lantern roof, Aldershot appeared suitable, although it was far from London. If a sentence of death were passed on Josef, he would face a long and difficult journey from Aldershot to the Tower of London on the morning of his execution. Carrying out the sentence of death at Aldershot was complicated by the fact that it was outside the jurisdictional boundaries of the military's London District. It was, however, the most promising option.

Hinchley-Cooke, Hippisley-Cox and Cussen visited Aldershot and met with Lieutenant Colonel D.A. Davison, the prison commandant. Hinchley-Cooke explained the purpose of their visit and asked if Davison could take charge of an enemy agent under sentence of death while ensuring secrecy, safe custody and the 'very special care necessary in the case of a condemned man'.[4] After brief consideration, Davison explained that the Glasshouse was not suitable. The prison was extremely overcrowded, with triple the usual number of prisoners. There was only one hall or wing of the prison and even if a cell for Josef were set aside on the top floor, most of the prisoners would quickly become aware that a 'special prisoner'[5] was detained there. If Josef became disturbed or hysterical during his incarceration this would disturb the other prisoners and that would be 'most unsuitable'.[6] On top of that, Davison told the officers that there were no convenient premises adjacent to the prison where an execution by firing squad could take place.[7]

In desperation, Hinchley Cook, Hippisley-Cox and Cussen turned their eyes back to London and took a tour of Chelsea Barracks in Westminster. After a careful inspection of the premises, the officers thought that one block might provide suitable accommodation for Josef from the beginning of the proceedings until their conclusion. The only caveat was that barbed wire and bars would need to be installed to provide adequate security, which would presumably take time.[8]

After much deliberation, the officers decided that the best option was to request that a portion of Wandsworth Prison be designated a military prison. According to Section 132(1) of the Army Act, it 'was lawful for a Secretary of State … to set apart any building or part of a building under the control of the Secretary of State … as a Military Prison or Detention Barracks.'[9] There would be a delay in prosecuting the case while they waited for the Secretary of State to issue a decree, but this particular option satisfied all of the criteria regarding Josef's incarceration. It had the added benefit that Josef could be brought to Wandsworth directly from Latchmere House and could be housed there during the entire proceedings up until the morning of his execution. Military policemen could also be attached to Wandsworth Prison to provide military custody, but it was also 'eminently desirable that [Jakobs] should be in the actual custody of the trained prison officers' who had experience in such matters.[10]

On 9 July, two weeks after the AG had directed that Josef be tried by court martial, Hinchley-Cooke was tasked with submitting a request through Sir David Petrie (Director General of MI5) asking the Secretary of State for War and the Home Secretary to set aside a portion of Wandsworth Prison as a Military Prison.[11] Back in May and June, one of the perceived benefits of trying Josef by court martial was that 'the trial could take place very quickly – within two weeks – far more quickly than by trial before a civil court'.[12] The reality was turning out to be something else and the logistics involved were complex. Having submitted their strongly worded request, the officers could only sit and wait.

The days passed and turned into a week but still there was no word. Finally, on the morning of 19 July, the Director of Personal Services (DPS) for the forces telephoned Hinchley-Cooke and asked if the governor of Wandsworth Prison had made the arrangements agreed upon. The DPS wanted Josef to be taken into military custody on 21 July so that the Summary of Evidence could take place that same day. The DPS had an officer in mind for the role of court martial president but the man's schedule was tight and the matter needed to be dealt with quickly.

Hinchley-Cooke reminded the DPS that the Home Secretary had not actually signed the decree and, as such, it would be best to wait until they had the document in hand.[13] While Josef could be handed over to military custody within an hour or two, it would take Hinchley-Cooke several days to assemble the witnesses for the Summary of Evidence. The DPS agreed to leave the matter with Hinchley-Cooke but again expressed his hope that the whole proceedings could start sooner, rather than later.

That afternoon a brief memo went out from Secretary of State; it was what they had been waiting for:

> In pursuance of the power conferred on me by Section 132 of the Army Act, I hereby set apart as a military prison the part of His Majesty's prison at Wandsworth described in the Schedule hereto.
> Schedule: The rooms known as F. 2/1 and F. 3/1.[14]

Given that it was a Saturday, the memo precipitated an inordinate flurry of activity. Preparations had been taking place behind the scenes and all that was required was the go-ahead for the plans to be put into action. On Tuesday, 22 July, a squad of military policemen (one warrant officer and eight non-commissioned officers), arrived at Wandsworth Prison and were given a tour of cell F3/1, the cell assigned to house Josef.[15]

That same day, Hippisley-Cox wrote a letter to the Officer Commanding the Holding Battalion of the Grenadier Guards. Since Josef was being treated as a military prisoner, he was subject to the Army Act for the purpose of his custody, trial, sentence and punishment; and while he would be kept in the custody of the Deputy Provost Marshal (DPM), he would be attached to the Grenadier Guards for disciplinary purposes.[16] As a result, it was up to the commanding officer, Lieutenant Colonel George Mervyn Cornish, to investigate the charge against Josef. A career soldier, Cornish had served with the Grenadier Guards since 1916, working his way up the ranks. Assigned command of the newly formed Holding Battalion Grenadier Guards[17] on 20 April 1940, Cornish missed the dramatic blitz-krieg of May and June, as well as the nailbiting evacuation from Dunkirk. He would, however, be ideally situated to oversee the trial and execution of a German spy.

After weeks of preparation, the authorities had everything that they needed for Josef's court martial. They had a military prison. They had a squad of military policemen. They had a commanding officer to take charge of the investigation. All they needed was the prisoner.

33

CHARGED WITH TREACHERY

On 23 July, Detective Inspector Grant drove to Latchmere House and, having passed through the security checkpoints at the front gates, entered the main building. After signing the requisite paperwork, Grant was taken to Josef's cell. When the door opened, Josef must have sensed that his situation had altered. He was told to gather his belongings and accompany Grant. No one explained anything, and he may have feared the worst. Driven through the streets of south-west London, his heart likely sank as the car drew up before the ominous edifice of Wandsworth Prison. As the massive front gates creaked open and the vehicle rolled through, Josef may have wondered what lurked behind the thick walls.

Standing on the front steps was a familiar figure, Hinchley-Cooke.[1] Climbing out of the vehicle, Josef was greeted by Hinchley-Cooke and ushered up the stairs and into the prison's administration wing (F Wing). Before them, F Wing opened up into the central rotunda from which radiated the other prison wings.

Having entered the prison on Level 2, Josef and Hinchley-Cooke climbed the spiral staircase along the right side of the rotunda and negotiated the narrow walkway to Cell F3/1. Located in the acute angle between F Wing and E Wing, the cell was a trapezoid shape, narrow at the doorway and wider at the window opposite. The cell was spacious and large enough to accommodate a bed, table and chairs, along with several guards, in this case, three members of the military police. Introductions were made, and Josef was told that this was his new home. Was it an improvement? Only time would tell.

The next morning dawned and Josef and his guards received a prison breakfast. The night guards went off duty and a new pair arrived under the watchful eye of their sergeant. The prison governor stopped by for a visit. It was all very civilised, and Josef had no complaints, other than boredom. A deck of cards was produced and before long, prisoner and guards were engaged in a brisk game of whist, language issues pushed to the side. The guards were friendly and treated Josef like a human being and a fellow soldier. In the afternoon, Josef and his guards were even permitted a walk in the prison yard. A day without interrogations by suspicious officers was a breath of fresh air, but it wouldn't last long.

At 6 p.m., Hinchley-Cooke and Cussen arrived at the prison, where they met the DPM, Lieutenant Colonel C.R.T. Gerard.[2] After signing in, the three men were escorted to Josef's cell. As they entered the room, the two military policemen leapt to their feet and saluted their commanding officer. Josef stood up more slowly and shook Hinchley-Cooke's hand. Perhaps now there would be answers to his questions. The guards were excused from the room and the four men sat down at the table. A pack of cards lay in an untidy heap and cigarette butts filled the ashtray. Cussen pushed the cards aside and laid folders and a notepad on the table. Hinchley-Cooke picked up a folder, opened it and read the following:

> On this day, Thursday, the 24th day of July, in the year 1941, you, Josef Jakobs, an enemy alien, are charged with 'committing a civil offence, that is to say, Treachery, an offence contrary to Section I of the Treachery Act, 1940, in that at Ramsey in the County of Huntingdon on the night of January 31/February 1, 1941, with the intent to help the enemy did an act designed or likely to give assistance to the naval, military or air operations of the enemy, or to impede such operation of His Majesty's Forces, namely did descend by parachute in the United Kingdom'.[3]

Hinchley-Cooke laid the folder on the table and cautioned Josef that he need not make any reply, but that if he did so, it would be taken down in writing by Cussen and would be given in evidence later. Josef nodded and asked Hinchley-Cooke to read the charge over again in German. After hearing the charge in his native language, Josef replied confidently, 'I have nothing to fear'.[4] He then asked Hinchley-Cooke to explain the legal procedure to him. Hinchley-Cooke told Josef that a Summary of Evidence would be taken on 28 July. The witnesses would give their statements and a list of exhibits would be presented. During that process Josef could question the witnesses if he wished.

The court martial would take place a week later and might last a day or two. Hinchley-Cooke said that a defence officer with legal qualifications would be provided and Josef asked if it was possible to request a German-speaking officer. While Hinchley-Cooke could make no promises in that regard, he said he would do his best. Josef asked what would happen if he was found guilty; would he be hanged or shot? Hinchley-Cooke explained that since Josef was being dealt with by military procedure, the penalty would be death by shooting. Josef was surprised and said, 'The others have been hanged.'[5] Hinchley-Cooke explained that they had all been tried by civil courts and that the penalty in those circumstances was death by hanging.

Josef believed that he had nothing to fear from the Treachery Act and the charge levelled against him. In truth, he had everything to fear. The charge was verbose, but the essence of it boiled down to one thing – Josef, with intent to help the enemy, undertook an act that was likely to hamper the British; namely, he parachuted into Britain. At first glance, it appeared to be a weak charge. Luftwaffe pilots parachuted into Britain after their aeroplanes had been shot down. None of them were charged under the Treachery Act. Rudolf Hess descended by parachute in Scotland in May 1941. He was imprisoned, not executed. The key lay in the wording of the Treachery Act.

It should be recalled that in May 1940 the Members of Parliament were told that the Treachery Act would only be used in the 'most grievous' cases of espionage and sabotage. Josef had no opportunity to commit an act of espionage or sabotage. He had landed with a broken ankle and that was the end of the matter for him.

It turned out that his case was by no means unique, at least not in terms of Second World War spies. Agents masquerading as refugees from Belgium and Holland who arrived on steamers, freighters and passenger liners in the latter years of the war were charged with 'arriving in the United Kingdom'. It didn't matter if the men performed an act of espionage or sabotage. That was, to a large extent, immaterial.

There were, however, two exceptions. The first four spies who landed from small boats along the coast of Kent in early September 1940 were all charged with two counts: landing in the United Kingdom and conspiring to transmit information on His Majesty's forces. In similar fashion, Druecke and Walti were also charged with two counts under the Treachery Act: landing in the United Kingdom and conspiring together and with others.[6] It is unclear why subsequent neutral and enemy alien spies were not charged with 'attempting' or 'conspiring' but simply charged with landing in the United Kingdom. As the Members of Parliament had pointed out in May 1940, during their discussion of the Treachery Act, intent was a slippery word and difficult to prove.

MI5 was not concerned. In the First World War, spies were executed because they had done something – sent a letter in code, used secret ink to send a message or drawn pictures of fortifications. During the early years of the Second World War, it was enough that an alien person had been associated with the German Intelligence Service. It was enough that they had a wireless transmitter, a code or material that could be used to make secret ink. Possession of espionage gear was enough to demonstrate intent. Josef, however, claimed that his intent had been to escape the Nazis and travel to America. Would his word stand up to the implacable intent of the British Security Service?

On 28 July, at the direction of Lieutenant Colonel Cornish, Commander of the Holding Battalion, Grenadier Guards, a Summary of Evidence took place at Wellington Barracks.[7] There is no evidence that Cornish conducted the investigation himself. It would appear that he authorised Major Anthony A.H. Marlowe, from the JAG's office, to undertake the proceedings, a man who would also serve as lawyer for the prosecution at Josef's court martial. The Summary of Evidence was standard procedure and allowed the commanding officer to determine if the evidence warranted a court martial. In Josef's case, the Summary of Evidence appears to have been a mere formality. Josef was not provided with a defence lawyer nor is there any record that a translator was provided.

According to the Army Act, the witnesses at the Summary of Evidence were to give their evidence, which would be taken down in writing. The defendant was to be given the opportunity to question each witness if he so desired.[8] After the prosecution witnesses had given their statements, the defendant, his wife and anyone else he wished to call could give statements.[9] Clearly, in the case of Josef, his wife was unable to attend the Summary of Evidence. There is also ample evidence to suggest that the witness statements were typewritten beforehand and provided to each of the witnesses to read.

The Summary of Evidence statements were based on the original statements made to the police in early February, but in all instances, the statements had been modified. Information was added, deleted and clarified to better present the prosecution's case. In addition to the witnesses, seventeen exhibits were produced:

1) Attorney General's fiat (directive authorising the court martial)
2) Revolver [*sic*][10]
3) Box of ammunition
4) Steel helmet
5) Parachute
6) Attaché case containing wireless
7) Flying suit
8) Leather wallet
9) Map
10) Blank ration book
11) Blank identity card
12) Completed identity card
13) Torn pieces of cardboard (from disc code)
14) Hand spade
15) Torch
16) Photocopy of reconstructed pieces of cardboard (disc code)
17) Jakobs statement of 18 June 1941[11]

The first witness was Charles Baldock, one of the farm workers who had heard Josef's pistol shots on the morning of 1 February and come to his aid. At the end of his statement, Josef asked, 'Is it right that I was unable to move?', to which Baldock replied, 'Yes'.[12] One after the other, the witnesses gave their statements: Coulson, Godfrey, Newton, Pottle, Mills, Marriott and Hinchley-Cooke.[13] Josef declined to ask questions of any of them, perhaps because he could not understand what had been said or could not formulate a response in English.

After the witnesses had given their statements, Marlowe asked Josef:

> Do you wish to make any statement or to give evidence upon oath? You are not obliged to say anything or give evidence unless you wish to do so, but whatever you say or any evidence you give will be taken down in writing, and may be given in evidence.[14]

In all likelihood, Josef simply shook his head or gave a simple 'no' in reply. In typical legal fashion, however, Marlowe noted that Josef 'does not desire to make any statement or to give evidence on oath at this stage, but states that he wishes to reserve his defence'.[15]

The proceedings from the Summary of Evidence were passed along to Cornish. As Josef's nominal commanding officer, Cornish needed to decide if the evidence warranted a court martial. As expected, on 29 July, Cornish confirmed the charge and Lieutenant General Sir Bertram N. Sergison-Brooke, the officer in charge of the military's London District, ordered that the court martial be convened.[16] That same day, Hippisley-Cox, the Assistant Adjutant General, sent a letter to Hinchley-Cooke with the Summary of Evidence documents.[17] Two days later, on 31 July, Hinchley-Cooke visited Wandsworth Prison and served Josef with copies of:

(a) the charge sheet
(b) the Summary of Evidence
(c) Exhibit 16 (photocopy of disc code)
(d) Exhibit 17 (Josef's statement from 18 June 1941)
(e) evidence to be given by Mr L.W. Humphreys (Radio Branch of the Post Office Engineering Department).[18]

It was official, on Monday, 4 August, Josef would be brought before a court martial in a fight for his life. What had been a distant threat in the previous months had suddenly become immediate. Josef asked Hinchley-Cooke if he might be visited by a Catholic priest prior to his court martial. Hinchley-Cooke promised to look into the matter. At the same time, Hinchley-Cooke asked the prison medical officer to complete a certificate of health for Josef. On each day of the trial, the medical officer would need to provide a similar certificate that acknowledged that Josef was fit to stand trial that day.[19]

On Friday, 1 August 1941 the JAG sent a certificate to Carl Ludwig Stirling, barrister-at-law and Deputy Judge Advocate General, appointing him to serve as Judge Advocate at Josef's court martial.[20] Stirling had the weekend to finalise preparations for Josef's court martial, which was scheduled to start three days later.

34

COURT MARTIAL BEGINS: 4 AUGUST 1941[1]

[NB: *I have added comments throughout the court martial proceedings regarding inconsistencies, inaccuracies, etc.*]

On the morning of 4 August, Josef woke behind the barred windows of Wandsworth Prison. It was the first day of his court martial and life continued as normal. Breakfast was served at the usual time. The military policemen changed shifts at the usual time. At about 8.30 a.m., Josef and his escort left the prison and were driven across the River Thames to the Duke of York's Headquarters in Chelsea. On that morning, a steady stream of vehicles arrived at the building carrying court martial members, intelligence officers, witnesses, court officials and policemen.

Josef and his guards were hustled off to a quiet room, where Josef and his defence lawyer, Captain Eric V.E. White,[2] sat down together to review the case. A barrister-at-law, White, had co-authored a book in 1935 entitled *The Practice Relating to Debentures; a Handbook of Legal and Practical Knowledge for Directors, Receivers, Secretaries, Accountants and Debenture Holders, with Full Appendix of Forms.* White would appear to have been more of a corporate lawyer than a criminal lawyer and it is a matter for debate if he had ever defended someone against a capital charge. He also lacked military experience, having only enlisted with the Leicestershire Yeomanry in the autumn of 1939 at the age of 32 years. Josef, unfortunately, did not have the luxury of shopping around for an experienced defence lawyer.

Elsewhere in the building, the members of the court martial panel gathered in their battle dress uniforms. The president of the court martial was Major General Bevil T. Wilson, Commander of the 53rd (Welsh) Division. While the Judge Advocate was legal advisor to the court martial panel, Wilson would direct the proceedings. Josef's court martial panel also included four members and two waiting members (in case one of the members was unable to continue).

The first member was Brigadier Frederick A.M. Browning, Commander of the 24th (Guards) Independent Brigade Group. Browning had served with the Grenadier Guards during the First World War and his company had played an active role in repulsing the German advance near Amiens in early April 1918. Neither Josef nor Browning, fighting on opposite sides during the Amiens conflict, could know that they would face each other again in 1941.

The second member was Colonel Edward W.S. Balfour, Officer Commanding Scots Guards. The third member was Lieutenant Colonel Henry H. Cripps, Officer Commanding Infantry Training Centre, Royal Fusiliers. The fourth member was Major Robert O.R. Kenyon-Slaney, Grenadier Guards. The two waiting members were Lieutenant Colonel Eric D. Mackenzie, Officer Commanding Holding Battalion, Scots Guards and Major R.C. Alexander, Irish Guards, Guards Depot. Neither of the waiting members would be required during the court martial, but Mackenzie would play a different role in Josef's story when he oversaw Josef's execution at the Tower of London.

In addition to the military officers, striding through the Duke of York's Headquarters were representatives from MI5: Petrie (Director General of MI5), Harker (Deputy Director General of MI5) as well as Hinchley-Cooke and Cussen. Detective Inspector Grant (Special Branch) represented the Metropolitan Police Force. Security officer, Major E. Walker had come on behalf of the military's London District. Standing out from the military and intelligence men were two lawyers in black robes, the lawyer for the prosecution, Marlowe, who we met at the Summary of Evidence, and the Judge Advocate, Carl L. Stirling.

A lot of preparation had gone into this court martial and it was Stirling's job to conduct the court martial, provide directions in law and generally ensure that the proceedings went smoothly,[3] a task for which he was eminently qualified. Admitted to the Bar of the Middle Temple in 1913, Stirling received a commission with the Royal Fusiliers two years later. During the last three years of the First World War, he spent most of his time sitting on military appeal tribunals hearing the cases of individuals requesting exemption from military service. Stirling was unsympathetic and believed that young men should be serving their country overseas, not trapping rabbits and herding cattle. During the interwar period, Stirling was appointed a legal assistant to the office of the JAG and took silk as King's Counsel. Stirling had a solid background in military law and even served as Judge Advocate at war crimes trials after the Second World War. On 4 August 1941, however, Stirling was focused on ensuring that everything surrounding Josef's court martial went smoothly.

Stirling entered the room in which the court martial was to take place and surveyed the scene. Quartermaster Sergeant B.A. Balment, RAOC, the shorthand stenographer, Lieutenant J.W. Thomas,[4] the interpreter, and several staff from Stirling's office were completing preparations. Stirling eyed the room and decided that everything was up to snuff. He had one last look at the table on which were displayed the court martial exhibits. He ticked off each item against a list identical to that of the Summary of Evidence, except for two additions: Exhibit G was the convening order issued by Cornish and Exhibit 19 was 498 £1 notes.[5]

Everything was in order and Stirling sent an assistant to gather the president and the members of the court who, upon entering the room, seated themselves at a long table. Their first duty was to review the order convening the court, the charge sheet and the Summary of Evidence. The officers needed to confirm the legality of the court (correct number and eligibility of convened officers) and the validity of the charge brought against Josef.[6]

Having satisfied themselves that the court was legal and the charge valid, the doors of the room were opened. The observers were invited into the room and seated along the back. Marlowe, lawyer for the prosecution, entered the room and took his seat at a table in front of the court. Finally, Josef and White entered the room and took their seats at another table near Marlowe. The witnesses were tucked away in various rooms down the hallway, awaiting their summons to testify before the court.

Stirling stood and acknowledged that the members of the court did not know how well Josef comprehended English. Stirling asked White to speak up if he thought the court did something that was unfair to Josef because he did not understand the proceedings. If White thought something needed to be translated, then he needed to inform the president. White acknowledged the request and admitted that Josef had only learned

English since coming to Britain. White would try to take Josef's testimony in English, but he might need to use the interpreter. Stirling reiterated that the court was relying on White to ensure that Josef understood the evidence presented.[7]

The order convening the court was read out and attached to the proceedings as Exhibit G. The names of the president and members of the court were read out and Josef was asked if he objected to being tried by any of them, to which he replied, 'No'.[8] The president of the court was duly sworn in by Stirling. Holding a copy of the New Testament in his uplifted hand, the president repeated the following oath after each phrase was spoken by Stirling:

> I swear by Almighty God that I will well and truly try the accused before the Court according to the evidence, and that I will duly administer justice according to the Army Act now in force, without partiality, favour or affection, and I do further swear that, except so far as may be permitted by instructions of the Army Council for the purpose of communicating the sentence to the accused, I will not divulge the sentence of the Court until it is duly confirmed, and I do further swear that I will not on any account at any time whatsoever disclose, or discover the vote or opinion of any particular member of this court-martial, unless thereunto required in due course of law.[9]

The members of the court were then sworn in collectively using the same oath, followed by the swearing-in of Stirling. Josef was then asked if he had any objections to Thomas acting as interpreter, or to shorthand notes being taken by Balment, to which he again replied, 'No'.[10] The interpreter and shorthand writer were duly sworn in by Stirling.

With all of the court officials duly sworn in, Marlowe made an application under Section 6 of the Emergency Powers (Defence) Act of 1939, that the proceedings be held in camera and the witnesses be forbidden to discuss the proceedings.[11] After discussion, the court agreed to the request. Marlowe also asked that Hinchley-Cooke be allowed to remain in the room, 'He is here in the nature of an expert witness; he has had the conduct of the proceedings from the start and I think his presence will be of assistance both to the Court, the prosecution and the defence.'[12] [*Hinchley-Cooke was not directly involved in Josef's case until mid June. Josef's possessions were sent to Butler, a colleague of Hinchley-Cooke in SLB, but there is no evidence of Hinchley-Cooke's direct involvement in the case until he took Josef's statement on 18 June 1941.*]

Marlowe noted that such a request had been previously granted when Hinchley-Cooke acted in a similar capacity in civil courts. The court asked White what he thought, given that Hinchley-Cooke was a witness for the prosecution. White replied, 'For my part, I do not object.' This point was presented to Josef by the interpreter, and he also had no objection.[13] The court then gave two orders:

(1)   No persons other than the following shall be admitted to the Court at any time during the hearing of the case: Lt Col W.E. Hinchley-Cooke, witnesses (as and when required), court officials, prisoner's escort, Brig. Sir David Petrie (Director General, Security Service), Brig. O.A. Harker (Deputy Director, Security Service), Mr E.J.P. Cussen (attached Security Service), Maj. E. Walker (Security Officer, London District) and Detective Insp. D. Grant (Metropolitan Police)

(2)   No Person who is present in Court during these proceedings shall disclose to any other person, save in the course of duty, any information whatsoever about such proceedings or any part of them.[14]

Stirling then turned to Josef and read out the charge through the interpreter.[15] In response to the question, 'Do you desire to plead guilty or not guilty to the charge?', Josef stated that he was 'not guilty.'[16] Stirling asked Josef (through the interpreter) if he wished to apply for an adjournment on the grounds that any of the rules relating to procedure before the trial had not been complied with or that he had not had sufficient opportunity to prepare his defence. Josef said, 'No.'

The president questioned the accuracy of the interpreter's translation of the word treachery during the reading of the charge. The German translation of the charge was read out again by Hinchley-Cooke.[17] At this point, Josef might have been justified in questioning the qualifications of his interpreter. Josef's ability to communicate in English was limited. His comprehension of the trial and his ability to defend himself were at the mercy of the interpreter.

Finally, Stirling noted that since they had a shorthand writer, they would not read over the evidence after it had been presented (as required by Rules of Procedure 83(b)).[18] The shorthand writer was an experienced professional and, as a result, none of the members of the court needed to take notes. If required, the shorthand writer could read back what he had written.[19]

Marlowe stood up and noted that since the court was empowered to try the case by the direction of the AG, he wanted to submit the AG's fiat as Exhibit 1. Having read the text of the directive out loud, Marlowe cleared his throat and began the case for the prosecution.[20]

Jakobs family, circa 1908: (left to right) Josef, Emma, Anna, Maria, Kaspar. (Jakobs family archives)

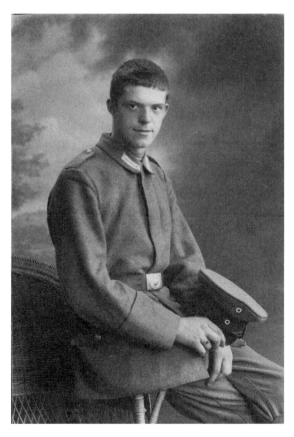

Josef Jakobs, circa 1917. (Jakobs family archives)

Josef and Margarete (Knöffler) Jakobs in summer 1934, Switzerland. (Jakobs family archives)

Children of Josef and Margarete (Knöffler) Jakobs, June 1941: (left to right) Raymond, Regine, Norbert at their First Communion. (Jakobs family archives)

Lily (Katz) Knips, circa 1938. (Sylvia Paskin – used with permission)

Hedwig Clara (Claire) Bäuerle, circa 1937. (Claire Robertson – used with permission)

Horace Jaikens (Ramsey Police), circa 1940. (Martyn Smith – used with permission)

Josef Jakobs, 2 February 1941, Latchmere House. (The National Archives)

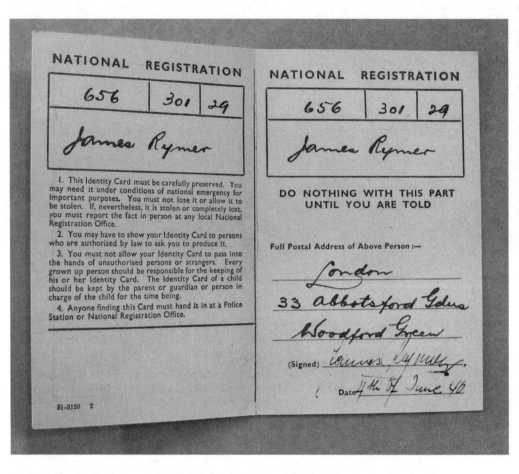

National Identity Card given to Josef Jakobs by the German Abwehr. (The National Archives)

William Edward Hinchley-Cooke (unknown date). (*After the Battle* magazine – used with permission)

Last letter of Josef Jakobs, 15 August 1941. Translation: 'Dear Gretchen, my little bunny, dear Norbert, dear Regine, dear Raymond. Adieu and Auf Wiedersehen into eternity. On 15 August, on the day of the Sacred Feast of the Assumption of Mary, London. [signed] Josef Jakobs. My last kiss to you all!' (Jakobs family archives)

Miniature Rifle Range, Tower of London, circa 1916. (*After the Battle* magazine – used with permission)

William Chidlow, circa 1938, in his Coldstream Guards uniform. (Kate Snell – used with permission)

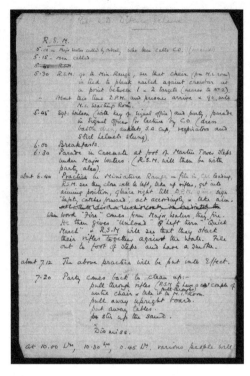

RSM Arthur Wilford's notes for the execution of Josef. (Royal Armouries – used with permission)

Chair in which Josef Jakobs was executed. Photo taken circa 1970s. (*After the Battle* magazine – used with permission)

Receipts of monthly payments made to Margarete (Knöffler) Jakobs by the Hamburg Abwehr. Payments would continue until just before the end of the war. Margarete kept a letter from Dr Beier (Boeckel) of the Hamburg Abwehr and M. Schröder was his secretary. (Jakobs family archives)

Josef Jakobs in April 1940. (Jakobs family archives)

Raymond Jakobs (son of Josef) in September 1964. (Jakobs family archives)

Giselle Jakobs and Kate Snell (daughter of William Chidlow) in October 2016 at the Tower of London. (Pamela Jakobs – used with permission)

Giselle Jakobs and Sylvia Paskin (granddaughter of Lily Knips) in November 2014 (Paul Robinson – used with permission)

35

CASE FOR THE PROSECUTION

Marlowe started by referring to Section 1 of the Treachery Act, which stated:

If, with the intent to help the enemy, any person does, or attempts or conspires with any other person to do,[1] any act which is designed or likely to give assistance to the naval, military or air operations of the enemy, to impede such operations of His Majesty's Forces, or to endanger life, he shall be guilty of felony and shall on conviction suffer death.[2]

Marlowe said that the facts would satisfy the court that the accused arrived in Britain and acted (landed by parachute) with intent to give assistance to the naval, military or air operations of the enemy or to impede the similar operations of Britain. Marlowe then summarised the facts regarding Josef's case:

The facts are that on the 1 February of this year, two farm labourers were walking across a farm in Huntingdonshire when they heard a series of shots, apparently fired from a pistol, which attracted their attention. At first they could see no signs of anybody but after a little while they found a man lying in a field about 150 yards from where they were. You will hear from those witnesses that the accused is the man they saw. They went over to him and as they approached him, he threw away the revolver [sic] with which he had been firing; he threw it into a steel helmet which was lying near him. It became apparent, both from the man's physical condition and from what he said, that he had broken a leg and it was also clear from what he said that he had come down from a German aeroplane, landed in that field and broken his leg in so landing. [*Josef did not say that he had come down from a German aeroplane, he simply pointed to his parachute.*] At that time his English appeared to be somewhat limited. He said to the farm labourers that his leg appeared to be broken and when he was asked what he was doing there, he said 'Me solo flying'.

That was the story he repeated to some members of the Home Guard who subsequently arrived on the scene. He was not unnaturally asked if he was solo flying where was his aeroplane. Then he told the story that he had come down by parachute from a German aeroplane. [*The farmers and Home Guard admitted that Josef spoke poor English and that much of the communication was by gestures. At no point did Josef 'tell a story' of how he had arrived.*] He was asked a few questions as to whether he was alone and he said he was. He was taken by members of the Home Guard to Ramsey Police Station, which was the nearest accommodation available for him.

The significant thing about this man at the time of his arrival is the articles which he carried with him. You will hear a list of the things which were found on him and near him when he arrived. It is a formidable list and you may think that every one of those things is something which a spy landing in this country would bring with him. The list consists of these articles (pointing to the exhibits), every one of which will be put before the court in due course. There is the pistol which you have heard he was firing to attract attention, a box of ammunition which fitted that pistol, a steel helmet, and a camouflaged parachute, being the one he came down in. Then there is something which you may consider of more importance, and that is an attaché case containing wireless equipment. You will hear evidence from an expert who has examined that outfit that that is a wireless set capable of transmitting messages to the Continent and of receiving messages from the Continent. He was dressed in a flying suit, which you will see, and he also had with him 498 £1 Bank of England notes – no doubt sufficient to keep him here for a considerable time. Those notes were contained in a leather wallet. [*This is not accurate. According to Newton's witness statement, most of the bank notes were found in wads in Josef pockets. A leather note case contained a few bank notes and the leather wallet only contained the ration book, the identity cards and the picture of Clara. Jaikens' report also noted that the leather wallet only contained the documents and a picture. There was no need to include the leather wallet within the list of exhibits since all of the documents were listed separately. As we shall see, there was something within the wallet that was not mentioned in the list of exhibits and which would be produced later.*] There

was also found on him a map of England which bore some rather significant markings. There was a pencilled triangle on that map; on one
side of the triangle was a cross and on another side a small circle. [*The
circle was on the east side of the triangle. The cross was within the triangle, not
on 'another side'.*] The triangle covers the area within which the accused
landed. The cross represents an RAF aerodrome and the circle indicates
a spot where an RAF satellite aerodrome is situated. [*The cross marks the
railway line between Peterborough and Huntingdon, several miles west of RAF
Upwood. The circle lies on the edge of the triangle and is close to RAF Warboys.*]
He also had with him a traveller's ration book, which you will see and
which you may think is an excellent forgery. You will hear that, in the
opinion of experts, it is a forgery and no doubt you will think it is a very
good one too. [*As the Registrar General noted, the ration card was a passable
forgery, but it had not been filled in and was out of date, which made it highly
suspicious.*] It was essential for him to have such a document if he was to
survive in this country for any length of time. He also had two identity
cards, one a completed one and one still blank. Those are both forgeries. You may find the completed one somewhat instructive because you
only have to look at it to appreciate that it is a forgery. Although the
document itself is an excellent forgery, the wording is not so good. You
will find the alleged address of the holder of that identity (whose name
is given as James Rymer) is written in the Continental fashion, the name
of the town being put first. [*No comment on the obvious registration number
error.*] The accused also had with him a hand spade, a small spade about
a foot to fifteen inches long, and an electric torch. That is not without
significance, because that electric torch, which you will see, was when
first seen, an extremely bright one. Although small it was very powerful.
Now, although it still works, the battery is not so powerful as it was some
six or seven months since this man landed. It was also fitted not only
with the ordinary switch but with a flashing device, which is capable of
being used for signalling. All those things found on him, the pistol, the
wireless set and the torch, were all in working order.

There were also found round where the accused was found lying,
a number of pieces of torn cardboard. Those, so far as possible, have
been reconstructed into their original form and you will hear from
Lt Col Hinchley-Cooke that they represent what is known as a disc
code. It is a method which you will hear is used by enemy agents arriving in this country. It consists of two discs fitted on top of one another,
one larger than the other, with a pin or a swivel through the middle so

that the smaller disc can be turned round on the larger one, thereby making a series of letters come opposite each other. You will hear from Lt Col Hinchley-Cooke, who is experienced in these matters, that that is one of the articles often found on enemy agents arriving here, and it is perhaps not without significance that the accused endeavoured to dispose of that code, which would be very incriminating for him, by tearing it up into small pieces. [*The disc code was only found on four out of the ten spies who arrived prior to Josef. The question to be answered is: Did Josef tear up the code because he was afraid that it would incriminate him as a spy and lead to abuse by the people who found him or did he tear it up to prevent it falling into enemy hands? Given the pain of his broken leg, was he even in a rational state of mind and capable of comprehending the consequences of his actions?*]

The accused was seen by various officials, including the police at Ramsey, and finally by Lt Col Hinchley-Cooke in which he admitted that he had come from Germany and had come by air. [*No mention of what happened between the Ramsey Police (1 February) and Hinchley-Cooke (18 June).*] He admitted that he was at that time the equivalent of a non-commissioned officer in the German Army, that he was employed in the German Intelligence [Service] and that he had come to this country for the purpose of studying the weather. You will hear there is no doubt as to this man's origin and there is no doubt at all as to the method by which he arrived. I think that really the only matter in issue here will be the intent with which he arrived. You will probably find it put forward in this case (the classic and usual defence) that he did not intend to spy. That is a defence which is open to any spy arriving in this country. Owing to the particular circumstances of this war, it is very easy for a spy arriving here to say 'It is quite true, I have come but all I was trying to do was to escape from the oppression of the Nazi Government, of which I disapprove.' No doubt you will find that defence put forward here. That will be the issue this court will have to try. It is whether this man arrived here intending to send back messages, as he was required to do, and to give assistance to the enemy or whether he arrived here as a fugitive endeavouring to escape from a Government of which he disapproved. I merely outline that defence at the moment as I apprehend (it being more or less common form) that it will be put forward here. That is really the matter with which this court will be concerned. I doubt whether the facts will be in dispute. If they were, I submit the prosecution would make it abundantly clear that this accused undoubtedly arrived in the manner which the prosecution submit and had it not been for the injury which he received on landing, one has no doubt he would have continued to carry out the duties which he was sent here to carry out. [*That is an assumption that ascribes intent to Josef.*] Those are the short facts of this case and I propose to call the evidence immediately. I will begin by calling Mr Baldock.[3] [*It is not clear from the transcript when, how, or even if, the interpreter translated Marlowe's opening statement to Josef.*]

Charles Baldock was called into the room, took his place near the front of the room and was duly sworn by Stirling, 'I swear by Almighty God that the evidence which I shall give before this Court shall be the truth, the whole truth, and nothing but the truth.'[4]

Marlowe began his examination of Baldock by asking a series of questions to which the farmer answered yes or no or gave short answers. The questions were based on Baldock's witness statement and were designed to prevent the witness from digressing or, worse, saying that he could not remember. For example, Marlowe did not ask, 'What is your name?' but rather, 'Is your name Charles Baldock?' He did not ask, 'What were you doing on the morning of 1 February 1941?', rather, he asked, 'Do you remember 1 February of this year?', to which Baldock simply replied, 'Yes'. Marlowe then asked, 'At about twenty past eight in the morning you were walking across Dove House [*sic*] Farm?' Such questions were technically leading questions and were not allowed during testimony except when they were used to establish facts that were not in dispute, or when questioning a hostile witness. Through this back and forth exchange, Marlowe extracted from Baldock the story of Josef's discovery.[5]

Marlowe established that Baldock had helped gather up some of the articles that were lying on the ground around Josef, including the pistol (Exhibit 2) and the box of ammunition (Exhibit 3). At this point, Stirling asked White, 'If you want to see any of these [exhibits], Captain White, will you ask?'[6] White replied in the affirmative. [*Had White not yet seen the evidence/exhibits prior to the court martial?*]

Baldock then identified the steel helmet (Exhibit 4) and the parachute (Exhibit 5) as Marlowe asked Baldock how Josef had arrived. 'He told you he had in fact come down in a parachute?' At this point, White intervened to say, 'May we have what the witness says?' [*An interesting interjection, given that Marlowe had been using leading questions up until that point.*] Marlowe rephrased the question. 'What did he in fact say to you?'

'He was solo flying.'

'And he told you how he had come down?'

'Yes.'

'How did he say he had come down?'

'With his parachute.'

At one point, Marlowe asked Baldock, 'Did you, while you were there, see a number of pieces of torn cardboard lying about?'

'Not until Captain Newton came.' [*A natural question upon cross-examination would have been, 'Why did you not see them before Newton arrived?' Were the pieces not noticeable? Trampled into the soil?*]

Baldock helped gather up the torn pieces of cardboard and identified them as Exhibit 13. Finally, Baldock identified Exhibit 6 as the wireless case that had been partially buried in the ground.

White cross-examined Baldock and asked if it was obvious, from a walking perspective, that Josef was helpless, and Baldock acknowledged that he had been in a great deal of pain. White then asked where the torn pieces of cardboard were lying and Baldock said they were lying all around Josef. [*White did not ask why Baldock had not noticed them initially.*] White asked if it was easy to converse with Josef, but Baldock said that the man didn't say much as he didn't speak fluent English. Much of the conversation was by dumb show and pointing. Baldock said, 'Alone?', to the man, who said, 'Yes', and then, 'solo flying'. Baldock asked the man where his aeroplane was, and the man pointed to the parachute.

Marlowe re-examined Baldock and asked if the accused made it plain to Baldock that he had come down by the parachute, and Baldock said, 'Yes.' Stirling interjected and asked about the weather on the morning of Josef's capture and Baldock said it had been very drizzly. According to Baldock, the ground surface showed no evidence that Josef had moved very far. It was obvious that he had landed, rolled over and lain there, not 12ft from his point of impact. The president then asked if Josef was in considerable pain, and Baldock said, 'Yes, and very cold'. The president asked if the man was incapable of movement and Baldock answered in the affirmative.

At the end of his testimony, the president warned Baldock to 'keep your mouth shut'[7] about the court martial. Baldock acknowledged the warning and was excused from the court.

Harry Coulson was called to the stand and, after being sworn in, was interviewed by Marlowe in a similar manner.[8] After a few factual questions, Marlowe made an aside to White, in which he asked, 'You do not mind my leading about these matters, do you?'

To which White replied, 'Not a bit.' [*Coulson may have been extremely nervous, or Marlowe may have been asking White's permission to use leading questions.*]

Marlowe drew out the story of how Coulson had helped to discover Josef but ran into a stumbling block. Marlowe asked Coulson, 'Did you hear the man say anything while you were there?'

'No.'

'Nothing at all?'

'No.'

This did not tally with Coulson's witness statement, nor did it corroborate Baldock's statement. Two witness testimonies differed and there was little that Marlowe could do. [*In his 1 February 1941 witness statement, Coulson said that he heard Josef say, 'Help, leg'. In his statement at the Summary of Evidence on 28 July, Coulson only heard Josef say, 'Leg'. Several days later, at the court martial, Coulson said he heard Josef say nothing.*]

Coulson identified several of the exhibits (parachute, steel helmet, attaché case, flying suit) as being similar to the ones found on Josef. Coulson said that he couldn't see what the man had on under his flying suit, testimony that again differed from that of Baldock, who stated that Josef was wearing civilian clothes underneath his flying suit.

Coulson was cross-examined by White and was asked if he had heard the man say anything at any point, even after Godfrey joined them, to which Coulson again replied, 'No.' [*This is perplexing as Godfrey and Newton asked Josef several questions to which Josef responded.*] The president admonished Coulson to say nothing about the trial and he was excused from the court.

James Harry Godfrey, farmer and Home Guard volunteer, was then called into the room and, after being duly sworn in, examined by Marlowe.[9] The court heard how Godfrey, after being notified by Coulson of the parachutist in the field, had telephoned the Ramsey Police. Godfrey identified some of the exhibits, including the wallet, money and road map. The president of the court asked to see the map and was told that Ramsey was about 11 miles north of Huntingdon and just 2 miles from Upwood. [*As we shall see during Mills' testimony, this is likely the moment when the president marked the map and underlined the word 'Ramsey'.*]

White cross-examined Godfrey, who admitted that he did not understand much of what Josef had said, only making out the occasional word. The words that Godfrey said that the man spoke were the only words that he could understand out of everything that Josef said. In effect, Josef said that he was a Frenchman from Luxembourg who had been made to come and, after flying alone, had come out at 300 metres [*sic*].[10] Godfrey had searched the man upon Newton's orders and noticed that Josef's flying suit was open. [*In which case, Coulson should have seen the civilian clothes beneath the flying suit. Compared to the other witnesses, Coulson was either less observant or had a poor memory.*] Although they did not remove the flying suit, Godfrey noticed that Josef was wearing a grey overcoat and a grey civilian suit. He was wearing a trilby hat and low boots [*sic*] with grey spats.

At that point, Stirling asked Godfrey, 'Did you see any signs of any uniform of any shape or form?', to which the answer was, 'No'.[11] Stirling also asked the distance to the nearest hedge (a distance of 150–200 yards), presumably to ascertain if Josef could have hidden any equipment before being found. A member of the court interjected and asked Godfrey if he had seen the steel helmet and Godfrey confirmed that he had.

'That is the only uniform you saw?'

Godfrey admitted, 'That is the only uniform I saw, the steel helmet.'[12] [*Godfrey contradicted himself. It required a member of the court to point out that the helmet was a uniform. No one at Josef's court martial suggested that the flying suit was a uniform, although Karel Richter's lawyer later tried to argue that point.*]

The members of the court wanted to see the trilby hat and the other clothes that Josef had been wearing but were told that they had been a terrible mess. The members of the court were perplexed as to how Josef could have landed by parachute wearing a trilby hat, but the president thought that he might have had it in his pocket and put it on as soon as he landed. There was a discussion about the hat and how it could be corroborated by other witnesses. [*The members of the court weren't as concerned about addressing the discrepancy between the testimony of Baldock and Coulson regarding the words spoken by Josef.*]

One member asked where Josef had broken his leg, but the question was not answered and there was more discussion on the veracity of Harry Godfrey. [*One gets the impression that people were talking on top of each other and that the stenographer could not keep pace.*] Josef spoke in German to the interpreter, who tried to interject, but was told that he could not speak. White was instructed to keep Josef and the interpreter quiet. At this point, Stirling asked Godfrey if the man's leg was broken and Godfrey confirmed that it was broken right through. Godfrey was reminded of the need for absolute secrecy and was excused from the court.

William Henry Newton, Captain of the Ramsey Home Guard, was called and sworn in by Marlowe.[13] Newton was able to corroborate that Josef had indeed been wearing a blue trilby hat. He also confirmed that a steel helmet had been found near Josef but he saw no other evidence of a uniform. Newton told the court that Josef had said he was a Frenchman from Luxembourg.

Newton had asked Godfrey to search the man and they found a wad of pound notes as well as a leather wallet. [*Marlowe refers to the wallet as Exhibit 5, but it was Exhibit 8 (the parachute was Exhibit 5). This may be a transcription error.*] At this point, Stirling interjected to say, 'I think the accused is rather worried on that point.' [*What did Stirling see on Josef's face? This may be the moment when Newton, or the president, upon handling the wallet, pulled a small notebook from within it. This will be discussed in detail during Josef's testimony.*]

Stirling asked Marlowe, 'Would you ask [Newton] where the money was found?'

Newton said the money was distributed about the man and that he collected two or three thick wads of notes from various pockets. There were banknotes in the note case and in the wallet, along with a blank ration book, a blank identity card and a completed identity card. [*This contradicts Newton's earlier witness statements (2 February and 28 July) as well as Jaikens' statement (2 February) in which the wallet contained no money, only two identity cards, a ration book and a postcard.*]

The president examined the completed identity card and remarked to Marlowe, 'Here is what you referred to, placing the town first. They always do that in Germany.' [*It is strange that neither the president, nor White remarked on the obvious registration number error. Perhaps they thought that the other spies had also had such obviously erroneous registration numbers.*]

White cross-examined Newton and asked if it was hard to understand Josef, and Newton acknowledged that while Josef said little, his English was poor, and it was obvious that he was a foreigner. Newton admitted that he spoke some French but, 'It did not occur to me to try him in French because I was quite satisfied in my own mind …' [*… that he was German?*]

Newton was abruptly cut off by White and told to just answer the question. At this point, Newton became reticent in answering White's questions. When asked if he was satisfied that the man could not have moved if he had wanted to – that it was impossible – Newton said that he 'would not go so far as to say that'. He was asked, 'Could he have walked?' to which he replied, 'Could he have walked?'

Asked if the man could have crawled, Newton responded with, 'That I could not say.' He eventually admitted that there was no evidence the man had tried to crawl. White asked Newton if at any point they had asked the man how he had got the attaché case down, but that question was never posed to the parachutist.

The president asked Newton if the man could understand English well, to which Newton replied, 'No'. The man spoke some words in very broken English, but Newton could not say if the man was simulating that. The president then asked, 'Anyhow, if he was simulating broken English, it was very well done?' to which Newton replied, 'Unquestionably'.

The president then asked White if he thought that Josef understood what had been happening. White acknowledged that it was doubtful whether Josef had followed it all, but he did not think it was necessary to stop and have it translated, as there did not seem to be any point that needed to be put to him.[14] The president suggested that after Newton's testimony, they should ask Josef if he needed clarity around any points.

White suggested that they might put the question to him immediately and the interpreter asked Josef if he had understood the witnesses and whether he wanted to ask them any questions. Josef, through the interpreter, said he did not understand what had happened between Stirling and Godfrey but there were no questions he wished to put to Newton. White asked if Josef was prepared to leave it to White to advise him on when he should put a question, and Josef, through the interpreter, said, 'Yes'. [*It would appear that the court, and White, did not consider it important or necessary for Josef to understand the evidence and proceedings of his own court martial despite Stirling's earlier admonition.*]

Newton was then advised to 'keep your mouth shut' and excused from the court.[15]

Ernest Pottle, acting police sergeant, was called and sworn in by Marlowe.[16] The court heard from Pottle that he had found a small hand spade in the field, along with more pieces of torn cardboard. Pottle was cross-examined by White, who asked him if the country in which the man was found was flat and remote from towns, to which Pottle agreed. It was a quiet part of the country, remote from industry [*apart from the nearby aerodromes*]. Stirling asked Pottle if he had examined the man's injury, to which Pottle replied, 'No.' Pottle saw the accused at the police station at about 10.30 a.m., and the man was lying on a stretcher dressed in a flying suit. Pottle said the man was wearing an ordinary lounge suit under the flying suit complete with collar and tie, a soft hat and spats. [*Another witness to corroborate the trilby hat.*] Pottle was told to 'keep your mouth shut' and excused from the court.

Thomas Oliver Mills, detective sergeant of the Huntingdonshire Constabulary, was called and sworn in by Marlowe.[17] Mills was shown the map and asked if the pencil marks on it were there when he first saw the map, to which Mills replied, 'Yes'. Stirling then spoke up and said that the president of the court martial, Major General Wilson, had made a mark under 'Ramsey' when he examined the map during Godfrey's testimony. The president denied that he had marked the map in any way and insisted that the line under Ramsey was already there. Mills disagreed and said that the mark under Ramsey was not there on 1 February. The president grudgingly admitted that he had underlined the word 'Ramsey'. [*The president tampered with a key piece of evidence. The line under the word 'Ramsey' is still present on the map archived within TNA: KV 2/27.*] After this clarification, Mills said that the triangle on the map marked the area within which the accused landed, or very near to it.[18] The cross was located near a large military RAF aerodrome. [*The cross was about 4 miles west of RAF Upwood along a railway line.*] The small circle marked the location of a satellite RAF aerodrome. [*The satellite aerodrome was RAF Warboys, although this could be coincidental. The circle was located on the edge of the triangle.*]

White, the defence lawyer, cross-examined Mills and asked him about his conversation with Josef at the police station. Mills said that the conversation was difficult owing to the fact that Josef spoke broken English. Josef had told him that he was a Luxembourger, but Mills thought that he was a German spy. Mills admitted that Inspector Jaikens had spoken with Josef in German. White asked if Jaikens was another police officer and Mills said, 'Yes, but not concerned with this case'. [*This is perplexing. Jaikens handled the initial phone call from Godfrey, despatched Newton to Dovehouse Farm and received the prisoner when he arrived at the police station. He spoke at least some German and likely had the most coherent conversation with Josef, in Ramsey. He also interviewed key witnesses and submitted a report on Josef's capture. Why was Jaikens not called as a witness?*]

Mills said that Josef's understanding of English fluctuated, which made Mills think that he was putting it on. [*It was just his impression, and yet White did not challenge that.*] Stirling suggested that they ask Josef whether he had understood the witness and if he had any questions. Josef said that he understood it as it appeared in the summary (of evidence) and he did not wish to ask any questions. [*Did Josef receive a German translation of the Summary of Evidence?*] Mills was advised to 'keep your mouth shut' and excused from the court.

John Hayes Marriott, civil assistant attached to the General Staff at the War Office, was called and sworn in by Marlowe.[19] Marriott stated that he was present at Cannon Row Police Station with Robertson when Josef arrived on 1 February. Marriott took possession of the articles found on Josef [*he confirmed that the wallet contained the two identity cards and the ration book*] and handed those over to Hinchley-Cooke. [*Not entirely accurate. The torn-up code fragments, for example, went from Butler to Stephens, back to Robertson and then on to Cowgill (MI6) for reconstruction. As well, Marriott technically handed the items to Richard Butler of SLB, not to Hinchley-Cooke personally. Some of the items were subsequently sent to Latchmere House, the Registrar General, MI6, the Post Office Engineering Department, the National Institute for Medical Research and the RSLO in Reading. In the process, Butler would lose the Catholic badge.*]

White cross-examined Marriott and asked him if he had looked at the items more closely. For example, did he try to investigate the person named on the identity card, James Rymer? Marriott said he did not, as that was not part of his duty.[20] White's next question was a pivotal moment in Josef's court martial. Had Josef had a better defence lawyer, it is possible that he might have escaped with his life:

[White] Were you present at his interrogation on Sunday, 2nd February? [*This was the two-hour interrogation conducted by Stephens at Latchmere House. It was at this interrogation that Josef was told that if he did not co-operate, his family would be liquidated. He agreed to work for MI5 and shared his emergency code.*]

[Marriott] No.

[White] Have you seen a transcript of that interrogation?

[Marriott] I have seen it, yes.

[White] I do not know whether I am going to be able to put this to any other witness, so I feel that I must put it to you. It may be that Lieutenant Colonel Hinchley-Cooke has seen the transcript and it will be more convenient to put it to him.

[Marlowe] I do not know which transcript it is.

[White] I am talking about the interrogation on 2 February.

[Marlowe] You do not mean the interrogation by Lieutenant Colonel Hinchley-Cooke?

[White] No.

[President] This has been brought forward for the first time; it has not been brought forward before about the transcript on 2nd February.

[Marlowe] No.

[Stirling] I do not see how you can put it to this witness if he was not there.

[White] It may be important, but the accused is going to make a number of statements about what he said on that day and I do not want it to be raised against him that those statements have not been put to the witnesses who can deal with them.

[Stirling] As far as I can see no witness has been called to whom you could have put it.

[White] So far, no.

[President] He [Marriott] was not there on 2 February, was he?

[White] No. Then I shall not put it.[21] [*White could have called Latchmere House officers as witnesses and/or requested that a transcript of the interrogation be entered into evidence.*]

There then followed a perplexing exchange between Stirling and Marriott:

[Stirling] Then where was [Jakobs] – still with the police authorities at New Scotland Yard [on 1 February]? Perhaps you do not know.

[Marriott] I do not think I am in a position to say. [*This was a dangerous moment. Marriott, as Robertson's right-hand man, knew that Josef had been interrogated at Latchmere House. Had he admitted what he knew, the door would have opened for White to question him further on Latchmere House.*]

[Stirling] I will not ask you if you do not know. [*Marriott did know; he just didn't want to say.*] Had the accused got an opportunity, as far as you know, about six o'clock when he came to New Scotland Yard [on 1 February] of getting somebody who could speak German and having an opportunity to make any sort of statement he liked voluntarily? [*Stirling was aware of the voluntary statement to Robertson. His purpose in bringing it up here is unclear as it had not been included in the Summary of Evidence nor entered as evidence on the list of exhibits. It may be that Stirling recognised that Josef had been interrogated prior to giving his statement to Hinchley-Cooke in June. Stirling may have been trying to establish that there was another statement taken under caution before Josef was interrogated.*]

[Marriott] Not in German.

[Stirling] He had no opportunity to do that?

[Marriott] He had not got a fluent German-speaking interpreter.

[Stirling] Did he ask where an interpreter might be obtained as he wanted to make a statement of his own?

[Marriott] No. He spoke in English.

[Stirling] You are not following me. So far as you are concerned, have you any recollection of the accused asking for facilities to make a statement about himself on that night?

[Marriott] No.

[Stirling] I am not on questions that were asked him, but whether he took any action to say, 'I want to tell you something' and whether he might be allowed to do so.

[Marriott] No.

[Stirling] So far as you know he did not do that?

[Marriott] No.[22] [*Marriott was either confused or not recalling the past accurately.*]

One can understand Stirling's frustration; it was clear from Robertson's report that Josef had asked to make a voluntary statement and one of the police officers, who spoke German, translated Josef's words into English. At this point in the court martial Josef, through his interpreter, interrupted the proceedings to say that he had never seen Marriott before, neither at the police station on 1 February nor at Latchmere House on 2 February:

[White to Marriott] The accused suggests you were not there on 1 February, on the Saturday?

[Marriott] At New Scotland Yard?

[White] Yes.

[Marriott] I was.

[White] Were you the only other person apart from Major Robertson?

[Marriott] From my department, yes.

[Stirling] Did you see the accused?

[Marriott] Yes.

[White] How many persons were there in the interrogation?

[Marriott] Major Robertson, myself and I think two police officers [Sergeant Grey and Constable Templeman].

[White] Did you sit in a place where he could see you or not?

[Marriott] Certainly.

[White] Do you agree there was an interpreter there on 1 February?

[Marriott] There was a police officer [Constable Templeman] who spoke German. What I said was that he did not speak German fluently.

[White] He did the interpretation?

[Marriott] Yes.

Stirling seized his moment:

[Stirling] May I try and get this quite clear? At this interrogation was there some individual who spoke German?

[Marriott] Yes.

[Stirling] You did not think it was very fluent; is that right?

[Marriott] Yes.

[Stirling] But could he carry on a reasonable conversation with the accused, as far as you could see, in German?

[Marriott] Yes. [*But Constable Templeman was not fluent and there is no evidence that he was a certified translator. Hinchley-Cooke, on the other hand, was 'Qualified as 1st Class Interpreter in a Modern Foreign Language'.*][23]

[Stirling] Who was that person? Was he a police officer?

[Marriott] He was a police officer [Constable Templeman].

[Stirling] Did the accused have an opportunity, through that German-speaking officer, of telling Major Robertson anything he liked that he wanted to volunteer?

[Marriott] Yes.

[Stirling] Did he volunteer about who he was or anything of that kind?

[Marriott] Yes.[24]

Stirling finally extracted the truth from Marriott. Josef had given a voluntary statement to Robertson on the evening of 1 February but the interpreter, Constable Templeman, did not speak fluent German. Given that the first statement to the police was of critical importance to the prosecution, one could wonder if a statement taken by an unqualified interpreter would have stood up in court.

With a sigh of relief, the court bid farewell to the confused Marriott who, although he already worked in a secret job, was still warned to say nothing about the court martial.

Leonard William Humphreys, an inspector in the Radio Branch (Post Office Engineering Department), was called, duly sworn and examined by Marlowe.[25] Humphreys said that Josef's wireless set was in perfect working order, capable of sending and receiving signals to and from the continent. White had no questions for Humphreys, but Stirling and the president asked for details on the wireless set. According to Humphreys, the set was of German construction and could stand a lot of 'knocking about'. While he couldn't say if it had ever been used, it was in working condition and used longlife batteries, replacements for which could be purchased in England. Humphreys was sworn to secrecy and excused from the court. The court adjourned for lunch from 12.55 p.m. to 2 p.m.[26]

After the court reconvened, Stirling asked White if he was planning on calling any witnesses for the defence, as the court needed to arrange for witnesses, and that might be difficult at short notice.[27] White said that the accused would tell the same story as he had in his interrogation (on 2 February), and, 'For my own part I am content to leave it at that.'

Stirling pressed further and said, 'The point that troubles me is that if Jakobs wants it we may not be able to get the witnesses at short notice.'

White replied, 'I do not think Jakobs wants it.'[28] [*But, in his appeal to His Majesty the King, Josef requested a postponement of his sentence until the end of the war so that he might have access to German witnesses and documents that were not available to him because of the war. Did White speak for Josef or was he speaking for himself? Josef could have called Lily Knips as a witness.*]

And there it lay. Josef was going to base his testimony on his 2 February statement to the officers at Latchmere House, but none of those officers would be called as witnesses to corroborate his story. White had attempted to cross-examine Marriott about the 2 February statement, but Marriott had not been present at that interrogation. White had been given the chance to call witnesses and turned down the opportunity to request the presence of Latchmere House officers. As we shall learn from other spy trials, had he pursued that course, Josef's court martial might have ended before it even began.

The next witness, Lieutenant Colonel W.E. Hinchley-Cooke, was called, duly sworn in and examined by Marlowe.[29] Hinchley-Cooke was on the General Staff at the War Office, a delicate way of saying that he worked for the British Security Service (MI5). On 1 February he had received the exhibits from Marriott. [*Technically, Butler received the exhibits from Marriott, not Hinchley-Cooke.*]

According to Hinchley-Cooke, the pistol and ammunition were both of German manufacture and in working order. The parachute, parachute harness and steel helmet were also of German manufacture and the helmet was a special one for parachutists. The ration book was a 'forgery throughout', as were the two identity cards. When asked how he knew the documents were forgeries, Hinchley-Cooke said that he would rather not say since the accused might not be convicted, in which case the information might get back to the Germans. [*This was probably a reference to the doctored identity papers BISCUIT had handed over to Ritter in Lisbon. Genuine cards were hand-folded, whereas the forged cards were machine-folded. MI5 had also sent over false registration numbers via SNOW.*] Hinchley-Cooke concluded by stating that he had twenty years of experience in 'these matters' and, 'I submit my evidence is taken without explanation.' [*Even though Hinchley-Cooke was testifying as an 'expert witness', he was a witness for the prosecution and it is difficult to understand how he could be immune from cross-examination or challenge.*]

Hinchley-Cooke reconstructed the torn pieces of cardboard into two discs, which had been photocopied 'in my presence'.[30] [*This is not accurate. The experts at the Government Code & Cipher School reassembled the torn fragments of the disc code and sent the results back to Robertson.*] Hinchley-Cooke referenced the two photocopies of the reconstructed discs (Exhibit 16) and admitted that some pieces could not be accommodated because the cardboard had been torn sideways and some fragments were dirty. Hinchley-Cooke had several similar disc codes in his possession and explained how the smaller disc revolved on top of the larger one to create a simple transposition code. The agent would write out the message on graph or ruled paper and then encode it with the aid of the two discs. [*Such a code was easily broken and the same was said of Josef's emergency code words, Winterhilfswerk and Marinesoldat. They were not valuable because they were simple transposition codes. The prosecution would argue that the cardboard disc code was much more valuable than the code words, even though the disc code was, by Hinchley-Cooke's own admission, a simple transposition code.*]

On 18 June 1941, Josef made a statement to Hinchley-Cooke, which was taken down in shorthand and then transcribed. Hinchley-Cooke cautioned Josef near the beginning of the questioning and never threatened or induced him to make the statement. [*Perhaps not, but Josef had, for months, been threatened by the officers at Latchmere House.*] Hinchley-Cooke produced the statement and it was marked Exhibit 17. Hinchley-Cooke said that he spoke German and acted as his own interpreter during the questioning.[31]

He asked Josef a question both in German and English. A police officer wrote down the question in English, and when Josef replied in German, Hinchley-Cooke would translate his response into English, which was also taken down by the police officer. Josef made the statement voluntarily and signed each page, the three alterations and the end of the document. Finally, Hinchley-Cooke had another German-speaking police officer check the translation. [*This was a more professional statement than the one taken by Robertson on 1 February, when there was only one German-speaking police officer, Constable Templeman, who was not fluent in German.*]

Marlowe then read the 18 June statement out loud.

According to Hinchley-Cooke, the exhibits in the courtroom comprised the usual equipment brought by German spies and Marlowe asked him about their instructions. White objected to this question on the grounds that instructions given to other agents would be hearsay for Hinchley-Cooke and had nothing to do with the accused and should therefore not be used as evidence against him. Stirling and the president agreed and told Marlowe that he should focus on the accused and leave out references to the usual practice.

Hinchley-Cooke was cross-examined by White, who began by asking about enemies of the Nazis in Germany. While Hinchley-Cooke acknowledged that there were enemies of the Nazi regime in Germany, he was not in a position to say how many, although he did admit that most were in concentration camps. Although Hinchley-Cooke had not been to Germany for some time, he was aware of conditions in the concentration camps and acknowledged that they were not designed to make the prisoners love the Nazis. Hinchley-Cooke had heard that neither Jews nor Catholics were fond of the Nazis and acknowledged that the accused had told him that he was a Catholic and had even asked to see a Roman Catholic priest.

When asked if he knew that the accused was of Jewish origin, Hinchley-Cooke said, 'No'. White said that the name 'Jakobs' was, of course, Jewish, but Hinchley-Cooke said, 'Not necessarily'. He said that while some

Jakobs were Jews, he had met others who were Christians. White said that although Josef's parents were Christian his grandfather was a Jew. [*During his interrogation at Latchmere House on 2 February, Josef stated that he was not a Jew. Research has shown that Josef's maternal and paternal lineages were Catholic well into the 1600s.*] White asked if the fact that the accused's grandfather was a Jew would make him non-Aryan in the eyes of the Nazis, but Hinchley-Cooke said not necessarily, otherwise Josef would not have received an officer's commission in the Great War. When pressed, Hinchley-Cooke acknowledged that it could have happened, but that it would have been unusual, as even during the Great War, the Germans were very strict with Jews. [*German Jews could become officers of the reserve army, but not the regular army.*][32]

Hinchley-Cooke admitted that there were anti-Nazi movements in existence, some of which did not originate in Germany. He felt that the questions were 'getting into very dangerous water'[33] and White then focused on the *Zentrale* (the anti-Nazi organisation to which Josef claimed to belong). Hinchley-Cooke had never heard of the *Zentrale* but acknowledged that he would hope there were organisations in Germany whose purpose it was to oppose the Nazis. He admitted that getting out of Germany required courage and ingenuity and that joining the German Intelligence Service was certainly one way to do it. Hinchley-Cooke had interrogated some of the agents who had come over and said that the Germans were 'not very particular' about their secret agents.[34] He agreed that it was a dangerous job and probably hard to get volunteers. While many had said that they were pressed or coerced, Hinchley-Cooke believed that they were all volunteers. [*He had just admitted that it would be hard to get volunteer spies and yet stated that all of the spies were volunteers.*]

Hinchley-Cooke had not heard that some people were released from prison in order to come on such errands [*Richter claimed to have been released from a concentration camp to join the German Intelligence Service*], but it would not surprise him that a non-Aryan would be sent on such a mission. Hinchley-Cooke admitted that if the Nazis had Josef's family in Berlin, they had something tangible in the way of hostages to make sure that he behaved himself while he was on his mission.

When asked about how Josef broke his leg, Hinchley-Cooke acknowledged that he could have broken it exiting the aeroplane. White suggested that Josef was not a very useful agent, given his poor language skills, but Hinchley-Cooke said there were 30,000 German refugees living in England. Some of them spoke very bad English and once Josef got away from Ramsey, he would not have drawn undue attention. Hinchley-Cooke said that he and Josef spoke primarily in German, as it was easier. It was obvious, when Josef spoke English, that he was a foreigner. Josef had told Hinchley-Cooke that he had never been to England before and Hinchley-Cooke had no reason to doubt that statement.

White asked if a spy who landed in England was liable to be manhandled by the farm labourers who first met him, and Hinchley-Cooke said, 'Yes, unless he has already buried his parachute and hidden his gear'. Hinchley-Cooke said the spy would be fine if he approached a farm labourer with his hands in the air and said he wanted to give himself up to the police. [*Although Grace, one of the loose-lipped letter writers, said, 'If they came down near us when George was home I'm sure he would shoot them on the way down.'*[35]]

White asked if the wireless set and code would be useful to British intelligence services and Hinchley-Cooke said, 'Yes'. Hinchley-Cooke said the best thing would be to hand them over and to tell people to look after them as they were valuable. [*Unless one couldn't speak English very well and had trouble making oneself clear.*] White asked if it would be wise for a German to hand them to a 'peasant' as opposed to an officer, but Hinchley-Cooke said it would make little difference.

Since the interrogation on 1 February, White asked if the accused had shown any indication of subterfuge, any attempt to conceal information, and Hinchley-Cooke said, 'Not to my knowledge'. The only inconsistency in his story was that he told one officer that he broke his leg on landing, whereas he told Hinchley-Cooke that he broke it while exiting the aeroplane. [*There were other inconsistencies in his story, e.g. his recruitment into the Abwehr.*] Hinchley-Cooke said that he 'had nothing whatever to do with the other interrogation'[36] and he had only glanced at the other interrogation statements as they were not made under caution and therefore were inadmissible as evidence. [*He is probably referring to the Latchmere House statements. The statement to Robertson on 1 February at Cannon Row Police Station was made under caution.*]

White then asked him a series of questions about another agent (Richter) that Josef had described, and about the verbal code words, but Hinchley-Cooke professed no knowledge of any of those matters. [*In essence, White was asking about the emergency code words that Josef had revealed during the 2 February interrogation. He was also bringing forward the way in which Josef had helped to break Richter. This was the point where White needed to ask, 'Well, who does have knowledge of these matters?' White, however, did not pursue this line of questioning to its logical conclusion nor did he request the presence of Latchmere House officers as witnesses. Given Hinchley-Cooke's role as an 'expert witness' who had had 'the conduct of the proceedings from the start', he managed to sidestep many questions by professing to have no knowledge of certain matters.*]

White asked if someone else, in the guise of the accused, could get in touch with the Germans via wireless, but Hinchley-Cooke said that wireless telegraphy and signals were more difficult to fake than handwriting and an experienced wireless operator would recognise the substitution at once. Hinchley-Cooke said the agents were trained with a specific wireless operator who would receive their messages and recognise them at once.[37] White asked if the accused were to co-operate with England, whether or not he might be of considerable assistance and Hinchley-Cooke said, 'Yes, if he genuinely co-operated.' White suggested that if he were to co-operate, when he ran out of money, and his German superiors told him to go somewhere and meet someone, he could then uncover some enemy agents. Hinchley-Cooke agreed that this was possible. White asked if the accused had been living in a special interrogation camp and Hinchley-Cooke acknowledged that such was the case. Stirling then picked up the same line of questioning:

[Stirling] As far as I understand it, presumably you saw him for the first time in June. Is that it?

[Hinchley-Cooke] I did.

[Stirling] But between February and June other people must have seen him?

[Hinchley-Cooke] Oh, yes.

[Stirling] What I wanted to get at and I am not going into it in any way deeply is: Has this man had an opportunity between 1 February and now of saying exactly what his own version of his coming here was?

[Hinchley-Cooke] Undoubtedly.

[Stirling] Are you in a [position] to tell us to whom he would have made a statement which is his version for coming here, or whether he has, or has not?

[Hinchley-Cooke] I do know that he has made statements to a number of officers in that interrogation centre.

[Stirling] All you are dealing with are your interrogations which you yourself administered to him?

[Hinchley-Cooke] Yes.[38]

[*This might have been the moment where White could have asked whether Josef had been offered inducements, threats or promises at the interrogation centre. Hinchley-Cooke would likely have stated that he had no knowledge of the matter, but it would have, again, given White a chance to ask who did have knowledge of such matters.*]

Marlowe re-examined Hinchley-Cooke and asked him if he believed that the accused's name was Jakobs. Hinchley-Cooke admitted that he had seen no identity papers to confirm that name. As a possible non-Aryan, Josef might be trusted by the Nazis on secret and confidential work, or not – it was a difficult question to answer. [*Josef was sent by the Abwehr, not by the Nazis.*] Hinchley-Cooke acknowledged that he had not tried the accused with French [*Why not?*], and that he had no way of confirming whether the accused was working for the German Intelligence Service or whether he had been born in Luxembourg.

Hinchley-Cooke admitted that a person by the name of James Rymer did exist and this information was known to the German authorities. More than that, Hinchley-Cooke did not want to say, claiming 'privilege', saying it was 'rather a delicate matter' that brought 'other things into operation'.[39]

White spoke up in the face of Hinchley-Cooke's reticence, 'I do not know whether the silence of this witness on that point is going to be taken to the injury of the accused.' Stirling waved off his concerns, saying it would not affect Josef's case. [*In many ways, White was fighting an uphill battle. He couldn't ask things about which he did not know. When he actually did question things that strayed too close to 'dangerous waters' or 'delicate matters', Hinchley-Cooke could retreat into silence as the 'expert witness' or profess no knowledge of the matter being discussed.*]

White cross-examined the witness again and asked about the woman (Lily Knips) who claimed to know the accused and whether she knew him as Jakobs. Hinchley-Cooke said she did know him as Jakobs, but this was not proof that it was his real name, rather than his nom de plume.

[*Here was another opportunity to call a witness for the defence, and yet White did not try to call Lily Knips. Perhaps this was the only defence witness he and Josef had considered, and Josef did not want to drag her into the mess. Hinchley-Cooke clearly knew about the results of Lily Knips' interrogation.*]

Hinchley-Cooke withdrew, and the prosecution's case was closed.[40]

In summary, Hinchley-Cooke's testimony was key to the prosecution's case and White did a less than stellar job in his cross-examination. Hinchley-Cooke said that he took a statement from Josef on 18 June. He cautioned Josef and never threatened or induced him to make the statement. Clearly, a threat or an inducement would have invalidated the statement. White knew that Josef had been held in a secret interrogation camp and, had he been an adequate defence lawyer, he would have known that Josef's family was threatened during the interrogation on 2 February. Once that threat was made, it hung over Josef's head and would forever colour all subsequent statements. That threat, made by Stephens, would have effectively negated any future statements from Josef, including the one made to Hinchley-Cooke.

White asked Hinchley-Cooke questions about Richter and the code words that Josef had given the interrogators. Hinchley-Cooke professed no knowledge of either topic. A competent defence lawyer would have asked, 'Who did have knowledge of such matters?' and would have called that person as a witness. Again, we are back to the summoning of Latchmere House officers as witnesses.

White had tried to ask Marriott about the 2 February interrogation, but Marriott had not been there and could not answer the questions. White had said that he would hold his questions on that particular interrogation for Hinchley-Cooke. When Hinchley-Cooke was on the stand, he stated that he had no knowledge of the 2 February interrogation and yet he knew the content of Lily's interrogation (that she knew Josef as 'Josef Jakobs'). This calls into question Hinchley-Cooke's assertion that he had no knowledge of some of the other interrogations and/or statements made by Josef during his time at Latchmere House.

36

CASE FOR THE DEFENCE

Stirling, through the interpreter, explained Josef's rights to him. Josef could, if he chose, give evidence under oath. If he did, then he would be questioned to see if he was speaking the truth. Josef replied that he wished to testify under oath. White confirmed again that he would not be calling any other witnesses. [*What would have happened if Josef had requested the presence of his Abwehr handlers from Germany? Would the proceedings have been suspended until such time as the witnesses could attend?*]

Josef took the stand and was duly sworn in by Stirling. White began to question Josef in English but quickly needed to use the interpreter, from which the following facts emerged.[1]

His name was Josef Jakobs, a 43-year-old dentist living in Berlin with his wife and three children: a 13-year-old boy, a 10-year-old girl and a 9-year-old boy.[2] Josef stated that he was not a member of the Nazi Party and, according to the Nuremberg Laws, would be considered a non-Aryan because his grandfather was a Jew. [*This is not accurate. Josef's paternal and maternal lines are Catholic well into the 1600s. In addition, having only one Jewish grandparent meant that one was considered a* Mischling, *not a Jew.*]

Josef went on to tell the story of how he had been imprisoned in Switzerland for gold forgery and had been put into a concentration camp in Germany for doing business with Jews (passports). Josef described how he had been tortured at the concentration camp and then described the Nazi treatment of himself and his family. He said that he sacrificed himself for his children. Every week, Josef had to report to the Gestapo. He could not speak freely in his own house and in front of his children, because they, in their innocence, might repeat something at school. Josef would have been arrested and sent back to the concentration camp. At church on

Sunday, Gestapo agents listened to the pastor, who could be arrested and sent to a concentration camp if he said something 'wrong'.

Josef's youngest son's name was Raymond, an English name. After Josef returned to Germany from Switzerland, a policeman came to his house and told him to report to Gestapo headquarters. When he arrived, they had begun the process of changing Raymond's name, but Josef would not complete the process. When Josef was sent to the concentration camp, the authorities told him, 'You are not a good German because you did not change your son's name as we asked.'

Josef then related the long and convoluted tale of how he had become involved with the anti-Nazi organisation, was recruited into the German Intelligence Service and then sent to Hamburg for his training. Josef claimed that he received no money from the Germans, so that he could be free, and brought up the issue of the confiscated foreign bonds. [*This is not accurate. His wife received monthly payments of 200 RM[3] from the Abwehr, beginning in October 1940. Later the payments increased to 300 RM.[4]*]

His downfall came when he confided in Van Hees about his plan to work against the Nazis in England. [*Josef makes no mention here of trying to get to America.*] Van Hees denounced him to the Gestapo. The German Intelligence Service decided to send Josef to England anyhow, but told him that if they heard that he had done anything against them, his family would be shot.

Josef told the court that the German Intelligence Service used various kinds of people as their agents. Some were volunteers, but others were prisoners who had been offered freedom if they worked for the Abwehr. Josef had no special qualifications to be a secret agent and he had no connections in England, except the ones of which they had already heard [*presumably Frau Knips and Karel Richter*]. Josef regarded England as the most free country in the world and thought that he would be treated fairly in England, while in Germany all his movements were watched. Josef stated that he came to England to help the British. He suggested that he could help expose future agents who would be sent to bring him more money. [*Josef was naive in the extreme to think that the Germans would send other agents with money for basic weather reports.*]

At this point in the typewritten transcript, there is a disruption in the line spacing and the following pages (54 to 59) are labelled 'rp2/1' to 'rp2/6'. Page 54 in the transcript, labelled 'rp2/1', begins in perplexing fashion. Josef is being questioned on how he would contact the Germans for more money. He answers while 'referring to the document which is to be found inside the wallet, Exhibit 8'. There was no reference to Exhibit 8 on the preceding page, nor was there any reference to the moment when the 'document' was produced from the wallet. This would suggest that something has been omitted from the transcript. The pages labelled 'rp2/1' to 'rp2/6' may be 'replacement pages'.

Josef explained that he would have contacted the Germans by wireless, 'referring to the document which is to be found inside the wallet, Exhibit 8'.[5] According to the transcript, the document in question read, 'Zoological Gardens at 2.00 either on the 2nd or the 16th of the month. Derby Station waiting room on the 3rd or 17th of the month.' He could also meet agents on the 1st and 15th of the month at the corner of Oxford Street and Edgar Road. Josef had written the note at The Hague before he left.[6]

The document that Josef referenced has a problematic history. None of the witness statements taken from the farmers, Home Guard and Huntingdonshire Constabulary in early February mention a notebook amongst Josef's possessions. The first reference to the notebook in the Security Service file at the National Archives is a 23 June interrogation report by Sampson in which Josef stated that he had written Boeckel's telephone number into a small notebook that he brought with him. Sampson wrote a marginal note that stated, 'There was no notebook among Jakobs' [possessions].'[7]

In an earlier report on 14 June, Josef said that Boeckel had told him that if he ever needed more money, they would send some to him.[8] He just had to tell them where to meet, for example, at the Zoological Gardens or a restaurant. This was an oblique reference to the notes he had written in the notebook, but not clear enough for the officers to question Josef about the existence of a notebook. The day after Sampson's report, on 24 June, Josef was questioned extensively about the missing notebook:

> He said this was a small note block, which he thought was in his wallet together with the identity cards, etc. In addition to the telephone number of The Hague Dienststelle, he had also noted some private particulars regarding questions which his wife had asked him in letters. He strenuously denied having destroyed this block and said that if it was not amongst his possessions, he must have put it by mistake in the suitcase which he left behind at The Hague.[9]

Memos flew and on 27 June, Milmo wrote a note to Stimson at Latchmere House stating, 'We have never seen the scribbling pad referred to by Jakobs, and there is no record of it in the list of his property.'[10]

There were no follow-up reports on the status of the notebook until 22 July. A handwritten list of suggested exhibits for the court martial, dated 22 July, made no mention of a wallet or a notebook.[11] A copy of Robertson's original list of possessions, however, includes handwritten annotations dated 22 July, one of which is the addition of a 'graph paper pad small' by Cussen, preceded by a check mark.[12]

That same day, Stimson wrote a letter to accompany the operational items being sent to Cussen, including a blue leather wallet with an attached key chain.[13] This is likely the blue leather note case listed by the Huntingdonshire Constabulary and Robertson. There is, however, no mention of a notebook in Stimson's letter, nor on the aforementioned lists. It would appear that sometime between 23 June and 22 July, the errant notebook had been found. The only person who mentions the notebook prior to 23 June is Chief Constable Rivett-Carnac (Huntingdonshire Constabulary) who, in a letter dated 17 February, refers to a 'small note book'.[14] How he knew of the notebook, while MI5 was apparently unaware of it, remains a mystery.

Cussen had tracked down the notebook but it would not be entered into the list of exhibits in the traditional manner. At the Summary of Evidence and court martial, Josef's two identity cards and his ration book, all of which had been contained within one of the wallets, were listed as separate exhibits. The notebook was not mentioned in the list of exhibits. During the Summary of Evidence and court martial, the list of exhibits simply stated 'wallet'. It did not state 'wallet containing small notebook' as did, for example, Exhibit 6, 'Attaché case containing wireless'. This is extremely perplexing and naturally calls into question the chain of custody for this piece of evidence and why it had been placed into the wallet for the court martial.

None of the witness statements from early February nor the Summary of Evidence in late July mention a notebook. Newton, for example, in his witness statement dated 2 February, noted that they found 'a brown leather wallet containing a ration book, identity cards and a photograph of a girl'.[15] At the Summary of Evidence on 28 July, Newton stated, 'inside the leather wallet I found a blank ration book [Exhibit 10], a blank identity card [Exhibit 11] and a completed identity card [Exhibit 12]'.[16] And, in another copy of witness statements associated with the court martial,

Newton stated that Godfrey 'also found a leather wallet which I examined and found to contain amongst other things a blank ration book and two identity cards'.[17]

During the court martial, Godfrey was asked if he had found a wallet and said, 'Yes', at which point the wallet was entered as Exhibit 8.[18] Godfrey was not questioned about the contents of the wallet.

During Newton's testimony at the court martial, he stated that he had found some documents in the wallet: a ration book and identity cards.[19] It would appear from the court martial transcript that the notebook was contained within the wallet and came to light during Newton's testimony when the wallet (Exhibit 8) was handled by Newton and/or the president. Josef had a reaction to something during Newton's testimony, a reaction noted by the Judge Advocate, and it is possible that he was shocked at the reappearance of the notebook that he had thought missing or left behind in The Hague.[20]

There are many unanswered questions surrounding Josef's notebook. Where was the notebook between 1 February and 22 July? How could the notebook be entered into evidence given its poor chain of custody? What discussions – possibly redacted from the transcript – took place during the court martial prior to Josef discussing the significance of the notebook? And finally, who placed the notebook into the wallet prior to the court martial and for what purpose? We will likely never know the answers to these questions, but they do raise some concerns about the proceedings surrounding Josef's court martial.

As his testimony continued, Josef said that he had a cardboard disc code, but he also had code words in his head that he had revealed during the interrogation on 2 February. Josef said there was one wavelength he was to use for daytime and one for night-time, and his call sign was 'MZU'. He couldn't remember what letters the Germans would use when calling him. Josef had given a demonstration of the code words to the officers during the interrogation on 2 February. [*No officers were called who could corroborate his statements.*]

The markings on the map had been drawn by the flying officer on the night they left Holland. The officer told Josef that he would land within the triangle, in a quiet spot. Josef thought that the pilot could not have known about the aerodromes for they would have presented a very high risk. The aeroplane could have been heard or seen and the British would have seen where he landed. [*It does seem remarkable that the aircrew dropped Josef in close proximity to two RAF aerodromes, and lends credence to the idea that he was being sent as a 'canary in the coal mine' and that the Germans wanted him captured. Another possibility is that the circle marked the point at which the aircrew expected to enter the triangle (drop zone) and that the cross marked Josef's anticipated landing point. Either way, the aircrew dropped Josef near two RAF aerodromes, which seems irresponsible if they were setting him up for a successful start to his espionage mission. Or perhaps the aircrew had simply miscalculated the drop zone due to poor navigation.*]

Josef then told the story of how he had hurt his ankle during his exit from the aeroplane. Josef suspected that his leg was broken but he jumped anyway. He said that he could have stayed in the aeroplane by notifying the flight officer, but he was glad to jump and get into England. He said that he landed on his left knee on the soft, freshly ploughed soil. [*Josef clearly did not understand the mechanics of a parachute landing.*]

When Josef landed, he lay in the same spot all night in great pain. He buried the wireless set because he was not sure what sort of men would find him. He thought that civilians would find him and say, 'There is a Nazi spy', and do him harm. He wanted to hand the set over to the British authorities, so he did not bury it completely but left a little corner sticking out. The German authorities had told him to destroy the wireless set if anything happened to him, but he did not do that even though he could have destroyed it with the pistol. [*I'm not entirely sure a pistol would have done much damage to the set. He'd have been better off burying or throwing away the quartz crystals.*]

When asked why he had torn up the disc code, Josef said that he was in great pain, at the end of his rope (finished) and had simply lost his head. He tore up the code after he fired shots the next morning and saw some men coming. [*This does sound plausible. Any spy in his right mind would have destroyed the code much earlier either by eating it, burning it with the lighter or burying it deep in the ground.*]

According to Josef, he never told the farmers or the Home Guard that he was a Frenchman but said that he was from Luxembourg. [*Later he will admit that he did say he was a Frenchman.*] He didn't want to admit who he was to a civilian, but in his first interrogation with an officer (Jaikens), he said who he was. When asked what he would have done if he had not broken his leg, Josef said he would either have gone to the military or to the police and handed everything over to them. [*Rather doubtful. He would probably have tried to get to London and find Lily Knips.*]

In coming to England, Josef claimed he had no intention of helping the Nazis or any other enemy of Britain, or any German operation, or of impeding any British operations. Josef had given the British Security Service a good description of another agent (Richter), who was arrested before he could do any harm.

Josef was then cross-examined by Marlowe, who expressed a wish to ask him 'one or two questions'.[21] Marlowe focused on Josef's financial situation and wanted to know if, at the start of the war, Josef was quite poor. Josef denied this and said that when he came out of the concentration camp, he had all his money.

Marlowe then asked Josef if he had lived for some time as a money changer, but Josef had trouble understanding the question, and said that if he did say that, it was because he was exhausted. [*This question was based on the 1 February statement to Major Robertson – which had not been included in the Summary of Evidence and was not included in the court martial's list of exhibits. According to the Manual of Military Law, Rules of Procedure, 'If the prosecutor intends to call a witness whose evidence is not contained in any summary of evidence or abstract of evidence given to the accused, notice of such intention shall be given to the accused a reasonable time before the witness is called, together with an abstract of his proposed evidence.'[22] It would appear that if Marlowe wanted to introduce into evidence the statement Josef made to Robertson, he should have called Robertson as a witness and given Josef and his lawyer time to review the evidence and cross-examine the witness. It is difficult to understand why Marlowe would choose to bring this statement into his line of questioning, particularly since White had not even seen the document. The reference to Josef being a 'money changer' is, in all likelihood, a reflection of the fact that Josef's statement to Robertson was not well translated by Constable Templeman who, by Marriott's own admission, was not fluent in German.*]

When asked if he earned a living for part of the time by getting people false passports, Josef denied that. [*Josef may not have understood the question. Or he may have believed that the passports he helped procure for the Jews were authentic not false.*] Marlowe put it to Josef that, when he was released from the concentration camp, he was short of money, but Josef denied this was the case.

Marlowe circled back and, after getting Josef to acknowledge that he had spent time in a Swiss prison for fraud, suggested that Josef would do anything to get money, including volunteering for the spy mission. Josef denied this and said that he had come voluntarily to make a connection between British Jews and the *Zentrale* in Germany. Marlowe then asked him why he had said that he was 'made to come' when he was found in the field. Josef said that he never said, 'made to come', and that he only came to help England against the Nazis. [*In all likelihood, he did use those words in a bid to prevent the farm labourers from doing him harm.*] In the very next breath, Josef said that he never took money from the Germans and never signed a contract with them. [*This is inaccurate. Josef's wife received a monthly payment from the Abwehr before and after Josef departed on his mission. This strongly suggests that he did indeed take money from them and that, like other agents, he had signed a contract that would ensure his loyalty and provide a stipend to his family.*]

Josef said he took employment with the German Intelligence Service in order to escape Germany, and no one ever checked to see if he could speak English. Josef said that in his wireless training they used some English words that, given his schooling in Latin, Greek, French and Spanish, meant he could work out their meaning. Marlowe asked Josef why he had not been sent to France or Spain, but Josef said that the Abwehr officers were looking for people to send to England. Josef stated again that he had been anxious to help the British against the Nazis. Marlowe then asked him why he had not kept his disc code intact as that would have helped England, but Josef said he lost his head on the morning of 1 February.

Josef argued that the wireless set would be more useful to England than the disc code, and he had the code words in his head. Marlowe pointed out that Josef had had enough sense to bury the wireless set and suggested that the Germans had told him to tear up the disc code if anything happened to him. [*It is rather doubtful that the Germans would have told him to tear up the code, thereby leaving enough evidence for it to be fully, or partially, reconstructed. Far better to burn it, soak it in water, eat it or bury it.*]

Josef repeatedly stated that he had been told to destroy the wireless set but not the code. Josef admitted that if he had wanted to serve his German masters faithfully, he would have destroyed the wireless set and himself with the pistol. Marlowe said that no one could know whether or not the code words in Josef's head were genuine, but Josef said he gave proof of it during the interrogation on 2 February. [*Had White called the Latchmere House officers as witnesses, they could have corroborated this aspect of Josef's story.*]

Marlowe asked him about telling Robertson that he had broken his leg upon landing [*Marlowe was asking Josef a question based on the 1 February statement that had not been put into evidence*], and suggested he hadn't thought his story through at that point, but Josef said that he was in great pain during that interrogation. He stated that he broke his leg exiting the aeroplane, although Marlowe suggested that he only made that up to justify his story that he had chosen to jump even with the injury. Marlowe persisted in asking Josef why he had told Robertson that he broke his ankle upon landing, and produced the statement made on 1 February [*but did not enter it into evidence*]. Josef admitted, 'Yes, this is my signature, but on this evening, I was not me, I could not give expression because it was impossible for me. I was in too much pain.'[23] [*The presentation of this statement during the middle of the court martial seems odd. The purpose of the Summary of Evidence was for the prosecution to present all of their evidence, thereby giving the defence a chance to review it. In introducing the 1 February statement during the court martial, Marlowe caught White flat-footed. One could wonder at the admissibility of this evidence. Hinchley-Cooke had been called to testify regarding the statement he had taken under caution from Josef. If the statement made to Robertson was being presented as evidence, then Robertson should have been called to testify.*]

The president wanted to call Robertson before the court, but Marlowe said that he was away and it wouldn't add much. [*On the contrary, Robertson could have clarified the issue of the translator and spoken to the physical condition of Josef that evening. Unfortunately, MI5 would likely have frowned on Robertson being placed on the stand, given his extensive knowledge of the double-cross system. White, however, could have demanded that Robertson be called as a witness and that the court martial be adjourned until such time as Robertson was available.*]

Marlowe said that he was challenging Josef's credibility by highlighting inconsistencies in his story and suggested that Josef had told the truth to Robertson and then later made up the story about breaking his leg in the air. [*In challenging Josef's credibility, Marlowe was using a statement that had not been presented at the Summary of Evidence, had not been entered as an exhibit at the court martial and was taken down by a translator of questionable fluency.*]

At Marlowe's request, Josef again demonstrated how he had been sitting in the aeroplane and how the air pressure pushed his leg backwards and forwards thereby breaking it. Marlowe slyly admitted that he only asked Josef to show him again to see if it matched his earlier demonstration. Marlowe asked how his leg could be blown backwards and forwards and Josef said that the aeroplane was circling at the time, and that the direction of the wind was shifting. [*Given that this was Josef's first time in an aeroplane, he was not familiar with the effect of slipstream along the fuselage of the aeroplane. It wasn't the wind that was the issue, but the fact that air moving past an object will generate turbulence around that object. No surprise that Josef's legs were snatched by that turbulence.*]

Marlowe then changed focus and asked Josef about his wife and children. Josef stated that his wife was not a Nazi and that she had a Jewish stepfather. Josef said he had tried to get his children out of Germany, but he had no hope. [*I'm not sure when Josef planned an escape with his family – perhaps during his time in Switzerland, prior to his arrest for gold counterfeiting?*] Marlowe then put it to Josef that he had left his family in order to save his own skin, but Josef said he was waiting for the end of the war to get them out of Germany. Josef argued that he could not wait for himself because he was not safe in Germany. His whole family was therefore in danger, because when the Nazis arrested one member of the family, they usually arrested others.

Marlowe fired his questions at Josef rapidly and at one point Josef said, 'I cannot understand the interpreter. Will you speak with me slowly?'[24] Josef said that the German Intelligence Service was more powerful than the Gestapo and, as a member of the Intelligence Service, he was relatively safe. [*Several other German agents interrogated after the war admitted that they were Jews or* Mischling *and had entered the German Intelligence Service as a way to escape the Gestapo.*]

Marlowe said that Josef had endangered his family by joining the German Intelligence Service and becoming a traitor to Germany. Josef acknowledged the 'Nazis do not know what my intention is'.[25] [*This is inaccurate. Josef admitted that he had told Van Hees about his intention to escape to America, who, in turn, reported it to the Gestapo.*] Marlowe said there was a chance that they might find out, but Josef said at his first interrogation in Britain, he asked for a guarantee that whatever he said should not be divulged in case of an invasion by the Germans.

Marlowe asked him if he believed that the Germans would invade, and he said, 'No', although the Germans were telling people this in Germany. Josef said the Nazis had arranged for a celebration in August of 1940, to celebrate the victorious invasion of England. Josef said he did not expect the Germans to invade and save him. [*This is not accurate. In the spring of 1941 both Josef and Richter were terrified that the Germans would invade. As the months wore on, however, with no sign of invasion, they began to realise that the Germans were not coming.*]

And once more, Josef asked Marlowe, 'Please will you speak with me slowly?' [*This calls into question, again, how much of the proceedings Josef comprehended.*]

At this point, White finally interrupted and asked the court about the statement made to Robertson, whether it was in evidence or not [*given that Marlowe had mentioned the Robertson interrogation at several points, this delayed response from White is perplexing*]. Stirling said:

No, as I understand it, he has put to the witness whether he has not made another statement on a different occasion and picked out one portion of it and the witness has said he may or may not have said it, but if he did, he was not in a fit condition to know what he was saying.[26] [*Stirling himself had brought up the issue of a voluntary statement made on 1 February during his questioning of Marriott.*]

White asked if he could see the entire document and Stirling asked Marlowe to hand the document over to the defence. Marlowe replied, 'I understood that Captain White had seen it before,'[27] but White replied in the negative. [*Given that the document had not been presented at the Summary of Evidence and was not entered as an exhibit, one could wonder how Marlowe came to the conclusion that White had seen it.*]

The court was adjourned for the day at 5.15 p.m. and would reconvene at 10 a.m. the next day.[28]

Several questions arose from the case for the defence up to that point.

The first dealt with the statement that Josef made to Robertson on 1 February. Earlier in the day, Marriott had admitted that Police Constable Templeman, who served as an interpreter for Josef's voluntary statement on 1 February, was not fluent in German. That necessarily called into question the validity of the statement. The fact that the statement was taken from Josef while he was suffering a broken ankle, with no access to pain relief, also called the statement into question. Josef's defence lawyer touched on neither of these issues.

Marlowe casually slipped several references to the Robertson statement into his cross-examination of Josef in order to call his character into question. Marlowe thought that White had seen the statement, but White denied any knowledge of it. One would naturally presume that Marlowe would have presented the statement at the Summary of Evidence, but such was not the case. According to the Rules of Procedure, Marlowe should have called Robertson to testify to the statement taken from Josef and allowed him to be cross-examined by White. It would appear that Marlowe pulled a fast one on Josef and his defence lawyer.

The second question dealt with the actual transcript of the court martial. The transcript was taken down in shorthand and transcribed afterwards. Based on the page numbering and line spacing, it would appear that the transcript has been redacted. The spacing on page 53 is much looser than on the preceding and following pages. The following six pages (pages 54–59) are labelled 'rp 2/1 to 2/6'. On page 53, Josef spoke about how he could help the British by meeting other agents in England. Pages 54 to 58 return to normal spacing. On page 59, Josef spoke about Richter and how he encountered him at the 'special interrogation centre'. This page also has much looser spacing. It would appear that something was removed from the transcript of Josef's court martial, possibly references to double agent TATE, whom Richter was to meet.

The alterations were most likely done at the request of MI5, as they were desperate to quash all references to their double agents. One has only to peruse the Security Service files at the National Archives to find numerous documents in which the code names and real names of TATE/ Schmidt and SUMMER/Caroli were redacted.[29]

However, the transcript of Josef's court martial goes beyond the simple redaction of a name; the transcript was rewritten to exclude any reference to a sensitive subject. The pages numbered 'rp' were likely 'replacement pages'. One would naturally wonder how a document could be altered in such a fashion, a document that recorded for posterity the procedure involved in sentencing a man to death.[30]

Stirling would later send the proceedings of the court martial to the General Officer Commanding, London District, on 7 August 1941 noting that 'the delay ... is due to the fact that the transcript of the shorthand note taken at the trial has been received by me only today'.[31] The delay in delivery of the transcript may have been due to the fact that it was being reviewed and/or redacted by MI5.[32]

The third question surrounded Josef's claim that his grandfather was Jewish. According to the Nuremberg Laws implemented by the Nazis, one Jewish grandparent was enough to make one non-Aryan. Given that all of Josef's ancestors, as far back as the 1600s, were Catholic, it is highly unlikely that he was persecuted for being a Jew or a *Mischling*. The only Jew in the family was Josef's stepfather-in-law, Abraham Wolfgang Elkan. It is possible that the translator and/or transcriptionist got confused during the court martial, that 'stepfather-in-law' was translated as 'father-in-law' or simply 'father'.

37

COURT MARTIAL ENDS:
5 AUGUST 1941

The court reconvened at 10 a.m. on 5 August and Josef was brought before the court and further cross-examined by the prosecution.[1]

Marlowe began[2] by asking Josef about the money and whether it was his intention to get some of his money out of Germany. Josef confirmed that had been his intention and that the £498 he had with him was part of the £2,000 that he had requested from his Mexican bonds. Josef claimed that he had refused to accept money from the German Intelligence Service from the beginning because he wanted to be free for himself. This refusal to accept money did not arouse any suspicion with the Germans because other agents did not take money either. Josef stated, 'No Aryan in the secret service takes money.'[3] [*This seems to be, at the very least, stretching the truth. Most of the other spies sent to England were paid while in the employ of the Abwehr and/or their families were to receive monetary compensation after the spies left on their missions. Josef's wife received 200 RM beginning in October 1940 and the amount was later increased to 300 RM. His assertion that 'no Aryan in the secret service takes money' is interesting, as it implies that he was an Aryan and yet earlier in the court martial, he portrayed himself as being a* Mischling.]

Marlowe then asked Josef about the marks on the map. According to Josef, the *Feldwebel* (sergeant) on the aeroplane said that he would be dropped 'in this square' and that from there Josef could get a rail connection to London. [*There is no 'square' on the map. This could be a translation or transcription issue. The area marked on the map was a triangle that contained a circle along the eastern edge and a cross further within the triangle. Given that the cross was on a rail line, it might be that the sergeant was simply trying to point Josef in the direction of a rail connection. It was odd, given the large triangle, that there were no other marks within its boundaries.*]

Josef said that the marks indicating the location of the aerodromes were just a coincidence. The German Intelligence Service would never drop agents in dangerous locations, such as near an aerodrome, where searchlights might see the aeroplane and the parachute. [*Unless, perhaps, the German Intelligence Service wanted the spy to be caught.*] Regarding the cross and the circle, Josef said that he had been told, 'You will land near these points.' The sergeant on the aeroplane drew the two marks and Josef did not know why one was a circle and one was a cross. [*It was unlikely that the Germans could drop an agent with such precision. It was odd to draw a triangle in which the agent was going to land, and then narrow that down to two small areas.*]

Marlowe asked about Van Hees and Josef admitted that he had told Van Hees he was undertaking the mission in order to escape. Van Hees informed the Gestapo, who then contacted the German Intelligence Service in Hamburg. The captain of the German Intelligence Service (possibly Boeckel) asked Josef if the information was correct, but since he was also a member of the 'revolutionary party', he told Josef that if he brought 'two sureties' then he would take Josef.[4] [*A recent book on Operation SEALION by German historian Monika Siedentopf has put forward the idea that the Hamburg Abwehr office was staffed by anti-Nazis.*] In light of Van Hees's denunciation, Josef would receive neither a passport nor the £2,000 he had hoped to take and, more seriously, his family would serve as surety.

Marlowe asked Josef about his parachute landing. Josef said that he landed at around 9 p.m. and first tried to attract attention in the morning. Marlowe suggested that Josef had waited until daylight because he had hoped that his ankle might only be sprained, but Josef said that he could tell his leg was broken and that he could not move at all. [*If there was any doubt as to the severity of Josef's injury, perhaps one of the physicians could have been called as a witness.*] When the farm labourers approached, Josef said he could not speak English, so he told them he was a Frenchman from Luxembourg. [*The previous day of the court martial, Josef had denied that he ever claimed to be a Frenchman. Poor translation, or lack of comprehension on his part?*] He first told someone he was a refugee when he was interrogated by Robertson. When asked if he would have carried out his mission if he had not broken his leg, Josef said, 'Never'.[5]

Before White re-examined Josef, he asked the court about the statement that Josef had made to Robertson on 1 February.[6] Hinchley-Cooke had said that the first statement made under caution by Josef, was the one made on 18 June, and yet the one made to Robertson was made under caution. White could not understand why it had not been included in the exhibits. Marlowe said that it was now included [*when was it added to the list of exhibits?*], but White wanted to know why it had not been included at the start. Marlowe admitted that the first statement did not differ in substance from the one made to Hinchley-Cooke. [*If it did not differ in substance, why had Marlowe brought it up and used it to point out inconsistencies between the two statements?*]

White wanted to know why the statement had not been put in as evidence, and Marlowe said it was put in, but Stirling said it had not been exhibited so it was added as Exhibit 19. [*This is unclear. It was never put in at the Summary of Evidence, so the comment that it was put in as evidence, just not exhibited, makes no sense. Was it appropriate to allow new evidence to be entered as an exhibit during the court martial, particularly as Robertson was not called as a witness?*]

White re-examined Josef and asked him about the statement made to Robertson on 1 February.[7] Josef said that he was completely 'finished' and in great pain and asked for an injection from the doctor. He thought that he might have received the injection after the interrogation. [*This contradicts an earlier comment in which he said the police surgeon bandaged his leg and gave him an injection before the interrogation. There is no reference in the police reports or Robertson's report as to when an injection was given. An injection of painkillers could have relieved Josef's pain but altered his state of mind. Perhaps the police surgeon thought a statement made while in pain was better than one made under the influence of medication?*]

Josef gave his statement in German, which was translated by a man in civilian clothes who could speak German 'very well'.[8] In that statement, Josef said he had one son and two daughters, but Josef corrected that later to two sons and one daughter. White asked for the names of his sons, Raymond and Norman [*sic*]. [*Another transcript error: Josef's son was named Norbert, not Norman.*] In the statement, Josef said that he broke his ankle, but that was not accurate. Josef said that he broke it 'here', but he was not sure if that was the foot or the ankle. [*The medical reports state it was a fracture of the tibia and fibula which would be ankle and/or lower leg.*]

Josef said that he was in great pain after he landed and he was worried that civilians would treat him harshly. When he attracted the attention of the farm labourers, he threw away his pistol and put his hands up, to demonstrate that he was not an enemy. They treated him well and Josef was glad to be found, as he was in great pain. Josef said he tore up the code during the night and dropped the pieces beside him. [*Elsewhere, he said he tore it up shortly before firing his pistol in the morning.*] Had he wished, he could have destroyed the code card by burning it. [*Except for the fact that his lighter had run out of fuel during the night.*]

White asked him about the code words, and Josef said they were more than a simple substitution code and he had demonstrated the code during the 2 February interrogation. [*This claim by Josef would have carried far more weight had the Latchmere House officers been called as witnesses. On its own, Josef's claims to have helped the British were met with disbelief.*]

White then turned to the president and said that this was the case for the accused.[9] [*A very weak case given that no witnesses for the defence were called.*] The president asked Josef what information he had given to 'our intelligence branch' and Josef said that he had told them about Richter and the organisation of the German Intelligence Service in Hamburg.[10] [*These statements could have been corroborated by Latchmere House officers. As it was, the court only had Josef's word for it.*]

After admitting that he didn't speak much French, only what he had learned in school, Josef was asked to quote something in Latin or Greek. Josef quoted *Cicero* in Greek and then recited the Lord's Prayer in Latin. Questioned again about his landing, Josef said that he landed gently and that he came down on his left leg while holding up his right leg. [*There is no such thing as a 'gentle' parachute landing unless one is an expert, and perhaps not even then. A gentle night landing would be virtually impossible.*]

The president asked Josef how he would have burned the disc code and he said he would have used his lighter. [*Certainly, except his lighter ran out of fuel during the night.*] The president wondered where the lighter was, as it was not among the exhibits, but Marlowe said there were immaterial exhibits with which the court had not been burdened.

Stirling asked Josef a few questions.[11] Josef stated again that he had come to help England against the Nazis. He had hoped that, with the permission of the British, he could establish a connection between English Jews and the *Zentrale*. He had told the interrogators at Latchmere House that if they did not want to employ him, then he wanted to try to get to America, to his aunt in Illinois. Josef acknowledged that, as an agent to England, he was supposed to be able to speak excellent English. Josef said the German Intelligence Service had no idea that he couldn't speak English. The court was puzzled by this, as one would expect the German Intelligence Service to test the English skills of their England-bound agents. [*Not necessarily. In late 1940, Germany was throwing agents at Britain without much training or language skills. It wasn't just an issue with Josef – as Hinchley-Cooke had noted earlier, the Germans were 'not particular' about their secret agents.*]

Josef said that during his training as a wireless operator, he was given sentences in English, which he understood, and his instructor then thought that he knew English. The court asked, 'That is the answer you want to give, is it?' and Josef said, 'Yes.' [*This, at least, was the truth. The Germans didn't care about his lack of language skills. After the war, Boeckel admitted that none of the agents spoke perfect English but, 'Berlin insisted that they be despatched as rapidly as possible.'[12]*]

When asked if he thought that Captain Newton was an officer on the morning of 1 February, Josef said, although he was in uniform, Josef did not know that he was an officer, as he was not familiar with British uniforms. [*Perhaps to call into question Josef's claim that he waited until he saw an officer before admitting he had come as a refugee from Nazi oppression. He did tell more of the truth when he saw police officers Jaikens and Mills, but the language barrier may have confused the situation.*]

The president wanted to know if Josef spoke good German and Hinchley-Cooke was called back to the stand on his former oath and questioned.[13] Hinchley-Cooke said Josef spoke north German and sounded like a well-educated man of the professional class. According to Hinchley-Cooke, Josef had not given any really important information to the military authorities. [*Earlier, Hinchley-Cooke had disavowed knowledge of a number of things. Given that he was supposed to be an 'expert witness' and had had 'the conduct of the proceedings from the start', one wonders why he had 'no knowledge' of so many things regarding Josef's case. If he had 'no knowledge', how could he know if Josef had given important information or not?*]

Hinchley-Cooke said the code words represented an ordinary transposition cipher [*sic*] and could be broken easily, whereas the disc code was very valuable. [*Not accurate. Earlier, Hinchley-Cooke said the disc code was a simple transposition code. That would mean that it too could be broken easily. TATE's disc code, which was virtually identical to Josef's, was also referred to as a simple transposition code according to the MI5 file on TATE. Sampson noted on 25 June 1941 that the disc 'code was not essential for his work as he had an emergency code'.[14]*]

Hinchley-Cooke also said that the disc codes from other agents had slight variations, so Josef's assertion that they were all the same was false. [*Perhaps not, but they were all simple transposition codes that could be easily broken by the cryptographers at Bletchley Park.*] He said that, in his experience, German agents were only told what they needed to know for carrying out their jobs and would not have much valuable or confidential information about the German Intelligence Service. [*They did, however, have valuable knowledge about other agents. Caroli for example, had information about Wulf Schmidt, who would go on to become double agent TATE. Josef had information about Richter, and Richter had information about TATE. Unfortunately for Josef, Hinchley-Cooke would divulge none of this because the double-cross system was of utmost secrecy.*]

Hinchley-Cooke acknowledged that they had had quite a few similar cases and agents were sent with a minimum of £200, sometimes as much as £500. He concluded by saying that £500 was a 'normal sum'. [*This is not accurate. Prior to Josef's arrival, agents generally received £100 or £200. In preparation for the civil trial of Druecke and Walti, Hinchley-Cooke prepared a statement of his planned testimony that read, 'It is within my knowledge that German agents operating in this country are given approximately £200 per head in English currency notes' (KV 2/1705). By the time Druecke and Walti were brought to trial in June 1941, however, that statement was removed from Hinchley-Cooke's testimony. When Josef arrived at Latchmere House, the MI5 officers were convinced that he must be an important person because he was the most highly paid agent to arrive in Britain up to that point. John Moe, who arrived in April 1941, arrived with £100 and US$100.*[15] *No one in the court, however, could challenge this point.*]

White asked Hinchley-Cooke if Josef had come to Britain with any information of value, and he said, 'No.' [*This is inaccurate. Josef knew Richter and helped the MI5 officers break him, and reveal his true mission: to establish the bona fides of TATE. Stephens had thought that this was highly valuable, given the importance of TATE to the double-cross system.*] White then wanted to know why, if Josef was of such little importance, was there such great secrecy surrounding his trial?

Stirling said, 'The court have decided to hold it in the interests of the country,' but White replied the secrecy began before the sitting of the court. The president said trials like Josef's were always kept secret as a matter of policy and were not open for discussion. When White pressed the issue again, he was told that the British did not want the Germans to know how their agents were caught.

Stirling asked each lawyer if they were satisfied that they had placed all the evidence they wished before the court, and both answered in the affirmative.[16] [*This was White's last chance, but he simply did not know how to help his client.*]

There were several items of note during this portion of the court martial. On the one hand, Josef was caught out in a lie. The previous day he had said, 'I never told the farmers I was a Frenchman,' yet on the second day, he said, 'I told them I was a Frenchman from Luxembourg.' Josef also said he could have used his lighter to burn the disc code, and while this would have been true in the middle of the night, by the morning, his lighter had run out of fuel.

Hinchley-Cooke was also caught out. He said several times that Josef had not provided any important information to the British. Yet Stephens, at the end of May, had admitted that, without Josef's assistance, it was doubtful whether or not Richter would have been broken. Hinchley-Cooke also stated that the £500 found in the possession of Josef was a 'normal' amount. This too was a stretch of the truth. Upon Josef's capture, several MI5 officers had noted that Josef was the highest paid agent to arrive in Britain up to that point, but Josef's defence lawyer did not know that and took Hinchley-Cooke's statements at face value.

38

SUMMARY FOR THE PROSECUTION

Marlowe then stood up and summarised the case for the prosecution:

To come to the facts of this case, one is struck by the oddity that out of all the people available to them for this mission the enemy selected a man whom they had under suspicion apparently, who they knew had no intention of spying for them, but who had only the intention to escape. [*As Hinchley-Cooke said, the Germans were 'not particular' about their secret agents and they had Josef's family under threat.*] That is the man that they selected for this mission according to his story. Among other suitable qualifications for this mission, he was unable to speak the language of the country to which he was sent. The court may think it rather surprising when they hear this story from the accused. One knows in the occupied countries, apart from their own country, there are a number of people ready to undertake these missions. [*It is not clear how Marlowe would know this.*] Out of those people, they selected a man who could not speak the language and who announced his intention and that intention was known to them, that he was not going to carry out his mission but was going to escape and at the same time was taking out of the country currency to which he was not entitled. That is a most surprising story and the court may find it quite incredible. It is put before you by a man who you may think, having seen him give his evidence, is an extremely cunning rascal who has no hesitation in thinking of a story which will fit the facts. You see that emerging time and time again. [*Marlowe's strategy was to portray Josef as a liar by highlighting the incredibility of his story, even though much of it was true.*]

For instance, just little things like the wireless case. Evidence is given that that was discovered because a small corner was left exposed or just under the surface. A story is immediately invented to fit it. The story is that he did that purposely and intentionally because he wanted to be able to find it again, because he wanted to tell those in authority where it was. In my submission, that is the story of an extremely cunning man who said to himself, 'That is an unfortunate thing that that wireless has been found and I must try and invent a story to fit it.' It was an absurd story because there was no necessity to bury the wireless set at all. The reason given by him is that he thought if somebody came and found him with a wireless they might set about him before he could explain what he was and who he was. The attaché case itself is a perfectly innocent looking attaché case from the outside. It was locked up at the time and no farm labourer arriving there would have any immediate suspicion it contained a wireless set. There was no need to bury it unless you carried out your instructions.

Is not the truth this, that this man had not really appreciated his position and that he was facing something which was quite outside the routine which he expected to follow? He anticipated that he would land here and carry out his instructions, either dispose of his wireless by burying it in a convenient place or taking it with him if he took that risk. But he was making his way to London and if he got into a difficult position he would destroy the most incriminating evidence and certainly destroy that which would be of assistance to this country. Those were the instructions rooted in his mind. He was faced with a position he had not anticipated. He had a broken leg. That is why you find this position of these instructions being carried out in a sense by a man who is in a position to remember what he has been told and who is trying to do his best to serve his masters. That is what this man was doing.

Yet he asks you to believe the story that he came here purely to help the English against the Nazis. Supposing that were a true story. He was there for some twelve hours. He was sufficiently conscious – certainly at some time whatever his condition was – to be able to dig a hole large enough to take that wireless, to see that it was buried beneath the surface. He was able to cut away his harness and parachute as he has told you. He was able to get his hat out of his pocket and put it on his head. He was conscious enough to do all those things and yet he tells you he has no idea why he tore up that disc code. It is rather remarkable, because that is one fundamental thing in this case which you can put your hand on which helps you to determine what this man's intention was, and it is the one thing throughout for which he has no answer at all. He has an ingenious explanation for everything else which has been put to him, but when you come to the question of the code he can think of no other answer than that he was unconscious and another that he lost his head. That is the only answer he can think of and the reason for that, in my submission, is that there is no answer. That is the one thing he could have brought to this country which might have been of assistance and which he could, if he were anxious to help this country, have put at the disposal of this country. [*He helped break Richter, which the interrogators at Latchmere House considered quite valuable given Richter's admitted connection with TATE.*] He could even have operated the wireless set himself with the use of the code and sent such information as he was requested to do by the authorities. [*This statement comes perilously close to the double-cross system.*] He put that beyond his power by destroying the code. [*No, he did not. Even with the disc code destroyed, MI5 was still prepared to use Josef as a double agent.*]

Then he tells you since then he has rendered valuable service by giving them another code which he says he carried in his head. I must ask the court not to accept that account of it. The prosecution do not accept it. [*They only had the word of a German spy and yet Josef had given Stephens the code words. Other agents, including SNOW, had also been given code words, a fact that the officers at Latchmere House knew very well.*] There is the essential fact that there was that document and he destroyed it. He put it out of his power to give the only help which he could to this country. [*This is inaccurate. He could have used the code words to contact the Abwehr. The MI5 officers knew that Josef had torn up the disc code but were perfectly prepared to use him as a double agent. Kurt Karl Goose was not equipped with a disc code and MI5 had him send wireless messages back to Germany.*]

You have heard his extraordinary story of how he is an anti-Nazi, how he is apparently known to be an anti-Nazi, he has been in a concentration camp, he is known to have been under sentence in Switzerland. These are the things he tells you. He is known to have apparently Jewish blood in him somewhere, to have a wife who is in some way connected with a Jewish relation, he cannot speak this language, he has no intention of spying, he has every intention to escape and he has every intention to escape with some money which he is not entitled to take out of the country. All these facts are known to the authorities and they facilitate his design by providing him with an aeroplane, they get his money and hand it to him, they give him an identity card and they send him here knowing he has no intention of serving them. That is the story he puts before you and, in my submission, that is quite a ridiculous story and one which no court could possibly accept. [*Marlowe was not aware of the desperate state of the German Intelligence Service.*]

The plain facts are that this man came down in a place where his map was marked and where two aerodromes were marked. He tells you a conflicting story about first not knowing that the marks were on the map and then that the marks were put there as two points where he might land. It is a little difficult to understand. It is just pure coincidence that those marks were on the map according to him, and he himself really has no idea what they mean except possibly landing points. It is an extraordinarily long chance that they happen to mark the two aerodromes which are within that area. All of those facts to my mind, in my submission make this man's story incredible. [*This would naturally presuppose that the German Luftwaffe could drop their agents with pinpoint precision – highly unlikely.*]

But you do not decide whether or not you convict on whether his own story [is] or [is not] incredible. [*The court would convict on exactly that point. In emphasising the incredibility of Josef's story, Marlowe had questioned his veracity, thereby calling Josef's true intent and motivation into question. Whatever Josef said about his intent, Marlowe had laid the foundation for the court to view Josef as a liar.*] The essential point is: Has the case for the prosecution satisfied you as to whether or not he came here with the intention to spy. [*The fact that Josef was equipped as a spy does not necessarily mean he intended to spy. The Germans intended him to spy. What was in Josef's mind is another story.*] In my submission the evidence is very clear. He arrives here with all the equipment of a spy. At first he does not tell this story which he now sets out. His first story is that he is a Frenchman and he endeavours to indicate he is a civilian who is in no war, as he puts it. He does not act as a refugee would. He does not say, 'I am a refugee from Nazi oppression.' [*Given that he could not speak English and the farmers and Home Guard could not speak German, 'made to come' was, perhaps, as much as could be communicated.*] He does not behave as you would expect him to do. [*Very few people behave as one would* 'expect' them to behave. Particularly when they are stressed, injured or in fear of their life.] He has this essential equipment and he buries the wireless and tears up the code.

In my submission, those facts alone are ample to indicate what was in his mind and only when it became apparent to him he was so incapacitated he would not be able to carry out his mission, and when he was caught, did he put up this story that he was here as a refugee.

In my submission, this case is amply made out and there is no alternative here but to convict the accused.[1]

39

SUMMARY FOR THE DEFENCE

Captain White then stood up and gave the summary for the defence:

May I please the court. I find myself in the strange and novel position of standing to put before you, in the best possible light, the case of an enemy alien. I think you will agree it is one of the glories, if not the greatest glory, of the English law, that the case of this man Jakobs can be investigated here by you and can be prosecuted by Major Marlowe and defended by myself just as if it were the case of the most loyal subject of the Crown. [*This is not accurate. Loyal subjects of the Crown would have had access to witnesses and family members. Josef was unable to call key witnesses as they were all in Germany.*] The English law applies to it in all its detail and in all its careful regard for the interests of the accused. In the heat of battle we, as soldiers, are to seek out and kill the enemy wherever he may be found. In the cool atmosphere of this court, enemy, or not enemy, he stands innocent until proved guilty, and it is the burden of the prosecution to prove to you beyond reasonable doubt that he is guilty of the offence which is alleged against him. Before the law he is just a fellow human being.

Now the essence of his case, as I see it, and as Major Marlowe put it in his opening, is not that he came down by parachute; the question in this case is: what was in his mind when he descended? The only direct evidence of that is his own story and to that story must be applied the tests of the surrounding circumstances and I know that test will be applied by this court with an open mind until it comes to its decision.

I should like, if I might, first to examine the story as he has put it here. He says he did not come as a secret agent. He says that when he left the aeroplane he had a broken leg, he had scarcely any knowledge of the English language and he had never been in the country. If those statements be true, can you imagine anybody worse equipped for the purpose of spying here and of helping the Germans. [*Captain White could have pushed the 'poorly equipped' piece by referring to the glaring error on Josef's identity card. Even if he had not broken his leg, he would have been picked up extremely quickly.*] As to the question of his leg and whether it was broken when he left the aeroplane, I will deal later. But suppose that it was not broken and suppose that he left the aeroplane with a poor knowledge of English and with no knowledge of the country, still can you imagine that he was well equipped for his task? Could he or could he not speak English. Well, you have heard as much of him as I have and it is for the court to decide whether his ability to speak our tongue here in this court has been feigned or whether it has not. No suggestion has ever been made that he has been in this country before. Now imagine falling in a foreign country from an aeroplane where you can hardly speak the tongue – and remember he has had six months to learn it [since arriving in England] – and where you do not know your way. I respectfully suggest the members of the court may put the question to themselves as to how they might react if they were put into the position of, shall I say, falling in Germany. One cannot conceive of oneself being less well equipped with the task of living which he had to do from day to day in this country in order that he might pass on the information which was required.

Now supposing his motive was not what he has sworn it to be, namely to come here and to help this country. I pause to remark that he has told you he is a Roman Catholic. He has told you he understands the solemnity of an oath. He has taken the oath fully realising that every part of his story would come under review and that he could be cross-examined by the Prosecution. He chose that, rather than to make a statement from the safety of his position there from which he could not be cross-examined. Supposing his motive were not what he has sworn it to be, what other motive was there in these particular circumstances? A hot headed adventurer? Surely he can hardly be that. He is a man of 43 years of age with a wife and family established in Germany. Is he a man coming over here seriously intending to help his country? He has little knowledge of the language and no knowledge of the country. Could he honestly say, if that were his real intention, 'I can best help my country in this way'? Can we not imagine a dozen ways by which he could help it and for which he was better equipped to help it than by coming here in those circumstances?

It was suggested by Major Marlowe in cross-examination that he was prepared, I think he said, to turn to any living which would bring him money. I do not know whether it is suggested he turned to this job so that he could get his £500. What use on earth is £500 to a German in England for the purpose of his everyday living? Personally I would not accept 10,000 Marks [*sic*] to be dropped in Germany for the enjoyment of life. In my submission the whole story of his life corroborates what he has told this Court. He need not have told you these things but he has and he has gone into them fully. Has not what he has said shown you he has every reason to hate the Nazis? Why he should love this country [Britain] one does not know and in my submission it does not matter. The important thing is that he should hate the Nazis and want to help those who are their enemies. Perhaps the most important thing of all is that he is a Roman Catholic. I submit this detail has a ring of truth. He said that one of his objections to the Nazis was that he could not take his children to Church on Sunday mornings and that they had to go shooting. We all know the importance which the Roman Catholic attaches to the upbringing of his children. Does not that bear a ring of truth? Why invent that of all things 'I cannot take my children to Church.' He is a non-Aryan. The whole story is full of Jews. His wife's father-in-law, his own father, his business associates, and the man with whom he was landed in prison in Switzerland. [*The transcript says, 'his wife's father-in-law, his own father', but this could be a mistake by White or a mistake by the transcriptionist. It was his wife's stepfather (Josef's stepfather-in-law) who was Jewish. Earlier, Josef had claimed his 'grandfather' was Jewish, but this is not borne out by genealogical research.*] It is a Jewish circle. It does not require any evidence placed before this Court to tell you that the Jews hate the Nazis. It does not require any stretch of imagination to imagine a man of Jewish origin should have every reason to detest the members of that party.

Now he says he was in a concentration camp. He was not cross-examined about that. Let us accept that he was in a concentration camp. Surely, enough is known in this country, again without any evidence at all, of the life in concentration camps to leave this Court under no misapprehension as to the feeling of one who has been in one on the orders of the Nazis and has come out again to live in Germany. Is it surprising then that when he left the concentration camp after the torments he has described, even showing in action what was done to him, that he should seek out a secret society about which again a Jew had told him in the concentration camp? Is it surprising that he should have gone to the *Zentrale* and put himself in league with those who detest the Nazis and seek to run them out of Germany? Again I submit that this has the stamp of truth. [*Even if Josef was not Jewish, there were many other groups who the Nazis persecuted. Given his background in fraud and shady deals, Josef would have been considered an undesirable individual.*] The story that he has told about the activities of the *Zentrale* must itself have struck the Court. Why make up a tale about liniment to make soldiers' feet swell [*part of Josef's testimony*]. That surely is not the story of a man who has come here as a liar. In my submission there are a number of little points and so often it is the little points that count running through this case which point to his having told the truth. Did you notice that in describing the *Zentrale* he could not remember, or I think he said he did not know, the names of the leaders? He said, 'I only know Dr Burgos [*sic*], my own leader. I cannot tell you the leaders of the movement.'[1] Is that the story of a facile liar? Surely a liar would have said, 'Yes, I know them all and here are the names.' Similarly, when I was asking him about the code letters for calls from Germany to him, he said, 'No, I have lost them. I cannot remember them.' He remembered his to Germany but not those from Germany to him. Again, liars do not do that sort of thing.

Why on earth should he tell you that this £500 was his own? Why adopt, if it is not true, this extraordinary story that he refused money? It is so easy and it requires no proof from anybody for him to tell you, 'I was given £500 by the Secret Service when I left Schipol Aerodrome.' It is what we should expect him to say. We should expect him to say, 'The Germans gave me money to do work in this country,' but he does not. He elects to tell you that it was his own and to go into the story of the £86,000[2] worth of bonds and the 10,000 Marks [*sic*] and the amount taken away. [*These were the Mexican securities, but it appears that during his interrogations, Josef or his interrogators converted their value into British pounds.*] He goes into all that. I suggest that liars do not adopt such a course as that when they are trying to hoodwink a Court. [*Stephens had used the money aspect to imply that Josef was a traitor to Germany. He had accepted money from the Germans and then was prepared to skip out on them. Stephens used this tactic with other spies.*]

Then did not you think the story about Raymond, his son, sounded a truthful story, something which really has nothing to do with this case at all and yet enough bearing on it to assist the Court in deciding whether this man is the liar he is said to be or whether he is telling the truth? Why should he tell you he was denounced by Van Hees and that he was under suspicion? It only tends to raise a doubt in the mind of the Court as to his standing with the German authorities. The only effect of his telling you about Van Hees's denunciation of him to the Gestapo is for the Court to say, 'How can this possibly be true. How can the Germans send over to this country as their agent one who had been denounced to them?' [*A very good question; one that will be answered later.*] Yet he tells it. He need not have said a word about his denunciation by Van Hees but he tells it because I suggest it is the truth and a part of his story. He even was prepared to face the questions about the map, the circle and the cross. It was so easy for him to say, 'That is just what they wanted me to do, to go and spy on these aerodromes and they marked those aerodromes.' That is not an answer which would have aroused any suspicion at all. But he said, 'That was not my job. I was not told to spy on aerodromes and I do not know why they marked the aerodromes. My job was to go to London and that is what they told me to do.'

Now he has told his story covering a period from 1935, when he went to Switzerland with his Jewish friend and was imprisoned, until February 2, 1941. I would challenge anybody to give a story of his life over a period such as that without that story containing and showing apparently some inconsistencies. Nor is it surprising that in this case and under those circumstances Jakobs' story should contain inconsistencies and most rightly those inconsistencies have been put to him in cross-examination by Major Marlowe.

The first of them is about his leg. It is suggested to him his leg was not broken in the aeroplane. First of all, I would point out that it is not so very unlikely that it should have been broken in the aeroplane. It was foul weather, it was very cold, and he has told you it was his cold side. The side of the aeroplane was heated against which he was lying and the other side was cold. He put his cold leg out and it blew back and forth in the wind. It is not surprising, is it, that it did blow back and forth? Under the pressure of the wind it was suggested it would blow only back. One has merely to think of a flag flying in a high wind or a public house sign in a strong wind. It does not blow one way; it blows back and forth. He has told you that is how his leg was broken. All of the witnesses here have agreed that the ground was very soft and indeed in his condition it must have been soft for him to have been able to take that spade and to dig in that wireless set. I suggest it is more a probability that his leg was broken in the air rather than by the fall. [*Or the fall simply made a small break significantly worse*]

Then a doubt arose as to the statement he made to Major Robertson on February 1, 1941. I find it difficult to understand all about this statement. I must confess I still do not understand why it was not put in [as an Exhibit]. We have had no evidence on the point but it may well be it was realised that although the statement was made under caution, it was made by a man who was extremely sick and in great pain and that therefore, even from the point of view of the prosecution, it loses that value which would be attached to a man who was in perfect health. [*That may be, but in bringing the statement into the court, Marlowe was able to point out the inconsistencies in Josef's initial statement and the one given to Hinchley-Cooke on 18 June. If it was not considered a valid statement, then it should not have been brought in at all.*] However, that may be, here is this statement. You will remember it was made on the same day as the day on which he was found. It was made after he had spent a night in the cold when there was snow and rain descending, with a broken leg, now broken for many hours, and you will remember his story, which has not been denied, that after the statement was made the doctor had to give him an injection. [*White has gone with Josef's later version, that he received an injection after giving his statement to Robertson.*] On probability it would not be surprising if a statement made in those circumstances contained inaccuracies. Search the statement and find how many there are. The substance of the thing is the same as the story which he has told throughout and as the story which he has told in this court. He mentions there that he was put out of business [selling passports] by the Gestapo. He mentions there the concentration camp, the height from which he jumped and the fact that he was a Catholic and an anti-Nazi. He has one or two inaccuracies. You notice he says, 'I have one son and two daughters.' He says that is wrong and he has given you the names of the sons. He says, 'I broke my ankle on landing.' If it is material – the court may think it is very material because of other evidence that can be applied to the surrounding circumstances of his descent – is it not possible that a man in those circumstances, in the agony of the moment, may not have made himself clear? [*Or that the non-fluent translator did not make it clear? It is perplexing that so little attention is paid to the language skills of Constable Templeman. He could have been called as a witness.*] Is there a great difference between saying, 'I broke my ankle on landing' and 'I had a broken ankle on landing'? It was not an ankle at all. It was his leg, as he knew and everybody knew. My submission about that statement therefore is that perhaps it is not to receive as much value as the statement of a man who was in a sound, healthy and undisturbed mind. But if his story is really different now from the story then – remember that he had all night in which to consider what he was going to say, if lies were to be put forward; he had had all night and the following day – that he had broken his leg in the aeroplane before he left it, he had ample opportunity and ample time in which to prepare that story before he gave the statement to Major Robertson on the evening of February 1.

Then it was put to him that he told lies to the farm labourers. Of course he told lies to the farm labourers. Here is a man – I know the court will forgive me if I reiterate it – who has no knowledge of this country and who has no knowledge of what peasants would do to him on finding him and suspecting that he was a spy. He had spent the night in agony, he had spent the night in the cold and exposure, he had spent the night, as you have now heard, with his clothes soaked in excreta and he had been unconscious for periods of the night. Is it surprising in a strange land and in such pain [that] he should fear those who found him and should want to tell them, until he could reach the officials, a story which would be less likely to arouse their suspicions? For all he knew a spy on being found by a burly farm labourer in this country might have been lynched and therefore he said he was a Frenchman. [*This is not all that farfetched. Recall Grace, one of the loose-lipped letter writers, who said, 'If they came down near us when George was home I'm sure he would shoot them on the way down.'*] He admits now that he said he was a Frenchman and that he told a lie and he told a lie deliberately. Perhaps the court might think it was a lie anyone might have told in the circumstances before he could get before the authorities whom he could trust. At last, when the dawn came and there was a likelihood of somebody hearing him – remember this place had been specifically chosen by reason of its being a quiet spot and a place in which to land a secret agent – he fired his shots. Before he did so he buried his wireless set. Is it really to be said that the burying of the wireless set in its case with the corner of the case protruding is the act of a guilty man, the act of a man who did not want his equipment to fall into the hands of his enemies? He has told you, and it seemed rather a vivid description, that his instructions were to shoot the set with his pistol if it were liable to fall into the hands of the English. Obviously it would have been an easy and simple way. You will remember this man had hardly moved from the time he fell. There was water lying in the hole where his fall was made. Any movement must have been painful. The digging of that spade into the ground must have been agonising. How much easier, if he did not intend it to fall into English hands, that he should have taken out the pistol and shot it. But no; he chose the harder course. Then just before he shot off the pistol, can you see him in that state of mind which I have described and bodily pain, realising he had on him for anyone to see this incriminating code which would suggest immediately to anyone, however poor his education, that this was a spy with a cipher on him. What does he do? He does not burn it; he does not bury it with the wireless set. He just tears it up and scatters the fragments around him in a place which one could see. What is the explanation of that? Is not it panic in the fear and agony of the moment? It is quite irrational. He just, as I submit, panics. Is it going to be suggested to Jakobs, 'Why on earth did you not do at that moment what a normal rational man would have done, that is to say, if you had wanted to prevent the code getting into English hands, burn it, or if you wanted to preserve it for the English, why did not you put it in your pocket?' He did neither of those things. This is such a personal matter. It is a matter in which only the imagination of those who have to decide on his act can help, and I ask the court in considering this very vital point to try and picture clearly and vividly the state of body and mind in which Jakobs was when in his panic he tore up that card and scattered it around him in a place which everyone could see.

When he got to Major Robertson of course he immediately told a different story. [*When he was taken to the police station in Ramsey and faced with two police officers (Jaikens and Mills), Josef told them that he was a soldier and had been sent to report on the weather. Essentially the same story that he told Robertson. So his story of being 'made to come' was only told to the farm labourers and Home Guard. When he saw the police, he came clean. It also needs to be kept in mind that neither Jaikens nor Mills were fluent in German. Mills said that Josef had been instructed to contact a woman in London, but Josef was likely referring to Lily Knips and may have been attempting to communicate his plan to enlist her aide in escaping to America.*] He says that that is his story and it is true. The court will, I know, bear in mind the fact that in substance, in spite of the state he was in, so that he had to be injected almost as soon as he made the statement, it is the same as the story he has given in this court today. It has been suggested that the code itself was a vital code. That is again a matter for the Court to decide. [*How can the court decide if a code would be vital? That is a matter for intelligence officers and cipher specialists.*] It is a matter for the Court to decide whether the card or the [Marinesoldat] code was the more important. [*It might have been beneficial to have a cryptographer called as a witness, rather than relying upon the court to decide which was more important.*] Perhaps it is only a minor issue in the case. The fact remains that Jakobs did reveal the [Marinesoldat] code and he revealed it apparently because it was a code that was hidden in his head and it could have remained there without the knowledge of any of the English authorities. He gave it of his own volition from a place from which none could have taken it unless he wished that they should. [*This was a telling point. Josef revealed the code words on 2 February, during an interrogation in which Stephens threatened Josef's family.*] It is said, 'Oh, you left your wife in the lurch.' He told you he put the matter to his wife at the time, he put it to the *Zentrale*, and his wife agreed. The power of the secret service [German Intelligence Service] in Germany at the moment – and the Court may not be disposed to dispute it – is such that his family would be safe when he was supposedly doing work of the secret service than when he was living with them under observation and suspicion reporting weekly to the police as he has already described to you.

Now I know it will not be considered presumptuous of me when I remark with what restraint the prosecution in this case has been put forward but it is the duty of the Prosecution to foresee the Defence and if possible to meet it in advance. Way back in his opening Major Marlowe told the Court that others have done this sort of thing, come over here, been caught and I suppose told the tale that they wanted to help this country. What if they have? It may be so but that does not go to the length of saying that every time that story is told it is untrue. You may remember I put to Lieutenant Colonel Hinchley-Cooke when I first began my questions to him the point that there must, in Germany at this time, be many opponents of the Nazi regime, there must be many who wish to get out of Germany and to fight their Nazi rulers and it would not be surprising in those circumstances if some of them reached this country. It would be a dangerous assumption – and I know without proof the Court will assume no such thing – that any man just because he arrives from Germany here is a spy. Lieutenant Colonel Hinchley-Cooke agreed with me in this that the Secret Service [German Intelligence Service] is a good way of getting out of Germany. You come out of Germany with the protection of, I suppose it is, the most powerful organisation and not only that but you can bring money with you. There are very few other ways so I imagine of getting money out of Germany at the moment. A Nazi hater if he wants to leave Germany and to bring with him something with which he can help his friends in this country might well choose that way. Do you remember Lieutenant Colonel Hinchley-Cooke again agreeing that the Nazis [*the Abwehr was not affiliated with the Nazi Party*] are not particular about the people whom they choose as their secret agents? It may sound incredible to this Court but from what Lieutenant Colonel Hinchley-Cooke has said and from what Jakobs has said it appears to be true. I suppose the reason is: this is a dangerous job and you can only use volunteers in it. If that is so, volunteers may come from all over the place. They have got to get people to come to England. They may take them out of prison and they may accept non-Aryans. But it appears that the evidence for the Prosecution and the Defence agree in this matter that surprising people are chosen and it may well be therefore that this would be the way that would appeal to an opponent of the Nazi regime to leave his country and come over here. I submit, in spite of all that has been said, that a secret agent arriving in this country in the frame of mind which Jakobs said brought him here could be of help to us. I have put it in my examination in chief, I have put it in my cross-examination, and I do not propose to deal with the point at any length. I only wish to say that it does not require any great strength of imagination to help one to realise that Nazi agents here working in co-operation with the secret service of this country must be of value. It may be he is not told much of the secrets of Germany and of his fellow workers; but when he is here surely it is one of the most useful things that can be done in the realms of secret service to be able to denounce to the authorities in this country those either of German origin or of English who are working here in league with the enemy. Jakobs has described how he would meet those people here. I do not know whether anybody had seen it before, but when the pocket book [Exhibit 8, leather wallet] was produced and looked at I noticed the President of the Court pulled a note-book out. [*This may have happened during Newton's testimony when Josef had a reaction as the wallet was handled.*] I was interested at once. It was shown to the accused. [*This perhaps happened later, during Josef's own testimony (court martial transcript pp. 53–59), where the transcript has possibly been redacted.*] You saw the interesting facts that arose from that. The accused has not had that thing since it was taken from him on arrival here. [*If White recognised that Josef had not seen the notebook since he arrived in England, why did he not question its absence at the Summary of Evidence or the way in which it was omitted from the court martial exhibits?*] He says that before he left The Hague he wrote in his own handwriting assignations, places and dates for meeting people in this country and he says those people would have given him money because he has to live here. [*Or was Josef to meet them and hand over money? There is always the possibility that Josef, sent with a much larger sum of money than previous spies, was to have passed along funds to another agent, as Stephens suspected. Was he supposed to meet an agent such as TATE or Jan Willem Ter Braak/Engelbertus Fukken? TATE requested funds on 14 January 1941. Josef was sent on 31 January with three possible rendezvous dates in his notebook: the 1st, 2nd and 3rd of the month. By 4 February, the Germans were arranging for SNOW to send money to TATE. Had the Germans perhaps given up on Josef making a rendezvous?*] What a valuable thing to the Secret Service here, to have a man in league with them who can go to those places of which they have particulars in writing on the dates of which they have particulars in writing and track down and arrest those be it of one nationality or another who are working against the interests of this country in league with the agents of Germany. [*Very true, except MI5 already had that system set up and populated with a variety of double-cross agents.*] I submit that even if there be no other way – and there may be many ways to which my imagination does not lend me – that is a most valuable piece of assistance which he could give us and he says that if his assistance were not accepted or if his work was done then he has this relative in America to whom he could go. The Court may think there is very little suspicious about that. [*White didn't know, or didn't understand, that Josef had agreed to assist MI5 on 2 February. Josef operated from the assumption that he had a deal with them. MI5 just didn't honour that deal.*]

Now I feel I must not delay the Court any longer but is it a fantastic speculation that the brutality and the sordid venality of the Nazis should produce in the heart of a man a hatred of their rule? Is it surprising that a man who is a Roman Catholic and a non-Aryan in particular should come to detest his masters in Germany? Of course if he comes here and lands and is found, then suspicion must attach to his landing. We must face that. But it would be a dreadful thing if, having left his country with all those risks taken and all those hardships borne he should arrive here with intent to help and find that his expectation leads him only to the firing squad.

The Court I know will weigh these grave matters, for grave they are. The Court has to decide in cold blood for this man Jakobs the question of life or death and unless the Prosecution has proved to you beyond reasonable doubt that Jakobs is guilty of the offence which is alleged against him, death it cannot be. Has not the story of this man Jakobs unfolded to you yesterday and today, voluntarily and under the sanctity of an oath, sown in the minds of each of you such a doubt as to his guilt that you must say, 'I cannot condemn this man to die'.[4]

40

JUDGE ADVOCATE'S SUMMING UP

Stirling, the Judge Advocate, then stood and summed up the case for the court:

May it please the court. About half past 8 on the morning of Saturday 1 February of this year, some revolver [*sic*] shots were heard by Mr Baldock and Mr Coulson in the neighbourhood of a sparsely populated district in Huntingdon near the little town of Ramsey. Interested at hearing these shots they proceeded to a field and there they found lying in the field a man. This was no ordinary man as you have learned during the last two days. He apparently was dressed in civilian clothes and had brought with him a curious collection of articles. One thing that stands out beyond any dispute in this case is that that man's right leg had been damaged.

Now the prosecution have not thought it necessary in this case to place medical evidence before you as to the kind of injury he had suffered and the extent of it, but I think you will be satisfied that there is only one thing you can say from all the surrounding circumstances that you have heard and that is that that man had an injury to his right leg which prevented him from moving any distance at all from the spot where he was lying.

Now, gentlemen, I am going to ask you later on to consider two questions, mere questions of fact. The first one I would ask you to consider when you have the whole of the evidence clearly in your mind is: Who exactly was that man who was lying in that field? Secondly, when you are satisfied about that, ask yourselves: Why did he come there? I am not going to detain you long on the first question. There is ample evidence before you, if you accept it, to establish that that man is one Josef

Jakobs, that he is a German national, that he was born in Luxembourg something like 43 years ago and that he is a married man with a Roman Catholic religion.

Now he is lying there in the field unable to move and when he is accosted by Mr Baldock and Mr Coulson and by Mr Godfrey of the Home Guard and by Captain Newton, who was also in the Home Guard, on that morning, he is naturally asked certain questions. On this occasion, gentlemen, you need no reminding from me that none of the people who were asking questions could speak German and it is for you to decide how much English Jakobs could in fact speak at that time. It is not for me to surmise on those matters; it is for me merely to remind you what emerged from those initial conversations with Josef Jakobs. They are the first conversations and they are very important in this case. [*The first conversations with the farmers, the Home Guard and the Ramsey Police were all hampered by language issues. By their own admission, the witnesses stated that Josef said much more that they could not understand, and they simply reported the words that they could understand.*] But I want to remind you that this is a human problem that you have to consider. This man undoubtedly had been flown over to this country in an aeroplane from Germany and he had landed by means of a parachute. Whether he broke his leg getting out of the [aeroplane] or whether he broke it on landing is for you to decide. But it seems to follow he had suffered a severe physical ordeal of lying in this field on a cold night in the way he has described and you may think that with regard to anything he says at that time there is room indeed for a man not to make his meaning very clear and understandable to English people who did not speak German.

Now he has admitted and given reasons for his stating what was not true and it is for you to say whether you are satisfied that his explanations are reasonable. What apparently he did say in answer to Mr Baldock was: 'Me solo flying. I have come from Hamburg. I am in no war. I am a Frenchman and I came down in a parachute.' Apparently Mr Coulson did not hear him say anything, but Mr Godfrey – and I think I must point out in fairness to the accused that there is a point on Mr Godfrey's evidence which should have your consideration – says what he got out of the accused was this. He was asked 'What are you doing?' and he said, 'Me solo flying. I came out at 3,000 metres.' He was asked where his [aeroplane] was and got no answer. Then he is supposed to have said, 'Me in no war. Me from Luxembourg. Made to come. Me French.' And then he said his leg was broken. Rightly or wrongly, it is for you to decide what that means, but it is my duty on behalf of the accused to point out that one witness, Mr Godfrey, said on that morning he was saying 'Made to come'. Gentlemen I do not think there is anything further to be obtained from Captain Newton. He merely discovered from the accused that he was a Frenchman and came from Luxembourg.

Now, gentlemen, it is admitted that that is not altogether a true statement of who the man was and I think having heard the evidence in this court you are satisfied that what he said there was incorrect, and if you accept what he says – and there is no reason to disbelieve him on these matters – you will presumably accept his own version as to who he is. If that be so, are you satisfied that Josef Jakobs came over to this country in an aeroplane and that he landed by parachute in the night of the 31 January and the 1 February and that he broke his ankle and that he was found in that field and that he was there for some purpose which you have to discover? Let me remind you very shortly that you have had a detailed description from the mouth of the accused as to his life as he tells it now. I am going to tell you this, gentlemen, that, of course, you will not disbelieve the story told by the accused merely because he is the accused. You will consider what he has sworn on oath and if you are satisfied that is true, you will accept it. If you do not believe it because it is inherently impossible, or you cannot accept it, because there is other evidence which shows it cannot be true, then, gentlemen, you will not accept it.

One of the difficulties in a case of this kind is obvious and that is that it is not possible to check up the statements as to the accused's life in Germany before he arrived here. [*Would the trial have gone differently if Josef had had access to witnesses for the defence?*] Let me very shortly remind you of a few of the matters which he says happened to him there. It appears, if you accept it from him, that he has been an officer in the old German army; it appears also from his own statement that he has been in trouble in Switzerland. He tells you that he was called up for military service, I think it was in June 1940, and that he was returned back and not made use of. He tells you that he was in a concentration camp in Germany when this war broke out. He tells you quite a lot about himself and finally he says that he was a member at this time of the Intelligence Service of the German General Staff, 5th Section. He tells you that he had unhappy experiences in Germany because he was an anti-Nazi, that he has certain Jewish antecedents, and that he has suffered at the hands of the Nazis and he is no friend of the Nazi regime and not working with them. I do not propose to take up any time in dealing with his history. You have heard it and you have made your notes and it is for you to decide. [*Did they make notes? They had been told at the beginning of the court martial that they did not need to take notes.*] The real point you have to consider about that history is whether you are going to accept the case for the prosecution and that is that it did not cause him in any way to become anti-Nazi and that he was at no time working against the Nazis, or whether you are going to accept the suggestion of the defence that by reason of his experiences and by the way he had been treated it was obvious he would not work loyally and faithfully for such a regime. Are you satisfied beyond all reasonable doubt who this man was who was lying in that field? I may suggest to you there is ample evidence there to satisfy yourself on that point.

We now come to what is the real important question in his case: Why did he come to England? What was his object in coming to England? What had he in his mind when he descended by parachute near Huntingdon on the night of the 31 January? Gentlemen, I am not going to take up your time in telling you what he brought. You have had it detailed to you at great length. You have heard about the pistol, the ammunition, the steel helmet, the parachute, the forged ration book, the [identity cards], the map that was marked, the torch which was useful for signalling, the code or cipher, whichever way you like to have it, and the £500 in money. It seems to me, gentlemen, there can be no question at all what that man had been fitted out for or what he was supposed to do. It is for you to decide. But is it not an irresistible inference that those are the tools of a man who has come here in order that he may signal back useful information to those who sent him to this country. I do not think that will really trouble you at all. The accused himself has given you a detailed account of how his masters taught him Morse, how they told him what to do, that these things were provided for him, and in fact he told you his instructions were that when he came to England, by means of these surreptitious codes, he was to notify appropriate authorities in Germany weather reports as to the weather in this country. It seems to me there can be no question at all in your mind—of course, it is for you to decide and it is your responsibility—but are you perfectly satisfied that this man, Josef Jakobs was sent over to this country for the purpose of spying and sending back information to the Germans.

Let me remind you of this, and this is the important point of my directions to you. As you know, it takes two people to make a bargain and what this case really reduces itself to is this: The defence agree, as I understand it, that Jakobs was ordered and was furnished with the necessary equipment and that he was sent out by his masters for the purpose of sending back information and that the accused agreed with his masters to do so, but that in his own mind he never intended to carry it out, that he himself was playing a part to deceive his masters. The case for the defence shortly is this – that whereas on the face of it he was here as a spy and his masters believed he had come here as a spy, he, Jakobs had come here to get away from the Nazi regime or for any reason which he has made clear to you in the witness box. But he says, 'I never came here to assist the German Reich in the prosecution of the war. I was coming here for the purpose of helping England and making it bad not for Germany but those who control it.' That is the real point. It seems to me there can be no dispute that he was sent here again I emphasise it is for you – as a spy. The sole question for you to decide is: Have the prosecution satisfied you with what motive the accused was in fact coming here.

Now I do not think I need go through the arguments for and against what has been put to you by the prosecution and the defence on this point. The prosecution, very restrained and very ably, have cross-examined Jakobs and they suggest that the story he has told you is one which you cannot believe. On the other hand, Captain White, who has put his case most ably to you, submits that Jakobs is a witness of truth and that you should accept from him on his oath that the true position was that he was coming here not to help the Germans in any way but for the reasons which he has told you in the witness box. It is of course proper to consider statements made by the accused when you come to try and answer the question why he came here. I know you will be absolutely fair to the accused when you come to consider any statements and in what circumstances they were made.

Now mention has been made of this statement which was made on the evening of the 1 February to Major Robertson. I do not propose to deal with it in any way; it speaks for itself. My duty to the accused is to remind you that no person could possibly have been in good mental and physical shape at that time of night after the experiences that Jakobs had been through, and in considering that statement and weighing it up, whether it is in favour of the accused or against him, I know you will consider what this man had been passing through from, roughly, something like half past 8 on the previous night. There is the statement before you and you will naturally consider it. It gives a reason there, if you accept it to be accurately taken down, for the accused coming to England. It does also suggest that he broke his leg on landing rather than the story he tells now in court. Those are matters which you will have to consider in the light of his physical condition at the time he was making it. [*There were actually two issues: (1) Josef's physical condition and state of mind and (2) the quality of the translation by Constable Templeman.*]

Now, Sir, in this court the accused has been given ample opportunity to tell you what his version under oath is of his coming to this country. You know that it is rather difficult with a witness who does not speak English very well to make the court understand what he is trying to say and, therefore, in considering what he has told the court it would be only right and fair to remember under what disabilities Jakobs is speaking. Sometimes he tells you a little bit in English and then it fails him and we have to have recourse to the interpreter. Gentlemen, it is for you to decide what he was trying to tell you and, if I have got it correctly, I understood one of his reasons for coming to this country was to establish a liaison between the Jews who were in the *Zentrale* Party and the Jews who were in England. Whether that is right or not, it is for you to decide. You have heard the evidence and you alone have to decide what he was trying to say. He also told you, as I understand it, that he was coming to this country so that he might help the Secret Service and so that he might do harm to the Secret Service in Germany. Those are all matters which I know will receive your careful consideration. You have heard them all and it is for you to decide what the accused's version is of his coming to this country. Those are the versions which you have had, the written version from Major Robertson and the version which is given in this court. [*Stirling makes no reference to the statement made to Hinchley-Cooke but seems to revert back to the questionable statement made to Robertson. Why emphasise the statement made to Robertson as opposed to the one made to Hinchley-Cooke?*]

Let me now remind you a little of the law which applies in this case. As you know, this country has endeavoured to arm itself in every way to resist German aggression. It has naturally obtained munitions and it has made a large army. It has protected itself in every possible way. One of the ways in which it has attempted to protect itself is by legislation. In 1940 Parliament decided to pass what is perhaps in this case rather an ineptly named Act called the Treachery Act of 1940 and under that Act they passed a short and drastic section which I am going to read to you.

The effect of this Act was to say that if an alien enemy in the United Kingdom with intent to help the enemy does or attempts with any other person to do any act which is designed or likely to give assistance to the naval, military or air operations of the enemy, to impede such operations of His Majesty's Forces or to endanger life, he shall be guilty of felony and shall on conviction suffer death. An alien enemy is defined under Section 5 as a person who possesses the nationality of a state at war with His Majesty not being either an English subject or a person certified by the Secretary of State to be an English protected person. The actual charge against the accused which you have had read to you and which I think must be quite clear, alleges that at Ramsey in the County of Huntingdon on the night of 31 January and 1 February, 1941, with intent to help the enemy the accused did an act designed or likely to give assistance to naval, military or air operations of the enemy or to impede such operations of His Majesty's forces, namely, did descend by parachute in the United Kingdom.

What the prosecution have to prove in this case, putting it in simple language, is that you have to be satisfied beyond all reasonable doubt that on this night this alien enemy, Josef Jakobs, landed by parachute in the United Kingdom and that when he did so he was coming with the intent to help the Germans, to help his own nationals, and coming here with the intention to send back messages which would be helpful to the Germans and a disservice to the forces here. If he was coming down in his parachute for that purpose, then, gentlemen, I think you would say clearly it came within the wording of those particulars. [*Returning to the MPs who questioned the Treachery Act in late May 1940, one is naturally left to question how 'intention' could be proved with any certainty*]

That, gentlemen, brings you back to the question of why did Jakobs come here? If he came here, and you are satisfied of that beyond all reasonable doubt, for the purpose of sending back these messages, then clearly it would be open to you to convict. On the other hand, if you are not satisfied of that and you think he was coming here, as it were double crossing his own masters, that he was coming here in truth and in fact so that he might give himself up and would do no harm in this country but to help them, then he is entitled to be acquitted of this charge because you will see that the act must have been with intent to help the enemy and the act itself must have been one designed as set out in the particulars of the charge.

Having dealt with the law, you come back again, as I say, to this all-important question which you must decide in the light of the evidence: Why did Jakobs come to this country? I do not think I need deal with the facts more in detail, but I am going to give you this very important direction in law: The prosecution have in this case to satisfy you beyond all reasonable doubt why Josef Jakobs came to this country. They must satisfy you that it is an irresistible inference that as reasonable men the only inference you can draw from the evidence you have heard in this case is that he was coming here for the purpose of sending back messages and spying and that is really why he came and that is what he would have done if everything had not gone wrong owing to the injury to his leg. [*Can the determination of intent ever be anything other than an 'inference'? Is an 'irresistible inference' actual 'proof'? This was exactly the concern raised by MP Silverman when the Treachery Act was discussed on 22 May 1940. Essentially, the court had to decide if they believed Josef's story or not. Was he a liar or not?*] If you are satisfied that that is the real and only inference you can draw, then you must convict the accused. On the other hand, if you are satisfied that the story told by the accused on oath is convincing and is the truth, then clearly you must acquit the accused of this charge. In the third event, if you are unable to say why he came here at all, that it might be one reason or it might be another, that it is possible he came here to spy or it is possible he came here, innocently, so far as this country is concerned, in the way he says; then he is entitled to be acquitted.

I do not think in the case of a court-martial such as this I need say very much more. If this were a case being tried at the Central Criminal Court with a Jury and one of His Majesty's High Court Judges, he would naturally warn the Jury that they must deal with this German just as they would with an Englishman. But, gentlemen, you are officers of long service. As you know perfectly well, this man, though he be a German, an alien, is entitled according to the law of this country to a trial just in the same way as if he were an English person and I know you will carry out your duties with complete impartiality. [*Except for being unable to call witnesses for the defence from Germany.*]

Now you have had addressed to you observations put forward for your assistance by the learned prosecutor and by the learned defending officer. They have each put forward those points which they would like you to consider when you come to discuss this case in closed court. My duty is to make sure that you appreciate what the law is, but the responsibility, gentlemen, is upon you and you alone. You have to consider the evidence which you have heard in this court. I am not going to detain you any longer. I am going to ask you to consider the evidence and say whether it satisfies you or not that on this night, the 31 January and the 1 February, the accused was in fact intentionally coming down in this country and making a breach in that legislation of the Treachery Act to which I have referred, and if so, he must suffer the consequences set out. If you are satisfied, you will convict. If you have a reasonable doubt such as I have indicated, you will acquit.

Now, Sir, I must ask you to close the court to consider the finding in this case.[1]

41

VERDICT AND SENTENCE

After closing the court at 12.35 p.m., the president, the four members of the court, and Stirling retired to consider the verdict. Stirling did not vote but was simply there to offer legal advice if required. The president read out the charge and asked each member of the court, beginning with the most junior officer, to voice their opinion as to the guilt or innocence of Josef.[1] In order to sentence Josef to death, all five officers needed to find him guilty. After ten minutes of deliberation, the president reopened the court.[2]

Stirling told Marlowe that they had no findings to announce (publicly) in the case.[3] That was not a good sign. Had Josef been acquitted, the findings would have been announced in open court. Stirling asked Marlowe if he had anything to offer regarding Josef's character, but Marlowe admitted that they had no access to Josef's military service records. Stirling then turned to White and asked if he wished to put anything on the record or if Josef would like to say anything. At White's invitation, Josef stated, 'I can only say that I was under oath and I have stated the truth.' White had nothing to add, feeling it had already all been said.

Stirling and the president asked that Josef be withdrawn from the court, although he was not to go away, and he was asked one last time if he had anything he wished to say to the court. Josef replied, 'Except when the court find me not guilty I will do all I can to help England. More I cannot say.'[4] It was already a moot point; Josef had been found guilty.

After Josef had been removed from the court, Stirling requested that the president close the court so that they could discuss the sentence. The president congratulated White, acknowledging that he had done extremely well under difficult circumstances. He also thanked the interpreter and that formed the conclusion of the proceedings in open court.[5]

After everyone had left the court room, including the lawyers for the prosecution and the defence, the president of the court wrote the only possible sentence on the court martial form:

> The Court sentence the accused, Josef Jakobs, to suffer death by being shot.[6]

Stirling then laid a piece of paper before the president entitled *Communication to an Accused Person upon whom a Sentence of Death has been passed by Court-Martial*. The paper was divided into two columns: the left-hand side was in English and the right-hand side was in German.[7] The paper had been typed up ahead of time by Hinchley-Cooke. Presumably a second version, one that found the accused not guilty was also available. The form stated:

To Josef Jakobs

The Court have found you guilty of the following charge:

[the same charge as earlier]

The Court have passed a sentence of death upon you.

The Court have made a/no recommendation to mercy in the following terms,

You should clearly understand:

(1) That the finding and sentence are not valid until confirmed by the proper authority.

(2) That the authority having power to confirm the finding and sentence may withhold confirmation of the finding, or may withhold confirmation of the sentence, or may commute or remit the sentence, or may send the finding and sentence back to the Court for revision.

If you do not clearly understand the foregoing you should request to see an officer, who will fully explain the matter to you. Lt Col W.E. Hinchley-Cooke will do this if you so desire.[8]

The communication was placed within a sealed envelope and Josef was called back into the room to receive it.[9] Josef may have already sensed the verdict. His military policemen were still hovering around him.

His defence lawyer had not congratulated him. He may have opened the envelope in the court room, or he may have waited until he arrived back at Wandsworth Prison. When he did open it, all hope vanished. He had been found guilty. He had been sentenced to death. The court had made no recommendation for mercy. There were no surprises. There was no hope. Or was there?

Josef asked Hinchley-Cooke about the 'proper authority' that would confirm the finding. Hinchley-Cooke said that in England, the confirming authority was usually the General Officer Commanding, in this case of the London District. Josef stared at the piece of paper in front of him and knew that another army officer would most likely confirm the finding. Was there no hope? There was – he could always appeal to the highest authority in the country, in this case, His Majesty the King. His words in court had not been enough, but perhaps his written word would alter the course of events. Josef thanked Hinchley-Cooke for his assistance and asked for a German-speaking priest.

42

MINISTERING TO A GERMAN SPY

From 23 July to 15 August Josef was held in a special cell at Wandsworth Prison, segregated from the other inmates. While most prisoners were permitted to attend chapel on Sundays, Josef remained locked in his cell. Despite the secrecy surrounding his arrival at the prison, whispers about the 'man in F3/1' circulated among the inmates and staff. On Sunday, 27 July, a few days after Josef's arrival, the prison's Catholic chaplain, Father Edward Daly got wind of the rumours. Daly approached the prison governor that afternoon and asked if he could have access to Josef regarding spiritual matters.[1] Grew told Daly that it wasn't up to him because the man in F3/1 was a military prisoner. He agreed to follow up with the military authorities and see if Daly could be granted access.

Grew was as good as his word and sent a memo to Hinchley-Cooke that afternoon. The following day, after the Summary of Evidence had been taken at Wellington Barracks, Cussen and Gerard (DPM) drove to Wandsworth Prison to speak with Daly but were told that he was away. Two days later, on 30 July, after phoning the priest, Cussen and Gerard met with him and explained the delicate situation.[2]

Although Josef was being held at a civilian prison, he was a military prisoner and all visitation arrangements had to be made through the DPM.[3] Gerard and Cussen were both happy to have Father Daly minister to Josef as long as certain conditions were met: (a) Daly could not speak about the prisoner to anyone, (b) Daly could not give the prisoner information of any kind on any subject and (c) if the prisoner gave information to Daly, other than under the seal of the confessional, they hoped that Daly would communicate it to them.[4]

Daly listened to the conditions and agreed to them. As a full-time prison chaplain, he was already subject to the Official Secrets Act and would have no trouble maintaining the veil of secrecy around Josef's case.[5] All three men agreed that Daly should see Josef as soon as possible and definitely before the following Sunday (3 August).[6] Josef's court martial started on Monday and the men agreed that he would derive great comfort from a chaplain's spiritual care. Cussen also asked Daly, if sentence of death were passed, would he make himself available to see Josef every day up until the date of his execution.[7] Daly was satisfied with the arrangements and everything was in order.[8]

Although the arrangements had been made and Father Daly had Gerard's express permission to minister to Josef, something still wasn't working. On 3 August, Bishop James Dey (Roman Catholic Vicar Apostolic of Great Britain, Military) wrote to Guy William Lambert, Assistant Undersecretary of State for War, regarding the Catholic chaplain at Wandsworth Prison.[9] The bishop said that Daly was having great difficulty dealing with prisoners sent to the prison by War Office regulations. The men[10] were sent to Wandsworth Prison to await trial but, during the period before their court martial, Daly was not permitted to have access to them. If they were found guilty and sentenced to death, then the sentence was generally carried out within forty-eight hours and it was only during this time that he was allowed to have any communication with them. Father Daly complained that this was too short a period for him to be of real spiritual service. Bishop Dey wanted to know the official attitude with regard to the matter, as Daly had a case under his care at that moment.[11]

On Tuesday, 5 August, Hinchley-Cooke was told about the letter and, perplexed, called Cussen into the room.[12] Cussen was at a loss to explain it – unless Daly had written the letter to the bishop prior to their visit on 30 July. Cussen couldn't understand where Daly got the impression that the sentence of death was carried out within forty-eight hours of a guilty verdict.[13] It is possible that Father Daly visited Josef prior to the court-martial proceedings but that the language issue was a barrier, hence Josef's request on 5 August for a German-speaking priest.

On the evening of 5 August, Hinchley-Cooke asked Butler to find a German-speaking priest for Josef. Since Josef was in military custody, Butler contacted the army chaplains' office the next day and spoke with the Right Reverend Monsignor John Coghlan, Senior Roman Catholic Chaplain to the Forces. Coghlan listened to Butler's problem and agreed that, given the circumstances surrounding Josef's incarceration, his spiritual care was definitely within the jurisdiction of the army chaplains. Coghlan suggested that Father Edward J. Griffith, an army chaplain formerly of the Brompton Oratory, would be an ideal candidate as he spoke excellent German. Griffith was currently stationed at a hospital in Liverpool where he ministered to German prisoners of war and was reliable in every way. With Hinchley-Cooke's approval, Butler asked that Griffith report to London that evening (6 August).[14] Coghlan immediately telephoned Griffith[15] and told him that his services were urgently required for a special duty. All would be explained that evening. Mystified, Griffith packed his bags and boarded a train for London.

After a long train ride, Griffith disembarked at a busy London railway station. A car had been sent to pick him up and he was whisked off to Hobart House, Grosvenor Place, and shown to the offices of Monsignor Coghlan. At around 7 p.m. Cussen and Butler arrived and explained Griffith's special duty. Griffith was exhausted from his trip, but he also understood the urgency of the situation. A man had been charged with espionage, undergone a court martial and been sentenced to death, all without proper spiritual support. Griffith was a young priest, only three years ordained, and life had not prepared him to offer spiritual guidance to a condemned man, but he knew that he could rely on God. Cussen and Griffith left for Wandsworth Prison while Coghlan telephoned Bishop Dey to explain the situation. Guy Lambert from the War Office also wrote an official letter to Bishop Dey to sooth ruffled episcopal feathers.[16]

Upon arrival at Wandsworth Prison, Cussen escorted the priest to Josef's cell, called the guards out and left the two men alone. After about twenty minutes, Griffith came out of the cell and told Cussen that he would say Mass in Josef's cell every day and visit with him whenever he could be of greater service. Cussen thanked Griffith for his time and asked him to liaise with the DPM.[17]

As for Josef, one can only imagine his relief. It was virtually a certainty that during his incarceration at Latchmere House he had had no access to a Catholic (or non-Catholic) chaplain. Latchmere House was a top-secret facility and visitors, be they ambassadors, clergymen, relatives or legal advisors, were prohibited.[18]

In May 1941, the *Catholic Herald* published an article entitled 'Conditions of Political Prison Life in Britain'. The article highlighted the complaints of some Latchmere House inmates detained during the summer of 1940. These were Britons who, for one reason or another, had come under suspicion and been interned under Regulation 18B. One man, Philip Shelmerdine, had acted as an election agent for a British Union (of Fascists) parliamentary candidate. Shelmerdine spoke of his own experience of internment with undisguised bitterness, 'I was never allowed to attend Mass or practice my religion during the five weeks I was at this camp, neither were detainees of other denominations permitted to attend services.'[19] Isolation was the name of the game at Latchmere House, a tactic designed to break prisoners quickly and completely.

Finally, in the last ten days of his life, Josef was once again able to hear Mass in his native tongue. He was able to have his confession heard. He could clear his soul of any lingering darkness. Josef knew that the end was coming. There was still the chance of a royal reprieve, but if that failed, Josef would go to his death.

43

A PLEA FOR MERCY

On 7 August 1941, Stirling, the Judge Advocate, sent the court martial proceedings to the General Officer Commanding, London District. Stirling apologised for the delay but noted that he had only received the trial transcript that day.[1] The General Officer Commanding, reviewed the court martial proceedings and returned them with a note stating that he saw 'no reason to dissent from the finding and sentence of the Court'.[2]

With the military's final stamp of approval, Josef's only chance for life lay with George VI. On 6 August, possibly with the assistance of Father Griffith, Josef wrote a handwritten plea for mercy to the king. Josef knew that his life hung in the balance and he wrote with great care. He knew that George VI was a father, and so Josef tried to garner sympathy by mentioning his wife and three children in Germany. Once Josef was satisfied with the letter, it began its journey into the hands of the king.

The letter was likely sent to Hinchley-Cooke, who translated it from German into English.[3] From there, the letter made its way to the office of the General Officer Commanding from whence, on 8 August, it was sent to the JAG to be transmitted to the proper authority.[4]

That same day, the JAG sent a letter to the Secretary of State for War with the proceedings of Josef's court martial.[5] Within the letter, the JAG noted that he was also forwarding a petition from the accused, about which he had this to say:

I have the honour to state for the information of His Majesty the King, that the charge was well laid, that there was evidence to justify the finding of the Court and that the sentence was according to law.

I have considered the Petition, and I have the honour to state for the information of The King that, in my opinion, no legal grounds are disclosed in it for interference with the finding of the Court-Martial.[6]

The JAG noted that the recommendation of the General Officer Commanding, London District, was attached. At the base of the letter was a handwritten note from Lieutenant General Ronald F. Adam, the Adjutant General to the Forces. The note, dated 9 August, was succinct:

I recommend that His Majesty be advised to confirm the finding and sentence of the Court and I further recommend that His Majesty be advised not to issue a special instruction in regard to the Petition.[7]

On 9 or 10 August, the petition was submitted to the king. The cover letter outlined the charge, the finding and the sentence, and was signed by the Secretary of State for War, David Margesson. The final paragraph noted:

The attached Petition has received the careful consideration of the Judge Advocate General, who states for the information of Your Majesty that it discloses no legal grounds for interfering with the finding of the Court. It is therefore not recommended that Your Majesty may be pleased to issue any special instruction in regard thereto.[8]

The submission to the king included a three-page summary of Josef's case as well as the main points brought forward in his petition. The summary concluded with the question, 'Do you consider, please, that it should be recommended to His Majesty that he be pleased to confirm the finding and sentence of the Court?'

A brief handwritten note below the question simply stated, 'I recommend confirmation.' The note was signed by C.J. Wallace, the Director of Personal Services, on 9 August 1941.

Josef's petition to the king spoke for itself:

The humble petition of Josef Jakobs, a prisoner under sentence of death.
   To His Majesty The King
   May it please your Majesty,
   A most unhappy man makes this appeal for mercy at the hands of Your Majesty. On the 5th of August, 1941, Your Majesty's Court-martial

condemned me to death, convinced that I came to Your Majesty's country with the intent to do her harm by transmitting information to the Nazis.

Your Majesty, in the face of death, I once again give the assurance which I have already given under oath before the Court-martial, I swear by the dearest and most precious thing I possess, the life of my three children that this never was and never could be the case, that it is just the opposite, that I came to Your Majesty's country with the sole purpose of fighting on England's side against the Nazis. I came to Your Majesty's country with the sole purpose of joining in the fight for personal freedom, for religious freedom for my children, for freeing the German people from the frightful enslavement of the Nazi tyranny and not to die for the Nazi tyrants.

Your Majesty can obtain a clearer idea from the speech of my defending officer, Captain White, of the unfortunate circumstances of my landing, a landing which at the time, however, I considered fortunate. I have nothing to alter in his descriptions, for they are entirely in accord with the facts.

Should your Majesty, however, believe that I am not worthy of Your Majesty's mercy, I beg Your Majesty to postpone the execution until the termination of the war, in order thereby to make it possible for me, at a fresh trial, to prove to the full my innocence by obtaining the attendance of witnesses now living in Germany and the production of documents. In the very nature of my case such evidence, which in fact exists, is by reason of the war not available to me. It is a difficulty which must face every enemy of the Nazis who leaves Germany and comes to this country. But surely England will not, for lack of such evidence, condemn to death a friend and one who will gladly help her. [*Josef actually brings up a very good point. He did not have access to German witnesses and documents for his defence.*]

Your Majesty, as the very facts of my arrival in this country will show Your Majesty, I am no coward, I am not afraid of death. I would accept the verdict of the Court-martial without this appeal for mercy, if I felt myself even in the least guilty of the charge brought against me. But the opposite is the truth and for that reason I beg Your Majesty mercifully to refuse to confirm the sentence passed on me. A wife and three young children join with me in this appeal.

I do not want to close this appeal for mercy without assuring Your Majesty once again that Your Majesty would show mercy not to an enemy agent but to a friend, a true friend of England.

Your Majesty's most humble servant,

[signed] Josef Jakobs[9]

The king had been advised to reject Josef's plea for mercy and he did just that. The plea of one father and husband to another was not granted. George VI had a wife and two children, but he was also a monarch. George VI had German ancestors, but he was also the ruler of a country at war with Germany. The king was governed, not so much by his royal authority, but by the recommendations of civil and military authorities: the Judge Advocate General, the Secretary of State for War, the General Officer Commanding (London District), the Adjutant General of the Forces and the Director of Personal Services. Ruthlessness, not mercy, was the order of the day in a nation besieged by a loathsome enemy. By Wednesday, 13 August, the king had confirmed the findings of Josef's court martial and commanded that the sentence be carried into effect.[10]

Was Josef's petition to the king a waste of time? Did any petition to the king succeed? The answer was, 'yes'. At least one man escaped death through a successful petition to the king. His circumstances were, however, very different from those of Josef.

44

FOOLISH GUNNER JACKSON

In October 1941, two months after Josef's court martial, Gunner Philip Jackson, Royal Artillery, wrote a letter to the Spanish Embassy asking for an interview with the German Minister in Ireland as he wanted to offer his services to the Germans.[1] A copy of Jackson's letter was secretly intercepted by the British and passed along to MI5.[2] The intelligence officers learned that Jackson was a disgruntled soldier and 'mentally he was of a low order'.[3] Jackson had committed an act with intent to help the enemy, namely sending a letter. MI5 decided to launch a sting operation against Jackson.

In December 1941, Jackson met a man named Marshall in the Imperial Hotel in Birmingham. Jackson thought Marshall was connected with the Germans, but he was actually Chief Inspector Sanders of the Birmingham City Police. At the end of the conversation, during which the unsuspecting gunner had incriminated himself, Jackson was arrested and sent to London. The hapless gunner was charged under Section 1 of the Treachery Act, court-martialled in early February 1941, found guilty and sentenced to death by being shot. Liddell was 'rather appalled at the disparity of justice between a case of this sort for example and that of Gerald Hamilton who was interned under [DR] 18B and has subsequently been released under [DR] 18A'.[4]

Unfortunately, MI5 realised rather belatedly that the execution of Jackson could be a problem:

It is imperative for security reasons that no information should leak in certain quarters that this man's communications have become known to the British authorities. If he were shot, or if the sentence were commuted and he were detained in a civil prison, there is no guarantee that it would not become known that his activities had come to light.[5]

In other words, the Spanish and Germans could not learn that Jackson had been busted. If the Spanish even caught a whiff of Jackson's execution, they would undoubtedly smell a rat. While the circumstances aren't clear, it would appear that the Spanish still had Jackson's original letter and someone within the Spanish Embassy had leaked a copy to the British.[6] News of Jackson's execution would raise red flags with the Spanish and create trouble.

Jackson's death needed to be avoided and two avenues lay open to the authorities. In the first case, two medical practitioners could evaluate Jackson and, if they concluded that he was insane at the time of the offence, he could then be locked up in Broadmoor Criminal Lunatic Asylum. If that failed, then Jackson's sentence would need to be commuted to penal servitude for life in a military prison, and the only way that could happen was via a petition to the king.

Jackson was assessed by two medical practitioners, who concluded that he was not insane at the time of his offence. Option one, committal to the anonymous padded cell of a lunatic asylum, was off the table. Option two it would have to be, but Jackson was a stubborn man. Jackson refused to submit a petition to the king. He had heard of life in prison and wanted no part of it. He preferred 'Death to such an Inhuman Life'.[7] MI5 would not, however, be diverted from their plan. Jackson received a visit from Hinchley-Cooke, after which he, in his own words, 'very foolishly gave consent'[8] to submit a petition to the king.

Jackson's petition was not, however, an impassioned, handwritten letter. It was a well-crafted legal document drawn up by a lawyer. The petition pointed out the mitigating factors of Jackson's life (volunteered for the army; sole supporter of his widowed mother) but also raised 'a point of law of great constitutional importance … that my conviction under Section 1 of the Treachery Act was bad in law'.[9]

Jackson, via the lawyer, supported his assertion with the following points:

(a)   Before a conviction under charge 1 of the Charge Sheet could be sustained, the prosecution has to prove that the act charged against me 'was designed or likely to impede … operations or endanger life.'

(b)   The act charged was 'writing and sending a letter to the Spanish Embassy.'[10]

(c)   It is submitted that this is no more than an act 'preparatory' and therefore falls under Regulation 90 of the [Defence Regulations] and not the Treachery Act, 1940.

(d)   The particulars of Charge 1 of the Charge Sheet which state that the letter 'asked for arrangements to be made … with a view to offering my services to the enemy' support this contention.

(e)   Further it is humbly submitted that the writing of a letter to a neutral Embassy was not in this case and cannot be 'an act designed or likely to impede … operations or endanger life' but is of necessity an act preparatory to the commission of further acts which might constitute an offence under Section 1 [of the Treachery Act].[11]

Finally, Jackson, through the lawyer, humbly admitted his foolishness and lack of education and while acknowledging that he was 'deserving of severe punishment',[12] submitted that a term of imprisonment was an act of mercy. Jackson signed the petition and, on 17 March 1942, with the strong recommendations of various civil and military authorities, the king commuted Jackson's sentence of death to penal servitude for life in a military prison.

It was a win for MI5 and national security but a definite loss for Jackson. He was held in solitary confinement for seven and a half months, for 'security reasons'.[13] Solitary confinement and the idea of penal servitude for life did not agree with Jackson. In September 1942 he wrote another petition to the king, this time a handwritten one, in which he asked for his sentence to be reduced so that he could regain his honour, either in the services or on war work or 'failing this, that the commutation of his death sentence to one of penal servitude for life be rescinded and the death penalty be carried out'.[14] Jackson 'preferred death to the mental agony of life imprisonment'.[15] His petition was denied. A few months later, in March 1943, Jackson had a mental breakdown, was declared insane and was admitted to Broadmoor Criminal Lunatic Asylum, where he remained until May 1945.[16]

Early in 1946, Jackson, and many other wartime detainees, were being considered for release. MI5 was contacted in relation to Jackson's case and Hinchley-Cooke admitted that there was no longer a security objection to the man's release. He also admitted that the actual offence was 'foolish rather than vicious'.[17] In fact, no harm had been done but, 'in view of the state of the war in 1941/42, an example had to be made'.[18] Jackson was finally released from prison on 23 March 1946, a victim of his own foolishness and a ruthless Security Service.

While Jackson had longed for death, Josef longed for life. But it was not to be. Josef, a man who desired life above all else, was destined to be shot in the Tower of London while Jackson, a man who desired death above imprisonment, escaped the firing squad but succumbed to the mental anguish of a sentence of life imprisonment. Petitions to the king were written by both men, but in Josef's case, his death was in the best interests of national security. In Jackson's case his death would not have been in the best interests of national security. MI5 stacked the cards against Josef and pulled a fast one on Jackson. Undoubtedly, had Jackson stuck to his guns and refused to submit a petition to the king, other medical practitioners would have been found to declare him insane and send him to the lunatic asylum. In either case, both men were simply pawns in a game far larger than either one of them could imagine.

Jackson's case, however, and his well-crafted legal petition to the king, raises some questions. Each and every neutral or enemy alien agent who landed in England during the Second World War, and was subsequently charged under the Treachery Act, was charged under Section 1 with an offence that varied slightly but always came down to 'landing in the United Kingdom'.[19] They did this 'with intent to help the enemy', an act that was 'designed or likely to give assistance to the naval, military or air operations of the enemy, or to impede such operation of His Majesty's Forces'. If we look at Jackson's petition to the king, however, so eloquently argued by the lawyer, one is left to ask, was not the act of 'landing in the United Kingdom' simply an 'act preparatory'? Could not a lawyer have argued against Josef's conviction using the same points:

(a) Before a conviction under charge 1 of the Charge Sheet could be sustained, the prosecution has to prove that the act charged against me 'was designed or likely to give assistance ... to the enemy or to impede ... operations of His Majesty's Forces or endanger life.'

(b) The act charged was that Josef did 'descend by parachute in the United Kingdom'. (Jackson's petition made no reference to 'intent'. Whether he wrote his letter to the Spanish Embassy offering his assistance 'with intent' to assist the Germans is immaterial to the legal argument of the appeal which focuses on the 'act' as it is laid out in the charge. It would be similar in Josef's case. Whether he descended by parachute with intent to help the enemy is immaterial to the legal argument that follows.)

(c) It is submitted that this is no more than an 'act preparatory' and therefore falls under Regulation 90 of the Defence Regulations and not the Treachery Act, 1940.

(d) The particulars of the charge which state that the accused 'landed in the United Kingdom' support this contention.

(e) Further, it is humbly submitted that descending by parachute in the United Kingdom was not in this case and cannot be 'an act designed or likely to impede … operations' but is, of necessity, an act preparatory to the commission of further acts (e.g. sending weather reports) which might constitute an offence under Section 1 of the Treachery Act.

During the First World War, many spies were charged under the Defence of the Realm regulations with 'acts preparatory'. Under those regulations, such acts were punishable by death, but this was not the case during the Second World War. The parliamentary lawmakers had made a distinction between acts committed with the intention to assist the enemy or impede His Majesty's forces and acts preparatory to such acts. The first were prosecuted under the Treachery Act, with death being the only option if convicted. The second were prosecuted under the Defence Regulations, with life imprisonment being the most serious option if convicted. Interestingly, as late as 14 March 1940, a draft version of the Treachery Act included a Section 1.2 which stated:

> If, with intent to assist an enemy, any person does an act which is preparatory to any such act as is mentioned in the foregoing subsection [(1)(1)], he shall be guilty of felony, and shall, on conviction, be liable to penal servitude for life.[20]

By 9 May 1940, that subsection had been removed and all that remained was the 'act … with intent to assist the enemy … or impede operations by His Majesty's Forces'.

In following the argument to its logical conclusion, one is left with the distinct impression that Josef Jakobs was wrongly charged under the Treachery Act when, in fact, he should have been charged under Section 90 of the Defence Regulations. Perhaps if he had had as eloquent a lawyer at his disposal as the one who crafted Jackson's appeal, things might have turned out differently. Unfortunately, as the JAG had noted on 8 August regarding Josef's appeal, 'In my opinion, no legal grounds are disclosed in [the appeal] for interference with the finding of the Court-Martial.'[21]

Churchill and the Swinton Committee demanded that lives be sacrificed in the battle against Nazism, particularly during the dangerous years of 1940 and 1941. Josef was just one of those lives – collateral damage in a war that took so many. When national security was at stake, some things were thrown aside: civil liberties, justice, compassion and mercy. It didn't matter if it was a German spy or a British soldier; anyone who threatened the State was bound to pay the price, some with their lives, some with their sanity.

45

PREPARATIONS FOR AN EXECUTION

The king had confirmed the sentence of death for Josef and ordered that it should be carried out. With the king's blessing, the military wheels began their final rotation.

In preparation for Josef's execution, Hinchley-Cooke and Assistant Adjutant General Hippisley-Cox were keen to avoid the publicity associated with a formal coroner's inquest, which usually involved a jury. On 12 August, the two men met with the Northern District Coroner, William Bentley Purchase, who put their minds at ease. Since the Tower of London was technically not a prison, but rather a royal palace and a fortress, the inquest could be carried out by the coroner alone. If the execution took place in a prison, of course, a jury would be required and the notice of death would need to be posted on the prison gates, but such was not the case with the Tower of London. In the case of the Tower, since the death was unnatural, a coroner's inquest was necessary to determine the legality of the execution (that there had been a legal sentence of death) and whether it had been carried out in a proper and humane way. To that end, the coroner might order a post-mortem examination by a qualified person (e.g. a pathologist), but both officials could be bound by the provisions of secrecy.[1]

The next day, Hippisley-Cox wrote a letter to Lieutenant Colonel E.D. Mackenzie, the Officer Commanding Holding Battalion, Scots Guards, who had also served as a waiting member at Josef's court martial. Hippisley-Cox summarised the case and let Mackenzie know that the king had commanded that the sentence be carried into effect. Josef was therefore attached to the Scots Guards for the promulgation of the sentence and punishment.[2] The DPM had also been instructed to take the necessary steps to carry out the sentence and Mackenzie was to act in conjunction with him.[3] Hippisley-Cox also attached a copy of the *Procedure for Military Executions* and asked that it be returned to him in due course.[4] Once the sentence had been carried out, a secret record of the proceedings was to be sent to Hippisley-Cox as soon as possible.[5]

The letter arrived on Mackenzie's desk on 13 August. He wasn't all that surprised, for he had known that barring a royal pardon Josef was destined for the firing squad. Given that the Tower of London was home to a company of soldiers from the Scots Guards Holding Battalion, Mackenzie knew that Josef would likely end up before a squad of his men.

Having received their orders, Mackenzie and Gerard (DPM) probably met late on 13 August, or first thing on 14 August, to discuss the logistics of Josef's execution using the *Procedure for Military Executions* as their guide. Mackenzie suggested that command of the firing squad be given to Major Philip D.J. Waters of the Scots Guards. A veteran of the Great War, Waters had rejoined the Scots Guards in the autumn of 1939 and been assigned the Training Battalion. It was his job to turn a mob of raw recruits into a squadron of keen-eyed guardsmen. A year later, Waters was transferred to the Holding Battalion, Scots Guards. It would now be Waters' duty to arrange for the execution, to select the guardsmen for the firing squad and to ensure that everything was carried out in an efficient and humane matter. While the execution was Waters' responsibility, he was assisted by Regimental Sergeant Major Arthur Wilford.

When Wilford reviewed the *Procedure for Military Executions*, he learned that there were no firm rules around military executions, simply notes on suggested procedures. Circumstances and locations could vary dramatically, and the main object was to carry out the sentence as rapidly and humanely as possible.[6] Wilford knew that the location and time for the execution had already been set. Josef's execution would take place within the Tower's miniature rifle range at 7 a.m. on 15 August. In reviewing the procedures, Wilford learned that eight rifles would be required, along with some live ammunition and at least one blank round. Wilford may have shaken his head at the notion of blank rounds. Some people believed that blank rounds (ammunition cartridges from which the bullet projectiles had been removed) allowed each member of the firing squad to harbour a glimmer of doubt – 'Did I fire the lethal round?' That might have worked during the days of muskets when it was easy to tell the difference between a musket loaded with wad and ball and one just loaded with wad.

With modern rifles and ammunition however, any skilled marksman would notice the difference between the recoil of a live round versus the weaker recoil of a blank round. Apparently, over time, the mind could convince itself that the recoil was softer, but Wilford probably doubted that. Blank rounds were possibly issued so that, should the firing squad ever be brought before a tribunal (e.g. by the Germans), each could plausibly deny that he had fired the lethal shot. Wilford also noted that the execution could take place either standing against a post fixed in the ground (if available) or seated and strapped to a chair.[7] Wilford may also have gone in search of two yeoman warders who had served at the Tower during the First World War: Chief Yeoman Warder Alexander Smoker and Yeoman Warder John Fraser.[8] These two men had been present at some of the First World War spy executions and could have shared their recollections with Wilford.

While Wilford was reviewing the procedures and making preparations, Gerard (DPM) informed the Tower's medical officer that an execution was to take place the following morning and a sedative might be required. Gerard already knew that Josef would arrive at the Tower in the company of a Catholic chaplain and so the Tower's chaplain would not be required. Finally, Gerard arranged for an army ambulance and a stretcher.[9] A post-mortem was required and after some discussion, it had been decided that it would take place in the mortuary under the Tower Bridge. Gerard also made two calls, one to W.E.J. Heddy, the East London Coroner and the other to Sir Bernard Spilsbury, the renowned pathologist, ensuring that they would attend the post-mortem.

When Lieutenant R.W. Taylor, the medical officer, received word that an execution by firing squad was to happen early the next morning, he pulled out a prescription pad. Three months earlier, Taylor had written out a sleeping draught prescription for Rudolf Hess. As far as he knew, Hess was still alive, but the man arriving tomorrow was destined to die. Picking up his ink pen, Taylor wrote quickly – tablets of Leptandrinae Comp to sooth the stomach and capsules of Sodium Amytal to calm the spirit. He usually put the name of the patient at the top of the form, but in this instance, none had been provided, so he simply wrote 'A. English Esq.'.[10]

Tearing the form out of the book, Taylor tucked it into a small envelope and gave it to a corporal to deliver to the local chemist. The corporal went to the shop of pharmacist Harold A. Rowe, who filled the prescription quickly and handed it to the corporal. Upon the departure of the corporal, Rowe held the paper in his hand. He knew the reputation of the Tower as a place of execution. True, the prescription might be for a nervous Scots Guard … but it equally might be for a British traitor or a German spy. He took the form, opened his desk drawer and tucked it into a folder with another prescription, the one for Rudolf Hess. Time would tell if this new prescription had a German connection.[11]

46

TOWER OF LONDON

On the morning of 15 August, while Josef's motorcade was en route from HM Prison Wandsworth, final preparations were under way at the Tower of London. RSM Wilford walked down to the miniature rifle range for a final inspection.[1] A Windsor chair from the MI Waiting Room[2] had been tied to a vertical beam that had been nailed against the crossbar between the first and second targets. A table stood at right angles to the door, ready to receive the rifles of the firing squad.

Around 5.30 a.m., as Wilford was examining the rifle range, Josef's cavalcade pulled up at the East Gate of the Tower and, after a brief consultation with the guard, the gates creaked open. A short drive, another guard, another gate. A sharp turn to the right and they were within the massive outer walls of the Tower. The car stopped and Josef, Father Griffith and his guards climbed out. The DPM exited the other vehicle and a guardsman invited the party to enter the MI Waiting Room. Once they had settled, Taylor, the medical officer, approached Josef and asked him if he needed any assistance. Josef declined and said that he was fine. Taylor informed Josef that, if required, he had something to calm the nerves and the stomach. Josef thanked him and repeated that he was fine.[3]

At 5.45 a.m., RSM Wilford met the sergeant and guardsmen of the firing squad at the Signal Office.[4] The men were in battle dress, complete with anklets, service dress cap, respirators and steel helmets slung.[5] A few minutes later, Mackenzie arrived and gave the group a short lecture. Execution by firing squad was an honourable death and one that needed to be carried out with speed but also humane precision. If any one of the men was squeamish, they could step down in favour of another. None did. Mackenzie possibly told them that the 'greatest service they [could] render the prisoner [was] to shoot straight at the mark'.[6] Mackenzie dismissed the men and they filed out to the breakfast hall. Undoubtedly, there were some who decided they couldn't stomach breakfast that morning.

In the MI Waiting Room too, nerves were getting the better of Josef, who asked the medical officer if he could have something to calm him.[7] Taylor picked up his valise and pulled out the vial of Sodium Amytal. A glass of water was produced, and Josef slipped a capsule into his mouth and swallowed it.

At 6.30 a.m., the firing squad and RSM Wilford paraded before Waters at the foot of the Martin Tower steps. Waters performed a brief inspection of the guardsmen.

The eight soldiers of the firing squad were all professional marksmen but none had ever participated in a firing squad. The *Procedure* had strongly suggested that there be a practice run and so, with a nod to Wilford, commands were given and the RSM led the squad of men into the relative dimness of the rifle range. Wilford made sure that the men closed up well to the left, after which each man picked up a rifle from the table. The Lee–Enfield rifles had been preloaded and one contained the obligatory blank round. The men lifted the rifles into the aiming position and glanced right to where the DPM would be standing. The DPM would give the sign to release the safety catches. The men would act accordingly and then, on another signal from the DPM, take aim, their target a white disc on the prisoner's chest. For the practice, the men aimed at the bare wooden spindles of the chair. With their eyes firmly on the empty chair, they knew that in less than half an hour, a man would be sitting in their sights, a man they would have to shoot. Their training would take over at that point and they would simply squeeze their triggers when they heard the command to fire. While the men did not fire a practice shot, perhaps to avoid upsetting the prisoner, Wilford then walked them through the post-execution procedure. Major Waters would order the men to unload, do a right turn and quick march out of the rifle range. As they exited, Wilford would ensure that the men stacked their rifles together against the wall.

The practice completed, the men were formed up outside the rifle range. Wilford and the corporal placed the rifles back on the table and joined the men outside. Seeing that all was in readiness, Waters marched down to the MI Waiting Room[8] and opened the door. He saluted the DPM and stated, 'Sir, we are ready'. With that, the DPM, Josef and his guards, Father Griffith and Lieutenant Taylor, stood and made their slow procession along the outer ward towards the rifle range.

Father Griffith murmured prayers in Latin while Josef took care not to stumble as his crutches caught between the cobblestones. Soon it would all be over. He saw the squad of soldiers standing at attention opposite the rifle range. The sun cast a warm glow around him. Major Waters, Chidlow and Saul led Josef into the dimly lit rifle range and towards the chair. Josef sat down in the chair and handed his crutches to the priest. Chidlow and Saul took up the two ropes and tied one around Josef's arms and chest, with the other going around his legs. The medical officer, Taylor, produced a black hood and was going to place it over Josef's head but Josef asked that he be allowed to face what was to come.[9] Taylor looked at Waters, who shook his head – request denied.

The medical officer placed the black hood over Josef's head and then, after listening to Josef's chest with his stethoscope, pinned a white disc to the front of Josef's coat above his heart. Father Griffith murmured a last prayer and made the sign of the cross on Josef's veiled forehead.

The men retreated to the far end of the rifle range. A nod from Wilford and the firing squad filed into the building, closing well to the left as they had practised. The rifles were picked up, the sign for safety catches was given and a series of soft clicks reverberated in the space. Hearing the sound, knowing what it meant, Josef spoke his last words, urging the 'Tommies' to 'shoot straight'.[10]

Josef had timed his last message perfectly. As the order to fire rang out, eight rifle blasts shattered the peace of the enclosed space. Seven bullets smashed into Josef's chest, five hitting the white disc. The DPM, accompanied by Chidlow and Saul, walked down to the far end of the rifle range as Waters dismissed the men. Pulling out his loaded handgun, the DPM bent over and shot Josef through the head.[11] There may have been lingering signs of life, or perhaps the DPM considered the *coup de grâce* a simple insurance policy.[12]

The medical officer came over, placed his stethoscope against the undamaged portion of Josef's chest, and listened for several seconds. There was no heartbeat and he pronounced Josef dead. As the medical officer withdrew, Wilford, Chidlow and Saul stepped forward. Wilford pulled the hood off Josef's head, while Chidlow and Saul undid the ropes holding the limp body to the chair. Wilford unpinned the bloodstained target and took the ropes from the military policemen as they placed the body onto a stretcher. Chidlow and Saul lifted their burden and carried it outside, loading it into the waiting army ambulance.[13] Wilford placed the ropes, hood and lint circle into a sack he had brought with him and stepped outside the firing range for a moment of fresh air.

The guardsmen of the firing squad stood at a distance, at the foot of the steps of the Martin Tower, smoking their cigarettes nervously. It was one thing to shoot someone in battle, quite another to serve on a firing squad. With the body loaded into the ambulance, the men were ordered back into the rifle range at 7.20 a.m. The rifles were cleaned. The chair was removed, the upright plank was pulled down and the table was put away. Finally, the sand was stirred up, covering the darkening pool of blood. The men were dismissed, their duty done.

Having loaded the body of Josef into the back of the army ambulance, Chidlow and Saul climbed into one of the cars that had brought them to the Tower. Their mood was sombre, and Chidlow fingered the leather case that Josef had given him. They had done their duty as soldiers, but Josef had left a lasting impression on Chidlow, one that would echo through the coming decades.

47

DUST TO DUST

While the duty of the military policemen and the firing squad was done, other individuals were just beginning their role in the execution of a German spy.

The ambulance had not far to go. It drove slowly down through the outer ward of the Tower, out onto the Tower Wharf and then through the East Gate. It pulled to the side and the two army medics stepped out of the vehicle and had a smoke while they waited for one of the Wharf Guards to open the heavy wooden door set within the base of Tower Bridge. A few yards away stood several police officers, there to ensure that the curious kept moving.

Smokes finished, the two medics opened the back of the ambulance and slid the stretcher out, the corpse covered with a rough woollen blanket. Sliding the stretcher all the way out, the medics each grabbed an end and manoeuvred their way through the doorway and down the stairs into the main chamber of the mortuary. Water dripped in the corners of the room and the entire place smelled damp and unused. With a shiver, the medics placed the corpse on the table in the middle of the room and slid the stretcher out from underneath the body. Their duty done for the moment, the medics followed the Wharf Guard back up the stairs and headed to the ambulance as the guard locked the door behind them. The Wharf Guard returned to his post and reported to the sergeant on duty. It would be a few hours yet, but several visitors were expected and it would be the duty of the Wharf Guard to escort them to the mortuary.

Meanwhile, the Spur Guards, on duty at the main entrance to the Tower, had been warned to expect two visitors: William R.H. Heddy, coroner for the East London District and Sir Bernard Spilsbury, the renowned pathologist.[1] When the two men arrived at around 10 a.m., an orderly escorted them to the Wharf Guard, where they were joined by Taylor, the Tower's medical officer.

The Wharf Guard ushered the three men into the mortuary. While Spilsbury examined the body, Heddy examined the paperwork he had been given. Spilsbury tut-tutted at the head wound and asked the medical officer if a *coup de grâce* had been administered. Taylor admitted that it had, but in his opinion the firing squad had done their job well.

With meticulous care, Spilsbury removed the clothing from the body and placed each item on a clean sheet on another table. When the corpse was naked, Heddy and Spilsbury peered at the chest wounds and agreed that death had been caused by 'injuries to the heart due to the passage of bullets'.[2] Each man made notes, Spilsbury for his own records and Heddy for official records. It was he who would have to complete the official death registration forms and deliver the verdict of 'execution of judicial sentence of death in accordance with military law'.[3]

While they were in the midst of their examination, an officer of the Scots Guards entered the mortuary. He had been ordered to examine the prisoner's clothing. Heddy and Spilsbury gestured to the other table and continued with their work. The officer examined each piece of clothing with minute care. He was searching for something small and flat.

As it turned out, after Hinchley-Cooke had left Wandsworth Prison, he had gone to his office at 58 St James Street and opened the envelope containing Josef's final letter. He had read the letter with dispassion, a seasoned MI5 officer who had no time for compassion and mercy. He was looking for anything that might be of national security interest. He had read many such letters in the last nine months, written by spies going to their deaths. There had been impassioned pleas of innocence, final bequests and declarations of undying love. Hinchley-Cooke thought that nothing could surprise him and yet, when he read the final line in Josef's letter, he was bemused:

Dear, dear Gretchen, the pictures from the medallion accompany me on my last journey!![4]

Josef had been searched repeatedly, by the police, by MI5, by the prison authorities, and yet it appeared that he had kept a secret. Hinchley-Cooke rang Hippisley-Cox, the Assistant Adjutant General, who in turn called Mackenzie of the Scots Guards. Orders were passed down the chain of command and an officer was sent to the mortuary to search for something that had escaped the keen eyes of the British authorities.

Finally, in the lining of Josef's jacket, tucked through a small tear in the seam, the officer felt stiffness where elsewhere was only supple fabric. He teased two small pieces of paper through the opening: oval photographs, one of a girl and one of a woman. The officer tucked the photographs into a small envelope, which arrived at Hinchley-Cooke's office a couple of hours later. Hinchley-Cooke stared at the two photographs. The woman was most likely Josef's wife, and the girl must be his daughter, Regine. Hinchley-Cooke tucked the photographs back into the envelope and added it to his case file on Josef Jakobs. The final letter was also there, now enclosed within a wax-sealed envelope bearing the address of Josef's wife Margarete. A note on the front of the envelope stated that it was to be delivered at the cessation of hostilities. It never was.

Hinchley-Cooke rang up Liddell (Director of B Division) and informed him that Josef Jakobs had been executed, having shown remarkable 'pluck and calm bearing'[5] at Wandsworth Prison. He had also heard that Josef's final words to the firing squad had been 'Shoot straight, Tommies.'[6] Word of Josef's final utterance would make its way to Latchmere House, where it made an impression on Stephens, one that would linger for years. Elsewhere, Gerard and Mackenzie both wrote statements to Hippisley-Cox, the Assistant Adjutant General, declaring that the sentence of death had been promulgated at the Tower of London that morning.[7]

Back at the mortuary, Heddy and Spilsbury had completed their work and now it was simply a matter of disposing of the body. All the spies who had been hanged in Pentonville and Wandsworth during the previous nine months were buried in unmarked graves within the grounds of those two prisons. The First World War spies were buried in Plaistow Cemetery in East London. Given that Josef was a Catholic, Father Griffith may have campaigned for a burial within the hallowed grounds of a Catholic cemetery.[8]

Josef's body was held in the mortuary over the weekend and on Monday, 18 August, an army ambulance arrived at the mortuary to transport the body to St Mary's Roman Catholic Cemetery in Kensal Green.[9] Griffith had promised Josef that he would be with him to the bitter end and met the ambulance at the chapel in the cemetery. Griffith was joined by the Reverend Charles Bernard Flood, from St James', Spanish Place Parish. Josef's body had been placed in a simple wooden box, which was carried into the small chapel. Griffith and Flood celebrated the funeral Mass and commended the spirit of Josef Jakobs to the mercy of God. At the conclusion of the service, the casket was carried out to the ambulance. Josef was to be laid to rest in Plot G, where those who could not afford a marked grave were buried. The gravediggers had done their job well and with no further ado, the casket was lowered into the ground. A few more prayers from the two priests and it was over. No stone would be laid to mark the final resting place of the last person executed in the Tower of London.

48

HOUNDS ON THE TRAIL

Josef was executed on a Friday morning, in what was to have been a secret event, but MI5 knew that they couldn't keep a tight lid on everything; even Churchill wanted espionage executions trumpeted from the roof-tops. For months, the British had been warned to prepare for a German invasion, to be on the lookout for anything out of the ordinary. It was a hot scoop for the press to provide people with the good news of captured and executed spies. It was good for morale. It was good for politicians. It wasn't good for the Security Service or national security.

In a bid to balance the demands of the press against the requirements of national security, MI5 decided to provide the War Office with a short blurb that contained safe information on a spy. In late July and early August 1941 the editors of Fleet Street were informed of the new policy and warned that any attempt to dig up more information about spies would be a waste of time, since everything would be censored. They were reminded of the Defence Regulations, which stated, 'No information should be published without submission to censorship concerning the activities of spies or enemy agents in the United Kingdom.'[1] The procedure worked well for the executions of Walti and Druecke on 6 August 1941. Unfortunately, the wheels came off the cart with Josef's execution.

On the morning of 15 August, the War Office issued a press release on Josef's execution. The release was factual but dry:

> German Spy Shot at the Tower – Speedy Capture by Home Guard
> A German Secret Service agent, Josef Jakobs, a German National, born at Luxembourg on June 30, 1898 was executed at the Tower of London yesterday morning.

He was convicted under the Treachery Act, 1940, after trial by General Court-martial on August 4 and 5. The trial was held in camera.

Jakobs was a non-commissioned officer in the Germany Army attached to the Meteorological Service. He was dropped by parachute from a German aeroplane in the Home Counties area, dressed in civilian clothes over which he was wearing a flying suit and parachutist steel helmet. He was fully equipped for espionage and had a wireless transmitting set, a large sum of English money and an emergency food ration, which included brandy and a German sausage. He also carried a small hand spade for the purpose of burying his parachute and flying kit.

He was taken into custody by members of the Home Guard approximately 12 hours after his descent.

Jakobs was tried by General Court-martial by direction of the Attorney General under the provision of the Treachery Act and the sentence of death was carried out by shooting. A barrister-at-law, at present serving in HM Forces, and an interpreter were placed at his disposal for the purposes of defence.

Jakobs is the first execution at the Tower of London by shooting during the present war.[2]

While *The Times* was content with the official press release, the rest of Fleet Street was less than pleased. Several editors protested to the newspaper censor but were told that further details would not be approved for publication. Despite these admonitions, several newspapers learned that Josef had been captured near Ramsey. By 10.30 a.m. on 15 August, three hours after Josef's execution, the village was caught like a deer in the headlights. Several eager reporters descended upon Ramsey, all on the hunt for 'the man who caught the spy'.[3]

A woman from *The Star* newspaper rang up Mrs Lilian Coles of the Lion Hotel in Ramsey and asked her for the name of the Home Guard volunteer who had caught the German spy. Mrs Coles, taken aback at receiving a phone call from a London newspaper, gave the woman Harry Godfrey's name and address. A couple of hours later, a reporter from *The Star* telephoned Godfrey and asked him some questions. The reporter apparently knew all about the trial and since the man had the correct information, Godfrey simply answered, 'Yes, that's right', to most of the questions.[4]

The *Daily Express* newspaper wasn't content with a phone call. One of their reporters visited the Huntingdon representative of the *Express* and motored off towards Ramsey with a photographer's assistant from

Whitney's Studios. A few enquiries in the neighbouring village of Warboys directed the reporter to Harry Godfrey. Lulled into a false sense of security by the reporter's extensive knowledge of the case, Godfrey expanded on his role in the capture of the German spy. The reporter took Godfrey to Whitney's Studio in Ramsey, where the photographer took several photographs of him in his Home Guard tunic and cap. Having been told by the reporter that Josef had been executed that morning, Godfrey thought it was quite in order to talk to the pressman, although he did stay away from the court martial proceedings.[5]

While Godfrey was being courted by the *Daily Express* reporter, two other newspapermen, Philip Johnson from *The Star* and W. Garstang from the *News Chronicle*, arrived in Ramsey after the midday meal. Their first stop was Ramsey Police Station, where they attempted to glean information from Inspector Jaikens without success.

Jaikens told them that he could not divulge any information and simply refused to discuss the matter with them. Jaikens even rang up the Deputy Chief Constable of Huntingdon, Superintendent Afford, who confirmed that Jaikens was 'definitely forbidden to give the newspaper representatives any information concerning the matter'.[6]

Afford even spoke to Johnson and told him that, according to MI5, they could get 'as many of the particulars, as would be allowed, from the Ministry of Information'.[7] Johnson complained that he had already been to the Ministry of Information and they had told him to visit Ramsey for further information.[8]

Shifting tack, Johnson and Garstang said that they simply wanted to boost the profile of the Home Guard and asked Jaikens for the address of the local Home Guard commander (Captain Newton) as well as that of Godfrey. Jaikens remained firm and refused to give them any information. The reporters left in a huff but Jaikens knew that village gossip would soon put them on the trail of both Newton and Godfrey.

As soon as the door closed behind the two men, Jaikens phoned Newton and warned him that several reporters were prowling the streets of Ramsey. Jaikens emphasised that Newton should give them no information. The warning was timely, for soon afterwards the two reporters showed up at Newton's office. Having produced their press cards, the reporters handed Newton a copy of *The Star* newspaper published that morning. Newton was careful not to give them any information that was not already contained in the article. Although, when the reporters asked for Baldock and Coulson, Newton helpfully told them that the two farmers lived on Puddock Road. Perhaps aware of his gaffe, Newton sent his clerk (Benjamin Greenwood) with them to ensure that the farmers didn't reveal too much.[9]

The reporters and Greenwood drove to Puddock Road to interview Baldock and suggested that a pint of ale might be in order. Baldock was amenable to free ale and sent a message to Coulson to meet the group at the nearby public house, the Farmer's Boy, a few hundred yards from Josef's landing site. Johnson and Garstang plied Baldock, Coulson and Greenwood with ale and questions.

Afterwards, each person had a different recollection of what transpired. According to Greenwood, Baldock readily answered questions about the spy's capture. According to Baldock, the reporters took photographs and asked questions, which Baldock steadfastly refused to answer. According to Coulson, there was no mention of Josef and, obviously, no questions.[10]

At around 6 p.m., Johnson and Garstang ran Godfrey to ground and asked him questions, to which he replied, 'Yes'. It was a short conversation and the reporters never introduced themselves properly, although Godfrey presumed that they were newspaper men.[11] With that, the reporters left the area and peace once again descended upon Ramsey. Such was not the case in London.

On the afternoon of 15 August, *The Star* newspaper submitted a story to the newspaper censor that told the story of Home Guard volunteer Harry Godfrey, and how he had helped to capture the German spy, Josef Jakobs.[12] The story was likely based on the lunchtime phone call with Godfrey and was approved for publication by 'a fool censor'.[13] Other newspaper editors read the story with disbelief.[14] They had been told that additional information would not pass the censor and yet here was a headline that trumpeted 'Parachute Spy Shot in Tower – Landed in Home Counties, H.G.s Captured Him'.[15] Fleet Street was not amused. *The Evening Standard* published a protest piece:

Home Guard Capture

A Home Guard has captured a German parachute spy. After this official announcement today the *Evening Standard* – without giving information to the enemy about the time or place of the capture – wanted to tell you something about this man: his name, his wife, his children. What he does in the daytime.

It was pointed out to the appropriate department of the War Office that here was a fine recruiting story for the Home Guard. Thoughts of adventures like this add credit to the Home Guard, and will bring comfort to many a volunteer bored with his routine patrol on a wet winter's night.

The Public Relations Department of the War Office agreed; the Ministry of Information agreed. The Service Department concerned said: 'You've got all you're going to get.'[16]

Other newspaper editors were not so willing to toe the censorship line. The editor of the *Daily Express* told the newspaper censor point-blank that they intended to publish more details and that they would just 'take a chance'.[17] Thus it was that on the morning of 16 August, Harry Godfrey's smiling face was plastered across London news stands as several newspapers praised the bravery of the Home Guard. Several MI5 officers opened their morning newspapers and read the headlines with dismay: 'Had No Chance to Do Spying'[18] and 'Dandy Joseph, Spy in Spats, Caught by H.G.'.[19]

MI5 was not amused. Hinchley-Cooke rang up Dixon, the RSLO officer in Cambridge, and asked him to investigate. Dixon turned around, phoned Jaikens and told him of MI5's extreme displeasure at the security breach. Dixon asked Jaikens to track down and interview the offending parties. Slowly a picture emerged, one that Dixon was able to send to Hinchley-Cooke on 17 August.[20] Somehow or other, the London reporters had learned that Josef had been captured in Ramsey. In Dixon's opinion, it was clear that the newspaper men had obtained that information in London, possibly from someone at the Ministry of Information. Hinchley-Cooke reported back to Liddell (Director of B Division), who took it up the line to the Director General of MI5, Sir David Petrie. Someone had opened the barn doors and the press had flown the coop.

Word of the fiasco reached Lord Swinton, Chair of the Home Defence (Security) Executive. It was Swinton who had told Petrie and Liddell that, wherever possible, all spies should be prosecuted and executed. On the morning of 19 August, having read the growing pile of press articles about Josef, Swinton wrote a short note to Petrie:

This is the kind of thing I want to avoid if I can. I think we have been unduly reticent. We should have put ourselves in a good position, if we had said: 'You may interview the man [Godfrey], provided you show us what you propose to publish.' As it is we get both publication and vilification![21]

The ultra-secret approach was not working and on 28 August 1941, the Swinton Committee met with representatives from the Home Office, the three service departments (army, navy, air force), the Ministry of Information, General Headquarters (Home Forces) and the Security Service (MI5). The information published by the press after a spy execution was of 'very great importance to security'.[22] The entire counter-espionage network could be imperiled by an indiscreet disclosure of some tiny piece of information connected with the spy's capture, a piece of information that no layperson would suspect of being of any importance. Only the Security Service could determine what information should be revealed but they needed to obtain the co-operation of the press. After much discussion, it was decided that a press officer (Home Office or War Office) would take information on a spy from intelligence officers and draw up a draft press release to be submitted to the Ministry of Information, who were most aware of what would satisfy the press. After revisions, it was hoped that the official report would be enough for the press.[23]

49

CZECH IN THE MIDDLE

The new press release policy would be tested three months later when Karel Richter was hanged at Wandsworth Prison. Richter's journey to the gallows was not one trodden with any degree of tranquility. Richter would rage, both in writing and in action, against the perceived injustices dealt to him.

In May 1941, while preparations were under way to try Josef by court martial under the Treachery Act, a similar discussion took place about trying Richter the same way. The problem with Richter was twofold: (a) there was no evidence that he was a member of an armed force and (b) there was some question as to his nationality. The Lord President of the Privy Council, Sir John Anderson, who had been involved in the parliamentary debate when the Treachery Act was passed, felt that 'strong reasons would have to be shown for trying by court martial an alien who is not a member of an Armed Force'.[1]

In a memo to Petrie (Director General of the Security Service) on 30 May 1941, Lord Swinton suggested that Richter was a prime candidate for a court martial, except for the fact that he was a Sudeten Czech.[2] The Sudeten area of Czechoslovakia had been invaded by Germany, but did that mean that Richter was a German? Or was he a Czech? England was not at war with Czechoslovakia, so technically Richter was not an enemy alien.

A few days later, Swinton had a chat with the AG, who told him that it was very important they should be sure that a person was an enemy alien (i.e. 'a person who possesses the nationality of a State at war with His Majesty') if they wanted to proceed via court martial. In the case of Richter, Swinton admitted that unless the Foreign Office was absolutely satisfied that the case was watertight, then they should probably proceed with civil trial.

Despite this admission, Swinton did not give up easily. He had another chat with the JAG, who said that if they tried a person who was not an enemy alien by court martial, the lawyer for the defence would have to speak up at the start of the trial – the defence would not be able to claim it later in the court martial. While they could try to slip Richter through the cracks, if his defence lawyer was on the ball, the whole court martial could fall apart.[3]

In another memo to Petrie, Swinton said:

> I told [Dick] White this morning that I wished every case, where we had finished with the man, to be submitted to the DPP. I want this done in every case of a man whom we are certain is a spy but where your people feel the evidence is insufficient to sustain a prosecution. I have given an undertaking that any spy or enemy agent whom we no longer require to retain at Latchmere for intelligence purposes shall be brought to justice if the charge against him will lie. The right man to decide whether a charge can be brought is the DPP and we should certainly have the insurance of his opinion and advice in every case.[4]

As early as August 1941, MI5 recognised that prosecuting Richter would be a delicate matter. His connection with TATE was a cause for concern. Some within the ranks of MI5 had a few qualms about the way in which Richter had been lured to England. The British had told TATE to request more money of the Germans. In response, the Germans sent over Richter. There was also some concern about what Richter might say about TATE during the trial; but such concerns were not enough to deflect the pursuit of justice.

In mid September, Richter was transferred from Latchmere House to Brixton Prison, a move that must have filled him with uncertainty. On 18 September, Richter was taken to Bow Street Police Court and charged under the Treachery Act. A short while later, he appeared before Magistrate Fry and was remanded in custody until 10 a.m. on 25 September and returned to Brixton Prison.

Several days later, on 23 September, Richter put pen to paper and wrote a letter to Short at Latchmere House. Richter had learned that his capture and interrogation had been kept completely secret and the Germans were not aware of his capture.[5] He had started to put pieces together and realised that his reticence in sharing information due to his fear of German retribution had been misplaced. Richter begged for an interview with Short; a chance to come clean. He received no response.

Two days later, on 25 September, Richter appeared before Magistrate Fry at Bow Street Police Court. Evidence was given by several witnesses, including Hinchley-Cooke. (This was the civil equivalent of the Summary of Evidence.) Richter was not represented by a lawyer and made no application for legal aid. At the end of the proceedings, Richter was given a chance to respond to the charge. Richter complained, 'The witnesses gave their evidence so quickly I didn't understand them all, that is not right. I don't mean here today, but when I was questioned at the police station by the police [likely several days previously].'[6] When asked if he wanted to give any evidence on his behalf or call any witnesses, Richter 'said nothing further'.[7]

Richter waited a good week before writing another plea to Short. He had learned a few things in the meantime and his nimble mind had begun to make connections. His letter dated 2 October was desperate, for he knew that his life hung in the balance:

> I really do not know what to think about all this. I expected understanding from you, and hoped that as in the case with many others, things could be settled without court proceedings being taken against me; but now, since hearing that Jakobs has been shot, I no longer know what to think. I do not even believe that he had been a German soldier, and even if he was, he was certainly no Nazi. He placed himself at your disposal. He had been told that he could save his life if he could give you enough information. You got information from him, and not only that; you also caught me through him, as you told me yourself, a fact for which the Germans would have shot him out of hand, if he had fallen into their clutches again. In spite of everything he is now dead.[8]
>
> I have not met [TATE] either in the camp [Latchmere House] or in court or here in prison, despite the fact that he has been working against England for perhaps months or years … You have got this man through me and in spite of everything have given or are giving him the opportunity to work for England, yet I sit here and must perhaps die … It almost drives me mad; it is as if I must soon wake up out of a nightmare. I cannot and will not lose hope.[9]

In addition to learning about Josef's execution, clever Richter had figured out that TATE was working for the British. He erroneously suspected that

TATE had been caught through the information that he (Richter) had provided to MI5. What Richter didn't know was that TATE had been a double agent long before Richter arrived in England. Richter was baffled as to why he was being brought to trial and yet TATE was not.

At the conclusion of another letter, Richter avowed:

> As you can see, I have done everything to be useful to you, I went as far as to humiliate myself, but everything has an ending. You will see at the coming main proceedings I shall not apply for counsel for the defence. Whatever the judgement may be – death penalty or perhaps years of internment – in any case fate has stopped the clock of life for me. You will see, and you can rely upon it that I shall not be less brave than Jakobs; I too will know how to die, yet not as a Nazi spy on your gallows, but as a man.[10]

Richter's letters to Short were passed along to Stephens who forwarded them to Hinchley-Cooke. In Stephens' opinion, little would be gained from a meeting between Short and Richter. The legal machinery turned and a few weeks later Richter's trial was on the docket.

On 21 October 1941, Karel Richard Richter was tried under Section 1 of the Treachery Act 1940 at the Old Bailey. After the preliminaries, Richter was asked if he wanted counsel, and he answered in the affirmative. The case was adjourned to the next day and a defence lawyer was found. On 22 October, Richter pleaded not guilty and, after some discussion, the prosecution was permitted to give their opening statement, after which the court was once again adjourned so that the defence lawyer could prepare his case. The next day, the witnesses were called by the prosecution, but the defence lawyer chose not to cross-examine two key ones, Hinchley-Cooke and Inspector Grant of Special Branch.

After the prosecution rested its case, the defence lawyer, Charles G.L. DuCann, stood up and said, 'There is no case for the defence to answer here.'[11] He argued that the onus was on the prosecution to prove their case, to prove that Richter had come with intention to help the enemy. In DuCann's opinion, the prosecution had not proved their case and he laid out his logic in fine legal form.

Firstly, he argued:

> That intention must be strictly proved as laid. It is clear from the Indictment that the Prosecution rely on the landing by parachute as

proof of the intent, but, in my submission, the mere landing in this country, whether by parachute or boat, does not prove intent to help the enemy. One is therefore thrown back on the other parts of the evidence given by the Prosecution, and I submit to your Lordship that the possession of equipment unused proves no intent to help the enemy. Indeed, its non-use by this man proves the contrary. The rest of the evidence consists simply of his statement to the police, which may, indeed, show some intent to help himself but shows no intent to help the enemy, and if the intent is not proved, and if there is no evidence before the Court which is evidence from which an intent can be logically inferred, as I am submitting to the Court there is not, an essential ingredient in the offence is not proved by the Prosecution. That is the first part of my submission.[12]

Secondly, DuCann argued:

It is necessary for the Prosecution to prove that the act on which they rely to satisfy Section 1 is an act which, in the words of the Indictment, is 'designed and likely to give assistance to the naval and military operations of the enemy and to impede such operations of His Majesty's Forces'. I am quoting the exact words of the particulars in the Indictment.[13]

Under Section 1, of course, it would be sufficient to prove merely an act either designed or likely to give assistance, and it would be sufficient to prove that that assistance was either to the naval, or military, or, indeed, air operations, or, of course, to hamper any of the three kinds of operations of our own forces. The Prosecution have chosen to select naval as well as military operations, and to omit air operations, and they have added, of course, the operations of our own forces. In my submission, having chosen to lay the indictment in that way, they must prove the case in that way, and my submission is that no act such as the one they have relied on, landing by parachute, is calculated to do the things which they have alleged. In my respectful submission, landing by parachute is not an act of the kind aimed at under the Section. Landing in this country, whether by parachute or by any other means, is a mere antecedent or preliminary preparation for an act of the kind contemplated by the Statute, because the act contemplated by the Statute is, of course, an act of treachery. A mere landing by parachute cannot be an act of treachery. I hope I have made that point clear.[14] [*DuCann had indeed made a clear point – landing by parachute was an act preparatory to an act to commit treachery,*

but would his point sway the judge? He needed to refer to Defence Regulation 90,
which would been used so effectively in Philip Jackson's petition.]

In his third point, DuCann noted:

The Prosecution have to prove an act which is done. The words of the
Statute are 'did an act'. If a man lands from a boat or steps from a train,
he undoubtedly does an act, but if he falls from an aeroplane it may be,
not an act which is done, but an experience which happens to him; it
may be something passive, and not active. For instance, if he fell from an
aeroplane, either with or without a parachute, that might be a passive
thing, not in accordance with his will, not a voluntary act, but an invol-
untary act. Of course in coming from an aeroplane in any way, whether
voluntarily or involuntarily, he must, if the [aeroplane] be over England,
necessarily land in this country, because the force of gravity attends to
that. It is not an act which he does; it is a thing which happens to him
in accordance, of course, with the laws of gravity, and, in my respectful
submission to your Lordship, it is not doing an act, something in the
active voice, if I may use a grammarian's expression. It is not sufficient
to prove that something has happened, as it were, in the passive voice.[15]
[*Our friend DuCann is a philosopher, although this is not his strongest point.*]

DuCann had hit on several key points and, in his final point, noted:

This [Treachery Act] under which this man is charged is an Act dealing
with treachery. It is entitled 'An Act to make further provision for the
trial and punishment of treachery', and while, of course, the heading of
it is no part of the Statute itself, it is clear from the whole Act and from
its title that the act contemplated under the Statute must be an act of
treachery. [*It is unfortunate that DuCann did not know about the discussions
in the House of Commons when the Treachery Act was passed in May 1940.*]
It is true that Section 4 of the Act reads 'This Act shall apply to anything
done' – then I can ignore (a) and (b) for the purpose of this case – '(c)
by any person in the United Kingdom'. I need not go further; I am
reading the words which apply to this particular case. Of course, those
words taken by themselves, and not read in conjunction with the rest
of the Act, make nonsense, because it would mean, if one took those
words apart from the context of the rest of the Act, that the Act would
apply to any person doing something quite innocuous. The words of the

Section are extraordinarily wide. 'Anything done by any person' might apply to a man eating his breakfast, or saying his prayers, or something equally innocuous. Obviously, that must be read in conjunction with the rest of the Act, and, if that be so, the Act applies only to acts of treachery. [*DuCann had given some thought to the Treachery Act and its application.*]

My submission is that landing by parachute or in any other way is not, and cannot be, by itself an act of treachery, though it might be an essential preliminary to such an act. What I am saying, my Lord, is that landing is no more an act of treachery than going to a house would be an act of housebreaking or burglary. In each case it would be an essential preliminary, it may well be, to the act contemplated.[16]

DuCann then expanded on his understanding of 'an act of treachery':

I should have said that the meaning of those words, 'an act of treachery', was that person owing a duty is false to that duty, and is not merely passively false to it, but actively does something which shows that falsity. Under this particular Act it goes a little further than that.

It must be something actively done in breach of a duty or a faith – 'allegiance' perhaps would be a better word – which he owes to the Crown or to the State. [*The authorities had created the Treachery Act to avoid using the Treason Act, which was seen as requiring allegiance. DuCann is arguing that charging someone with treachery means that they had an allegiance.*]

In the case of an enemy alien it would be necessary for him to be doing something while he is in this country and under the King's peace which is actively calculated either to assist the military, naval or air force operations of the enemy …

The evidence before your Lordship goes to show that this man is an enemy alien, a subject at present, whether with his will or against his will, de facto of the German State, and that he was, at the time when he landed, dressed in the uniform of the forces of a belligerent enemy, and that therefore he is a prisoner of war who has surrendered, and that therefore he is entitled to all the privileges and protection accorded under both national and international law to prisoners of war. [*DuCann considered Richter to be an enemy alien whereas Swinton had admitted that Richter's nationality was not clear.*] Although I cannot say that the terms of this Act do not apply to prisoners of war in uniform, in my respectful submission the Act does not so intend, because under it, on a liberal interpretation of its terms, every prisoner of war would be guilty under its provisions of felony and liable to the death sentence at the hands of a civil court. [*DuCann considers Richter's flying suit and helmet to be evidence of a uniform whereas at Josef's court martial, only the helmet was considered to be a uniform.*]

My Lord, on all of those grounds, or on any of them, I ask your Lordship to rule that I have no case to answer.[17]

Mr Justice Tucker's response to DuCann was swift and short, 'My ruling is that you have a case to answer [on all those grounds].'[18] [*Did Tucker follow DuCann's arguments? It is unfortunate that Tucker did not provide his reasoning for dismissing DuCann's arguments. This stands in contrast to the case of Oswald John Job, whose defence lawyer, Mr Gordon, engaged Mr Justice Stable and Mr L.A. Byrne (prosecution) in a lengthy legal discussion about the admissibility of a statement not made under caution.*[19]]

And so the case proceeded. Richter was called as a witness and said that even though he was a civilian, he was attached to the German army, General Kommando 10, Hamburg. The German army recruited civilians as military employees to ensure that they were subject to military law. At several points, Richter had told the Abwehr that he didn't want to go but was told:

> Don't play any tricks. Don't be stupid. It is no use whatever you refusing, because you will not only spoil everything for yourself, but that can and may have the worst consequences for you, and not for you alone. You know that you are subject to military law and war law, and more I need hardly tell you.[20]

Richter was a smart man and understood that if he didn't follow orders his family would be in danger.[21] Once he was in the aeroplane, Richter told a similar story to Josef. The aeroplane was icy cold and when he put his legs through the trapdoor, he felt as if they would be torn away. Richter was pushed through the trapdoor and a static line, attached to the aeroplane, opened his parachute for him.

In his closing arguments, Richter's lawyer suggested that in order to contravene the Treachery Act, one had to do an 'act' of treachery. DuCann argued that landing by parachute (Richter's offence under the Treachery Act), over which Richter had no choice or control (being pushed out of the aeroplane and having the parachute open via static line), was not in and of itself an act of treachery. The defence also argued that Richter had been in uniform (the flying suit and steel helmet) when he landed and should therefore have been treated as a prisoner of war who had surrendered. Unfortunately, unlike the lawyer who would craft Jackson's appeal, DuCann did not quote Defence Regulation 90, which referred to 'an act preparatory'. Even if he had, it remains doubtful that he would have been successful in achieving an acquittal. The difference between Philip Jackson and Karel Richter was that MI5 wanted to keep the first alive and wanted to kill the second.

DuCann had done well as a defence lawyer, far better than Josef's defence lawyer, White. Even Inspector Grant, in his report on the trial, acknowledged, 'DuCann made a very eloquent speech for the defence, stressing that Richter had been sent against his will. He claimed that the prisoner had done no act likely to assist the enemy, and asked the jury to acquit him.'[22]

On 24 October, after deliberating for thirty-four minutes (one of the longest deliberations of all the spy trials – most were eight to eleven minutes), the jury returned their verdict: guilty. Richter's punishment was, 'To be hanged by the neck until he be dead and his body to be buried within the precincts of the prison in which he shall have been confined before his execution.'[23] Upon hearing the verdict, Richter burst into tears and appealed for mercy, 'You should think of my parents and my child. I cannot even write [to them].'[24] His outburst availed him nothing.

Richter was not taken back to Brixton Prison but transferred to Wandsworth Prison, under the watchful eye of Governor Grew. Unlike Josef, Richter would not be a model prisoner. He arrived at the prison in a nervous state – understandable, given that he had been found guilty and sentenced to death. All was well on 25 October, but sometime during the night Richter attempted to commit suicide by scratching the inside of his elbow with a small flake of metal. The medical officer at Wandsworth Prison noted in his report that it was a genuine attempt at suicide, though 'not a very determined one'.[25]

The Catholic chaplain, Father Daly, reported that Richter had been in a terrible state of mind but now regretted his action and appeared much calmer.[26] However, Richter would not appear calm for long, nor would he remain calm at the end.

Richter's execution was provisionally set for 12 November 1941 but, as with other condemned spies, Richter was permitted to write a letter of appeal to the Home Secretary. Richter wrote several letters to DuCann, his defence lawyer, begging for a meeting. Finally, on 1 November Richter completed his appeal and sent it off. A couple of days later, he submitted an addendum. Several more letters were sent to DuCann, again begging for a meeting, but there is no evidence that DuCann offered Richter any assistance. In one impassioned line, Richter wrote:

> In short, the time at [Latchmere House], during which I was completely cut off from the world, was not mentioned [during the trial] and I could have proved that I have helped the English Secret Service as far as I was able to do so and that I am not guilty of high treason.[27]

It was all too little, too late. Unlike Jackson, whose appeal was crafted by a lawyer, Richter's appeal consisted of a handwritten letter in German. The appeal naturally had to be translated into English and passed through the hands of Hinchley-Cooke. In his appeal, Richter said that he had not intended to harm England in any way and that, in fact, no harm had been done by his arrival in England. He had acted under duress. The Gestapo had made threats against himself and his family. The Nazis had used him as a 'sacrifice'[28] and sent him to his death. He complained about the 'old man' who had served as his interpreter at the trial. Finally, Richter referenced Latchmere House, Short and double agent TATE, all of which was highly concerning to MI5.

Much discussion ensued about what to do with Richter's appeal. If it went ahead, it would be seen by various judges and MI5 was concerned about the security of the double-cross system.[29] They circumvented this by deciding that it was best to censor Richter's appeal and summarise the redacted sections. Hinchley-Cooke took Richter's appeal and struck out any reference to Latchmere House, the British Security Service, Captain Short, the Regent Palace Hotel (where Richter was to meet TATE) and LEONHARDT (TATE's German code name). Repeated assertions that Short could confirm the truth of what Richter had said regarding TATE were removed. Any references to the information Richter gave to Short were also removed.[30] Gutted of any reference to his co-operation with the authorities, Richter's appeal was sent on its way.[31]

The Court of Appeal received Richter's letter and dismissed it. They noted that there was ample evidence to infer from Richter's actions that he had come to England with intent to help the enemy and that there were no legal grounds to appeal his original trial and verdict.[32] Most damning was the fact that he had made no attempt to give himself up to the authorities. Richter's appeal was denied, and his execution date was rescheduled for 10 December.

Interestingly, in a letter dated 1 December, one individual (illegible signature) wrote:

> I agree that there is no case for interference with the sentence on Richter. *The mere fact that a man has been brought into this country by the Germans equipped to act as a spy does not of course necessarily show that he landed here with intent to help the enemy.* [author's emphasis] If this Czech had deceived the Germans and had satisfied the authorities that he had come to this country without any intention of helping them he would not have been prosecuted, but the circumstances of this case seem to me to show clearly that Richter did come here with intent to help the enemy, though he appears to be an irresolute type of person whose intentions may have been somewhat half-hearted.[33]

While the Court of Appeal was considering Richter's letter, MI5 was reconsidering the wisdom of going through with Richter's execution. As early as 5 November, Robertson (head of the double-cross system) strongly recommended that Richter be given a reprieve. Robertson thought that it was extremely dangerous for Richter's obituary to appear in the news as it might cast doubt on TATE.[34]

Several weeks later, on 23 November, Liddell (Director of B Division) picked up the same gauntlet and wrote to Petrie (Director General of MI5) about the dangers of bringing Richter to trial. 'I should like to emphasise once more how much I deprecate from the Intelligence point of view the present procedure by which it is necessary to make public details of every execution carried out.'[35]

Liddell and Robertson were particularly concerned about Richter's links to double agent TATE, the perceived pearl in Germany's spy network. Richter had told Short in mid July 1941 that he had come to check up on TATE and see if he was free of control. An Abwehr officer had said that if TATE was false, then the whole string of agents was false. That statement had sent shivers through MI5's double-cross system. They had already had to fold up the SNOW network because of suspicions about SNOW's loyalty and how much the Germans suspected about his work for MI5. If the TATE network collapsed (TATE, MUTT, JEFF, RAINBOW), the entire double-cross system was in serious danger.

The MI5 officers debated two key points. If Richter was executed and the story was published in the newspapers, would the Germans then infer that Richter had given TATE up? Or would they conclude that Richter had remained mute and TATE was safe? On the other hand, if they acquitted Richter and he quietly disappeared into solitary confinement in a military prison (as did Jackson), would the Germans simply presume that he had fallen foul of weather and/or terrain? The debate raged back and forth for several days, with some MI5 officers in favour of acquittal and others in favour of execution. In the end, it was decided to let events take their natural course and control the facts released for publication.

Late to the party, on 30 November, Stephens wrote a note to Dick White (Liddell's deputy) grumbling, 'I have in fact mentioned this danger [of prosecuting Richter] to you and Colonel Hinchley-Cooke, but the decision has gone against us, and as far as I can gather, we cannot do more in the matter.'[36] Richter's execution would be allowed to proceed.

Liddell, in his letter to Petrie on 23 November, had raised a second point of concern regarding the execution of spies:

From a strictly intelligence point of view we have benefited considerably by keeping spies, so to speak, on the shelf of a reference library. It is rarely possible to say at any time that all information has been extracted from an agent. He may have a conscience which makes him reluctant to give away other agents, but if at a later date he finds that somebody else has done so and that we are in possession of the information this may ease his conscience and may cause him to be more forthcoming. An enemy agent may also have a faulty memory which can only be stimulated by facts which have come to light from the interrogation of other agents. It happens fairly frequently that after questioning a new arrival we re-interrogate a number of other enemy agents who, from a knowledge of their former activities and places of training, will be able to confirm and possibly supplement statements made by the later arrival.[37]

Stephens also subscribed to the 'human reference library' school, but both he and Liddell were overruled by Petrie, who argued that agents in the human reference library became stale, with out-of-date information.

Finally, a niggling doubt still rattled around the file on Richter. He had come to England with wireless components, supposedly meant for double agent TATE. The only problem was that the wireless crystal earmarked for TATE was the wrong frequency for TATE's set. Was it a German mistake or was there another spy? For months, the British had been concerned that an unknown German agent was at work in East Anglia. It was possible that Richter had brought the crystal for this unknown operative. Or perhaps the Germans had simply made another major faux pas. After all, when TATE had asked them for advice on new batteries, the Germans had recommended ones with the wrong voltage for his set. Perhaps the crystal was a similar mistake.

On 2 December, Richter received a visit from Hinchley-Cooke. Richter was less than impressed. Hinchley-Cooke tried to get him to talk, but Richter was resigned to his death. He knew that Hinchley-Cooke was only there to extract information and basically said, 'I am going to be hanged next week and I am not going to tell you anything which will only assist you to catch and hang somebody else.'[38] This statement and the context in which it was given indicated to Hinchley-Cooke that the crystal was indeed intended for delivery to an unknown agent, an agent about whom Richter possessed information. The MI5 officers admitted that Richter was stubborn:

> It is believed that Richter will divulge nothing further unless he has a firm assurance that his life will be spared and it is strongly submitted that the necessary authority should be obtained to enable us to go to Richter and put to him a concrete proposition that if, and only if, he supplies us with information which will enable us to identify, and may reasonably be expected to assist in the apprehension of, another German agent who is at large we undertake that he shall be reprieved.[39]

Discussions within MI5 leaned towards the idea that reprieving Richter at that late a stage would make TATE look good. If Richter appeared to cave at that point, and divulged information on TATE, MI5 would be unable to identify him as the dates for the meetings were long past.[40] It could be a win–win scenario for all concerned. Snatch another spy out of the hands of the Germans, take the heat off TATE and save Richter's life.

With some authority to back him up, Hinchley-Cooke visited Richter again on 4 December, but this time the meeting went very differently. Hinchley-Cooke spent several hours with Richter, trying to extract more details about the recipient of the crystal, but it was all for nought. Richter made a series of rambling statements in which he admitted that the crystal was to be used by TATE with a different aerial.[41] Hinchley-Cooke wrote a disgusted report in which he concluded that Richter could be of no of assistance in solving the question about a spy in East Anglia.[42] Richter had made so many rambling statements that no one was clear on what to believe.

On 8 December, Richter wrote another handwritten plea for mercy to the Home Secretary. It did nothing to deflect the inevitable. On the morning of 10 December, Richter was hanged at Wandsworth Prison. He did not go to his execution like a lamb but like a lion. He fought the guards when they came into his cell and resisted the hangman's noose for seventeen minutes.[43] An instant before the trapdoor opened, Richter leapt and the noose slipped from under his chin, barely catching under his nose.[44] Despite the drama, the coroner noted that it was a clean death.

Two very different men, Josef and Richter, were charged, tried and executed by the British authorities. Their cases, while dissimilar in some respects, shed light on two issues that, in one way or another, touched every foreign agent executed in Britain during the war: (a) inducements and (b) fair trial. One author has recently gone so far as to suggest that in the cases of Josef and Richter, 'the outcome edged uncomfortably close to state murder'.[45]

50

THE ROAD TO A SUCCESSFUL PROSECUTION

Earlier, we touched on the issue of inducements in relation to the case of Josef, but how MI5 handled other espionage cases is highly instructive.

In September 1940, the Home Defence (Security) Executive, led by Swinton, had laid it down that spies who were destined for prosecution should not be offered any inducement during their interrogations. At the same time, Swinton agreed 'that it was completely within the discretion of the Services [MI5 and MI6] whether they would forego prosecution and use the agent in any particular case for their own purposes'.[1] Liddell (Director of B Division) and Robertson (head of the double-cross system), therefore felt that they had free rein in how to handle newly arrived spies. Flush with their success with Wulf Schmidt (TATE) and Gösta Caroli (SUMMER), Robertson and his officers were anxious to increase their stable of double agents. If a spy met certain criteria (captured quickly and secretly, equipped with a wireless transmitter/receiver, amenable to being turned) then, in MI5's opinion, it was better to have another double agent rather than a dead spy.

In March 1941, Swinton visited Liddell and appeared to retract the earlier statement that prosecution of spies was at the discretion of MI5. The hounds were baying for blood and Churchill in particular, wanted to know why more spies had not been executed, as in the previous war. Swinton made it clear that 'nothing should be done or omitted which could in any way jeopardise a successful prosecution'.[2] That would apparently include inducements.

There were many ways in which a successful prosecution could be obtained. One of the easiest was for the suspect to make a voluntary confession or a voluntary statement in which he admitted his intention and/or his guilt. A voluntary confession was a hole-in-one for the prosecution. If a confession wasn't obtained, then the prosecution had to work harder to convince the judge and jury that the suspect was guilty.

There were, however, a few pitfalls to be avoided in obtaining a voluntary confession. English law has a long and storied history, one that alters but gradually with the passage of time. A dusty tome entitled *A History of the Criminal Law of England* provides helpful references based on the *Digest of the Law of Evidence*.[3] A confession is an 'admission made at any time by a person charged with a crime, stating or suggesting the inference that he committed that crime'.[4] Such confessions, if they are voluntary, 'are deemed to be relevant facts' against the person who made them.[5]

As it turns out, there are a number of other categories of confessions, those caused by inducement, threat or promise:

> No confession is deemed to be voluntary if it appears to the judge to have been caused by an inducement, threat, or promise, proceeding from a person in authority, and having reference to the charge against the accused person ... and if (in the opinion of the judge) such inducement, threat, or promise, gave the accused person reasonable grounds for supposing that by making a confession he would gain some advantage or avoid some evil in reference to the proceedings against him.[6]

Thus, for the prosecutor, the best scenario would be for the accused to be brought to a police station where he would make a voluntary confession. Failing this, the accused would be questioned by the police (without the use of inducements, threats or promises) and make a voluntary statement/ confession within which the suspect's guilt was inferred or admitted.

In late 1940 and early 1941, however, MI5 was not so much concerned with obtaining a guilty verdict as they were with obtaining intelligence from a potential double agent. Time was of the essence and the MI5 officers had to break an agent quickly. One of the fastest ways to get a stubborn agent to change their mind was to offer them an inducement: a threat or a promise: 'Co-operate with us, and you can save your life. Fail to co-operate with us and you're as good as dead.'

The MI5 methods were crude but effective. Unfortunately, their methods did not always produce confessions or statements that could be considered voluntary. In the first half of 1941, MI5 was still hammering out a procedure whereby they could get the intelligence that they craved yet not compromise the subsequent prosecution of a case. It was a delicate balance, and, in many cases, MI5 did not succeed in walking that tightrope. It was common practice that, once Latchmere House had finished extracting information from an agent, Hinchley-Cooke would have the agent brought to a police station, where he would take a voluntary statement from the agent. One has only to review some of the spy cases to see the problem with this approach.

Consider the case of Vera Eriksen, Karl Druecke and Werner Walti, who were captured in the autumn of 1940. Early on in their incarceration, Vera was separated from the two men and sent to Holloway Prison while Druecke and Walti remained at Latchmere House. Stephens had learned that Vera was enamoured with Druecke and fearful for his life. Neither Vera nor Druecke were impressed with Stephens' methods, but did respond to Latchmere House's doctor, Harold Dearden. Stephens was not too proud to use Dearden as the 'good cop' to his own 'bad cop'. Dearden was sent to Holloway Prison, where he had several conversations with Vera, the most successful of which took place the day after two of the Kent spies, Waldberg and Meier, were executed in early December 1940. Vera was encouraged to write letters to Druecke urging him to co-operate with the interrogators. Druecke revealed his real name but little else.

In February 1941, MI5 decided that they had wrung as much information out of the trio as they were likely to get. In late February, Hinchley-Cooke visited Holloway Prison to obtain a statement from Vera. During the course of their conversation this exchange took place:

[Hinchley-Cooke] Where did you get the idea to come to this country?

[Eriksen] You see I would rather not answer at all really. I would rather speak with the people from [Latchmere House] and they told me I did not need to answer any more because I told them everything.

[Hinchley-Cooke] Who told you that?

[Eriksen] Dr Dearden. I do not know the other people. There were six gentlemen there. Dr Dearden came here [Holloway Prison]. He told me that I would off trial[7] if I told them everything and that I would not be shot or hanged.

[Hinchley-Cooke] I know nothing about that. Do you remember when you left Stavanger?[8]

Hinchley-Cooke was to be commended for recovering his composure so quickly, but he was less calm afterwards. Hinchley-Cooke called up Stephens in 'a flap'. What had Dearden said to Vera? Stephens got off the phone with Hinchley-Cooke and wrote a note to Dearden, providing a summary of Hinchley-Cooke's encounter with Vera. Uncharacteristically, Stephens wrote in a conciliatory fashion:

> Knowing Vera [Eriksen] to be a prize liar I assume that you never held out the inducement or promise which she mentions but I must have the matter confirmed by you. Colonel Hinchley-Cooke is troubled about the position as he feels the impression which would be caused by her statement true or untrue might vitiate the trial not only of [Eriksen] but of Druecke and Walti also. A solution is that you should appear as a witness for the Crown but there are obvious objections to this course. Will you please let me have a note on this subject as soon as possible.[9]

That same day, Dearden sent a memo back to Stephens, firmly stating:

> At no time have I held out any promise to this prisoner that she would not be sent for trial, nor have I at any time promised her that she would not be shot or hanged if she were sent for trial. I have advised her on many occasions to be frank and to tell the whole truth about herself and others, on the grounds that by doing so she was doing that which was wisest in her own interests. I give this advice as a routine practice to every prisoner but I am invariably careful to make it clear that I have no connection with the Intelligence Branch of the Service and therefore no power to do other than give them friendly and disinterested advice.[10]

Stephens was pleased with Dearden's answer, content to remain secure in his estimation that Vera was a 'prize liar'.[11] Stephens wrote a memo to Dick White (Liddell's deputy) in which he noted:

> Col. Hinchley-Cooke's contention is that a jury would be affected by the statement of a prisoner that an inducement has been held out to her, notwithstanding the fact that the statement might be false. From the point of view of a prosecution the normal procedure would be to call Dr Dearden as a witness for the Crown to give the lie direct to Vera [Eriksen]. This procedure however, is open to extreme objection

in view of the character of Latchmere House. [*MI5 went to great lengths to ensure that no Latchmere House officer was called as a trial witness.*]

Colonel Hinchley-Cooke's solution is that he should be permitted to question a prisoner magisterially between the time of apprehension by the local police and admission to Latchmere House. From his point of view there are advantages but from our point of view there are considerable disadvantages and in view of our recent arrangement that we should have a Black Maria to fetch prisoners from the RSLO's direct I think the whole issued should be discussed between us?[12]

The problem of what to do with Vera ended up on the desk of prosecutor L.A. Byrne on 1 April 1941. MI5 had decided not to prosecute the woman while proceeding with the prosecution of Druecke and Walti. Byrne was less than pleased and noted that:

I understand that there are reasons why [Vera Eriksen] should not be prosecuted and I have therefore only considered the matter in relation to Druecke and Walti. I should however in passing like to draw attention to the fact that in a statement made by [Vera] to Lieut-Col. Hinchley-Cooke she appears to have said, 'I do not wish to say anything more because I have been interrogated on several occasions by Dr Dearden and other persons. Dr Dearden said it was all finished and that I should be "off trial" and would not be shot or hanged.'

If it is true that Dr Dearden held out any such inducement it appears to me that it was a highly dangerous action on his part and one that should not be repeated as I can well imagine a case in which such an inducement might render inadmissible a statement of great importance.[13]

Three months later, another lawyer weighed in upon the matter in a memo dated 23 July 1941. According to the memo, MI5 had decided that Vera would not be prosecuted because she had given them certain information, was likely to give them more, and was of more value to them alive than dead. The unknown author noted:

In my opinion this was a foolish way of dealing with this matter … [It] may give rise to all sorts of rumours and suspicions … I think it is perfectly clear in a case of this kind that the proper course would have been to proceed against the woman and to get a conviction.[14]

It then would have been open for MI5 to argue against the desirability of the sentence being carried out and she could have been reprieved without awkward questions:

> Counsel's opinion communicating upon this matter is herewith. If it is true that Dr Dearden who, I believe, holds himself as a psycho-analyst or something of that kind, used the expressions which the woman attributes to him, he is certainly not fit to have the handling of suspects or persons against whom criminal proceedings are likely to be taken in the Courts.[15]

This unnamed individual hit the nail on the head with regard to Vera. She was detained for the duration of the war and held in a variety of prisons and internment camps. At the end of the war she was repatriated to Germany and disappeared in the flood of returning refugees. Rumours about Vera have run rampant for decades.

A final note on the prosecution of Vera was written in October 1941 when Cussen noted, 'The case of this woman was reported to the DPP and he decided not to take proceedings against her under the Treachery Act.'[16] While there was likely more to the story than that, it was clear that just the faintest hint of inducement (true or not) was enough to make the lawyers skittish.

In Richter's case, he was questioned by the local police but there is no evidence that he made a statement under caution. From the police, he was transferred directly to Latchmere House, foregoing the traditional interview at Cannon Row Police Station by Robertson. Richter did eventually make a statement to Hinchley-Cooke on 31 May, under caution, but only after several days of intense interrogation at Latchmere House. He would not be the only one.

By the summer of 1941, Germany had seemingly given up on the idea of sending spies to Britain via parachute, in part due to the RAF's growing mastery of the skies.[17] The next wave of spies arrived camouflaged within the flood of Belgian and Dutch refugees who had risked much to escape Continental Europe via Spain. Erstwhile refugees who arrived on the shores of Britain were first sent to the London Reception Centre at the Royal Victoria Patriotic Schools (RVPS). Here, refugees were questioned by a series of trained officers who were on the lookout for anything out of the ordinary.

On 15 August 1941, the same day that Josef was executed, a Belgian named Alphons L.E. Timmerman boarded a ship in Spain bound for Britain. Timmerman arrived in Glasgow on 1 September and told both the immigration officer and the security control officer that he was a refugee. Arriving at the RVPS a few days later, Timmerman admitted that he had been recruited by the Germans as a spy and was equipped with secret ink. He told the RVPS officer that he had wanted to wait until he arrived in London and spoken to a solicitor before revealing the truth and he had no intention of carrying out his mission.

Timmerman's was an open-and-shut case. He made a statement to Hinchley-Cooke before being sent to Latchmere House. He was charged under the Treachery Act with having 'voluntarily entered the United Kingdom' with intent to assist the enemy.[18] Timmerman's civil trial took place in late May 1942. The jury took twenty minutes to return a verdict of guilty. He was executed on 7 July 1942.

The case of Florent Steiner played out differently. Steiner (Dutch-Belgian) was a marine engineer who was contacted by German agents while in port in Lisbon. The Germans gave him secret writing material and suggested that he send them information when he arrived in England. In June 1941, Steiner landed in England, overstayed his seaman's landing permit, and ended up living in Liverpool, working as a mechanic in his brother's garage. He kept the secret writing material and the two cover addresses but did nothing with them. Seven months later, MI5 got wind of Steiner's contact with German agents in Lisbon and arrested him.

During his initial statements, Steiner denied that he had had any connection with the Germans. He was sent to Latchmere House, where he eventually broke and admitted that he had secret writing material in his flat. MI5 wanted to prosecute Steiner under the Treachery Act but the DPP warned against it. There was no evidence that Steiner had sent any letters to the Germans. His passivity would suggest that he had had no intention of carrying out his mission.

This stands in stark contrast to Richter's case, where his passivity was held against him. In MI5's opinion, however, 'had Steiner's intentions been innocent it is considered that he would either have informed the authorities or thrown away his [secret writing] materials. As it is, he kept them.'[19] However, as the Members of Parliament had noted in May 1940, determining a man's intentions was fraught with uncertainty. The DPP recognised that the case against Steiner was not a strong one and suggested that he be prosecuted under the Defence Regulations and the Aliens Order instead of the Treachery Act. MI5, however, was less than happy with this possibility. On 30 June 1942, Milmo noted:

> I would respectfully but strongly submit that in this case it would be contrary to the national interest to proceed against Steiner on anything other than a capital charge. It would in my view be quite disastrous if it became known that a man who is proved to have been sent here as a German agent, and to have brought with him secret ink and writing materials, and who has failed to disclose these facts to the authorities over a period of many months, should only render himself liable to a term of imprisonment or to penal servitude. A further objection to prosecuting Steiner on a non-capital charge is that in the event of a conviction he would have to go to a penal servitude prison where precautions necessary for security reasons and for the protection of [Latchmere House] in particular could not be observed.[20]

Given that the DPP thought prosecution under the Treachery Act was inadvisable, MI5 admitted that prosecution under the Defence Regulations was also less than desirable. In a report to the DPP, MI5 respectfully suggested:

> It is highly undesirable for such minor charges to be preferred in a case such as this. It is essential that all persons who land in this country, having been in contact with the enemy, should be impressed with the fact that they are likely to be charged under the Treachery Act, and any proceedings under the Defence Regulations would have the effect of destroying this impression. It is felt, therefore, in all the circumstances that it is undesirable for any proceedings to be taken against this man.[21]

Steiner was a lucky man, simply detained for the duration of the war. Others would not be so lucky.

In mid May 1942, while MI5 wrestled with the Steiner case, a Dutch man, Johannes M. Dronkers, and two other men, arrived in Harwich after being rescued from a yacht off the coast of England. Claiming to be refugees, the three men were questioned at the RVPS. Dronkers' story was the least believable and its complexity revealed a number of gaping holes.

At Dronkers' first interview, the interrogating officer was blunt in his assessment of the middle-aged Dutchman:

> Dronkers, in my opinion, is a mental case … The man is a dithering fool, old before his time, a bundle of shaking nerves, maudlin and sentimental, who nearly weeps when the talk comes to Holland or the House of Orange, unintelligent, a typical piece of flotsam, with no special qualifications whatsoever, utterly useless and worthless as an Agent. His two companions are, in my opinion, genuine escapees, in good faith.[22]

The officer thought that Dronkers was an enemy agent, except for the fact that he was completely useless. By the seventh interview, however, Dronkers cracked, and it turned out that he had been recruited by the Germans to send secret ink messages back to Germany. He claimed that he had had no intention of carrying out his mission. Hinchley-Cooke was brought in to obtain the necessary voluntary statement from Dronkers, after which, he was sent to Latchmere House. Little else was extracted from the sad Dutchman and in August 1942, Hinchley-Cooke sent the case on to the DPP. Dronkers was tried in mid November 1942. The jury deliberated for eleven minutes before returning a verdict of guilty.[23] He was executed on 31 December 1942.

MI5 had seemingly found its stride with the successful prosecution of spies. Refugees were sent to the RVPS, where suspicious individuals were cut out of the crowd and subjected to rigorous interviews. After the RVPS officer had achieved a break in the case, Hinchley-Cooke was called in to take the voluntary statement and then the hapless spy was sent to the tender mercies of Stephens at Latchmere House. MI5 and the DPP were happy, but even this foolproof system began to unravel.

In mid July 1942 a Belgian seaman, Franciscus J. Winter, arrived in Scotland via Gibraltar. He claimed to be a refugee, was refused leave to land and was sent to the RVPS. After several interviews with Lieutenant Ray, one of the RVPS interrogating officers, Winter admitted that he had been sent to Britain on behalf of German Intelligence. Unlike Dronkers and Timmerman, Winter made no excuses. On 14 and 15 August 1942, Hinchley-Cooke took the usual statement in anticipation of prosecution. Winter was sent on to Latchmere House, but little more was extracted from him and he was deemed to be a low-grade agent. Winter's trial was scheduled for mid November 1942 but, along the way, the prosecutors discovered a slight hiccup in the case.

During one of the interrogations Lieutenant Ray at the RVPS had used the word 'help'. The stenographer during that interrogation wouldn't speak on the record but 'she had the impression, though she could not point to any particular fact, that Winter had been offered an inducement to confess ... she was inclined to wonder how Winter could "help himself."'[24] If Lieutenant Ray had offered Winter this vague inducement, then Hinchley-Cooke's statement could be ruled inadmissible. Prosecutor L.A. Byrne examined the case and indicated that, in his opinion, 'the confession obtained by Mr Ray did, in all probability, amount to an inducement which rendered his evidence on this point inadmissible'.[25] Byrne felt that Hinchley-Cooke's statement, however, was admissible since it was not connected with the first statement, to Lieutenant Ray.

The case went to trial in December 1942 and the defence didn't push the issue of inducement. The defence argued that since Winter had been refused leave to land in Scotland, he hadn't really landed and therefore he was not guilty of having 'entered the United Kingdom'.[26] Winter's jury returned a verdict of guilty after ten minutes. He was executed on 26 January 1943.

MI5 had dodged a bullet with the Winter prosecution, but this would not always be the case. In late 1942, Johannes DeGraaf arrived in England, supposedly a refugee from Nazi oppression. Born in Canada, to Dutch parents, DeGraaf and his family had moved back to Holland when he was 10 years old. He ran afoul of the Germans in 1941 and escaped to Spain, where he worked at the British Embassy in Madrid for several months. At his fourth RVPS interrogation, DeGraaf broke and admitted that he had been sent by the German Intelligence Service.

Given that DeGraaf was a citizen of the Commonwealth, MI5 had to tread lightly. They received Home Office permission to send DeGraaf to Latchmere House for a week or two, but the moment he asked for a solicitor, he would have to be transferred back to Brixton Prison.[27] Under Stephens' ministrations, MI5 learned that DeGraaf was one of the best trained agents to arrive on the shores of England.[28] He was highly trained in sabotage and it turned out that while he was working at the British Embassy in Madrid, he had passed along information about the refugee escape routes to the Germans. This information had not been revealed to the RVPS officers.

DeGraaf was clearly a candidate for prosecution, except for the fact that he had been employed at the embassy for eight months. MI5 realised that at trial, DeGraaf could argue his real mission had been to reach South Africa. Unable to accomplish that, he had resolved to work for the British, and would be able to provide evidence of satisfactory employment at the embassy.[29] It was a tough case. The DPP reviewed the papers and concluded that a charge under the Treachery Act would have to be based on the fact that DeGraaf entered Britain with intent to help the enemy. 'The evidence in support of a charge would be that on his arrival … he told an untrue story of his escape here.'[30] However, MI5 got the full story out of him:

> The details of the facts on which this admission was based were obtained from him by means of interrogations [at Latchmere House] in circumstances which, in my opinion, it would be undesirable to attempt to prove … On a broad view of the facts, I feel obliged tentatively to forecast the possible failure of the prosecution to prove the suggested charged under the Treachery Act and you will probably agree with me that a failure to convict in a case of this character would be highly undesirable.[31]

That was putting it mildly. In March 1943, Milmo (MI5 officer and barrister) noted:

> It would not, in our view, be in the public interest that it should become generally known how very difficult it is to establish a strong enough case for prosecution against a spy, or that there are in this country in detention a very large number of spies who are not and cannot be dealt with under the Treachery Act.[32]

Liddell noted:

> The Director of Public Prosecutions turned the case down because the formal statement given to Hinchley-Cooke at a later stage had been preceded by a number of other interrogations. This might lay the prosecution open to attack on the grounds that the story had been extracted by third degree methods [threats, etc.]. Personally, I feel inclined to agree with Milmo that a weak statement in the first instance [from RVPS] followed by interrogations by military intelligence

[at Latchmere House] and then another official statement [to Hinchley-Cooke] would have laid the prosecution open to the criticism that the original story was the true one and that the subsequent story had been extracted under duress.[33]

One could argue that this line of reasoning also applied to Josef's case. A statement taken by Robertson on 1 February was weak due to the extreme pain of the suspect and the lack of a certified translator. The second statement, taken by Hinchley-Cooke on 18 June, was preceded by months of interrogation at Latchmere House.

In late April 1943, DeGraaf was interned for the duration of the war and sent to Dartmoor Prison. Stephens was most unhappy, and in a note dated 3 May 1943, wrote, 'I reported at considerable length … on this case as the evidence was extremely strong for prosecution under the Treachery Act.'[34] DeGraaf was, in the words of one MI5 officer, 'an extremely lucky man to be alive'.[35] DeGraaf was released from prison in 1945 and by 1948 had made his way back to Canada.

Another man would not be so lucky. Pierre R.C. Neukermans, a Belgian veteran, escaped the Nazis via Spain and arrived at Poole Airport on 16 July 1943. He made a good impression at the RVPS and was recommended for release to the Belgian Ministry of Agriculture in London. Five months later, MI5 got word (through decoded German transmissions) that a German agent and two other men had escaped Belgium via Spain. It didn't take long before Neukermans and the other two were detained and questioned.

In early February, Hinchley-Cooke took a statement under caution from Neukermans, who was then sent on to Latchmere House. Under more intense interrogation, Neukermans revealed that he had secret ink at his apartment (a block of alum) and that he had sent letters from England to Portugal using the secret ink. He had not admitted this to Hinchley-Cooke, but MI5 figured that Hinchley-Cooke could take another statement and focus on the block of alum and hope that Neukermans would readmit the secret letters that he had sent.

Neukermans was brought to trial in late April/early May. His defence counsel entered a plea of guilty by reason of insanity. After testimony from several doctors, the plea was withdrawn. The jury took nine minutes to return a verdict of guilty. Neukermans was executed on 23 June 1944.

While Neukermans was still working at the Belgian Ministry of Agriculture, in the autumn of 1943, another agent landed in the United Kingdom, but this one came via parachute. After the failure of the first wave of parachute spies in 1940 and 1941 (injured, lost, captured), the German Abwehr had seemingly abandoned the idea of parachute spies. A couple of years later, however, on the night of 30 September 1943, Norwegian Nikolai S.M. Hansen landed near Fraserburgh in Aberdeenshire. Hansen did something quite different from all the other parachute spies, he hailed down a passing lorry with his flashlight and asked to be taken to the authorities. He confessed to the police that the German Intelligence Service had sent him to Britain with two wireless transmitters. His instructions were to bury one and then give himself up with the other one. Once he was free to move about, he was to return, unearth the other transmitter and communicate with the Abwehr, but Hansen had chosen to come clean to the British.

Hansen was sent to Latchmere House and, given his statement to the police, both Stephens and Hinchley-Cooke agreed that he could not be prosecuted. Stephens was given the go-ahead to begin interrogation and found Hansen to be a 'dull, unobservant peasant type'[36] with a 'great deal of natural low cunning and shrewdness'.[37] Robertson rejected Hansen as a double-cross possibility and Stephens agreed he was unreliable.

Stephens was right on all counts. Subsequent interrogations revealed that Hansen had been given secret ink and several cover addresses. Hansen had evidently not been as forthright with the police as had been initially thought. Apparently, the Germans had told Hansen that if he ever divulged the cover addresses to the British, they would take reprisals against his wife.

Liddell, in his diary entry from 11 October 1943, noted that Hinchley-Cooke's:

> … blood lust has been aroused by the Hansen case. He thinks that we should prosecute and wants to interview certain of the officers at [Latchmere House]. Stephens is breathing fire. We have however tactfully persuaded [Hinchley-Cooke] that before he does so the question of principles must be decided.[38]

Hansen had already been through interrogations at Latchmere House, which likely included the usual inducements, threats and/or promises.

Any statement taken from Hansen at that late a stage would be challenged by the defence, even if the DPP allowed the case to go forward. The only other option was to allow an officer from Latchmere House to testify in court, but that was less than ideal. In an 18 October note on Hansen's file, E.B. Stamp (B1b) wrote to Liddell (Director of B Division):

> Hitherto no prosecution has even been launched where its success has been dependent upon the evidence of a witness from [Latchmere House]. On the contrary, matters have always been so arranged that such evidence was unnecessary and irrelevant. There has been at least one case where we have had to face the possibility of the Court or the Defence requiring the attendance of some witness from [Latchmere House], and this has been a risk which we have felt bound to take. There is however clearly the greatest possible difference between calling a witness from [Latchmere House] to give evidence in chief where he would be subject to an unlimited and no doubt roving cross-examination on matters connected with [Latchmere House] and having such a witness called by the Defence where he could not be cross-examined by the prisoner's counsel, although the latter is sufficiently undesirable in itself.[39]

A few days later, Liddell wrote to Harker (Deputy Director General of MI5) and admitted that he was certain it would lead to disaster if a witness from Latchmere House was called to give evidence in chief, for he would be subject to a searching cross-examination. Liddell strongly recommended that no proceedings be taken against Hansen.[40] Harker passed the message on to Petrie (Director General of MI5), who agreed.[41]

Just to cover their bases, Petrie wanted Hinchley-Cooke to get the DPP's opinion, since that was in line with the principles laid down by Lord Swinton.[42] The DPP evidently agreed with Liddell and no action was taken against Hansen. A month later, Stephens added his own sense of the Hansen case. In Stephens' opinion:

> I think a prosecution in this case was foredoomed to failure by the very fact that this man willingly handed over both wireless sets to the police authorities at the first available opportunity. The position, in my submission, is not altered by the fact that he withheld his cover address in Sweden. He was under threat from the German Secret Service of dire reprisals upon his family. That would be the inevitable rejoinder from any advocate.[43]

Hansen's case was a dud. He was detained for the duration of the war and deported back to Norway in 1945.[44]

A second Norwegian would also escape the clutches of MI5 through a similar route. Knut Brodersen made his way from Norway to Spain with secret ink hidden on his person. Arriving in Scotland in the spring of 1944, Brodersen was sent to the RVPS, where he quickly broke under questioning. On the morning of 8 May, Brodersen arrived at Latchmere House and gave a statement to Hinchley-Cooke that afternoon. It looked like another open-and-shut case and the DPP felt confident that they could proceed with prosecution under the Treachery Act.

Thus it was that, on 20 June 1944, Brodersen was arraigned before the court. Recognising the seriousness of the situation, Brodersen accepted the offer of a defence lawyer.[45] Just a few days later, however, the open-and-shut case began to unravel. On 24 June, Mr Head (Brodersen's lawyer) submitted a request to call the captain of the ship upon which Brodersen had arrived, and at least one of four officers who interrogated Brodersen at Latchmere House. If possible, Head wanted to get statements prior to the trial.[46]

Consternation reigned in MI5. Milmo, Stamp, Hinchley-Cooke and Sinclair (Hinchley-Cooke's colleague) met to discuss the telephone message from Head. Hinchley-Cooke admitted that the 'request made him a little anxious' and 'it seemed fairly clear that an adjournment would have to be asked for the defence so that the Captain of the vessel could be present, and for the prosecution to consider the position'.[47] Milmo agreed that the Latchmere House request was a matter of concern and the interests of Latchmere House must be protected 'at all costs'.[48] Head could not be allowed to take a statement from any Latchmere House witness.[49]

It would only get worse. On 26 June, Milmo, Stamp, Hinchley-Cooke, Cussen and Sinclair convened a hasty meeting after receiving a report from Stephens regarding Brodersen. As it turned out, on the morning of 8 May, when Brodersen was transferred to Latchmere House (but before he made a statement under caution to Hinchley-Cooke), Sampson had conducted a preliminary interrogation of the Norwegian. Sampson had used standard Latchmere House terminology and phrases. He warned Brodersen that 'it is a matter of life and death'.[50] Sampson told Brodersen that 'we have had hundreds of people here, and many of them have been executed' and then produced 'a few obituary notices' for him to examine:

You must understand we are at war, and we have no compunction with anyone who tried to hinder our war effort. Anyone who does that is liquidated pitilessly … Now you are in as dangerous a position as any man can be, and I make no promise to you, but what I do say is that you can help yourself by helping us. Have anything to say?[51]

The five MI5 officers sat in glum silence after reading the report. It didn't take a legal expert to recognise that Sampson's comments were dripping with inducements, threats and inferred promises. The matter would have to be referred to Crown Counsel. Hinchley-Cooke also consulted Petrie, who agreed that under no circumstances could any witness from Latchmere House be called; the case should be withdrawn.

On 27 June Hinchley-Cooke and Sinclair met with Vincent Evans (assistant to the DPP) to review the case. Evans was less than impressed and agreed that if Head found out what had happened at Latchmere House, he would have grounds for successfully contending that the statement made under caution to Hinchley-Cooke was inadmissible. MI5 didn't want Head to know the real reason for withdrawing the case (calling Latchmere House witnesses) and suggested that the whole burden of withdrawal be placed on the ship's captain from whom a statement would be taken. Brodersen's defence counsel would argue that the ship's captain had told Brodersen that he would be taken to London upon landing and thus Brodersen had waited before coming clean.[52]

On 28 June, Hinchley-Cooke and Sinclair met with a group of lawyers at the Central Criminal Court, who suggested it would be better to use a *Nolle Prosequi* (unwilling to pursue) order, which would allow them to simply withdraw the case without needing to give a reason. Head would have no idea as to the reason and the case wouldn't need to be adjourned while they waited to take a statement from the ship's captain. The group consulted with the AG who concurred. Thus, on 29 June, when the case came before the court, the DPP issued a *Nolle Prosequi*.[53] Brodersen and Head must have been ecstatic, if slightly perplexed. Brodersen was, however, not entirely off the hook and was interned at Dartmoor Prison for the duration of the war.[54]

Brodersen's case might have been over but the ramifications were huge. On 3 July Liddell and Milmo went to the Home Office to meet with Sir Alexander Maxwell and explain the reason for the withdrawal of charges. Maxwell listened to the tale and then said that he 'fully appreciated that in these matters intelligence must come first'.[55] He suggested, however, that 'it might be a question as to whether proceedings should ever be taken against any person who had been in [Latchmere House] if the success of these proceedings depend upon a statement taken from the man under caution at some subsequent date'.[56]

The three men talked about Maxwell's suggestion and the two MI5 men admitted that 'the Security Service, as a result of their experience in this case felt that this principle ought to be adopted'.[57] It had always been MI5's practice to try and complete the case for a man's prosecution and take a statement under caution before he went to Latchmere House. Unfortunately, it was often 'only by sending the man to [Latchmere House] that an admission was obtained of recruitment by the enemy intelligence service'.[58] If Brodersen had not been sent to Latchmere House, it was doubtful as to whether any confession would have been forthcoming from him. Maxwell approved in principle MI5's view that 'statements under caution should not be taken from the persons if they have once been admitted to [Latchmere House]'.[59] Rather too late for Josef and Richter.

51

INDUCEMENTS, THREATS AND PROMISES

[Jakobs] placed himself at your disposal. He had been told that he could save his life if he could give you enough information. You got information from him, and not only that; you also caught me through him, as you told me yourself, a fact for which the Germans would have shot him out of hand, if he had fallen into their clutches again. In spite of everything he is now dead.

Karel Richter[1]

By the autumn of 1941, MI5 had largely figured out how to achieve a successful prosecution and yet still obtain critical intelligence through interrogation. They had learned how to abide by Lord Swinton's directives, but in the case of Josef Jakobs and Karel Richter, MI5 strayed over the line.

Broken leg or not, the fact was that once Josef found himself before a military officer in Cannon Row Police Station, he asked to give a voluntary statement under caution. He admitted that he had been sent by the German Abwehr but stated that it was never his intention to carry through with his mission, but rather to make his way to America where he had an aunt. Given the fact that Josef was suffering from a shattered lower leg and had no fluent translator, one could naturally wonder at the admissibility of that statement made to Major Robertson.

The next day, on 2 February, Josef was brought to Latchmere House for a preliminary interrogation. Stephens didn't have much time with Josef but he and his team had created a 'calculated atmosphere' within which Josef agreed to 'work as the servant of his captors'.[2] Stephens admitted that he used Josef's affection for his family as a lever, giving Josef the impression 'that we can liquidate these persons if he fails to do what we require'.[3] Stephens had doubts about Josef's loyalty but felt 'the fact that he has responded to threat in a comparatively short period of time should not be misunderstood'.[4] Stephens thought Josef could prove to be a much more amenable double agent than some of the others the British had handled.[5]

Were inducements or threats or promises offered to Josef Jakobs on that fateful day of 2 February? Most definitely. 'Work for us or we'll liquidate your family.' Richter would go so far as to say Josef 'had been told that he could save his life if he could give you enough information'.[6] Even Stephens acknowledged that Josef responded to a 'threat'.

The verbatim interrogation transcripts have been weeded from Josef's file but if we look back at Brodersen's case, we can see the type of language used by Sampson, which was likely very similar to how the interrogators spoke to Josef.

Finally, there is the case of Florent Steiner, who was interrogated by Stephens, Short and Goodacre in early March 1942. The verbatim transcripts are rife with veiled threats and promises.

You must know by now where you are, and why you are here. As I have said, we shoot people, and we hang people. You may think that England proceeds on a democratic basis. That may be so in peace time. In war time spies come here, and because of that we either keep a good number, as you know, here, or we keep some more somewhere else, or else we send them off for this sort of thing [show documents].[7] There is only one way out of it, and that is the whole truth. [Stephens to Steiner.]

The only other point I have to make plain is that the privilege of being shot is reserved for Germans, and the penalty for people like yourself who are not Germans is hanging. That is all. It is not a very pleasant outlook, is it? [Stephens to Steiner.]

My interest is not to see that people should be shot, or hanged. That is the inevitable penalty for people who are obstinate, do you understand? People who help, we may be able to treat them differently. [Stephens to Steiner.]

I think the best thing you can do is to go off to your cell again, and your future treatment will be dependent upon the results you produce, do you understand? [Stephens to Steiner.]

No listen, you are obviously worried about saying too much. Don't you understand that the best thing to do is to tell absolutely everything. You have said what you have, so now tell everything and make the thing comfortable for yourself. Don't attempt to hide things, it does not matter. [Short to Steiner.][8]

The next day, Stephens and Goodacre had another go at Steiner. The promises and veiled threats continued.

I'm not making promises, but your best chance of trying to improve your position is by telling the complete truth. [Stephens to Steiner.]

You cannot make the case any worse, but you can make it better if you give information which can be checked. [Stephens to Steiner.]

Now, do you realise that, having admitted you came over here in Kromholz's service [a German agent in Lisbon] – that is as, technically, a spy – your position is a great deal worse if you admit that you came over here to do this work for nothing, without any reward, then if it were something you were paid to do. [Goodacre to Steiner.][9]

Given the statements made by interrogators to Brodersen and Steiner, all of which contained inducements, it is quite clear that Josef was threatened and given the impression that he could save himself and his family by turning against the Germans and actively working for the British as a double agent. He agreed 'to work as the servant of his captors'.[10] One would naturally conclude that such an agreement was at least bilateral – the British agreed to spare his life (and that of his family) if he agreed to work for them. As Masterman noted, the agent was turned into a double agent, 'convinced that he could save his life by working for [MI5]'.[11] Agreement made, but then later rescinded.

As the weeks progressed, it was clear that Josef would not be suitable as a double agent. His capture was too widely known. People had talked, and the Germans might hear of his capture. It wasn't worth the risk and Josef's name was removed from the list of potential double agents; unbeknownst to Josef. When he was released from hospital, he was still under the impression that he had an agreement with the British. He gave them information on Richter. He was brought into Richter's first interrogations as a living witness to Richter's lies, a tactic that helped to break Richter.

Weeks later, Josef was placed in a cross-ruff with Richter. 'Throughout their association, Jakobs was at pains to impress upon Richter that the officials [at Latchmere House] know everything, to work for them in fact. He encouraged [Richter] to make a typewritten statement.'[12] Josef thought he was fulfilling the terms of his agreement even if he sometimes needed reminders from Stephens and Sampson.

On 6 June, Stephens noted at the end of an interrogation:

> When Jakobs was leaving the room I warned him of his precarious position and advised him to give as much information as possible. During the night his memory apparently served him well for he asked for an interview this morning and Sampson interrogated him with some considerable effect … Jakobs is a slippery customer and is certainly anxious to save his neck. It is, therefore, difficult to tell whether he is telling the truth or whether he is romancing in order to curry favour.[13]

This dilemma was one of the reasons Stephens believed that violence during an interrogation was 'taboo, for not only does it produce answers to please, but it lowers the standard of information'.[14] It would appear, however, that even the threat of violence was enough for prisoners to tell interrogators what they thought they wanted to hear.

On 18 June, Hinchley-Cooke telephoned Stephens and asked that Josef should be available at 2.30 p.m. to be brought from Latchmere House to New Scotland Yard. Stephens told Hinchley-Cooke that Josef would be made available, but he had a favour to ask. He would be grateful if Hinchley-Cooke would avoid letting Josef know that he was going to be placed on trial shortly, since 'he was at present being used as an "associate" in connection with the collection of information from certain detainees at [Latchmere House]'.[15] Stephens reiterated that 'no promise of any kind had been made to Jakobs in connection with this work he was doing'.[16] Yet, Stephens had earlier acknowledged the use of threats.

Is there a difference between a threat and a promise? Or are they two sides of the same coin? If you do not co-operate with us, we will kill you and your family (threat). If you do co-operate with us, we will not kill you or your family (promise).

Semantics? Perhaps not. Some researchers have argued that the above threat and promise (which are conditional and meant to influence the victim) are strictly connected. In fact, a 'promise act is always and necessarily (although hidden) accompanied (and supported) by an act of threat, and vice versa'.[17] The critical feature in both is that the victim and the perpetrator both have a role. There is a mutual agreement of cause and effect, action and response, commitment. As it turned out, MI5 was not all that interested in fulfilling their side of the conditional promise vs threat equation.

In early September 1940, four German spies landed along the coast of Kent. They were captured and sent to Latchmere House. These were some of the first spies Stephens welcomed, and he was eager to get at them. Charles Albert Van den Kieboom was brought into the interrogation room on 5 September. Stephens was in fine form:

> You snivelling swine, what do you stand to gain by lying like this? Do you think you are so clever that you can tell any lie you like and we have to accept it? Have you enough intelligence to realise that you are going to be shot, and that the only way of trying to save your neck is by trying to tell the truth, or have you such faith in your Boche masters that you think that they will welcome you with open arms when they come into this country? How many more lies have you told?[18]

Kieboom, in an admirable feat of composure, simply replied, 'I think that is everything sir.'[19] And yet, Kieboom did eventually break, as most of them did. On 7 September, Kieboom, with coaching from MI5, sent a message to Germany using his wireless transmitter, saying that Pons (one of the four spies) had been shot and the rest of the party had been in hiding for three days.[20]

At that stage, MI5 was evidently thinking of using the men as double agents but in the end decided against it. The four had been equipped with two transmitters (but no receivers) which were of limited value to a double agent. Despite co-operating with the British and sending a message to Germany, Kieboom was tried, convicted and sentenced to death. Agreement made – and rescinded. Less than a year later, Swinton, MI5, the DPP and the AG would note that 'a promise once given had to be honoured'.[21] Such a decision came far too late for Kieboom, and for Josef.

Months later, Josef believed that if he co-operated with the British, if he helped them, he would save his life and those of his family. Richter spoke with Josef on numerous occasions and Josef had shared his advice on dealing with the British. Co-operate, tell them what they want to hear, and save your life. Call it a threat or a promise, either way the comments made to Josef by the staff at Latchmere House influenced Josef's thoughts and actions.

This leads us to Josef's statement made under caution to Hinchley-Cooke on 18 June 1941. Given the evidence from Stephens' own reports, and in light of the other spy cases, Josef's statement should not have been admissible in court. Inducements, threats and promises had been made to him prior to his statement to Hinchley-Cooke, yet this was the statement presented at Josef's court martial. Not only that, it was used as a counterpoint to the statement Josef had made to Robertson on 1 February.

Marlowe, for the prosecution, made much of the differences between the two statements, presenting this as evidence of Josef's intentions. It may explain why Marlowe introduced the Robertson statement during the court martial. The Robertson statement was not entered into evidence at the start of the trial, nor revealed at the Summary of Evidence taken at Wellington Barracks on 28 July. This did not follow the Rules of Procedure and one could naturally question the practice of introducing new evidence partway through the trial. On top of that, the Robertson statement was taken in less than ideal conditions and calls into question whether it was, in fact, a 'voluntary' statement.

In some situations, serious questions have been raised 'as to concerns about the defendant's physical or mental health in connection with the interrogation process'.[22] Questions around the voluntary nature of a confession in regards to a person's health normally arise in three settings: (1) was the defendant physically ailing when he was interrogated (either hospitalised or bedridden), (2) was the defendant under the influence of alcohol or drugs, (3) did the defendant suffer from serious mental illness?[23] Given that Josef had a broken leg and had lain exposed to the winter weather for more than twenty-four hours, one could naturally ask whether or not the first setting would apply to the statement given to Robertson. The fact that Josef mistakenly claimed to have one son and two daughters during that statement (when in fact he had two sons and one daughter) could lead one to suspect that his physical and mental state were less than ideal and may not have met the threshold for a voluntary confession. On the other hand, the Police Divisional Surgeon, Dr Marran, had examined Josef and stated that he thought he was fit enough to make a statement. After the statement, however, Dr Marran did give Josef an injection for the pain, which calls into question Josef's fitness.

If Hinchley-Cooke's statement was ruled inadmissible, Marlowe's tactic of comparing the two statements would have vanished. Similarly, the fact that Josef had surrendered as soon as he was able and gave a voluntary admission to the police, makes one think of Nikolai Hansen. He escaped prosecution because he surrendered and gave a voluntary confession to the police. It was only after he had been thoroughly interrogated at Latchmere House that MI5 realised he had been holding back. Josef had the misfortune to arrive in Britain during a period of extreme national danger. Britain was against the ropes and there was no room for mercy. Civil liberties were curtailed, and some legal niceties were skirted.

52

RULE OF LAW

At the same time, had Josef had a wily and cunning lawyer, he might have escaped death. Josef's defence lawyer could have brought forward several points. He could have challenged the admission of Robertson's statement with more vigour. He could have challenged the physical and mental health of Josef at the time that the Robertson statement was taken. He could have challenged the language skills of Police Constable Templeman who served as translator on 1 February.

White knew that Josef wanted to reference statements he had made to the officers at Latchmere House on 2 February. He asked Marriott if he could direct those questions to him and received a negative. He asked Hinchley-Cooke if he could direct those questions to him and received a negative. Josef repeatedly stated that he had told the officers at Latchmere House many things and had helped them in different ways. White could have asked that officers from Latchmere House be called as witnesses, but he did not, and Josef paid the ultimate price. Was it White's fault? Probably not.

If we look at the trials of the other spies, we uncover a disturbing pattern: legal representation for the defendants was often arranged in a hasty and cursory fashion. The trial of the four spies who had landed in Kent took place from 19–22 November 1940. Waldberg's lawyer led him to plead guilty to a capital offence. The other three pleaded not guilty. Realising his error, Waldberg was left with an appeal to the Home Office. It was unsuccessful.

Neither Walti nor Druecke had legal representation when their depositions were taken prior to their civil trial. On the first day of their trial, both men pleaded not guilty. The clerk of the court asked Druecke if he had a lawyer. Druecke did not, nor did Walti. The clerk of the court asked if they understood English and when he received an affirmative answer asked them if they understood it sufficiently to follow the proceedings.[1] At that point, the judge stepped in and said, 'This is a trial at which the accused are apparently unrepresented by counsel. That seems to be very unsatisfactory.'[2]

It was agreed that the court would adjourn and reconvene after lunch. Neither defendant had the funds to pay for counsel and so two legal aid lawyers were rounded up and brought into the court. Druecke chose one and Walti was left with the other. The lawyer for the prosecution (who was also the Solicitor General) sat down with the defence lawyers for 'five minutes' and briefed them on the documents.[3] The jury members were sworn in and the solicitor general gave his opening statement. An interpreter was sworn in and then the prosecution called their first witness. At the end of the trial, the jury found both men guilty and they were sentenced to death by hanging.

It would appear, however, that Walti's lawyer, Whitebrook, was wily and cunning. Towards the end of July, Whitebrook wrote several letters to the Secretary of State (Home Office) challenging Walti's conviction based on The Hague Convention. His argument was not accepted by the Home Office, although they did admit:

> Indeed if there were anything in Mr Whitebrook's point I think it would be that the British Government contravened the Hague Convention by allowing Parliament to pass the Treachery Act of 1940 in such a form as to render liable to a conviction of 'felony' persons who may be spies within the meaning of the Hague Convention.[4]

In early August, Whitebrook tried a different tack, arguing that the prisoners had not been represented by counsel either at the start of the trial or when the depositions were taken.[5] Whitebrook wrote to the Undersecretary of State again and said that his client had been under-represented at the police court. Whitebrook himself was called into the trial after it had already started. He had had no opportunity to see the depositions, 'save as they were passed to me whilst the witnesses were giving evidence at the trial'.[6]

In Whitebrook's opinion, when the case was heard before the magistrate (deposition), Walti would not have been able to understand the witnesses. While they spoke excellent English, it was with a Scottish accent that was difficult to understand, even for a southerner. As far as Whitebrook was concerned, it would have been utterly beyond Walti's power to cross-examine them. Finally, Whitebrook noted:

> The absence of legal aid, at the Police Court proceedings, of a proper brief, duly prepared by a careful solicitor, of time to weigh the course of cross-examination, and of study to determine the legal status of the accused, with reference to the Allegiance and the King's Peace, all weighed against the prisoner. In the words of the learned Judge, 'It was most unfortunate'.[7]

Whitebrook may have had a point, but the State would not be swayed from its course. Walti and Druecke were executed at Wandsworth Prison on 6 August 1941.

Josef, too, was not provided with a lawyer at his Summary of Evidence on 28 July 1941 and was unable to question the witnesses. This was similar to Richter's case, who had no legal counsel when he was charged at Bow Street Police Court. Richter arrived at his trial without any form of legal counsel. When asked if he wished to have such representation, Richter replied in the affirmative and, in his instance, court was adjourned until the next day. At least in his case, Richter's lawyer, DuCann, had half a day to review the evidence and depositions, and prepare a brief for the defence.[8] In all other instances after Richter's trial, it would appear that the accused spies were provided with counsel prior to their trial.

Finally, one comes to the matter of a compromised chain of custody in terms of the articles entered into evidence at trial. It was the role of the authorities to ensure that any evidence relevant to the case was stored securely and documented, to avoid damage and tampering. Thus, in Josef's case, there were meticulous lists of his possessions, passed from the Huntingdonshire Constabulary to Robertson to Butler (SLB) to Stephens and Stimson at Latchmere House, and back again. The evidence, in Josef's case, was not kept by the police but by staff at MI5. As it would turn out, MI5 was not always the greatest custodian of artefacts.

On 31 October 1940, Marriott wrote to an officer named Stringer asking him to search for a grey exercise book in which Waldberg (one of the four spies who had landed on the coast of Kent) had written down the messages that he had transmitted to Germany. Marriott was in quite a flap, 'I need hardly say that it is a most important piece of evidence and simply must be found.'[9] Misplacing such a critical piece of evidence does not shed a good light on MI5's practice of maintaining a secure chain of custody.

Early on in Josef's case, his Catholic badge (documented by the Huntingdonshire Constabulary) went missing. In late February, the RSLO officer from Reading asked Butler if he could have the loan of a spy wireless set to show to the local police. Butler loaned Josef's set, and other equipment, to the RSLO with strict instructions that it should not be tampered with in any way. In a postscript, Butler noted, 'I am sorry to write this formal letter but I am responsible for the safe custody of the various articles concerned and life is liable to be a little unpleasant for me if I do not keep a very watchful eye upon them.'[10] The notebook that Josef had in his possession when he landed was not tracked down until 22 July, with no explanation as to how, or when, it had been discovered, and where it had been in the interim. The paper trail was not complete.

On 14 August 1941, a member of staff from Hinchley-Cooke's office wrote to Milmo asking for the location of Richter's parachute helmet and knife, admitting that they had gone missing in mid May.[11] Even if the items were found, one could wonder at the legitimacy of presenting such items as exhibits during Richter's trial.

For the chain of custody to be secure, prosecutors generally wanted the police to be able to testify (a) that the evidence offered in court was the same evidence they collected or received, (b) to the time and date the evidence was received or transferred to another authority and (c) that there was no tampering with the item while it was in custody. This generally meant that the police who seized the evidence needed to mark it in a way that distinguished it from similar objects taken from other suspects.

The evidence must also be stored in a way that provided reasonable assurance that no one was able to tamper with it. If the evidence was transferred to a different authority, there must be a paper trail that supported the transfer. The prosecutor needed to show the evidence presented in court was the evidence collected at the scene of the crime. If evidence went missing at any point, or was open to tampering, it might not be admissible in court.

The Metropolitan Police Force was well versed in the art of maintaining an impeccable chain of custody. A savvy defence lawyer might have begun by questioning the chain of custody, given that it was clear the evidence had been in the custody of the military and not the police. Neither Josef nor Richter had such a lawyer, however, and such irregularities passed unnoticed.

Such mistakes and omissions were not the sole purview of the British authorities, however, for the German Abwehr made its own share of fateful errors in dispatching agents to the United Kingdom.

53

INEFFICIENT GERMANS

Four spies arrived on the shores of England in early September 1940, the first of many wartime agents to be sent over during the course of the following nine months. Most of the agents were apprehended within hours of landing. As the bedraggled spies were interviewed by the police, Latchmere House officers and Hinchley-Cooke, a picture began to emerge of the organisation that had sent them, the German Abwehr. It was a picture that left the MI5 officers bemused and befuddled.

On 8 September 1940, Liddell met with Kenneth Strong (head of the German Section at MI14). Strong had interviewed the four newly arrived spies (Waldberg, Meier, Pons and Kieboom) and was puzzled. Strong had spent many years in Germany and had a 'great regard for German efficiency'.[1] In the words of Liddell, Strong 'cannot bring himself to believe that [the Germans] could have been so stupid, as to send these men over here without having schooled them properly and worked out plans by which they could be really effective'.[2]

MI5 could almost think that those four spies, plus Caroli (SUMMER) and Schmidt (TATE), had been sent over as part of some diversion, except for the fact that the British had intercepted transmissions from the Germans that indicated otherwise. The Germans were worried about the six men they had sent over and Liddell noted, 'This is interesting confirmation that these six spies, who have been thrown into this country in the most inefficient manner, are apparently part of a serious German organisation'.[3]

At the end of September, Eriksen, Druecke and Walti arrived on the shores of Scotland from Norway. They too seem to have been thrown at Britain with little thought or preparation. A year and a half later, Dick White wrote a note to Petrie in which he acknowledged:

Doubtless the only satisfaction which the directors of the German Intelligence in Norway obtained from the venture was their ability to report to the High Command that they were dispatching spies to the United Kingdom in preparation for the invasion which was then the practical intention of the [German] High Command.[4]

At Druecke and Walti's trial, Hinchley-Cooke testified:

I am afraid that the Germans are very careless in the way they send these agents over. Considering that they make a German '1' on an English Registration Card, one must admit that they are very careless; and that would be happily, very consistent with their usual practice of being careless! They are also careless from the point of view of forgetting to put on a landing stamp of an immigration officer. That would be equally careless … But there is actually an intelligent explanation for these various mistakes, if I may explain it. That was at the time when an invasion was considered very possible, and the German Intelligence Service were in a great hurry to send over certain agents quickly to get certain information; and if I may so put it, my opposite numbers were very hard pushed for time, and therefore they made these mistakes.[5]

Hinchley-Cooke's explanation may have held up, were it not for the fact that Kurt Karl Goose was sent over in early October 1940 with a fine example of a identity card bearing none of the usual mistakes.[6]

This idea of 'German carelessness' was the story that Stephens told newly arrived spies. The hapless agents were barraged with such statements as, 'The Germans did a horrible job of training you, look at all the mistakes they made. They lied to you. Why are you still being loyal to them? You should shift your loyalty.'

Meier and Waldberg had been put together at Latchmere House on 11 September 1940 and had grumped about the various shortcomings of their trip.[7] Meier thought that perhaps the Germans wanted them to be caught so that the four spies could give false information about the planned invasion. Maybe that was why they had been sent without proper identity cards, other bona fides or even a water bottle! Waldberg condemned one of the German spymasters (Kohler), who had given them an entirely false idea of the ease with which their job could be carried out. Kohler had said that Britain was devastated by bombing and quoted Herman Goering (head of Germany's Luftwaffe), who stated that by 10 September 1940 not a house would be left standing in England.[8]

Two of the key hallmarks of German inefficiency and carelessness were the identity cards with which the spies were equipped and the poor language skills of the agents. The British National Identity Card system was fairly simple: a foldable card with a registration number, name of the bearer, address of the bearer and a date. Introduced by the registrar after the start of the war, the cards were an unknown for the German Abwehr. They asked one of their prized British spies, JOHNNY (double agent SNOW to the British) to supply them with registration numbers as well as addresses for bombed-out properties. MI5 happily supplied some registration numbers to the Abwehr via SNOW, some of which did not exist (e.g. Richter's registration number started with VXAQ, but the V series was not used).

A subagent of SNOW (double agent BISCUIT) brought a copy of a traveller's identity card and a ration book to a rendezvous in Spain with the German spymaster Nikolaus Ritter. The German Abwehr's documents department produced forged identity cards and ration books based on those examples. These were then filled in with the pertinent details and given to the agents. There were, however, a variety of problems with the forged cards. Some could be laid at the feet of the British, since BISCUIT's cards had been altered slightly to include subtle errors that the Germans reproduced faithfully. For example, the genuine cards were hand-folded, but the false ones were machine-folded. Other errors could be put down to German carelessness, inefficiency or perhaps something more ominous.

In the case of Josef Jakobs, an error was made; one of such monumental proportions that Liddell mused upon it for almost a whole page in his diary entry on 2 February 1941. All the other agents who had been equipped with identity cards had ones that used the numbers sent by SNOW, or were otherwise unremarkable.

CNSO 171/1 – Caroli – arrived Sept 1940
PNAG 217/3 – Schmidt – arrived Sept 1940
CNXV 141/1 – Walti – arrived Sept 1940
CNEX 141/2 (or CNIX 141/2) – Eriksen – arrived Sept 1940
CNFU 141/1 – Druecke – arrived Sept 1940
FMEG 296/1 – Goose – arrived Oct 1940
BFAB 318/1 – Ter Braak/Fukken – arrived Nov 1940
656/301/29 – Jakobs – arrived January 1941
VXAQ 195/1 – Richter – arrived May 1941[9]

One has only to glance over the list to recognise that Josef's registration number does not match the others. Was it a mistake, or something more sinister? The original registration number sent by SNOW to the Germans was ARAJ 301/29. The Germans had used the last portion of the registration number, but altered the first part and in such a way that it would not pass even the most cursory glance by the oldest, most near-sighted British bobby. Liddell was perplexed:

> Why did they give [Jakobs] a registration card with no letter prefix? Incidentally it was one of those about which SNOW sent numbers. If they had wished to alter the letters or the numbers, that would have been different, but to rule out the prefix and put in numbers instead would seem to rather more than a clerical error. Did they intend that Jakobs would be captured, on the assumption that they know that these [double-cross] agents send weather reports and other information which though limited is at least accurate. If he had a number and name submitted by SNOW and SNOW was not trusted, they might have sent him over to test SNOW in some way although it is difficult to see exactly how, since SNOW could perfectly well say that he had been captured owing to the blunder about his registration card. A better test would seem to have been to try and place him in direct touch with SNOW. Another point which occurs to me is that the Germans must now be wise to the game of collaring an agent and forcing him to use his wireless set in our interests. There is in fact evidence that they are doing it themselves. Surely therefore they would have some arrangement, for example the dropping of the first letter of the prefix by which an agent could indicate that he was not acting under compulsion. We know that in some ways the Germans are extremely crude and sketchy in their methods and this may of course be the explanation but I find it difficult to believe. Jakobs has already agreed to assist us to make use of his wireless set.[10]

Was Josef's registration number a deadly mistake due to a careless clerk, a mistake that made it past the Abwehr's spy handlers? Or was it something more sinister? Two facts come into play: (1) all of the other identity cards given to Germans spies bore normal registration numbers and (2) the numbers on Josef's card were part of a series sent by SNOW. Josef's identity card would seem to be a deliberate attempt to alter what had been a normal-looking registration number (ARAJ 301/29) to one that stood out like a sore thumb (656/301/29).

Josef claimed that he had been denounced to the Gestapo by Van Hees but the Abwehr had still decided to send him to Britain. Perhaps the Germans decided to stack the deck against Josef. The Germans were naturally wondering if some of their spies had been turned into double agents, and Josef was the perfect canary in the coal mine. If the Germans heard back from Josef via wireless transmitter, they could be certain that he had betrayed them and been turned into a double agent. The Gestapo could then take out their vengeance on Josef's family. By giving Josef such a registration number, the Germans were essentially pasting a sign to his forehead that read, 'SPY'! Even a cursory inspection of his identity card would have resulted in Josef being questioned intensively. He would have been brought to a police station, his belongings would have been searched (yielding a wireless transmitter, a code and German-made clothing) and he would have been arrested.

In the end, the plan went off the rails when Josef left the aeroplane. The flight crew recognised that he had injured himself badly. Ritter even sent a message to SNOW asking about the man who had parachuted south of Peterborough on 31 January. Given that the Germans had their suspicions about the loyalty of SNOW, Ritter must have known that such a message would be read by the officers of MI5. Rather than leaving Josef to die of exposure in some British field or forest, Ritter was essentially sending a message that said, 'SPY LANDED HERE'. All of this could indeed lead one to believe that the German Intelligence Service was inefficient, careless and irresponsible.

The fact that Josef carried a disc code in his pocket, rather than out of sight within the locked attaché case, is perplexing. One author has argued that the disc codes supplied to Josef and others (e.g. Walti and Druecke) would never have been supplied to legitimate German agents. The disc codes were proof of espionage intent and a death sentence for those found carrying them.[11]

At the end of the war, Hugh Trevor-Roper, a historian who had worked for the Radio Security Service during the war, wrote a report on *The German Intelligence Service and the War*. Trevor-Roper ascribed the Goose inefficiency of the Abwehr to a variety of factors, including the personal faults of Admiral Wilhelm Canaris (head of the Abwehr); a lack of centralisation in the Abwehr; a lack of co-ordinated deception; penetration by the British; Allied counter-measures (e.g. the double-cross system) and the *Führerhauptquartier* (working under policies implemented at the 'whim' of 'ignorant maniacs' – i.e. officials of the Nazi Party).[12]

This idea, that the failure of German Intelligence could be ascribed to 'Goose inefficiency', was easy enough for the British authorities to embrace. It bolstered their own sense that they had put one over on the Germans with the double-cross system. British skill, acumen and pluck had won the day. As early as the 1950s, however, a different story began to emerge, one that called into question the idea of German 'Goose inefficiency'.

A variety of authors have suggested that, instead of being inefficient, the German Abwehr were using any means at their disposal to actively sabotage Hitler's planned invasion of Britain. German historian Monika Siedentopf recently wrote a book entitled *Operation Sealion: Resistance in the German Secret Service*.[13] Siedentopf admits that the LENA invasion spies (sent from September 1940 to May 1941) were poorly trained and only marginally skilled. She suggests that this was a result, not of Abwehr inefficiency, but of anti-Nazi resistance within the Abwehr.

After German's blitzkrieg invasion of France and the Low Countries, Hitler turned his eyes towards England. Hitler admired the British and saw them as natural friends of the Germans. With the Allies pushed off the Continent by his troops, Hitler figured that he could reach a quick agreement with Britain and then turn his attention towards Russia. However, Churchill had other ideas. Hitler was in a predicament, wanting to gain *Lebensraum* (living space) in the east but not wanting to repeat the mistakes of the First World War when Germany fought a war on two fronts.

Invasion plans for Britain were pulled off the shelf and passed around for discussion. The German navy was against it, knowing that they didn't have the shipping capacity to ferry troops across the English Channel. They were also concerned about the Royal Navy and the Royal Air Force. The German Luftwaffe was all for it, arguing that they could pulverise the RAF within a few weeks. The German army was keen to continue across the Channel but recognised that the RAF and the Royal Navy needed to be neutralised.

After another rebuff from Churchill in mid July 1940 Hitler realised that Britain could only be brought to the peace table through force. In mid July Hitler ordered the initial preparations for Operation SEALION. The invasion was initially scheduled for August and then postponed until September. Part of those preparations included the need for accurate intelligence on what was going on in Britain. Wilhelm Canaris, head of the German Abwehr, passed the word down to the Abwehr office in Hamburg. They needed spies in Britain, and they needed them now. The officers in Hamburg scrambled to locate, recruit and train suitable agents.

Lieutenant Colonel Herbert Piekenbrock, the head of Abteilung I of the Abwehr (responsible for espionage actions against Germany's enemies), noted after the war that successful agents needed to speak proper English with a complete knowledge of English dialects and colloquial phrases and abbreviations. They needed clothing and other pocket items that would mark them as English. Finally, the agent needed a strong back story along with impeccable identity papers.[14] The LENA spies had none of those things. Many spoke poor English and they were flummoxed by British currency. They were clothed with German-made suits, trilby hats and spats. Their cover stories were virtually non-existent, and the spies were clueless about daily life in Britain.

By late September 1940, the plans for Operation SEALION were postponed until the spring. A few straggler spies were sent over in the first half of 1941 – Josef Jakobs in January, Moe and Glad in April and Richter in May. For all intents and purposes, Operation LENA was a failure. The Abwehr had sent twenty people to Britain and even German officers, after the war, noted that the LENA spies were 'poor spy material'.[15] Siedentopf argues that the poor quality of spies dispatched to Britain was not an accident but deliberate. The Abwehr had fulfilled the letter of Hitler's command but not the spirit of it.

Siedentopf noted that the Abwehr was a hotbed of anti-Nazi officers. During the Nuremberg trials after the war, Alfred Jodl, Chief of the Operations Staff of the Armed Forces High Command (*Oberkommando der Wehrmacht* or OKW), noted that the Abwehr was a 'nest of conspirators'.[16]

Wilhelm Canaris, a naval officer with an illustrious history, took command of the Abwehr in early 1935. Initially enamoured with the Nazis for their anti-communist stance, Canaris quickly lost faith in them with the outbreak of war. He recognised that Hitler was taking Germany down a dangerous path. Canaris was an old-school Prussian officer and loathed the thuggish, criminal methods employed by the Nazi Party. Canaris surrounded himself with officers who were of a similar mind. Still, Canaris was a good German and the Abwehr produced excellent intelligence for the invasion of France and the Low Countries. After the war, however, General Ulrich Liss (head of the Fremde Heere West (Foreign Armies West)) noted, 'The same could not be said for his [SEALION] operations. I thought then that, while he appeared to be trying to be efficient, he was not doing his job against England with conviction.'[17] Canaris recognised that the invasion of Britain was doomed to failure. As the orders went out to commence preparations for Operation SEALION, Canaris trod a delicate path. While outwardly giving orders to spy against Britain, Canaris made sure that his officers knew that inefficiency was the order of the day.

In looking at the Abwehr officers, Siedentopf focused on Herbert Wichmann, the head of the Abwehr office in Hamburg. Wichmann was a former naval officer with a good connection with Canaris. Upon receiving orders to launch agents against Britain, Wichmann had his officers round up a ragtag collection of potential spies. Wichmann asked one of his officers, Dr Harald Mandt, to proof the spies. Mandt vetted men who had no real international experience, were of low intelligence, could not speak English, had no knowledge of Britain or its customs, were friends of the Nazis or were criminals under pressure from the Gestapo.[18] The agents were then trained by men who had no espionage experience.

Josef was trained by Julius Boeckel (aka Dr Beier), an anti-Nazi businessman recruited into the Abwehr by Wichmann and Ritter. According to Siedentopf, Boeckel was privy to the LENA conspiracy and made sure that the spies were not well trained.[19]

Once the agents had been sent to Britain, the Hamburg office received their communications and screened the information before sending it on to Berlin. Ritter knew that SNOW was working for MI5 and yet continued to treat him as a treasured agent. Richter was sent to check on TATE because the Abwehr had their doubts about him, but those doubts were never passed along to Berlin. After the war, an SD (Nazi *Sicherheitsdienst* – Security Service) officer said that the Hamburg Abwehr office was closely watched because the officers undermined rather than supported the war efforts.[20]

Canadian historian John Bryden has also examined the remarkable inefficiency of the German Abwehr in his 2014 book *Fighting to Lose – How the German Secret Intelligence Service helped the Allies win the Second World War*. Bryden focuses on Canaris' actions during the war, as well as those of his subordinates. One of them, Erwin von Lahousen, an Austrian recruited to head the Abwehr's Abteilung II (sabotage), survived the war and was interrogated by the Americans. He said that he had discouraged sabotage against the British and the Americans. He admitted that he was a member of an inner circle around Canaris whose members had actively conspired against Hitler. The Americans admitted, 'It would seem that our views on the causes of the Abwehr's ineffectiveness and inertia should be revised.'[21]

As regards the LENA spies, Bryden argues they were essentially sacrificial agents. The errors in the identity cards were glaring and made no sense. The Abwehr's documents department was extremely sophisticated. They could imitate every ink, every piece of paper and every seal.[22] Several of the Abwehr officers had lived in the United States and Britain prior to the war (Ritter and Kramer).[23] They knew how to write an address in English, not Continental, fashion.[24] They knew that the British '1' was different from the German '1'.[25] Bryden goes so far as to suggest that Ritter knew that both SNOW and TATE were double agents working for the British. In sending additional agents over to England, Ritter often asked SNOW for suitable landing sites.[26] When TATE needed more money, Ritter arranged for SNOW to send him some. This broke one of the first rules of running espionage agents – allowing them to know of each other. The fact that SNOW and TATE were aware of each other, meant that when SNOW was blown, TATE was automatically blown as well. Despite these obvious issues, MI5 continued to believe that the Germans were inefficient and stupid, without a clue that TATE was working for the British. TATE would later become the paymaster of Dusko Popov (double agent TRICYCLE) and so the deception spread, but MI5 continued to believe that all was well within their double-cross system.[27]

In fact, the double-cross system was probably blown from the start but the anti-Nazi German Abwehr officers conspired to make it appear as if Germany had legitimate agents working in Britain. Bryden argues that the real inefficiency lay within MI5. The officers in charge of the double-cross system believed that some of their own wireless operators could mimic the 'fist' of a German agent transmitting Morse code via wireless transmitter. Bryden considered this to be pure folly.[28] Each German wireless operator listened for signals from two spies and their 'fist' would have been as familiar to them as their voices.[29]

Finally, Bryden noted that by the time Caroli (SUMMER) was sent over in early September 1940, Canaris, who was at Hitler's elbow, would have known that the RAF was undefeated and that the invasion of Britain was destined for the dustbin. Bryden argues, 'This is further evidence, along with the clumsily forged identity papers, that Caroli and the others who followed him were meant to be caught.'[30]

Some of the captured agents were executed. Some were turned into double agents who sent information back to the Hamburg office. The

Hamburg officers knew the information was suspect but sent the reports along to Berlin. Reports that detailed the invasion-readiness of the British armed forces. Reports that highlighted the morale of the British people. Reports that minimised the damage caused by German bombing.

In June 1941, Hitler turned his back on the west and focused his attention on Russia in the east. Britain was safe for the moment, thanks, in part, to the ill-fated spies of Operation LENA. Referred to as a *Himmelfahrt* (journey to heaven or suicide mission) by some of the Hamburg Abwehr officers,[31] Operation LENA sent twenty sacrificial men and women to Britain, including Josef Jakobs. They were unlucky, expendable pawns who had been drawn into a dangerous web of espionage.

54

CAUGHT IN A WEB

In all likelihood, Josef's initial story, told to Robertson and Stephens in early February, was one that he thought would save him from death. He claimed to be a soldier who had never intended to spy, but who was simply trying to escape Nazi Germany. He told a story that he thought would keep his neck out of the hangman's noose. He had no idea that the British would try to turn him into a double agent and use him against the Germans.

Over time, Josef's story changed. He told conflicting accounts of how he was recruited into the German Abwehr. He told conflicting accounts of his motivation. He was desperately trying to save his life. Wulf Schmidt (TATE) said it best when he told Stephens, 'Self-preservation must be the strongest instinct in man.'[1]

In all likelihood, self-preservation was what motivated Josef. After he was released from Sachsenhausen concentration camp in March 1940, Josef was likely called up by the German armed forces. Recognising that his life as a German soldier would probably be inordinately short, Josef sought to escape his conscription. He may have been excused from service due to health reasons, or he may have told them about his Swiss conviction. By hook or by crook, Josef was not going to serve in the German army, but his escape from the armed forces was followed by various run-ins with the Gestapo. Josef recognised that his life and those of his family were in danger. One day, he met an acquaintance who suggested that he sign up for the German Abwehr. A German citizen could fulfill their military service within the Abwehr and be safe from the Gestapo. It seemed like a perfect solution. Josef would be safe from enlistment within the army and he and his family would be safe from the Nazis. Josef expressed interest and met with an Abwehr recruiter, Walter Steffens (aka Inspector Frischmuth) from the Bremen Abwehr office.[2]

After the war, other agents testified that they had also been recruited by Steffens. A Jew named Helmut Oliver said that, in the latter part of 1940, he was introduced to Steffens, who said if Oliver joined the Abwehr he would be protected from the Gestapo.[3] Another agent, Ernst Otto Rodenberg, said his main reason for joining the Abwehr was for the protection Steffens gave him against the Nazis, who were trying to squeeze him out of his job due to his partly Jewish origins.[4] After the war, Steffens was never interrogated about his role in the Abwehr because he was only found through a source the British did not want to compromise.[5]

After several conversations with Abwehr representatives, Josef travelled to Hamburg, where he met Julius Boeckel, a novice spymaster. Boeckel negotiated a contract with Josef that, according to Ritter, stated Josef would be paid several hundred Reichsmark while undergoing instruction.[6] Once he was sent on his mission, his family would receive 200 RM per month.[7]

Josef repeatedly told MI5 investigators that he had not signed a contract with the Abwehr, his family would receive no money and he was not on the Abwehr's payroll.[8] At one point, Josef went so far as to claim that he had paid for his training himself and it had cost him 4,000 RM.[9] He insisted on this in order to prove he was working on his own account and he was not a traitor, an accusation Stephens threw at every spy, likely accompanied by a contemptuous sneer. Josef tried to weave a series of lies that would shed a better light on his motivations but failed miserably. He had signed a contract. He had been paid money.

Perhaps Josef never thought he would actually be sent on a mission to Britain. Perhaps he had thought he might be sent to Spain or Argentina or even to the United States. Perhaps he believed the Abwehr psychologist who told him that spying in Britain was a walk in the park. The British were inefficient. His accent wouldn't be noticed as there were tens of thousands of German refugees and immigrants in Britain. He could sit in cafés, listen to conversations and send reports back to Germany. It sounded romantic and adventurous. Josef may even have thought that, after a few weeks or months in England, he could enlist the assistance of Frau Knips and board a ship to the United States, the land of the free and the home of the brave.

Where Josef erred was in sharing his plans with his acquaintance, Van Hees. Word got back to the Gestapo and, soon enough, Josef was hauled back to Hamburg and brought before Boeckel. The Gestapo were tapping their feet impatiently, waiting to see how the Abwehr would handle the problem of Josef Jakobs. Boeckel didn't even blink. The Abwehr didn't need the Gestapo sniffing around their offices. Blackmail was one of the Abwehr's prime recruiting methods and Boeckel turned the screws. Josef was in trouble with the Gestapo. If he didn't go on the mission, and soon, his family was in serious danger.[10] In all likelihood, Josef swore an oath of allegiance prior to his departure, one that was used for other agents, 'I bind myself to fulfill the commands of the Intelligence Service and am fully aware of the consequences if I do not fulfil them.'[11]

Josef agreed to be dispatched to Britain as soon as the weather co-operated. Final preparations were made but the Abwehr altered the registration number on Josef's identity card. Josef could still be a useful guinea pig against MI5. How far would MI5 go in recruiting German spies as double agents? The Abwehr made sure that Josef would be arrested by the first person who saw his identity papers. If the Abwehr received transmissions from Josef, they could be assured that he had turned on them. The Gestapo could then be let loose on his family. If the Abwehr received no transmission, they could be assured that they would eventually read about Josef's execution in a British newspaper.

Josef was a pawn in the espionage game, sent on a one-way mission to Britain by a totalitarian regime that considered him, and other individuals, to be expendable. He might have thought that the British would treat him differently. He was mistaken.

In 1940 and 1941, Britain was faced with a terrifying spectre, the threat of imminent invasion by a totalitarian state bent on European domination. National security was at stake and sacrifices had to be made – at least in the eyes of MI5. On 25 May 1940, shortly after the Treachery Act was approved, Liddell noted:

> The liberty of the subject, freedom of speech etc. were all very well in peace-time but were no use in fighting the Nazis. There seemed to be a complete failure to realise the power of the totalitarian state [by the Home Office] and the energy with which the Germans were fighting a total war.[12]

A year later, on 10 June 1941, Liddell would lament about 'how difficult it is to carry out investigations properly in a democracy which is fighting a totalitarian enemy'. Decades later, legal historian, A.W. Brian Simpson would muse on the problem facing liberal democracies during times of grave crisis, 'Is it essential to their survival that they should temporarily cease to be liberal democracies until the threat is over?'[13] It would appear that 'when the security of the state, and the very survival of British liberty, is at stake, the rights and interests of individuals simply have to go by the board'.[14]

The British state made no distinction between German or British, Dutch or Czech. Anyone who was a threat to the State or to national security was dealt with ruthlessly. Some have argued that the bloodletting was necessary – spies needed to be executed in order to demonstrate to the Germans that some of their agents had been captured.[15] It would have stretched German incredulity too much to try to convince them that all of their agents were successful and escaped capture.

The road to execution, however, was not always a smooth one. Torn between a desperate need for information and intelligence and the politicians' demands for bloodletting, MI5 trod a fine line. The prosecution of Josef Jakobs was problematic.

His first statement to Robertson at Cannon Row was made while he was in physical pain and taken down by an uncertified translator. Even though it was made under caution, there remains doubt as to whether it was an admissible 'voluntary' statement. In addition, it was not entered as an exhibit at the Summary of Evidence, nor at the court martial but slipped in during the middle of the trial. This did not follow the Rules of Procedure.

His 'official' statement made to Hinchley-Cooke on 18 June 1941 was preceded by weeks of interrogations that were rife with threats, promises and inducements. In 1944, MI5 would agree with the Home Office that 'statements under caution should not be taken from the persons if they have once been admitted to [Latchmere House]'.[16] The statement to Hinchley-Cooke should have been inadmissible as evidence at Josef's court martial.

There were numerous instances in which key pieces of evidence were misplaced by MI5, including the notebook in which Josef had written possible rendezvous dates and times with other agents. How the notebook, which had been missing since 1 February 1941, could appear in the wallet during the court martial, when it had not been mentioned at any point during the Summary of Evidence, nor in the list of court martial exhibits, is still a mystery.

MI5 had admitted in 1941 that if they 'had used an agent or given him a promise: the risk that the agent's double-cross work would be revealed in court had to be considered; and a promise once given had to be honoured'.[17] Josef had agreed to work as a servant of his captors – as a double agent. His lengthy stay in hospital and the public nature of his capture meant that MI5's initial assessment of him as double-agent material needed to be revised. Did that, however, negate the agreement reached between Josef and MI5? Was it not a promise that, once made, had to be honoured?

Finally, it can be argued that the charge laid against Josef, and the other neutral and enemy alien agents, of 'landing in the United Kingdom' was an act preparatory, in which case the agents should have been charged under the Defence Regulations and not the Treachery Act.

Dorothy O'Grady and Philip Jackson escaped the grasp of MI5 with their lives, if not their liberty. Josef Jakobs and Karel Richter would not be so lucky. The circumstances surrounding their capture, interrogation, prosecution and execution, at a crucial time in 1941, leave one wondering – did they receive fair trials or were they victims of a perversion of justice? There is no doubt that the Nazi regime treated captured Allied agents and soldiers with far less regard for the rule of law and ethics, but that does not negate the question, particularly when it is levelled against a liberal democracy that prides itself on its sense of justice and fairness.

The question is not a mouldering one from the past either, for it still shows up today with regard to the treatment of terrorists, refugees and illegal immigrants. How much will we sacrifice – civil liberties, individual freedoms, the right to a fair trial – in the name of national security?

EPILOGUE

I started this quest more than thirty years ago, seeking the answer to a simple question: who was my grandfather? Such a question is ultimately unanswerable. The truth is, I cannot even answer the question 'who am I?'

Trying to piece together the story of my grandfather is like trying to reassemble a vase that has been smashed into a thousand pieces and being thwarted by the absence of 90 per cent of the pieces. I can say this – Josef Jakobs was a complex man. He was a husband and an adulterer. He was a father and a stranger. He was a businessman and a crook. He was the illegitimate son of a Catholic priest. He was a man with many character flaws.

During his time in Britain, Josef's character went through the crucible. He was tested in ways he had never imagined and ultimately forced to confront his own moral failings. He saw himself for who he truly was, and the picture was not pretty.

Ultimately, at the end, however, Josef Jakobs showed his true colours. Trials and tribulations can either break a person or strengthen them. One will see either the dross or the gold. Josef went to his execution with a clean conscience, at peace with his God and, more importantly, with himself.

William Chidlow, military policeman, told his daughter that Josef was a 'good man'. Stephens, cynical MI5 interrogator, wrote that Josef was a 'brave man'. Governor Grew remembered Josef for his 'soldierly manner, his courtesy and his quiet courage'.[1] Hinchley-Cooke was impressed with Josef's 'pluck and calm bearing'. With his last breath,

Josef absolved the soldiers of the firing squad, embraced his imminent death and their role in it, and asked them to 'shoot straight'.

Despite the gossamer image of Josef that has emerged, my quest has not been in vain. I have learned that I am much more than a scientist and a researcher. I have learned that I have much in common with my grandfather. I too am that disturbing blend of light and dark.

I have also, much to my surprise, discovered that the most fascinating aspect of Josef's story is not so much the facts, but the relationships between Josef and his contemporaries. The encounters between Josef and Lily Knips, Robin W.G. Stephens, William E. Hinchley-Cooke and William Chidlow fascinated me. During the last few years, I have been compelled to dig deeper, to learn more about these individuals. I have been surprised by what I discovered.

In 2014, I wrote a letter to Sylvia Lily (née Sauer) Paskin, granddaughter of Lily Knips. It was a hard-fought victory to even uncover the fact that Lothar and Hermine Sauer had had a child. I traced Sylvia to a Jewish cultural centre in London. Sylvia read my letter with bemusement and astonishment. She had heard rumours that her grandmother had been involved with a spy but had no details. My letter, and subsequent conversations between the two of us, have helped to shed some light on Lily Knips and her relationship with Josef.

Sylvia believes that Lily and Josef may have had a more intimate relationship than either admitted to their interrogators. It would not surprise me. News of Josef's execution on 15 August 1941 must have hit Lily hard and more bad news was to follow. On 15 April 1942, Lily's father passed away in Hannover. He had apparently avoided the Nazi death camps, but Lily's sister would not be so fortunate. Elsa (née Katz) Majewski was deported to the Sobibor death camp on 13 June 1942. Her death date is unknown. It may have all been too much for Lily. On 15 January 1943, Lily died of carbon monoxide poisoning (suspected suicide) in her apartment at 9 Compayne Gardens.

In 2016, I received an email from Adrian Birt, a second cousin (once removed) of Robin (Tin-Eye) Stephens. Adrian shared a couple of photographs with me of Stephens as a young boy. It is hard to envision the irascible Stephens as an innocent child, particularly given events later in his career. After the cessation of hostilities in 1945, Stephens was given command of an interrogation centre in Bad Nenndorf, Germany. Despite running the camp under the same rules as Latchmere House (violence is forbidden), numerous inmates were admitted to the local hospital in shocking condition. Allegations of beatings, starvation and exposure to extreme cold began to circulate. Ultimately, Stephens, the camp doctor and two other officers were brought before courts martial. Only the doctor would be found guilty. Stephens and the other two officers were acquitted. Stephens returned to the ranks of MI5 and served as a security liaison officer in Nigeria during the 1950s. In 1960, Stephens retired from the army and vanished. Stephens' father died in 1962 but the estate went to his sister (Stephens' aunt). In 1990, Stephens' second wife passed away in Lincolnshire. What happened to Stephens remains a mystery.

In 2014, I received an email from Richard Hall, whose wife is the great niece of William E. Hinchley-Cooke's wife. Born and raised in Germany, and sporting a German accent, Hinchley-Cooke had proved that he was an Englishman to the core. He would have happily executed all of the suspicious characters who landed on the shores of Britain via parachute or boat. During Josef's trial, Hinchley-Cooke admitted that the Nazis had put a price on his own head. He was *persona non grata* in the eyes of the Germans and was wanted dead or alive.

For the rest of the war, Hinchley-Cooke worked to bring treacherous men (and women) to justice. One of his crowning achievements was to testify at the trial of the infamous Lord Haw-Haw (William Joyce), a Briton who had defected to Germany prior to the war and broadcast English-language programmes on behalf of the Nazis. After the war, Hinchley-Cooke and his wife retired to a seaside house on Wellington Parade, Deal, Kent.

Hinchley-Cooke was as much a victim of the war as were the spies he prosecuted. His wife's nephew related a tale of being at Hinchley-Cooke's house one day for tea when the doorbell rang. Hinchley-Cooke wouldn't let his wife answer the door until he had taken out his revolver and concealed it under his newspaper. Hinchley-Cooke had made many enemies during the war and he was forever looking over his shoulder, waiting for his day of reckoning. On 3 March 1955, Hinchley-Cooke collapsed in the street outside his home, the victim of a massive heart attack.

In 2013, I received an email from Kate Snell, daughter of former military policeman William Chidlow. Kate told me that since she was a little girl her father had told her the story of how he had guarded Josef and accompanied him to his execution. Before he died in 2008, Kate's father made her promise that she would find Josef's family and return the reading glasses to us. Thanks to the blog I started in 2012, Kate was able to find us. Two weeks later, I received a package with Josef's reading glasses, complete with the blue leather 'Optiker-Ruhnke' case mentioned by the Ramsey Police. That August I wrapped up the spectacles and presented them to my father for his birthday. A gift given by Josef to Chidlow had finally come full circle and been placed in the hands of Josef's son. Kate had kept the promise she had made to her father.

Kate had wanted to return Josef's glasses to his family, and my father, Raymond, was the last surviving member of Josef's family. Josef's wife, Margarete, passed away in 1971 at the age of 68, the victim of a heart attack. By chance, our family was visiting Berlin at the time and my father made it to her bedside before she passed away. Margarete had been predeceased by almost every member of her family, many of whom died far from home. She, at least, did not die alone.

Norbert, Josef and Margarete's eldest son, passed away in 1963 in Bielefeld, at a home for the disabled. Josef's mother, Emma, passed away in 1952 in Berlin. Regine, Josef and Margarete's daughter, passed away in Meppen in January 1946 at the age of 16. Margarete's own mother, Therese (Knöffler) Elkan passed away in 1943, predeceased by her German-Jewish husband, Wolfgang Elkan.

Margarete had kept a small day planner book from 1941, in which she had written short notes to herself. Her entry for 27 May 1941 (the anniversary of Josef and Margarete) reads, 'Today is our 15th wedding anniversary and what lies behind me is unfortunately much sorrow and little joy. Still without any news. Are you also thinking of me a bit? Where could you be?'[2] Despite Josef's roguish character, his affairs with other women and his criminal past, Margarete clearly loved him. In early July 1941, she would write, 'For six months no sign of life. It is horrible. And for how much longer? Sometimes it's almost unbearable and one is so alone in many things, the children can't always be there and also can't help. I have no more reserves to draw upon.'[3]

Margarete would find those reserves, however, and she ensured that she and her three children survived the Nazi regime, the war and the occupation of Berlin by the Russian army. She was a strong, feisty woman who lived long enough to meet her two granddaughters. I was only 5 years old when she passed away and regret that I never heard her story or developed a relationship with her.

There is, however, one relationship, more than any other, that has been healed by my quest for Josef – the one between my father and myself. When I began my quest, the marriage of my parents was fracturing.

Never close to my father to begin with, I drifted even further away from him, unwilling to embrace a man who had wronged my mother in so many ways. They say that time heals many wounds, but I would say that time brings with it the wisdom to see that we can be both the wounded and inflicter of wounds. My quest for Josef helped me to see that people are not either/or but rather both/and. My father is distant and vulnerable. I am generous and vengeful.

Over the years, as I have worked on numerous iterations of this manuscript, I have shared my discoveries with my father. Through that process, my father came to know his own father, Josef Jakobs. My father always thought that Josef just disappeared and cared little for his wife and children. For decades, my father turned his back on his country and his family.

Josef's final letter did much to alter the way in which my father saw Josef. Reading Josef's letter, one cannot but hear the love of a father for his children. His letter gives us a brief peek into the mind of this complex man and speaks for itself:

London, the 15th August 1941
On the Holy Feast of the Assumption of Mary
My dear, dear wife,
When you, my much beloved Gretchen, receive this letter, I will already be standing before the eternal Judge! For today is my last night on this earth, on the Sacred Feast of the Assumption of Mary, I hope to be well prepared to take the journey to eternity. In just 5 hours, I will be shot at the Tower of London, after I was brought before an English War Tribunal on August 5 on charges of espionage and condemned to death. I want to quickly tell you, how it came to that. On the night of 31 January to 1 February, I landed on English soil with a broken leg. My right leg was already broken in the air from the sudden air pressure, as I was exiting the [aeroplane]. After I had lain helpless and in excruciating pain the whole night in rain and snow on the open fields, I was found the next morning after 14 hours. I was operated on 3 days later, two times in a row and lay for 8 weeks as a prisoner in a civil hospital. From there, I went as a cripple to a prison and I will die tomorrow as a cripple, for I can only walk with crutches.
On the 4 and 5 of August, I was tried, with the above result. The English have treated me quite good and I can't complain. Since the 6 of August, I have had Holy Mass celebrated in my cell daily, to

which I minister from my chair. Of course, I have received Holy Communion every day. The priest, an Englishman, who speaks very good German, is my true friend and helper this night and until the last moment. At 3 o'clock, he and I will celebrate the last Mass for me. I die then a good, nice death, a soldier's death, a better one I could not have hoped for. And now I want to take my leave from you, my dear, dear wife, my Gretchen, from you, the children, my mother, Maria, your mother, Peter etc. I greet them all heartily once more and ask that they keep me in their prayers.

Dear, best wife, 1000 and over 1000 thanks for all the good that you have done for me. But even so, I beg you 1000 times for forgiveness for all of the conscious and unconscious hurts that I have given you. You were too good for me, you deserved a better man, you angel. And when I failed, it was not out of ill intent, my Gretchen. You were always, for me, the dearest and most precious, that you were absolutely. I hope that you understand me without further explanation. The minutes race by so fast, especially now, and there is so much that I cannot write, as you can imagine. Except now, a few requests. Remain my good, steadfast wife. Endure your loss bravely, don't dwell on it, but think that you are also in God's hand, remember above all that you too must be prepared for a sudden death. For I hope above all, that we will see each other again in eternity. Be strong in our holy belief, never abandon it I beg you, pray instead with the children to the Sacred Heart of Jesus, consecrate yourself and the children to him, wholly and completely, and then he will never leave you, and will stand by you in your hour of death.

Dear Gretchen, remember instead, always, that, a loving, merciful God and eternity exist. That you only live on this barren world to look forward to eternity. Then will you endure all trials gladly. And then our children. Let them receive a good upbringing in the Catholic faith, as much as you are able. If they are raised in our holy faith well, then they will only bring you joy. With these lines, I bid farewell to Norbert, Regine and Raymond. I demand of them, in light of my death, that they are obedient to you in all things, that they fulfill your wishes and commands strictly. Moreover, they are to treat you with reverence and love. My last and most important wish that I ask of you, is that you pray 3 Hail Mary's for my poor soul daily, pray to the Sacred Heart of Jesus, and that annually, on my death day, at my death hour, 15 August at 7 a.m., that you go to church, hear Holy Mass and receive Holy Communion.

Take this request upon yourself, and hold it for your whole life. I also, in my situation, will pray for you before God, and naturally especially for you. And now, for the last time, Adieu and Auf Wiedersehen into eternity. Once more, many greetings and kisses, and last thoughts to my mother, your mother, Wolfgang, Maria, Peter, Tante Esch, Alfred.

Dear Norbert, dear Regine, dear Raymond, 1000 greetings, 1000 kisses. Remember your father, who loves you dearly. Show your gratitude to him, by obeying your mother and above all by holding fast to our sacred Catholic faith.

Be god-fearing, never let the world trap the light and deceive it. Never forget to pray for the poor soul of your father.

Auf Wiedersehen Norbert, Regine, Raymond!

Auf Wiedersehen Grete!!

Gretchen, my best, my dearest wife, 1000 last greetings and kisses. Once again, 1000 thanks for all the good. Be and remain steadfast, be and remain true and strong in our sacred Catholic faith.

Dear, dear wife, dear Norbert, dear Regine, dear Raymond, dear Mother and Maria, kneel down and receive the last blessing of a dead man but one on his way to Life.

May our all powerful, compassionate God, the Father, Son and Holy Ghost bless you all my loved ones. May his blessing follow you on your ways, protect you from all danger and lead you to eternal life. Amen!

Dear Gretchen, my little bunny, dear Norbert, dear Regine, dear Raymond

Adieu and Auf Wiedersehen

into eternity.

On 15 August, on the day of the Sacred Feast of the Assumption of Mary, London.

Josef Jakobs

My last kiss to you all! [a large circle is drawn on the page]

Dear, dear Gretchen, the pictures from the medallion accompany me on my last journey!!

Auf Wiedersehen. Jubs [Margarete's pet name for Josef]

Josef wrote that letter from Wandsworth Prison, in the early morning hours of Friday, 15 August 1941. Less than five hours later, he was sitting before a firing squad at the Tower of London. Seventy-one years later, on 15 August 2012 at 7.12 a.m., my father and I stood outside the east wall of the Tower, on the approach to the Tower Bridge.

I had brought my father to England (and Germany) to celebrate his 80th birthday. I wanted to show him the key places where Josef had spent his last days, as well as his final resting place. While not in the best of health or fitness, my father navigated the busy streets of London and its Underground.

We visited the Tower of London and stood before the display case containing the chair in which Josef was seated for his execution. I took my father to the Scots Guards Museum, where he held the circular target in his hands.[4] Finally, we made the trek to St Mary's Cemetery in Kensal Green. My father was able to stand near Josef's grave, and to light a candle in his memory in the cemetery chapel.

Alas, many of the other sites associated with Josef's captivity have altered over the decades. Latchmere House has been turned into a housing estate. The Duke of York's Headquarters has been converted into an arcade with shops, restaurants, offices and an art gallery. Brixton and Wandsworth prisons are both challenging to visit, although I did manage to gain access to Wandsworth Prison in 2014. Josef's former cell is now a chaplain's office.

During our visit to London in 2012, there was one pivotal location that I did not take my father, in part because of the logistical challenges in travelling to it – Dovehouse Farm, near the town of Ramsey. During my first visit to London in 1991, Winston Ramsey had planned to take me to Ramsey but time was short and I nixed the idea. I regretted that decision for many years. As it turns out, Ramsey is one of the few places associated with Josef that has altered little over the decades.

In 2010, I travelled to London and this time, Winston Ramsey and I made it out to Ramsey and Dovehouse Farm. The farmhouse might be new, but little has changed at the farm since 1941. To the west one can see Wistow Fen Farm where Harry Godfrey was hard at work on the morning of 1 February 1941. To the south, along Puddock Drove, one can see the brick facade of the former Farmer's Boy Pub where Baldock and Coulson regaled two newspapermen with tales of their spy-catching prowess. To the north-west, in the distance, one can see the church steeple and roofs that mark the town of Ramsey, where lies Ramsey Police Station. The real site of interest, however, is not a farm or a pub or a police station, it is an unmarked patch of earth, 500 yards south-east of Dovehouse Farm.

I never knew a patch of earth could be so poignant with meaning, so ripe with emotion, so full of significance. It was just a patch of earth and not even the same soil as in 1941. The dirt has shifted and changed, been ploughed under numerous times, moved by tractors and wind … and yet, there was something there.

I stood on that patch of earth in the early sunshine of May 2010 with a wind gusting from the east. It was cold and I felt chilled. It was only a bare patch of earth, and yet I could feel Josef's presence. I looked up into the sky, blue with scudding clouds and impending rain showers. Did Josef ever dream that one of his grandchildren would be standing in that exact spot, looking back at him over the years?

I have jumped out of an aeroplane, with nothing but a parachute between me and certain death. I have not jumped out of an aeroplane into the frigid darkness of a late January night.

I have landed in a farmer's field and tumbled to the ground in an ungraceful heap. I have not landed in the dead of night, unable to see the ground and unable to prepare for the bone-jarring jolt of contact.

I have picked myself up after landing, dusted myself off and been congratulated by fellow jumpers. I have not lain in pain, unable to move, frozen by the biting wind.

I have gathered up my parachute, taken off my harness, and headed to the pub for a congratulatory pint. I have not lain there wondering what the morning would bring, mourning the loss of all that I have held dear.

The truth is that I could never know what my grandfather experienced on that long, cold night when he plummeted out of the darkness and landed on British soil. I could not know what he thought. I could not know what he felt, but it did not take much, as a human being, to imagine the terror, pain and fear that gripped Josef during those twelve hours.

It was only a patch of earth, but for me it was a holy place in which I could stand and feel the spirit of my grandfather. His spirit was strong there, for it was on that patch of earth that he wrestled with his demons. Part of Josef died that night. His hopes, his dreams, his regrets, his visions for the future soaked into the earth like great drops of spiritual blood. He left something of himself behind in that field.

You can't see it, you can't touch it, you can't hear it … and yet it is there. It is just a patch of earth … and yet so much more than that.

APPENDIX

JOSEF'S PERSONAL PROPERTY

This is a list of the property found on Josef Jakobs. It has been compiled from several sources and marked discrepancies are noted.[1] Items have been grouped into categories.

Descent

Camouflaged parachute and harness.
Light brown parachute suit (overalls) with zip pockets.
Steel helmet marked '*Kopfwelte*: GR 59' (likely the helmet liner size).
Pocket knife marked 'Swing' with wide blade and brown, wooden handle.
Small hand spade about 15in long.

Weapons

Automatic pistol marked '*Mauser-Werke AG. Oberndorfe* A.N. V.1. No. 489356 Cal: 7.65'.
Two rounds of ammunition in pistol.
Seven rounds of ammunition in a cardboard box made for twenty-five.
One shell (ammunition casing) (only mentioned on Robertson's list from 02/02/1941).

Espionage

Attaché case (16in x 11.5in x 5.5in) – black imitation crocodile (fibre) case with chromium latches and handle – contained wireless transmitting set and accessories. Humphreys from the RSS wrote a report detailing the items (KV 2/26, no. 2a, 13/02/1941), none of which mention a small notebook (see Personal below).
Wireless transmitting set (an SE 88/5 – identical to Druecke and Walti's set).[2]
Two keys to attaché case.
Fragments of thin cardboard (remains of disc code).
£497 in £1 bank notes (old and new) (Huntingdonshire Constabulary list has £496 and the court martial has £498).
Shell Touring Map of Great Britain with red paper cover (9in x 5in folded) (10 miles to 1 inch).
Black electric torch – 5in long and 1in diameter.

Identity Papers

Pink traveller's ration book – C.A. 567927.
British National Identity Card – blank.
British National Identity Card – No. 656/301/29 – James Rymer, London, 33 Abbotsford Gardens Woodford Green – dated 4 June 1940.

Smoking

Automatic cigarette lighter marked 'KW'.
Packet of Cordon Rouge cigarettes (20), American Blend #3525.
Brown, square leather cigarette case with tuck-in flap – marked 'Zeka Wettig Geder'.
Cigarette holder.

Medicine

Aluminium tube (about 1.5in long and 5/16in in diameter) containing small white tablets.

Paper tube marked 'Tabl. Solvent 0.4 WCX 1.V.Z.' (to hold four tablets, each the size of an aspirin tablet).

Paper tube marked 'Phos 0.03 WS.PX.1' (to hold four tablets, each the size of an aspirin tablet).

Personal

Horn-rimmed reading glasses in blue leather case marked 'Optiker-Ruhnke'.

Oblong wristwatch with luminous dial on black leather strap – marked '*#9321 Fond Acier, Inoxidable*' and made by Marchal, le Haye.

Roman Catholic badge.

Comb (8in long) in brown-grey crocodile case.

Pair of scissors and nail file in leather case (Rivett-Carnac had a nail bone in the case as well).

German–English dictionary marked '*Metoula Sprachführer*' (blue with gold stars on cover – about 4in x 2.5in x 0.5in) – contained a piece of paper with English currency amounts.

(Notebook – mentioned only on Rivett-Carnac's list from 17 February 1941 and a handwritten note by Cussen on 22 July 1941.)

Propelling pencil with four colour leads (red, blue, green, black).

Coin – 2½ cent piece.

Postcard of a woman with a message on the back – 'My dear, I love you forever, yours, Clara, Landau, July 1940'.

Food

Packet of minced meat sandwiches.

Two ½lb packets of chocolate, marked '*Orange Fin Jonker*' – wrapper was blue and orange – one side had image of blue boy and an orange partly quartered – on the reverse was written '*Lekkere chococlate van Cacaofabriek De Jonker, Zaandijk*'.

Small bottle of spirit marked '*Beaulieu cie Cognac 15 Vos*'.

Portion of brown sausage.

Wallets

Brown leather purse with zip fastener.
Blue leather note case with chain guard attached.
Brown leather wallet (contained ration book, identity cards and post card).

(Jaikens references a fourth wallet, a leather note case that contained five £1 notes but every other list only mentions three wallets/note cases. The five bank notes were most likely found in the blue leather note case above.)

Clothing

(Rivett-Carnac stated that every item of clothing had a label from Germany or an occupied territory, e.g. Dresden, Zurich [not occupied], Hamburg, Berlin). He also noted that all of Josef's clothes were of a foreign cut. Only some of the items noted what was on the clothing labels.)

Light grey herringbone overcoat (tweed).
Dark grey-striped lounge suit.
Top shirt.
Semi-stiff collar.
Bright tie (marked '*Hemdenplatz – Berlin*').
Three woollen pullovers.
Two undervests (Rivett-Carnac said there were three shirts and may have considered these items to be 'shirts').
One pair ear pads (possibly ear muffs).
New pair grey socks.
Blue woollen socks.
Two woollen scarves (Rivett-Carnac had only one).
Blue silk handkerchief tucked into suit pocket.
Pair of leather gloves marked '*Eska Mk Nappa*' on press buttons.
Grey spats with zip fasteners.
Black pointed shoes with brown laces and padded socks inside (shoes marked '*Medicus – Dresden*')
Trilby hat marked '*Helium*' (Rivett-Carnac called it a 'Pork Pie' hat).

NOTES

All sources beginning with CAB, CRIM, HO, J, KV, LCO, MEPO, PCOM, PREM, RG, WO, WORK are from the National Archives at Kew.

Sources beginning with LMA are from London Metropolitan Archives.

1 – Broken from the Vivid Thread of Life

1 A line from Tower Green's execution site memorial by Brian Catling, dedicated to those who were condemned to death by order of the State.
2 The chapter is based on William Chidlow's memoir, Josef Jakobs' final letter, Benjamin Dixon Grew's book and RSM Arthur Wilford's notes.
3 Saul had asked Josef for his autograph and Josef complied. The piece of paper Josef signed and dated (14 August 1941) is contained within a small diary of the late Lance Corporal Henry Saul held by his son, Peter Saul.
4 Jakobs family documents, Josef's final letter dated 15 August 1941.
5 Josef's final letter would sit in the file of MI5 until 1993 when it was handed to his two granddaughters.
6 'The Rite of Extreme Unction' (1962). Accessed 27 August 2018 on https://acatholiclife. blogspot.com/2009/09/rite-of-extreme-unction.html
7 Grew, Benjamin Dixon, *Prison Governor* (London: Herbert Jenkins Ltd, 1958) p.124.
8 LMA, ACC/3444/AD/07/001, governor's journal entry for 15 August 1941. Grew was back at his office at 4.40 a.m. after a quick inspection of the prison. According to RSM Wilford's notes from the day of the execution, the prisoner was to arrive at around 5.30 a.m.
9 Grew, Benjamin Dixon, *Prison Governor* (London: Herbert Jenkins Ltd, 1958) p.124.
10 Ibid.
11 Chidlow, William, *A Second World War Guardsman's True Story* (unpublished, 2001).
12 Ibid.

2 – Skeletons in the Closet

1 Farago, Ladislas, *The Game of the Foxes* (New York: David McKay & Co., 1971) p.328.
2 West, Nigel, *MI5: British Security Operations 1909–1945* (Briarcliff Manor: Stein and Day, 1982).

3 Ramsey, Winston, 'German Spies in Britain', *After the Battle*, Vol. 11, pp.1–34.
4 Nigel West is the pen name of Rupert Allason, former Conservative MP of Torbay, Devon (1987–97).
5 Jakobs family documents, letter from Mrs E. Smith of the Lord Chancellor's office, 18 August 1993.
6 Simpson, A.W. Brian, *In the Highest Degree Odious* (Oxford: Clarendon Press, 1992) p.410.

3 – Inauspicious Beginnings

1 This chapter is based on historical and genealogical research and family documents as well as Josef's statements to the MI5 interrogators, primarily KV 2/25, folios nos 65a and 68a.
2 Jakobs family documents, marginal note on baptismal registration of Kaspar Jakobs.
3 Email dated 12 November 2008 from Diocese of Trier archivist regarding Kaspar Jakobs' clerical service within the diocese.
4 Ibid.
5 Ibid.
6 Ibid.
7 Jakobs family documents, birth registration of Josef (née Lück) Jakobs from the state archives in Luxembourg City.
8 Email dated 12 November 2008 from Diocese of Trier archivist regarding Kaspar Jakobs' clerical service within the diocese.
9 Jakobs family documents, birth registration of Emma Maria (née Lück) Jakobs.
10 Jakobs family documents, birth and death registration of Lucia Margaretha Lück.
11 Email dated 12 November 2008 from Diocese of Trier archivist regarding Kaspar Jakobs' clerical service within the diocese.
12 Ibid.
13 Ibid.
14 Jakobs family documents, birth registration of Anna (née Lück) Jakobs.
15 Jakobs family documents, school records from Dominican College, Vechta.
16 Jakobs family documents, marriage certificate of Kaspar Jakobs and Emma Lück.
17 Jakobs family documents, birth registration extract for Josef (néeLück) Jakobs issued by Luxembourg on 19 March 1908.
18 Jakobs family documents, school records from Dominican College, Vechta.
19 *Fußartillerie-Regiment von Hindersin (1. Pommersches)* Nr.2.
20 School-leaving exam similar to A-levels in the United Kingdom and high school graduation in North America.
21 *Garde-Schützen-Bataillon.*
22 *4. Garde-Regiment zu Fuß*, a senior infantry regiment.
23 The 4th Foot Guards were part of the Guard Corps and, within that, of the 1st Guard Division. Within the 1st Guard Division, they began the war with the 2nd Guard Infantry Brigade and finished the war with the 1st Guard Infantry Brigade.
24 http://de.wikipedia.org/wiki/4._Garde-Regiment_zu_Fu%C3%9F
25 This information is based on a statement made by Josef during an interrogation by MI5. It has not been corroborated.
26 http://de.wikipedia.org/wiki/4._Garde-Regiment_zu_Fu%C3%9F
27 Jakobs family documents, death registration of Anna (née Lück) Jakobs.
28 The Iron Cross recognised acts of heroism, bravery and leadership. During the First World War, the Iron Cross Second Class was widely awarded (5.5 million) whereas the

Iron Cross First Class was less common (220,000). While it is possible that Josef was awarded the Iron Cross, his family has no record of such an award and Imperial German Army records were destroyed during the Second World War.

29 *Deutsche Verlustlisten 1905. Ausgabe*, 21 May 1918. Accessed online via http://www.wbc. poznan.pl/dlibra/publication/182816?tab=1

30 http://de.wikipedia.org/wiki/4._Garde-Regiment_zu_Fu%C3%9F

31 *Freiwilligen Regiment Reinhard*, also known as *Freicorps Reinhard* – http://de.wikipedia.org/ wiki/4._Garde-Regiment_zu_Fu%C3%9F

32 http://de.wikipedia.org/wiki/4._Garde-Regiment_zu_Fu%C3%9F

4 – Dentist and Family Man

1 This chapter is based on historical and genealogical research and family documents as well as Josef's statements to the MI5 interrogators, primarily KV 2/25, folios nos 65a and 68a.

2 According to the personal particulars report at Latchmere House, Josef's teeth were 'all false, three gold capped in lower jaw'.

3 *Reichsverband Deutscher Freier Höherer Knabenschulen und Vorbereitungsanstalten.*

4 KV 2/25, no. 65a, 15 April 1941, statement by Josef, and 21 April 1941, report by Sampson.

5 KV 2/25, no. 65a, 15 April 1941, statement by Josef.

6 *Jahrbuch für Dentistik: verbunden mit dem Adressbuch der deutschen Dentisten*, 1933–34.

7 *Das Ehrenkreuz des Weltkriegs 1914–18.*

8 Jakobs family documents, certificate to accompany *Ehrenkreuz für Frontkämpfer* (Honour Cross for Front-line Veterans).

9 Jakobs family documents, marriage registration of Josef Jakobs and Alma Margarete Knöffler.

10 Jakobs family documents, business card of Erwin Ludwig Knöffler.

11 Jakobs family documents, death registration of Georg Köhne.

12 Jakobs family documents, birth registration of Alma Margarete Knöffler.

13 Personal communication from Martha Fitzner (granddaughter of Hans Fitzner).

14 Jakobs family documents and Martha Fitzner and Guillermo Fitzner (son of Hans Fitzner).

15 Jakobs family documents, marriage registration of Therese Knöffler and Abraham Wolfgang Elkan.

16 Jakobs family documents, Jakobs *Familienbuch* (Family Book).

17 Personal communication from Raymond Jakobs.

18 Jakobs family documents, Jakobs *Familienbuch*.

19 Raymond Jakobs.

20 Ibid.

5 – Desperate Times Call for Desperate Measures

1 This chapter is based on historical and genealogical research and family documents as well as Josef's statements to the MI5 interrogators, primarily KV 2/25, folios nos 65a and 68a.

2 Equivalent value in 2014 approximately £250,000. This and other currency projections have been calculated using the Historical Currency Convertor on www.historicalstatistics.org site. Worth is 'absolute worth' or purchasing power equivalent, not 'relative worth'. The conversion is provided to give an approximate sense of the amount of money Josef was referencing in comparison with 2014 (the most recent year for the calculation).

3 Equivalent value in 2014 approximately £1,750–£2,100.

4 Equivalent value in 2014 approximately £152,000 and £38,000 respectively.

5 Research has confirmed that a Ramon Artigas was a director of Banco de Espana.

6 The MI5 transcript states 'pennies' but it may have been the German equivalent '*pfennig*'.

7 KV 2/25, no. 65a, 15 April 1941, statement by Josef.

8 *Gesetz zur Verhütung erbkranken Nachwuchses.*

9 *Erbgesundheitsgericht.*

10 Equivalent value in 2014 approximately £12,600.

11 Jakobs family documents, passport of Alma Margarete (née Knöffler) Jakobs.

12 Confirmed by Jakobs family photographs.

13 Jakobs family documents, passport of Alma Margarete (née Knöffler) Jakobs.

14 KV 2/24, no.44a, 28 February 1941, statement by Lily Knips. Josef told Lily that he had been arrested for 'selling adulterated gold in dental products'.

15 Equivalent value in 2014 approximately £252,000.

16 Jakobs family documents, Fitzner pedigree research conducted by Otto Fitzner.

17 Bobrick, Benson, *A Passion for Victory* (New York: Alfred A. Knopf, 2012) p.94.

18 Ibid.

19 Equivalent value in 2014 approximately £48,000 and £200,000 respectively.

6 – A Different World

1 This chapter is based on historical and genealogical research and family documents, Lily Knips' statement to MI5 interrogators, as well as Josef's statements to the MI5 interrogators, primarily KV 2/25, folios nos 65a and 68a.

2 Jakobs family documents, marriage certificate of Therese Maria (née Knöffler) Köhne and Abraham Wolfgang Elkan.

3 *Verordnung zur Ausschaltung der Juden aus dem deutschen Wirtschaftsleben* (The Decree on the Exclusion of Jews from German Economic Life).

4 KV 2/25, no. 75b, 29 April 1941, statement by Josef. According to Josef, Rammrath was known as Baron von Buchwald. Genealogical research confirmed that Rammrath acquired this title by less than honourable means and that it was stripped from him.

5 KV 2/27, no number, 29 April 1941, statement by Josef. Ziebell was 34 years old and from a good family. He had been a colonel in the Argentine army and had served as a public prosecutor in Berlin for many years.

6 Equivalent value in 2014 approximately £120,000.

7 Equivalent value in 2014 approximately £88,000.

8 Equivalent value in 2014 approximately £48,000.

9 Equivalent value in 2014 approximately £40,000.

10 Equivalent value in 2014 approximately £120,000.

11 Equivalent value in 2014 approximately £32,000.

12 Equivalent value in 2014 approximately £12,000.

13 Equivalent value in 2014 approximately £600,000.

7 – A Jew Escapes to Albion

1 This chapter is based on Lily's statement to MI5 officers (KV 2/24), MI5's requests for information on Lily and Lothar from the Home Office Traffic Index and Aliens Register (KV 2/24, folios nos 19a, 24a, 35b and 36a), Josef's statements to the MI5 interrogators (primarily KV 2/25, folios nos 65a and 68a), genealogical research and personal communication with Lily's granddaughter, Sylvia (née Sauer) Paskin.

2 Presumably an accounting firm.
3 Lily had several relatives in England: Mr Caiden, director of Sears & Roebuck (KV 2/24, no. 19a, 12 February 1941, Home Office Records) and George Heilbron (KV 2/24, no. 47a, February 1941, address book of Lily Knips).
4 Equivalent value in 2014 approximately £120,000.
5 Equivalent value in 2014 approximately £100,000.
6 Equivalent value in 2014 approximately £320,000–£480,000.
7 KV 2/27, no number, 29 April 1941, statement by Josef. Rammrath didn't want to deal with Jews.
8 Equivalent value in 2014 approximately £120,000.
9 Equivalent value in 2014 approximately £1,300,000. The discrepancy between the 2014 equivalent value of 30,000 RM vs £27,000 can be perhaps explained by Josef's assertion that the exchange rate in England was 100 RM/£1, while in Germany the rate was 9 RM/£1. Although even this doesn't make sense, given his assertion that Seiler would convert Lily's Reichsmark at £900/1,000 RM.
10 Equivalent value in 2014 approximately £2,400.
11 Confirmed by Raymond Jakobs – Josef did buy a Chrysler car around this time, possibly Lily's.
12 KV 2/24, no. 19a, 8 February 1941, Home Office Records.
13 Hans Blum wasn't imprisoned for long, leaving for Britain in April 1939.
14 Equivalent value in 2014 approximately £800,000.
15 Likely the *Deutsche Zentrumspartei* or *Zentrum* (German Centre Party or German Catholic Party), a lay Catholic political party.
16 Jakobs family documents, *Generalstaatsanwalt Abschrift*, Berlin, 24 July 1939.
17 German records are fragmentary, and the length of their sentences is not clear.

8 – A New World

1 Hansard, HC Deb 4 June 1940, Vol. 361 cc.787–98.
2 Named after the wife of Colonel Hans F.M. Piekenbrock, head of Abwehr Abteilung I (espionage).
3 Kahn, David, *Hitler's Spies* (New York: Macmillan, 1978) p.346.
4 Ibid., pp.272–73. The Germans used a similar method during the First World War. 'There can be no doubt that Germany, probably through lack of choice, employed agents who very largely lived on their wits in normal times. It seems to have been a settled principle with their secret service to get hold of semi-destitute people with a penchant for extravagant living and induce them to spy on the promise of liberal remuneration according to results.' Felstead, Sidney Theodore, *German Spies at Bay* (New York: Bretano's, 1920) p.164.
5 KV 2/88, no. 119a, 5 December 1945, Preliminary Interrogation Report on Ritter by CSDIC (WEA).
6 Hayward, James, *Double Agent Snow* (London: Simon & Schuster, 2013) p.14.
7 KV 2/88, no. 119a, 5 December 1945, Preliminary Interrogation Report on Ritter by CSDIC (WEA).
8 Ritter, K.F., *Aurora* (Bloomington: Xlibris, 2006) p.20.
9 KV 2/88, no. 119a, 5 December 1945, Preliminary Interrogation Report on Ritter by CSDIC (WEA).
10 Ibid.
11 Hayward, James, *Double Agent Snow* (London: Simon & Schuster, 2013) p.14.

12 Ritter, K.F., *Aurora* (Bloomington: Xlibris, 2006) p.20.

13 Ibid., p.21.

14 Ibid.

15 Ibid., p.30.

16 Ibid.

17 Ibid., pp.30–31.

18 Hayward, James, *Double Agent Snow* (London: Simon & Schuster, 2013) pp.144–45.

9 – Soldier or Spy

1 Information in this chapter is combined from Latchmere House interrogation reports, Josef's statements to interrogators, Richter's interrogation file, genealogy research, as well as personal family papers.

2 Personal communication from Raymond Jakobs.

3 Macintyre, Ben, *Double Cross: The True Story of the D-Day Spies* (New York: Crown Publishers, 2012) ebook, Chapter 1.

4 Siedentopf, Monika, *Unternehmen Seelöwe* (München: Deutscher Taschenbuch Verlag, 2014) p.100.

5 Farago, Ladislas, *The Game of the Foxes* (New York: David McKay & Co., 1971) p.272.

6 Siedentopf, Monika, *Unternehmen Seelöwe* (München: Deutscher Taschenbuch Verlag, 2014) p.73.

7 KV 2/1333, no. 18a, 7 February 1946, CSDIC (WEA) BAOR FR (Final Report) 44 on Boeckel.

8 WO 208/5227, no. 18A, no date, summary sheet on Boeckel.

9 WO 208/5227, no number, 7 February 1946, supplement to FR (Final report) 44 from CSDIC (WEA).

10 Equivalent value in 2014 approximately £800.

11 Some of the other spies received similar deals. In 1942, the Abwehr agreed to pay Johannes M. Dronkers a monthly stipend during his training. Once he left on his mission, his wife would receive 150 Guilders per month (equivalent value in 2014 approximately £615 per month). Josef's wife would receive 200 RM per month (equivalent value in 2014 approximately £640 per month). This was later increased to 300 RM per month (equivalent value in 2014 approximately £960 per month). Knut Brodersen, who arrived in England in late 1943, negotiated an agreement with the Abwehr whereby his wife would receive 800 Krowns per month (equivalent value in 2014 approximately £1,300 per month).

12 MI5 later reviewed the transmissions of their double agents and concluded that two of the messages had probably come from double agent SUMMER (Gösta Caroli) and one likely came from double agent TATE (Wulf Schmidt). Two of the messages, however, could not be claimed by any of MI5's double agents. Had they come from an unknown agent? Or was one of their double agents triple-crossing them? Knowing the shiftiness of double agent SNOW, that was not outside the realm of possibility.

13 KV 2/1333, no. 14ab, 20 December 1945, CSDIC (WEA) memo to IB on Boeckel.

14 KV 2/30 to 2/33, information on Karel Richter based on his MI5 file.

15 Her surname is Bäuerle which is pronounced Boy-er-le. The umlaut over the 'a' is commonly omitted which means her name is then pronounced Bough-er-le.

16 Leimbach, Berthold, *Tondokumente der Kleinkunst und ihre Interpreten 1898–1945* (Göttingen: Leimbach, 1991). Stadt Ulm, Geburtseintrag (Birth Entry) #807/1905.

17 Released 21 March 1933.

18 Released 22 May 1940.

19 Personal communication from Raymond Jakobs – remembers Josef using the Morse sender in Berlin.

20 Leverkuehn, Paul, *German Military Intelligence* (London: Weidenfeld and Nicolson, 1954) p.42.

21 KV 2/27, no number, 29 April 1941, statement by Josef. Van Hees (unknown first name) was 50 years old and lived at Nestor Strasse 45.

22 Equivalent value in 2014 approximately £90,000.

23 According to WO 71/1240, 4 August 1941, Day 1, court martial proceedings, p.52, Josef received the call from Hamburg on 1 January and was sent to The Hague on 8 January. According to Josef's wife's diary, a call from Hamburg came on 3 January and there was a drive to Hamburg on 5 January, with Josef being 'at the front' on 7 January.

24 Malten was the alias of Carl August Johannes Merkel/Merker. Kluiters, Frans, De Abwehr in Nederland (1936–45) (unpublished manuscript, 2006), ebook - available at https://www.nisa-intelligence.nl/contributions.html

25 Equivalent value in 2014 approximately £48.

26 The rose is well preserved in an envelope with a brief note from Josef to his wife.

27 Personal communication from Raymond Jakobs, who read a letter from Josef to Margarete denying an affair.

10 – A Leap into the Unknown

1 This section is a compilation based on Josef's MI5 interrogations.

2 This could be an alias for *Hauptmann* Karl-Edmund Gartenfeld, a member of the German Luftwaffe. Gartenfeld also dropped Gösta Caroli and Wulf Schmidt.

3 Equivalent value in 1941 approximately £23,000 based on www.officialdata.org site, which uses United Kingdom inflation rates based on composite price index.

4 KV 2/24, no. 18b, 3 February 1941, letter by Rivett-Carnac to Dixon. Rivett-Carnac (Chief Constable of the Huntingdonshire Police) said that the circle was on the main road north of Warboys and that the cross was on the railway line near Woodwalton and Connington Fen. Detective Inspector Mills said that the circle was Warboys and that the cross was Woodwalton.

5 Josef thought it was a Junkers aeroplane (Ju 202), but there is no such model. Other sources suggest German agents were dropped from Heinkel aeroplanes (He 111).

6 Normally the time difference between Germany and Britain was one hour, but during the war Britain used Double Summer Time. During the summer, clocks were set two hours ahead of Greenwich Mean Time (GMT) and during the winter, clocks were set one hour ahead of GMT.

7 The pieces are sometimes described as paper, but elsewhere referred to as cardboard. I have used cardboard as a more accurate description of the material used. It was not, however, corrugated cardboard.

11 – Spy Catchers

1 The sequence and number of shots is based on statements by Baldock and Coulson – four shots, three shots, two shots – for a total of nine shots.

2 WO 71/1240, 4 August 1941, Day 1, court martial proceedings, pp.7 and 12. Baldock said that Josef lay 150 yards away from them, and 50 yards within the field of the Shaw Brothers. Coulson said that Josef lay 500 yards away from the Drove and 50 yards within the field of Shaw Brothers.

3 There is some discrepancy as to when Josef put his pistol into his helmet. One account says it took place when Baldock said, 'Don't shoot'. Another account says it took place when the farmers approached Josef. Baldock, Coulson and Newton refer to the weapon as a revolver, but it was a pistol. This error is propagated during the court martial, where pistol and revolver are both used to describe Josef's gun.

4 KV 2/24, no. 20b, 1 February 1941, witness statements by Baldock and Coulson. KV 2/27, no. 11a, 16 June 1941, MI5 report by Cussen including witness statements. Baldock said that he and Coulson approached the man together, but Coulson said that he held back.

5 KV 2/24, no. 20b, 1 February 1941, witness statements by Baldock and Coulson. KV 2/27, no. 11a, 16 June 1941, MI5 report by Cussen including witness statements.

6 KV 2/24, no. 20b, 1 and 2 February 1941, witness statements by Baldock, Coulson and Godfrey. Coulson said he told Godfrey about a 'man'. Godfrey said he was informed of a 'German parachutist'.

7 Curedale was a fertiliser manufacturer's representative.

8 KV 2/24, no. 20b, 2 February 1941, witness statements by Newton and Curedale. Wistow Fen Farm is about 500 yards south-west of Dovehouse Farm.

9 KV 2/24, no. 20b, 2 February 1941, witness statements by Newton and Curedale. The location is described by Curedale as being 'slightly SE of Ash Drain'.

10 KV 2/24, no. 20b, 2 February 1941, witness statement by Curedale.

11 KV 2/24, no. 20b, 2 February 1941, witness statements by Godfrey, Newton and Curedale. Godfrey said a road map was taken from the man.

12 KV 2/24, no. 20b, 2 February 1941, witness statements by Newton and Curedale.

13 Newton & Curedale drove back to police station in a car. Neither Baldock nor Coulson testified that they accompanied the cart to the police station. Pottle wasn't there. Witness statements were only taken from key individuals and it is likely that curious farm labourers gathered from the nearby farms.

12 – An English Gaol

1 KV 2/24, no. 21a, 10 February 1941, copy of Clara Bäuerle's postcard.

2 KV 2/24, no. 20b, 4 February 1941, report by Jaikens.

3 This was a glaring error and a puzzling one, although not unique to Josef's case. Engelbertus Fukken (alias Jan Willem ter Braak) and Karel Richter were also sent with identity cards written in Continental fashion. These stand in stark contrast to the addresses on Druecke and Walti's identity cards, which were written in the correct fashion: street address, city, post code. On the other hand, the identity cards of Fukken, Josef and Richter all had a British '1', while those of Druecke and Walti had a German '1'.

4 Hertzog was descended from German immigrants to South Africa. He emigrated to England in the mid 1920s, studied medicine and set up his practice in Ramsey in the mid 1930s.

5 There is no evidence that Josef was cautioned prior to answering those questions.

6 Josef said it was a Junkers (Ju 202) but there is no such aeroplane. It was likely a Heinkel 111 (He 111), although the two-engined Ju 88 can't be ruled out.

7 KV 2/24, no. 10a, 2 February 1941 report by Robertson stated the aeroplane flew at 9,000ft, but elsewhere, Josef said they flew at 10,000m.

8 Reports stated 3,000ft but elsewhere Josef said he jumped at 3,000m. A post-war report by H.L.A. Hart indicated that Caroli jumped at 15,000ft, Schmidt at 3,000ft, Jakobs at 9,000ft and Richter at 10,000ft. (KV 4/22, Appendix 1, 1945, *History of Work in the Security Service* by H.L.A. Hart).

9 It would appear that neither Mills nor Jaikens took an official statement from Josef. There is no evidence that Mills or Jaikens cautioned Josef prior to asking him any questions. Given the language issues, it is quite likely that they also misunderstood Josef and very unlikely that the Abwehr had instructed him to contact a woman in London (Lily Knips).

10 American Blend No. 3525.

11 Marked '*Jonker*'.

12 Wristwatch #9321.

13 The grooming items appear to have been contained in a separate leather case from the ones mentioned earlier.

14 KV 2/24, no. 20b, 2 February 1941 and 4 February 1941, witness statement by Newton and report by Jaikens.

15 KV 2/24, no. 20b, 3 February 1941, report by Mills.

16 KV 2/24, no. 20b, 4 February 1941, report by Jaikens. KV 2/27, no. 11a, report by Cussen.

17 Also known as Cecil Egerton Dixon.

18 KV 2/24, no. 20b, 3 February 1941, report by Mills; 4 February 1941, report by Jaikens; 1 February 1941, certificate by Hertzog.

19 KV 2/24, no. 20b, 4 February 1941, report by Jaikens. This suggests that other individuals were present at the time of Josef's capture, but did not give witness statements.

13 – Preparations to Receive a Spy

1 Masterman, J.C., *The Double-Cross System in the War of 1939 to 1945* (New Haven and London: Yale University Press, 1972) p.49.

2 West, Nigel, *The Guy Liddell Diaries, Volume 1: 1939–1942* (Abingdon: Routledge, 2005) pp.1–4. In mid 1941, B Division was restructured: B2a became B1a and B8a or BL (Latchmere House) became B1e.

3 As quoted in Elliott, Geoffrey, *Gentleman Spymaster* (London: Methuen, 2011) p.101.

4 While the lane is called 'Canon Row', the police station is known as 'Cannon Row'.

5 KV 2/24, no. 1a, 1 February 1941, letter from Robertson.

6 KV 2/24, no. 4a, 2 February 1941, report by Robertson. KV 2/26, no number, 2 February 1941, list of property sent from Robertson to Butler.

7 KV 2/24, no. 4a, 2 February 1941, report by Robertson. KV 2/24, no. 16a, 1 February 1941, report by Grey. KV 2/27, no. 11a, 16 June 1941, report by Cussen.

8 KV 2/24, no. 10a, 2 February 1941, report by Robertson. There is no mention of when or if Josef received an injection for pain. During his court martial (WO 71/1240, 4 August 1941, Day 1, p.57), Josef stated that the doctor bandaged his leg and gave him an injection. Within the context of Robertson's report, this would seem to indicate that the injection took place when the doctor attended to Josef prior to his voluntary statement. On the other hand, on the second day of the court martial, Josef said that he thought he received an injection after the voluntary statement (WO 71/1240, 5 August 1941, Day 2, p.6).

9 KV 2/24, no. 10a, 2 February 1941, report by Robertson. KV 2/24, no. 4a, 2 February 1941, report by Robertson. KV 2/24, no. 16a, 01 February 1941, report by Grey.

10 KV 2/24, no. 16a, 1 February 1941, report by Grey. KV 2/24, no. 4a, 2 February 1941, report by Robertson. KV 2/27, no. 11a, 16 June 1941, report by Cussen. KV 2/24, no. 16a, 1 February 1941, Josef's statement to Robertson.

11 Weather intelligence, Department 5.

12 Another option for the aeroplane would be a Ju 88, which had two engines and a crew of three.

13 The number of shots does not match those reported by Baldock and Coulson – four shots, three shots, two shots. It is possible that Josef had fired earlier shots that the farmers did not hear. Or Josef, in his extremity of pain could not articulate accurately how many shots he fired. Or it was simply an error in translation.

14 KV 2/24, no. 16a, 1 February 1941, Josef's statement to Robertson. This is a typewritten statement that just says, 'signed by Josef Jakobs'. There is no signature. A note on folio no. 4a notes that the original statement is missing. There is no mention in Robertson's accompanying report at no. 4a if the statement taken down in English by Constable Templeman was read back to Josef, or if he had the opportunity to suggest corrections. Contrast this with the 18 June 1941 statement made by Josef to Hinchley-Cooke in which Josef was able to read his statement, suggest alterations and initial them.

15 KV 2/24, no. 10a, 2 February 1941, report by Robertson. KV 2/24, no. 16a, 1 February 1941, report by Grey.

16 KV 2/24, no. 10a, 2 February 1941, report by Robertson. KV 2/24, no. 4a, 2 February 1941, report by Robertson. KV 2/24, no. 16a, 1 February 1941, report by Grey.

17 KV 2/24, no. 4a, 2 February 1941, report by Robertson. KV 2/24, no. 10a, 2 February 1941, report by Robertson. KV 2/24, no. 2a, 1 February 1941, unsigned memo.

18 KV 2/24, no. 3a, 1 February 1941, telephone message from Blackford to Robertson. KV 2/24, no. 2a, 1 February 1941, unsigned memo. KV 2/24, no. 10a, 2 February 1941, report by Robertson.

19 KV 2/24, no. 10a, 2 February 1941, report by Robertson.

20 See Appendix for complete list.

21 SLB dealt with the prosecution of spies. Staff included Butler, Cussen and Hinchley-Cooke. It was originally B13 and renamed SLB in mid 1941.

22 KV 2/24, no. 1a, 1 February 1941, letter from Robertson.

23 Robin Stephens was promoted to lieutenant colonel between 19 June 1941 and 11 July 1941 (based on references in Jakobs and Richter files).

24 KV 2/24, no. 4a, 2 February 1941, report by Robertson. KV 2/24, no. 5a, 2 February 1941, memo from Robertson to Dixon. KV 2/24, no. 6a, 2 February 1941, memo from Robertson to Stephens. KV 2/24, no. 7a, 2 February 1941, list of property sent from Robertson to Butler.

14 – Abandon Hope all Ye Who Enter

1 Friends of Latchmere House – http://www.latchmerehouse.com/#/building-history/4575723218

2 Dearden, Harold, *Medicine and Duty* (Kingswood: The Windmill Press, 1928) pp.vii–viii.

3 Dearden, Harold, *Time and Chance* (London: William Heinemann, 1940).

4 KV 2/24, no. 9a, 2 February 1941, personal particulars form from Latchmere House.

5 Jaikens had noted that Josef was 5ft 9in tall but given that Josef was lying down, this may not have been accurate.

6 Biography of Stephens based on various genealogy documents.

7 Macintyre, Ben, *Agent Zigzag* (London: Bloomsbury, 2007) p.113.

8 Andrew, Christopher, *The Defence of the Realm* (Toronto: Penguin Group, 2009) p.250.

9 Ibid., p.150.

10 Macintyre, Ben, *Agent Zigzag* (London: Bloomsbury, 2007) pp.113–14

11 Stephens, R.W.G., & Oliver Hoare (ed.), *Camp 020: MI5 and the Nazi Spies* (London: Public Record Office Publications, 2000) p.107.

12 Ibid., pp.117–19.

13 Ibid., p.117.

14 KV 2/24, no. 21a, 10 February 1941, report by Stephens.

15 KV 2/24, no. 9a, 2 February 1941, personal particulars form from Latchmere House.

16 KV 2/24, no. 18k, 6 February 1941, report by Sampson. This statement that Josef was not a Jew was reiterated in KV 2/25, no. 96a, 25 June 1941, liquidation report by Stephens.

17 KV 2/24, no. 9a, 2 February 1941, report by Stephens.

18 KV 2/24, no. 9a, 2 February 1941, report from Latchmere House.

19 Ibid.

20 Equivalent value in 2014 approximately £4,500.

21 KV 4/187, 2 February 1941, Guy Liddell diary entry. Liddell noted, 'This is more than any of the other agents have brought.' KV 2/24, no. 9a, 2 February 1941, report by Stephens. He too noted 'the £500 found in [Josef's] possession is a greater sum than that brought jointly by known and dangerous agents such as [Druecke] and [Eriksen].' This was of crucial importance during Josef's court martial when Hinchley-Cooke testified that £500 was a normal amount for the spies.

22 KV 2/24, no. 20a, 8 February 1941, report by Stephens.

23 Josef's call sign was MZU and his receiving sign was ILC.

24 KV 2/24, no. 9a, 2 February 1941, report from Latchmere House.

25 SNOW also had a code word 'CONGRATULATIONS', the use of which is explained in West, Nigel and Madoc Roberts, *SNOW: The Double Life of a World War II Spy* (London: Biteback Publishing Ltd, 2011) p.214.

26 Likely a mispronunciation of Acedicone, the trade name of the drug Thebacon.

27 KV 2/24, no. 9a, 2 February 1941, report by Stephens.

28 Ibid.

29 Ibid.

30 Ibid.

31 Ibid.

32 Ibid.

33 Ibid.

34 Ibid. Josef brought more money than Druecke and Eriksen combined.

35 Stephens and other MI5 officers often refer to the German SS, an abbreviation for the German Secret Service. Elsewhere, it is referred to as the GIS or the German Intelligence Service. Both are a reference to the German army's intelligence arm, commonly referred to as the Abwehr, which has no connection to the Nazi political party's Schutzstaffel (SS).

36 KV 2/24, no. 9a, 2 February 1941, report by Stephens. He requests that someone (name redacted) be sent to Latchmere House for the purpose of mutual recognition.

37 Cobain, Ian, *Cruel Britannia* (London: Portobello Books, 2012).

38 Stephens R.W.G., & Oliver Hoare (ed.), *Camp 020: MI5 and the Nazi Spies* (London: Public Record Office Publications, 2000) pp.57–58.

39 Ibid., p.118.

40 Ibid., p.20.

41 Cobain, Ian, *Cruel Britannia* (London: Portobello Books, 2012) p.37.

42 KV 2/24, no. 9a, 2 February 1941, report by Stephens.

15 – Medical Respite

1 Dick Goldsmith White would serve as Director General of both MI5 and MI6.
2 KV 2/24, no. 11a, 3 February 1941, letter from Dick White to Maxwell. KV 2/24, no. 12a, 3 February 1941, telephone message from Maxwell.
3 KV 2/24, no. 11a, 3 February 1941, letter from Dick White to Maxwell.
4 Ibid.
5 KV 2/24, no number, various dates, Josef's medical records from Dulwich Hospital.
6 Ibid.
7 Ibid.
8 Ibid.
9 Ibid.
10 Ibid.
11 KV 2/24, no. 18a, 6 February 1941, report by Robertson.
12 Ibid.
13 Ibid.
14 Built in Florence Nightingale style with 24–30 beds in the wards.
15 KV 2/24, no. 18a, 6 February 1941, report by Robertson.
16 A subsequent report sent to the Ministry of Health, Emergency Medical Services, noted that airman 'Josef Jacobs' had been admitted as a prisoner of war with a fracture of the leg, presumably due to descending from an aeroplane. (KV 2/24, no number, various dates, Josef's medical records from Dulwich Hospital).
17 KV 2/24, no. 18a, 6 February 1941, report by Robertson.
18 Ibid.
19 KV 2/24, no. 23a, 10 February 1941, report by 'John' (possibly John Marriott) for Robertson.
20 KV 2/24, no. 23a, 10 February 1941, memo from Robertson.
21 KV 2/24, no. 25b, 14 February 1941, report from Dearden to Stephens.
22 KV 2/24, no. 25b, 14 February 1941, report by Stephens.
23 KV 2/24, no. 37a, 24 February 1941, report by Dearden.
24 Ibid.
25 Ibid.
26 Ibid.
27 KV 2/24, no. 37a, 24 February 1941, report by Stephens.
28 Ibid.
29 KV 2/24, no. 41b, 27 February 1941, report from Dearden to Stephens.
30 KV 2/24, no. 47a, 5 March 1941, report by Stephens. In his report, Stephens noted that the original blood sample from Josef had been lost in an 'accident' (possibly a bomb) and that a second sample had been drawn from Josef and would be sent to the recipient of the report (it is not clear who). Did they keep a library of blood samples from espionage agents?

16 – The Cost of Loose Lips and Tittle-Tattle

1 KV 2/24, no. 1a, 1 February 1941, report by Robertson.
2 KV 2/24, no. 24a, 9 February 1941, report by Blackburn Police.
3 KV 2/24, no. 24a, 12 February 1941, letter from Baxter to Dick White.
4 www.ancestry.com – 1940 US Census – 2902 Halldale; www.ancestry.co.uk – 1901 United Kingdom census – Horace was born about 1886 and was a pattern maker at the age of 15. He boarded a ship for Canada in 1907 at the age of 21. By 1910, he

was married and living in New York with his wife Mary Elizabeth and his 1-year-old daughter Florence (information amalgamated from www.familysearch.org and www.ancestry.com).

5 KV 2/24, no. 32a (and after 29a), 2 February 1941, letter from Queenie to Mr H. Porter. Marriott wrote a short memo on 17 February 1941 in which he questioned whether or not the letter should be allowed to proceed to its recipient.

6 KV 2/24, no. 32a, 8 February 1941, report by Ministry of Information.

7 KV 2/24, no. 32a, 17 February 1941, memo from Dixon to Marriott.

8 Dutchman Engelbertus Fukken (alias Jan Willem Ter Braak) was operating in Cambridge from early November 1940 to end of March 1941. One naturally wonders if rumours of Josef's arrival and capture reached his ears.

9 'Poll' was boarding with Mrs Ward, of 53 Sturton Street, Cambridge.

10 KV 2/24, no. 37b, 16 February 1941, letter from Poll to Miss E. Boyd, p.6.

11 KV 2/24, no. 37b, 16 February 1941, report by Ministry of Information.

12 KV 2/24, no. 32a, 17 February 1941, memo from Dixon to Marriott.

13 Ibid.

14 KV 2/24, no. 42c, 28 February 1941, memo regarding Barton report.

15 KV 2/24, no. 51a, 11 March 1941, memo from Blunt to Ryde.

16 KV 2/24, no. 54a, 18 March 1941, postal censorship form. Grace's husband, George, had fought in Greece in the First World War. Their son, Paul, was 16 years old and in the Air Cadets.

17 KV 2/24, no. 46a, 3 March 1941, memo from Dick White.

18 West, Nigel, and Madoc Roberts, *Snow* (London: Biteback Publishing Ltd, 2011) p.131.

19 Ibid., p.133.

20 Not even close – perhaps to confuse the Germans as to the accuracy of their parachutist drops.

21 West, Nigel, and Madoc Roberts, *Snow* (London: Biteback Publishing Ltd, 2011) p.133.

22 KV 2/24, minute sheet, 2 February 1941, note by Dick White.

23 KV 2/26, no number, 2 February 1941, list of Josef's property sent from Robertson to Butler.

24 See Appendix for a full list of all items found in Josef's possession.

17 – Clandestine Communication

1 KV 2/26, no. 2a, 13 February 1941, report by Humphreys.

2 Humphreys said it was similar to the 'D-E' set which is the set from Druecke. See KV 2/1701, no number, 17 April 1941, note from General Post Office regarding 'D-E' set.

3 KV 2/26, no number, 25 February 1941, letter from Butler to Ryde.

4 KV 2/24, no. 14a, 4 February 1941, memo from Latchmere House to Robertson.

5 KV 2/26, no number, 4 February 1941, memo from Robertson. KV 2/24, no. 14a, 2 February 1941, memo from Latchmere House to Robertson and a handwritten note from Robertson noting that the disc code was sent to Cowgill (MI6) on 2 February 1941 for reconstruction. KV 2/26, no number, 7 February 1941, memo from MI6 to Robertson.

6 Walti, Druecke and Eriksen.

7 KV 2/24, no. 9a, 2 February 1941, report from Latchmere House.

8 KV 2/26, no number, 5 February 1941, memo from Butler to Rothschild. KV 2/24, no. 30b, 17 February 1941, Medical Research Council report.

9   KV 2/24, no. 30b, 17 February 1941, Medical Research Council report on tablets.

10 Ibid.

11 More information can be found in Ohler, Norman, *Blitzed: Drugs in Nazi Germany* (Penguin Books: London, 2017).

12 KV 2/24, no. 30b, 17 February 1941, Medical Research Council report on tablets. The wrappers of Group 2 and Group 3 contained red and black writing, but the meaning of W.S.P.XI or V.Z. was unknown.

13 Ibid.

14 Ibid.

15 KV 2/25, no. 64a, 23 April 1941, letter from Milmo to Smith.

16 Ibid.

17 KV 2/25, no. 66a, 25 April 1941, report from Smith to Milmo.

18 – A New Identity

1   KV 4/406, no. 44b, 13 February 1941, report accompanying letter by Dick White – Notes on the Detection of and Search for Enemy Agents, p.2.

2   KV 2/24, no. 17b, 3 February 1941, letter from Robertson to Vivian.

3   KV 4/187, 2 February 1941, Guy Liddell diary entry.

4   Josef had the James Rymer card and also a blank one.

5   KV 2/24, no. 17b, 3 February 1941, letter from Robertson to Vivian.

6   Ibid.

7   KV 2/24, no. 25d, 14 February 1941, letter from Vivian to Robertson.

19 – Dressing the Part

1   Cordon Rouge – American Blend No. 3525 – likely a product of A. Batschari, a cigarette company in Baden-Baden that operated from 1834 until the Second World War.

2   'Dandy Joseph, Spy in Spats, Caught by H.G.', *Daily Express*, 16 August 1941, p.2.

3   James Doohan of *Star Trek* fame was shot in the chest during the Second World War, but his silver cigarette case stopped the bullet (https://www.warhistoryonline.com/world-war-ii/james-montgomery-doohan-wwii-veteran-chief-mechanic-starship-enterprise.html).

4   Some reports say grey – he may have had two pairs.

5   KV 2/24, no. 20b, early February 1941, various witness statements. Newton and Curedale both stated that Josef had a wallet and a note case (two items). Jaikens' report notes that Josef had a leather note case, a brown leather wallet, a brown leather purse with zip fastener and a blue leather note case with chain guard (four items). The Huntingdonshire Police list of Josef's possessions includes a leather note case, a brown leather wallet, a leather purse (three items). Robertson's list (folio no. 4a) has a brown leather purse with zip fastener, a blue leather note case and a brown wallet (three items). Rivett-Carnac, in a letter to all of the police detachments (17 February 1941), references a 'small note book' but makes no mention of wallets, note cases or purses. (as quoted in Dodman, Dave and Roy Dudley, *Huntingdon County Police: A Brief History of the Force and Those Who Served with Honour (1857–1965)* (privately published by Dave Dodman, 2003) pp.129–31.

6   KV 2/24, no. 53a, 12 March 1941, report by Sampson.

7   Ibid.

8 Hayward, James, *Double Agent Snow* (London: Simon & Schuster, 2013) p.201. Hayward
   sources this quote as being from the SNOW files at the National Archives but does not
   mention which one, nor the folio number. He simply says that it was quoted in a memo
   dated 24 February 1942. It was not uncommon for the navigation to be off. Richter was
   to have been dropped on the outskirts of Cambridge and landed in London Colney, a
   discrepancy of 25 miles (40km), as noted in Levine, Joshua, *Operation Fortitude* (London,
   HarperCollins, 2011) p.128.
9 KV 2/25, no. 65a, 24 April 1941, report by Stephens.

20 – An Unsavoury Name

1 KV 2/24, no. 36a, 21 February 1941, Traffic Index, Central Aliens Register and Home
   Office extract on Lothar Sauer.
2 KV 2/24, no. 44a, 28 February 1941, statement by Lily Knips. Her son, Lothar, was living
   in Glasgow, working for Mr J.H. Robertson.
3 KV 2/24, no. 55a, 24 March 1941, report by Gale.
4 KV 2/24, no. 44a, 28 February 1941, statement by Lily Knips. She stated that she
   received the letter about two months after the occupation of Denmark (9 April 1940),
   so perhaps June, but both Short and Gale suggest that the letter arrived in August or
   September 1940.
5 Equivalent value in 2014 approximately £144,000.
6 KV 2/24, no. 44a, 28 February 1941, statement by Lily Knips. According to Josef, he and
   Martin Goldstein had been released from Sachsenhausen on the same day (22 March
   1940 – Good Friday). He said that Goldstein had emigrated to Russia in July 1940.
   (KV 2/25, no. 75b, 30 April 1941, statement by Josef.) Genealogy research confirms
   that Martin Goldstein and his family travelled through Russia to Shanghai where they
   remained until 1948, at which point they emigrated to the United States. There is no
   indication in Lily's statement that she met Goldstein.
7 KV 2/24, no. 47a, 1 March 1941, report by Short. He states that Lily had not heard from
   her 'sister' since 1936 but Lily did not mention a 'sister' in her statement from KV 2/24,
   no. 44a, 28 February 1941. She said that her second husband, Franz Knips had a daughter
   by a second marriage whom Lily had not seen since 1936. Short may have made an
   error in his report.
8 KV 2/24, no. 47a, 1 March 1941, report by Short.
9 Ibid.
10 KV 2/24, no. 55a, 24 March 1941, report by Gale.
11 KV 2/24, no. 47a, 5 March 1941, report from Stephens to B2.
12 KV 2/24, no. 47a, 1 March 1941, report by Short. Clara Gronau had lived a few doors
   down from Lily Knips at Freiherr-vom-Stein Strasse 15. She arrived in England on
   19 April 1939.
13 KV 2/24, no. 55a, 24 March 1941, report by Gale.
14 KV 2/24, no. 47a, 1 March 1941, report by Short. The Postal Service may have directed
   the letter to the correct address, 19 or 29 Compayne Gardens.
15 The accounts of Lily and Josef matched quite closely.
16 KV 2/24, no number, 26 March 1941, Josef's medical records from Dulwich Hospital.
   KV 2/24, no. 58a, 3 April 1941, letter from Dick White to Home Office.
17 KV 2/24, no. 56a, 1 April 1941, memo from Renton (B8).

21 – Once More unto the Breach

1 KV 2/24, no. 9a, 2 February 1941, report by Stephens.
2 Ibid.
3 KV 4/187, 2 February 1941, Guy Liddell diary entry.
4 WO 71/1240, 4 August 1941, court martial proceedings, Day 1, p.57. Josef said that he typed up the statements himself.
5 KV 2/25, no. 65a, 24 April 1941, report by Stephens.
6 KV 2/25, no. 65a, 17 April 1941, statement by Josef.
7 KV 2/26, no number, 29 April 1941, memo from Stimson to Butler.
8 Ibid.
9 KV 2/2593, 22 November 1943, List of Cases Investigated by Camp 020 [Latchmere House]. KV 4/188, 17 September 1941, Guy Liddell diary entry. 'Stephens rang me up early this morning to say that Saetrang … had committed suicide … I got hold of [Hinchley-Cooke] and Cussen in order that we could make arrangements for a coroner's inquest with the least possible publicity. They have made arrangements to do this effectively, through a tame coroner in the north of London.'
10 By 7 May 1941, TATE was recommended for an Iron Cross Second Class by his spymaster Nikolaus Ritter (KV 4/187, 7 May 1941, Guy Liddell diary entry).
11 Equivalent value in 2014 approximately £9,000.
12 KV 2/25, no. 65a, 22 April 1941, report by Sampson.
13 KV 2/25, no. 69b, 29 April 1941, interrogation of Josef.
14 Ibid.

22 – Oh, What a Tangled Web

1 Equivalent value in 2014 approximately £90,000.
2 KV 2/25, no. 68a, 25 April 1941, report by Sampson.
3 Based on April 1941 interrogations of Josef as recorded in KV 2/25, nos 65a and 68a.
4 KV 2/25, no. 65a, condensed from Josef's statements on various dates.
5 Genealogical information and personal papers.
6 KV 2/25, no. 65a, 16 April 1941, statement by Josef.
7 KV 2/25, no. 69b, 30 April 1941, report by Stephens.

23 – Stubborn Czech

1 Regent Palace Hotel, Tate Gallery and British Museum.
2 Jonason, Tommy, and Simon Olsson, *Agent Tate* (Stroud: Amberley Publishing, 2011) p.93.
3 Farago, Ladislas, *The Game of the Foxes* (New York: David McKay & Co., 1971) p.306. The words were ascribed to 'Hansen' by Farago who didn't have the correct name of Schmidt/TATE.
4 Equivalent value in 2014 approximately £25,000.
5 Equivalent value in 2014 approximately US$24,000.
6 KV 2/30, no. 18b, 16 May 1941, report by Police Superintendent Sidney Reeves.
7 Gertrud Wegmann, Ridgewood-Brooklyn, 3684 64 St, Long Island, New York. Richter was found with a black leather wallet that contained the photograph of a woman and the baptism certificate of his illegitimate son. The Americans followed up but could find

no such person at that address. The possessions are not in the KV file for Richter at the National Archives.

8 It would appear that Richter did not make a statement under caution to the authorities prior to being admitted to Latchmere House, where he was then subjected to interrogation. He did make a statement under caution to Hinchley-Cooke on 31 May 1941.

9 Macintyre, Ben, *Agent Zigzag* (London: Bloomsbury Publishing, 2008) p.117.

10 KV 2/30, no. 5a, 16 May 1941, report by Stephens.

11 Ibid.

12 KV 2/32, no. 3a, 28 June 1941, report by Short.

13 Imperial War Museum, HU66768 lists his name as does West, Nigel, *MI5: British Security Operations 1909–1945* (Briarcliff Manor: Stein and Day, 1982).

14 Stephens R.W.G. and Oliver Hoare (ed.), *Camp 020: MI5 and the Nazi Spies* (London: Public Record Office Publications, 2000) p.165.

15 KV 2/30, no. 14a, 19 May 1941, report by Stimson.

16 Could be identical to the Abwehr officer who recruited TATE, Lieutenant Huckriede (alias Scholtz), Jonason, Tommy, and Simon Olsson, *Agent Tate* (Stroud: Amberley Publishing, 2011) p.10. On the other hand, Richter's Scholz apparently told him that TATE was a 'pearl beyond price', a comment that has been attributed to Praetorius by the same authors. In KV 2/170, the file on Praetorius, he states that Richter was an agent of *Refereat I Wi*, of which Praetorius was the head.

17 KV 2/30, no. 19b, 21 May 1941, report by Stephens.

18 KV 2/30, no. 7a, 16 May 1941, report by Stephens.

19 KV 2/30, no. 19b, 21 May 1941, report by Stephens.

20 KV 2/31, no. 40b, 4 June 1941, report by Short.

24 – Treachery Act (1940)

1 KV 2/25, no. 69b, 30 April 1941, report by Stephens.

2 LCO 2/1383, 7 September 1939, memo by DPP on Emergency Powers (Defence) Act, 1939.

3 LCO 2/1383, 2 October 1939, as quoted in an anonymous report on Emergency Powers (Defence) Act.

4 LCO 53/54, 11 October 1939, Maxwell's meeting notes.

5 LCO 53/54, 31 October 1939, letter from JAG to Maxwell.

6 Ibid.

7 LCO 53/54, no. 23a, 5 January 1940, letter from Maxwell to Lambert.

8 LCO 53/54, no. 22a, 1 January 1940, report from War Office to Lambert. According to Felstead (Felstead, Sidney Theodore, *German Spies at Bay* (New York: Bretano's, 1920) p.56), Rosenthal attempted suicide twice after his conviction. On his way to the scaffold, he broke down and pleaded for his life, much to the disgust of the commandant, who called him a 'cur'.

9 LCO 53/54, no. 22a, 1 January 1940, report from War Office to Lambert. This is confirmed by Felstead, Sidney Theodore, *German Spies at Bay* (New York: Bretano's, 1920) p.56.

10 LCO 53/54, 28 February 1940, letter from Lambert to JAG.

11 Seaborne Davies, D., 'The Treachery Act, 1940', *Modern Law Review*, Vol. 4 (3), 1941, p.218.

12 LCO 2/1383, 23 May 1940, Treachery Act, 1940, Section 1.

13 Josef fit both categories, an enemy alien and a member of the military.

14 Following excerpts taken from Hansard HC Deb, 22 May 1940, Vol. 361, cc.185–195 and cc.196–235 as well as Hansard HL Deb, 23 May 1940, Vol. 116, cc.391–398.

15 From 1918 to 1950, a parliamentary constituency comprised of the graduates of all English universities (except Cambridge, Oxford and London), represented by two Members of Parliament. Eleanor Rathbone was elected as MP in 1929 and held one of the seats until her death in 1945. She was a formidable woman; a fierce anti-Nazi who campaigned for the acceptance of refugees from Germany and Austria. She pressured the government to publish news of the Holocaust.

16 Hansard HC Deb, 22 May 1940, Vol. 361, cc.189.

17 Hansard HC Deb, 22 May 1940, Vol. 361, cc.190.

18 Defence Regulation 2A dealt with 'any act likely to assist an enemy, or prejudice the public safety or the defence of the realm or the efficient prosecution of the war with an intent to assist the enemy.' As quoted in Hinsley, F.H., and C.A.G. Simkins, *British Military Intelligence in the Second World War, Vol. 4, Security and Counter-Intelligence* (New York: Cambridge University Press, 1990) p.22.

19 Hansard HC Deb, 22 May 1940, Vol. 361, cc.190.

20 Hansard HC Deb, 22 May 1940, Vol. 361, cc.193.

21 Hansard HC Deb, 22 May 1940, Vol. 361, cc.194.

22 Hansard HC Deb, 22 May 1940, Vol. 361, cc.207–209.

23 Hansard HC Deb, 22 May 1940, Vol. 361, cc.199–200.

24 Hansard HC Deb, 22 May 1940, Vol. 361, cc.213.

25 Hansard HC Deb, 22 May 1940, Vol. 361, cc.218.

26 Allen is likely referring to the Judge Advocate's role at a court martial, not the JAG.

27 Hansard HC Deb, 22 May 1940, Vol. 361, cc.229.

28 Hansard HC Deb, 22 May 1940, Vol. 361, cc.231.

29 Ibid.

30 Simpson, A.W. Brian, *In the Highest Degree Odious* (Oxford: Clarendon Press, 1992) p.190.

31 LCO 53/54, no. 43, extract from 24 April 1941 letter from Maxwell.

32 Hansard HC Deb, 22 May 1940, vol. 361, cc.231.

33 Hansard HC Deb, 22 May 1940, vol. 361, cc.218.

25 – Life or Death

1 In his appeal, Waldberg claimed that his real name was Henri Lassudry and that he was French.

2 HO 144/21471, 12 November 1940, Central Criminal Court. The four were the only executed spies to be charged with a concrete act 'transmitting information' on His Majesty's Forces. They, along with Druecke and Walti, would also be the only executed spies to be charged with two counts under the Treachery Act and the only ones to be charged with 'conspiring with others'.

3 The terms used by Sir John Anderson during the House of Commons debates on the Treachery Act – Hansard HC Deb, 22 May 1940, Vol. 361, cc.190.

4 At the end of the war, Caroli was sent back to Sweden. He married, had one son and died in 1975.

5 I have not been able to find a Security Service file on Kurt Karl Goose (aka Hans Reysen) in the National Archives. There is a summary of his case in KV 4/8 and KV 4/16. According to KV 2/2593, Goose was sent to Camp 020R for the duration of the war and sent to Diest on 2 July 1945.

6 In 1982, Nigel West wrote that Werner Heinrich Walti's real name was Robert Petter. I have used Walti, as it is more well known. Vera Eriksen's real names were Vera von Schalburg and Vera von Wedel. I have used Eriksen, as it is more well known. Druecke used the alias Franciscus De Deeker.

7 KV 4/187, 17 December 1940, Guy Liddell diary entry.

8 Searle, Adrian, *The Spy Beside the Sea* (Stroud: The History Press, 2012) ebook.

26 – Intelligence vs Prosecution

1 There were a number of other suspicious individuals who passed through the gates of Latchmere House between late July and early October, but we are limiting ourselves to the ones who were turned into double agents or prosecuted under the Treachery Act.

2 Hinsley, F.H., and C.A.G. Simkins, *British Military Intelligence in the Second World War, Vol. 4, Security and Counter-Intelligence* (New York: Cambridge University Press, 1990) p.96.

3 CAB 93/5, 10 September 1940, Security Intelligence Centre, 'Use of Enemy Agents Captured in this Country for Counter-Espionage Purposes'.

4 KV 4/187, 7 October 1940, Guy Liddell diary entry.

5 Ibid.

6 Ibid.

7 Masterman, J.C., *The Double-Cross System in the War of 1939 to 1945* (New Haven and London: Yale University Press, 1972) p.49.

8 Hinsley, F.H., and C.A.G. Simkins, *British Military Intelligence in the Second World War, Vol. 4, Security and Counter-Intelligence* (New York: Cambridge University Press, 1990) p.97.

9 KV 2/24, no. 9a, 2 February 1941, report by Stephens.

10 Ibid. He requests that someone (name redacted) be sent to Latchmere House for the purpose of mutual recognition.

11 Ibid.

12 KV 4/187, 3 February 1941, Guy Liddell diary entry.

13 Hinsley, F.H., and C.A.G. Simkins, *British Military Intelligence in the Second World War, Vol. 4, Security and Counter-Intelligence* (New York: Cambridge University Press, 1990) p.96.

14 Ibid., pp.96–97.

15 KV 2/25, 65a, 24 April 1941, report by Stephens.

16 KV 2/25, 65a, 22 April 1941, report by Sampson.

17 KV 2/25, no. 68a, 25 April 1941, report by Sampson.

18 KV 2/25, no. 69b, 29 April 1941, report by Sampson.

19 KV 2/25, no. 69b, 30 April 1941, report by Stephens.

20 KV 2/25, no. 88b, 6 June 1941, report by Stephens.

27 – The Truth Will Out

1 KV 2/27, no. 16a, 22 June 1941, memo from Stephens to Dick White and Robertson.

2 KV 2/25, no. 94b, 16 June 1941, report by Stephens.

3 Ibid.

4 Whether this was true or not was a matter for debate as some agents' code names did not follow the pattern: Schimdt/LEONHARDT, Caroli/NILBERG.

5 KV 2/25, no. 94b, 17 June 1941, report by Stephens.

6 Stephens, R.W.G., and Oliver Hoare (ed.), *Camp 020: MI5 and the Nazi Spies* (London: Public Record Office Publications, 2000) pp.57–58.

7 KV 2/30, no. 30a, 26 May 1941, report by Short.

8 Josef sent a letter to his wife from The Hague in January 1941 and it included the same *Feldpost* number as mentioned by Richter.

9 Short received a promotion between 15 June and 15 July 1941.

10 KV 2/31, no. 55a, 15 July 1941, report by Short.

11 Some authors have referenced a document entitled 'Major Ritter's Final Report on the Snow Case (translation)'. The document is located within SNOW's file at KV 2/451, no. 1360b, 31 July 1941. On page 7 and 9 of this report, there is mention of sending ROBOTER (Richter) to England to check up on TATE. This document is actually an imaginary scenario and is not based on an actual German document. It is appended to an analysis of the SNOW situation by Marriott and Gwyer. A subsequent report written by Masterman on 16 November 1941 confirms the imaginary and speculative nature of Ritter's 'Final Report' (KV 2/451, no. 1368b). In a CSDIC(WEA) interrogation report on Ritter, dated 18 January 1946 (KV 2/88, no. 124a), Ritter denies any knowledge of an agent named Richter.

12 KV 2/31, no. 55a, 15 July 1941, report by Short.

13 Ibid.

14 KV 2/25, no. 94b, 16 June 1941, report by Stephens. KV 2/25, no. 94b, 11 June 1941, report by Short. KV 2/27, no. 16a, 22 June 1941, memo from Stephens to Dick White and Robertson.

28 – Operation LENA – the Mission to Heaven

1 KV 3/205, Appendix I, report on Nest Bremen.

2 KV 2/11, no. 3a, 5 September 1940, examiner's report.

3 KV 3/205, Appendix I, report on Nest Bremen. KV 4/16, December 1940, German Secret Service, Report No. 2, p.7.

4 KV 4/16, December 1940, German Secret Service, Report No. 2, p.8.

5 Carl Meier, Jose Waldberg, Josef Jakobs and Karel Richter.

6 PREM 3/418/2, no. 13, no date. anonymous report on Caroli.

7 KV 2/1936, no. 80c, 21 November 1943, report by Henderson attached to report by Stephens.

8 PREM 3/418/2, no. 13, no date, anonymous report on Caroli.

9 KV 4/16, December 1940, German Secret Service, Report No. 2, p.7.

10 KV 2/1936, no. 80c, 21 November 1943, report by Henderson attached to report by Stephens.

11 KV 4/16, December 1940, German Secret Service, Report No. 2, p.8.

12 KV 2/11, no. 3a, 5 September 1940, examiner's report.

13 KV 4/16, December 1940, German Secret Service, Report No. 2, p.8.

14 KV 2/11, no. 6a, September 1940, summary of the case (incomplete document).

15 Farago, Ladislas, *The Game of the Foxes* (New York: David McKay & Co., 1971) p.272.

29 – Actress, Singer, Mistress, Spy

1 KV 2/24, no. 9a, 2 February 1941, report from Latchmere House.

2 KV 2/24, no. 21a, 19 February 1941, report by Stephens.

3 KV 2/24, no number (comes after 24a), 12 February 1941, Cowgill to Dick White.

4 KV 2/25, no. 75a, 17 April 1941, report by Allchin. KV 2/25, no. 74a, 2 May 1941, Milmo to Cowgill.

5 KV 2/25, no. 74a, 2 May 1941, Milmo to Cowgill. KV 2/25, no. 83b, 20 May 1941, Home Office records on Klara Sofie Bäuerle.

6 KV 2/25, no. 68a, 25 April 1941, report by Sampson.

7 KV 2/25, no. 69b, 29 April 1941, report by Sampson.

8 KV 2/25, no. 68a, 25 April 1941, report by Sampson.

9 KV 2/26, no. 101x, 1 July 1941, transcript of conversation between Josef and Richter.

10 KV 2/87, no. 55a, 23 August 1941, report by G. Powell to Stephens.

11 KV 2/26, no. 101x, 1 July 1941, verbatim extract of conversation between Josef and Richter. One could wonder if Major Malten was simply trying to give Josef an extra little incentive to go on the mission to England.

12 KV 2/26, no. 101x, 8 July 1941, report by Sampson.

13 KV 2/26, no. 101x, 9 July 1941, report by Stephens.

14 Landesarchiv Berlin, Berlin-Köpenick, #1141/1942, death registration of Hedwig Clara Bäuerle.

15 Veronal was used as a sleeping draught. Over time, the dosage needed to be increased in order to achieve the same effect, increasing the likelihood of accidental overdose/poisoning. The possibility that Clara died by her own hand cannot, however, be ruled out.

16 Recordings can be found on YouTube by searching for her stage name 'Claire Bäuerle'.

30 – Case for Liquidation

1 KV 2/25, no. 65a, 24 April 1941, report by Stephens.

2 KV 2/25, no. 69b, 30 April 1941, report by Stephens.

3 Ibid.

4 Ibid. KV 2/25, no. 65a, 24 April 1941, report by Stephens. KV 2/25, no. 94b, 16 June 1941, report by Sampson.

5 KV 2/27, no. 19a, 27 June 1941, report by Stephens.

6 KV 2/25, no. 88a, 6 June 1941, report by Stephens.

7 Ibid.

8 Ibid.

9 KV 2/25, no. 96a, 25 June 1941, Latchmere House liquidation report.

10 KV 2/25, no. 94b, 16 June 1941, report by Sampson.

11 Ibid.

12 KV 2/25, no. 96a, 25 June 1941, liquidation report by Sampson.

13 KV 2/30, no. 5a, 16 May 1941, report by Stephens.

14 KV 2/25, no. 65a, 24 April 1941, report by Stephens. KV 2/25, no. 71a, 1 May 1941, letter from Milmo to Cowgill. KV 2/25, no. 88b, 6 June 1941, memo from Stephens to Dick White.

15 Stephens, R.W.G. and Oliver Hoare (ed.), *Camp 020: MI5 and the Nazi Spies* (London: Public Record Office Publications, 2000) pp.155–56.

16 KV 2/25, no. 82a, 15 May 1941, memo from Stephens to Milmo.

17 Ibid.

18 Ibid.

19 Weather intelligence department.

20 KV 2/25, no. 82a, 15 May 1941, memo from Stephens to Milmo.

21 Likely Sjoerd Pons (acquittal), Dorothy O'Grady (after appeal, sentence reduced to fourteen years of penal servitude) and possibly Gertrude Hiscox and Norah Briscoe (charged under Treachery Act and DR on 16 June 1941 and found guilty under DR).

22 KV 2/27, no. 9a, 17 May 1941, Harker to B2.

23 KV 2/27, no. 9a, 18 May 1941, Dick White to B13 (SLB) (Hinchley-Cooke).

24 Despite the fact that Hinchley was a middle name, over the years, it became part of Hinchley-Cooke's surname.

25 Stadtarchiv der Landeshauptstadt Dresden, Dresden I, #372/1894 – Birth Registration of William Edward Hinchley Cooke.

26 Andrew, Christopher, *The Defence of the Realm* (Toronto: Penguin Group, 2009) p.56.

27 Ibid.

28 Ibid.

29 West, Nigel, *MI5: MI5: British Security Operations 1909–1945* (Briarcliff Manor: Stein and Day, 1982) p.39.

30 DNW Auctioneers, 22 September 2006 auction of Hinchley-Cooke's medals. Includes a lengthy biography.

31 West, Nigel, and Madoc, Roberts, *Snow* (London: Biteback Publishing Ltd, 2011) p.35. Guy Liddell diaries at the National Archives also reference Hinchley-Cooke as 'Cookie' (KV 4/185–196).

31 – A False Sense of Security

1 Edward James Patrick Cussen. A lawyer who, after the war, investigated P.G. Wodehouse's involvement with the Nazis. Cussen went on to become a high court judge.

2 KV 2/27, no. 11a, 16 June 1941, report by Cussen.

3 Ibid.

4 For example, in Newton's original statement, he said that when they opened the attaché case, they found a wireless set. In the modified statement, Newton said that when they opened the attaché case, they found a wireless set, headphones, a quantity of insulated wire and some blocks of paper. (KV 2/27, no. 11a, 16 June 1941, witness statements appended to Cussen report.) Based on information gleaned over the preceding four months, perhaps someone within MI5 decided that the witness statements needed to be altered into something smoother and more substantial. The original witness statements were made when events were still fresh in the minds of the individuals. The question naturally becomes, how far could MI5 go in modifying and clarifying witness statements before they deviated too far from the original statements?

5 KV 2/27, no. 12a, 18 June 1941, memo re: Hinchley-Cooke requesting Josef.

6 Ibid.

7 Ibid.

8 KV 2/27, no. 13a, 18 June 1941, statement by Josef to Hinchley-Cooke.

9 Ibid.

10 This line was added to the typewritten statement by Hinchley-Cooke. The correction/addition was signed by Josef in the margin.

11 KV 2/27, no. 13a, 18 June 1941, statement by Josef to Hinchley-Cooke.

12 KV 2/27, no. 27a, 25 July 1941, report by Grant. Statement was taken down in shorthand by Police Sergeant A. Smith.

13 KV 2/27, no. 14a, 18 June 1941, Josef to Hinchley-Cooke statement.

14 KV 2/27, no. 20a, 26 June 1941, memo from Dixon to Cussen.

15 KV 2/27, no. 15a, 21 June 1941, MI5 application to AG.

16 KV 2/27, no. 18a, 24 June 1941, letter from DPP to AG.

17 Possibly one of the four spies who landed in Kent. A juror had spoken to the press after seeing the story in the newspapers.

18 KV 2/27, no. 18a, 25 June 1941, letter from DPP to JAG.

19 KV 2/27, no. 18a, 25 June 1941, AG's direction.

20 Ibid.

32 – First Espionage Court Martial

1 KV 2/27, no. 22a, early July 1941, memo by Cussen.
2 Ibid.
3 Ibid.
4 Ibid.
5 Ibid.
6 Ibid.
7 Ibid.
8 Ibid.
9 Ibid.
10 Ibid.
11 Ibid.
12 KV 2/27, no. 18a, 24 June 1941, letter from DPP to JAG.
13 KV 2/27, no. 24a, 19 July 1941, memo by Cussen.
14 LMA: ACC/3444/AD/08/003, HM Prison Wandsworth, Governor's Confidential Letter Book, 19 July 1941, directive from Herbert Morrison, Secretary of State.
15 LMA: ACC/3444/AD/08/003, HM Prison Wandsworth, Governor's Confidential Letter Book, 22 July 1941, handwritten note from Prison Governor Grew.
16 KV 2/27, no. 25a, 22 July 1941, memo from Hippisley-Cox to Grenadier Guards.
17 Formed 4 March 1940.

33 – Charged with Treachery

1 KV 2/27, no. 27a, 25 July 1941, report by Grant.
2 KV 2/27, no. 29a, 29 July 1941, report by Hinchley-Cooke to AAG.
3 Ibid. Defence Regulation 2a, with a penalty of penal servitude also focused on intent 'any act likely to assist an enemy, or prejudice the public safety or the defence of the realm or the efficient prosecution of the war with an intent to assist the enemy'. The difference between life and death.
4 KV 2/27, no. 29a, 29 July 1941, report by Hinchley-Cooke to AAG.
5 Ibid.
6 HO 144/21636, 12 June 1941, Central Criminal Court Proceedings, Day 1, p.2. On 1 April 1941, Byrne recommended four charges: two under the Treachery Act (landing and conspiring), one under Defence Regulation 2a (landing) and one under the Official Secrets Act (OSA) (being in a prohibited area) (KV 2/1701). When Druecke and Walti were brought before Bow Street Police Court on 22 April 1941, the last charge (OSA) had been dropped (KV 2/1705). By the time they were brought to trial on 12 June 1941, the charge under the Defence Regulations had also been dropped (KV 2/1704). Druecke and Walti would not be charged jointly under the Treachery Act and the Defence Regulations as had been suggested during the parliamentary debates in May 1940.
7 KV 2/27, no. 30a, 28 July 1941, Summary of Evidence.
8 The War Office, *Manual of Military Law, 1929* (London: His Majesty's Stationery Office, 1929 and 1940 addenda), Part II, Rules of Procedure, Section 3, pp.616.
9 Ibid.
10 It was a Mauser pistol, not a revolver.
11 KV 2/27, no. 30a, 28 July 1941, Summary of Evidence (reprinted in WO 71/1240, 4 August 1941).

12 Ibid.

13 In response to Cussen's request, Dixon had indicated that Jaikens was available, along with the other witnesses. Why Jaikens was not called as a witness, given that he spoke some German with Josef, is a mystery.

14 KV 2/27, no. 30a, 28 July 1941, Summary of Evidence (reprinted in WO 71/1240, 4 August 1941).

15 Ibid.

16 WO 71/1240, 4 August 1941, Exhibit G.

17 KV 2/27, no. 30a, 30 July 1941, letter from AAG to Hinchley-Cooke.

18 KV 2/27, no. 31a, 1 August 1941, memo from Hinchley-Cooke to AAG. There is no evidence that a lawyer was present on 31 July 1941 when Hinchley-Cooke served the documents to Josef.

19 KV 2/27, no. 31a, 1 August 1941, memo from Hinchley-Cooke to AAG.

20 WO 71/1240, 1 August 1941, JAG appoints Judge Advocate for court martial.

34 – Court Martial Begins – 4 August 1941

1 I have added comments regarding inconsistencies, inaccuracies, etc. in square brackets.

2 KV 2/27, minute sheet, no. 37, 5 August 1941.

3 The role of the Judge Advocate in a military trial is similar to that of a judge in a civilian trial.

4 An intelligence officer.

5 The amount varies. Some lists have £497 while others have £496.

6 The War Office, *Manual of Military Law, 1929* (London: His Majesty's Stationery Office, 1929 and 1940 addenda), Part II, Rules of Procedure, Sections 22 and 23, pp.632–33.

7 WO 71/1240, 4 August 1941, court martial proceedings, Day 1, p.2.

8 One might think this was just a formality, but at another court martial, the accused asked if any of the members were Jewish. It turned out that one member was, and he was replaced by a member-in-waiting.

9 The War Office, *Manual of Military Law, 1929* (London: His Majesty's Stationery Office, 1929 and 1940 addenda), Second Appendix, p. 762.

10 WO 71/1240, 4 August 1941, court martial proceedings, Day 1, p. 2.

11 The spy trials in civil court were also held in camera, which meant that defence lawyers were limited in how much information they could glean from previous cases. In 2003, author and legal historian, A.W. Brian Simpson reflected on the proliferation of in-camera cases during the Second World War even for minor violations of the Official Secrets Act and the Defence Regulations. According to Simpson, the 'most ridiculous' cases occurred in 1940 and 1941 (including Dorothy P. O'Grady's case). After the war, in-camera trials continued and Simpson noted, 'In general, the judiciary appear to be perfectly comfortable with this aspect of the secret state, as with others. In participating in secret trials [the judiciary] have, perforce, joined [the secret state], in dereliction of their fundamental duty to respect and further the rule of law.' Simpson, A.W. Brian, 'Trials in camera in security cases', in *Domestic and International Trials, 1700–2000 – The Trial in History, Vol. 2*, R.A. Melikan (ed.), (Manchester: Manchester University Press, 2003) Ch.5, pp.98–99.

12 WO 71/1240, 4 August 1941, court martial proceedings, Day 1, p.3.

13 Ibid., Day 1, pp.2–4.

14 KV 2/27, no. 35a, 4 August 1941, court martial direction (also included in WO 71/1240).

15 WO 71/1240, 4 August 1941, court martial proceedings, Day 1, p.4. The charge was identical to the one read out to Josef by Hinchley-Cooke on 24 July but included a preamble: 'Joseph [*sic*] Jakobs, an enemy alien subject to trial by court martial under the

Army Act by virtue of Section 2(1)(b) of the Treachery Act 1940, attached Holding Battalion Grenadier Guards, is charged under Section 41 of the Army Act, with: committing a civil offence …'

16 WO 71/1240, 4 August 1941, court martial proceedings, Day 1, p.4.

17 Ibid.

18 The War Office, *Manual of Military Law, 1929* (London: His Majesty's Stationery Office, 1929 and 1940 addenda), Second Appendix, p.670. The Rules of Procedure 83(b) states, 'The evidence of a witness as taken down should be read to him after he has given all his evidence and before he leaves the court, and such evidence may be explained or corrected by the witness at his instance. If he makes any explanation or correction, the prosecutor and accused or counsel or the defending officer may respectively examine him respecting the same.' The following piece, 83(c), notes, 'In the case of a court martial at which a shorthand writer is employed, it shall not be necessary to comply with Rule 83(b), if in the opinion of the court and the judge advocate (if any) (such opinion to be recorded in the proceedings) it is unnecessary to do so, but nevertheless, if any witness so desires, Rule 83(b) shall be complied with.'

19 WO 71/1240, 4 August 1941, court martial proceedings, Day 1, pp.4–5.

20 Ibid., Day 1, p.5.

35 – Case for the Prosecution

1 Kieboom, Waldberg, Meier and Pons, as well as Druecke and Walti, were the only aliens charged with 'attempting an act' or 'conspiring with others'. All of the other neutral or enemy alien spies were simply charged with committing an act, namely arriving or landing in the United Kingdom.

2 WO 71/1240, 4 August 1941, court martial proceedings, Day 1, p.5.

3 Ibid., Day 1, pp.5–7.

4 The War Office, *Manual of Military Law, 1929* (London: His Majesty's Stationery Office, 1929 and 1940 addenda), Second Appendix, p.763.

5 WO 71/1240, 4 August 1941, court. martial proceedings, Day 1, pp.7–11.

6 Ibid., p. 9.

7 Direct quote from the court martial proceedings.

8 WO 71/1240, 4 August 1941, court martial proceedings, Day 1, pp.11–13.

9 Ibid., pp.13–18.

10 Ibid., p.16.

11 Ibid., p.17.

12 Ibid.

13 Ibid., pp.19–22.

14 Ibid., p.22.

15 Ibid., p.23.

16 Ibid., pp.23–24.

17 Ibid., pp.24–27.

18 Josef landed just outside the eastern side of the triangle.

19 WO 71/1240, 4 August 1941, court martial proceedings, Day 1, pp.27–30.

20 On the other hand, Grant had been asked by Hinchley-Cooke to investigate the ration card and identity card, even going so far as to question the 'real' James John Rymer, a radio maintenance engineer with the BBC. KV 2/27, no. 27a, 25 July 1941, report by Grant.

21 WO 71/1240, 4 August 1941, court martial proceedings, Day 1, p.28.

22 Ibid., pp.28–29.

23 British Army List, 1940, the War Office, p.10. Given Hinchley-Cooke's background, he was likely a certified German translator.

24 WO 71/1240, 4 August 1941, court martial proceedings, Day 1, pp.29–30.

25 Ibid., p.30.

26 Ibid.

27 Ibid., p.31.

28 This is a perplexing statement. Josef could have called Lily Knips as a witness, or Hans Blum, the Jewish lawyer who had been involved in the black-market passport business and had fled to England. In addition, during an interrogation on 16 June 1941, Josef told Sampson about Dr Paul List, a Russian Jew who had emigrated to Germany. He was a chess player and had run a club in the Café Trumpf that both Josef and Van Hees frequented. In 1938, List and his wife fled to England and he would have been able to confirm that Josef was anti-Nazi.

29 WO 71/1240, 4 August 1941, court martial proceedings, Day 1, pp.31–44.

30 Ibid., p.32.

31 According to the British Army List (1940), Hinchley-Cooke was 'Qualified as 1st Class Interpreter in a Modern Foreign Language', likely German, given his background.

32 www.germanjewishsoldiers.com/memorial.php

33 WO 71/1240, 4 August 1941, court martial proceedings, Day 1, p.38.

34 Ibid.

35 KV 2/24, no. 54a, 18 March 1941, postal censorship form.

36 WO 71/1240, 4 August 1941, court martial proceedings, Day 1, p.41.

37 He claimed that wireless telegraphy and signals were more difficult to fake than handwriting and an experienced wireless operator would recognise the substitute at once. Yet, the British double-cross system ran several double agents whose transmissions were sometimes sent by British wireless operators. How could the British trust that their double-cross agents were believable if they believed that a replacement operator was a dead giveaway to the Germans?

38 WO 71/1240, 4 August 1941, court martial proceedings, Day 1, p.42.

39 Ibid., p.43.

40 Ibid., p.44.

36 – Case for the Defence

1 WO 71/1240, 4 August 1941, court martial proceedings, Day 1, p.45.

2 Ibid., pp.45–59.

3 Equivalent value in 2014 approximately £640/month.

4 Equivalent value in 2014 approximately £960/month.

5 WO 71/1240, 4 August 1941, court martial proceedings, Day 1, p.54.

6 A small graph-paper coil-bound notebook is contained within the KV 2/27 file at the National Archives. The first page of the notebook has writing on it, including: 'Z.G. (2 u. 16)' and 'St. P.R. (3. u. 17)'. These are possibly the meeting locations and dates that Josef referenced during his court martial. There is nothing on the page that resembles Oxford Street and Edgar Road or the 1st and 15th of the month. Oxford Street does not intersect Edgar Road and it may actually be Oxford Street and Edgeware Road. There is no mention of Derby Station on the page, although 'St. P.R.' may refer to St Pancras Railway Station, the station from which trains departed for Epsom Downs Racecourse, the location of the Derby Stakes horse race. During 1940–45, however, the Derby was moved to Newmarket, although the Germans

may not have been aware of that. I have written several blogs about the notebook, one of which examines the notebook contents in detail (http://www.josefjakobs. info/2017/09/the-contents-of-mysterious-notebook.html).

7   KV 2/25, no. 96b, 23 June 1941, report by Sampson.

8   KV 2/25, no. 94b, 14 June 1941, report by Short

9   KV 2/25, no. 96b, 24 June 1941, report by Sampson.

10 KV 2/25, no. 96c, 27 June 1941, memo from Milmo to Stimson.

11 KV 2/26, no. folio, 22 July 1941, handwritten list of Josef's property.

12 KV 2/27, no. 26a, 22 July 1941.

13 KV 2/27, no. 26a, 22 July 1941, letter from Stimson to Cussen.

14 Dodman, Dave, and Roy Dudley, *Huntingdon County Police: A Brief History of the Force and Those Who Served with Honour (1857–1965)* (privately published by Dave Dodman, 2003) pp.129–31. Rivett-Carnac, in a letter to all of the police detachments (17 February 1941) references a 'small note book'.

15 KV 2/24, no. 20a, 2 February 1941, statement by Newton.

16 KV 2/27, no. 30a, 28 July 1941, Summary of Evidence.

17 KV 2/27, no. 32a, 1 August 1941, copy no. 4 of statements.

18 WO 71/1240, 4 August 1941, court martial proceedings, Day 1, pp.14–15.

19 Ibid., p.20.

20 Ibid., pp.31–34.

21 Ibid., pp.60–65.

22 The War Office, *Manual of Military Law, 1929* (London: His Majesty's Stationery Office, 1929 and 1940 addenda), Part II, Rules of Procedure, Section 76, p.666.

23 WO 71/1240, 4 August 1941, court martial proceedings, Day 1, p.63.

24 Ibid., p.64.

25 Ibid.

26 Ibid., p.65.

27 Ibid.

28 Ibid.

29 Blacked out, whited out or cut out.

30 In addition to the odd numbering scheme, there was also evidence that two typewriters were used to type up the proceedings of the court martial. One typewriter produced a Q with a wide tail and a G with a short crossbar. The other typewriter produced a Q with a tight tail and a G with a long crossbar. These irregularities could escape the casual reader. Harder to ignore would be the fact that the line spacing on pages 53 and 59 was much wider than the rest of the transcript. Pages 60 to 65 had yet another number sequence in the upper left hand corner – B1 to B6 – those pages corresponded with Marlowe's cross-examination of Josef.

31 WO 71/1240, 7 August 1941, JAG to Sergison-Brooke.

32 There is no record of who transcribed the shorthand notes, or what delayed their transmission to Stirling.

37 – Court Martial Ends – 5 August 1941

1   WO 71/1240, 5 August 1941, court martial proceedings, Day 2, p.2.

2   Ibid., pp.2–5.

3   Ibid., p.2.

4   Ibid., p.4.

5   Ibid., p.5.

6   Ibid., pp.5–6.

7 Ibid., pp.6–8.
8 Ibid., p.6.
9 Ibid., p.8.
10 Ibid., pp.8–9.
11 Ibid., pp.9–10.
12 KV 2/1333, no. 14ab, 20 December 1945, CSDIC (WEA) memo to IB regarding Boeckel.
13 WO 71/1240, 5 August 1941, court martial proceedings, Day 2, pp.10–13.
14 KV 2/25, no. 96a, 25 June 1941, liquidation report by Sampson.
15 KV 2/1067, no. 25a, 14 April 1941, report by Marriott.
16 WO 71/1240, 5 August 1941, court martial proceedings, Day 2, p.13.

38 – Summary for the Prosecution

1 WO 71/1240, 5 August 1941, court martial proceedings, Day 2, pp.13–15.

39 – Summary for the Defence

1 Spelled 'Bergas' in the Latchmere House interrogation reports.
2 Equivalent value in 2014 approximately £5,500,000.
3 KV 2/24, no. 54a, 18 March 1941, postal censorship form.
4 WO 71/1240, 5 August 1941, court martial proceedings, Day 2, pp.15–20.

40 – Judge Advocate's Summing Up

1 WO 71/1240, 5 August 1941, court martial proceedings, Day 2, pp.21–25.

41 – Verdict and Sentence

1 The War Office, *Manual of Military Law, 1929* (London: His Majesty's Stationery Office, 1929 and 1940 addenda), Part II, Rules of Procedure, Section 69, p.663.
2 WO 71/1240, 5 August 1941, court martial proceedings, Day 2, p.25.
3 Ibid.
4 Ibid., p.26.
5 Ibid.
6 WO 71/1240, 4 August 1941, Form of Proceedings for General and District Courts Martial.
7 KV 2/27, no. 36a, 5 August 1941, Communication of Sentence.
8 Ibid.
9 WO 71/1240, no number, 7 August 1941, letter from Stirling to Sergison-Brooke.

42 – Ministering to a German Spy

1 KV 2/27, no. 41a, 6 August 1941, memo from Cussen to Hinchley-Cooke.
2 Ibid.
3 Ibid.

4   Ibid.

5   Ibid.

6   Ibid.

7   Ibid.

8   Ibid.

9   KV 2/27, no. 39a, 3 August 1941, letter from Dey to Lambert.

10 Druecke and Walti were executed on 6 August 1941.

11 KV 2/27, no. 39a, 3 August 1941, letter from Dey to Lambert.

12 KV 2/27, no. 41a, 6 August 1941, memo from Cussen to Hinchley-Cooke.

13 Ibid.

14 KV 2/27, no. 40a, 6 August 1941, memo from Butler to Hinchley-Cooke.

15 Ramsey, Winston, 'German Spies in Britain', *After the Battle*, Vol. 11, pp.24–25, noted, 'Found guilty, Jakobs was taken to the Tower of London and held in a cell on the top floor of Waterloo Barracks at the east end of E-block, in the custody of the Holding Battalion, the Scots Guards. A priest, Father Josef Simmil of St Boniface Catholic Parish, Aldgate, a naturalised Briton, was made available, but Jakobs did not request to see him.' This information was also referenced in West's book on MI5 but is inaccurate. Josef was not held overnight at the Tower, nor did he refuse to see a priest.

16 Museum of Army Chaplaincy, War Office file no. 38, 9 August 1941, letter from Lambert to Dey.

17 KV 2/27, no. 41a, 7 August 1941, postscript note from Cussen to Hinchley-Cooke.

18 Stephens, R.W.G., and Oliver Hoare (ed.), *Camp 020: MI5 and the Nazi Spies* (London: Public Record Office Publications, 2000), p.41.

19 KV 4/81, no. 25a, 2 May 1941, *Catholic Herald* press cutting.

43 – A Plea for Mercy

1   WO 71/1240, 7 August 1941, memo from JAG to Sergison-Brooke.

2   WO 71/1240, 7 August 1941, memo from Sergison-Brooke to JAG.

3   According to the 1940 British Army List, Hinchley-Cooke was 'Qualified as 1st Class Interpreter in a Modern Foreign Language', likely German, given his background.

4   WO 71/1240, 8 August 1941, memo from Hippisley-Cox to JAG.

5   WO 32/18144, 8 August 1941, letter from JAG to Secretary of State for War.

6   Ibid.

7   Ibid.

8   WO 32/18144, no date, proceedings of court martial sent to His Majesty.

9   KV 2/27, no. 43a, no date, petition from Josef to King George VI (German & English translation) (also included in WO 71/1240).

10 WO 71/1240, 4 August 1941, Form of Proceedings for General and District Courts Martial.

44 – Foolish Gunner Jackson

1   KV 4/189, 5 December 1941, Guy Liddell diary entry. Jackson wanted to go to Germany and send broadcasts disparaging the British government. He was also prepared to share gun locations with the Germans.

2   KV 4/188, 3 November 1941, Guy Liddell diary entry. Liddell said, 'We succeeded in getting [the letter] out through a friend of Major Rawlinson (MI19).'

3   KV 2/3319, minute sheet, no. 38, note from Liddell.

4 KV 4/189, 5 February 1941, Guy Liddell diary entry. According to Liddell, Hamilton had been involved with the Casement Rebellion, was known to the Germans and wanted to go to Eire via clandestine means and start a peace campaign through the Vatican's Apostolic Delegate and the German Legation (KV 4/188, 19 July 1941, 5 November 1941 and 10 November 1941). The Advisory Committee released him under DR 18A, much to MI5's disbelief.

5 WO 32/21943, no. 9a, no date, unsigned report on the case of Gunner Jackson.

6 KV 4/188, 3 November 1941, Guy Liddell diary entry.

7 WO 32/21943, no number, 14 August 1942, handwritten letter of petition from Jackson to the king.

8 Ibid.

9 WO 32/21943, no number, probably March 1942, typewritten petition from Jackson to the king.

10 The Treachery Act allows for the prosecution of someone who (a) does an act, (b) attempts an act or (c) conspires with any other person to do an act. Only Kieboom, Waldberg, Meier and Pons (the four spies who landed in early September 1940 off the coast of Kent), and Druecke and Walti were charged under option (b) or (c). Although option (b) or (c) could be considered 'preparatory' acts, Jackson was not charged with attempting an act (giving information to the Germans) or with conspiring with others (meeting with an individual whom he believed was working for the Germans).

11 WO 32/21943, no number, probably March 1942, typewritten petition from Jackson to the king. In November 1940, George Johnson Armstrong, a British citizen, wrote a letter to the German Consul in the United States offering his services. While one could argue that his letter was also an act preparatory, he was charged under the Treachery Act with writing a letter, found guilty and executed in July 1941.

12 WO 32/21943, no number, probably March 1942, typewritten petition from Jackson to the king.

13 WO 32/21943, minute sheet, no. 73, 1 March 1946, case review by AAG.

14 WO 32/21943, no. 37a, no date, memo regarding case of Philip Jackson.

15 Ibid.

16 WO 32/21943, minute sheet, no. 73, 1 March 1946, case review by AAG.

17 WO 32/21943, minute sheet, no. 72, 27 February 1946, notes from Hinchley-Cooke.

18 Ibid.

19 There were several British citizens who were charged under the Treachery Act and executed during the Second World War: George Johnson Armstrong, Jose Estella Key, Duncan Scott-Ford and Oswald John Job. Armstrong was charged with writing a letter to the German Consul. Key was charged with recording shipping information in Gibraltar. Scott-Ford was charged with recording convoy information. Job, after discussion, was simply charged with landing in the United Kingdom, despite the fact that he was a British citizen.

20 LCO 53/54, 14 March 1940, Draft of a Bill – Assistance to the Enemy, Section 1.2.

21 WO 32/18144, 8 August 1941, letter from JAG to Secretary of State for War.

45 – Preparations for an Execution

1 HO 45/19086, 12 August 1941, letter and note by Purchase.

2 KV 2/27, no. 44a, 13 August 1941, Hippisley-Cox to Mackenzie.

3 Ibid.

4 Ibid.

5 Ibid.

6 The War Office, *Provost Training in Peace and War* (London: His Majesty's Publishing Stationery Office, 1950), Section 117a, p.213. Extracts from Section 117 on military executions kindly provided by the curator of the Royal Military Police Museum. While the museum did not have the equivalent manual for the Second World War, in essence it would have been the same procedure.

7 The War Office, *Provost Training in Peace and War* (London: His Majesty's Publishing Stationery Office, 1950), Section 117b, viii, p.214.

8 Sellers, Leonard, *Shot in the Tower* (London: Leo Cooper, 1997) p.42. As quoted in Sellers, John Fraser shared his recollections of Carl Hans Lody's execution in his memoir entitled *Sixty Years in Uniform*, published in 1939. According to the Yeoman Warders list on www.yeomenoftheguard.com, Fraser retired in 1947.

9 The War Office, *Provost Training in Peace and War* (London: His Majesty's Publishing Stationery Office, 1950), Section 117b, xi, p.215.

10 Royal Armouries Archives, 15 August 1941, prescription form purchased from the estate of Harold A. Rowe.

11 Rowe kept the two prescriptions and they were auctioned by Eldreds (Plymouth) on 20 October 2009 and acquired by the Royal Armouries.

46 – Tower of London

1 The timeline for the morning of the execution and the preparations are based on RSM Arthur Wilford's notes (Royal Armouries Archives) and the memoir of William Chidlow.

2 Likely the Medical Inspection Waiting Room in Casemates #29.

3 Chidlow, William, *A Second World War Guardsman's True Story* (unpublished, 2001).

4 RSM Arthur Wilford's notes (Royal Armouries Archives).

5 Standard army phrase.

6 The War Office, *Provost Training in Peace and War* (London: His Majesty's Publishing Stationery Office, 1950), Section 117b, ix, p.214.

7 Chidlow, William, *A Second World War Guardsman's True Story* (unpublished, 2001).

8 This may be Casemates #29, where the First World War spies were held prior to their execution.

9 Chidlow, William, *A Second World War Guardsman's True Story* (unpublished, 2001).

10 Stephens, R.W.G., and Oliver Hoare (ed.), *Camp 020: MI5 and the Nazi Spies* (London: Public Record Office Publications, 2000) p.165.

11 Chidlow, William, *A Second World War Guardsman's True Story* (unpublished, 2001). A corroboration of secondary sources which note that Sir Bernard Spilsbury reported one bullet had entered the head (Browne, Douglas G., and E.V. Tullett, *The Scalpel of Scotland Yard: The Life of Sir Bernard Spilsbury* (New York: E.P. Dutton and Company, Inc., 1952 p.463.

12 Given that five bullets had pierced the target, one might expect an instantaneous death, but such is not the case. The person loses consciousness due to a drop in blood supply to the brain. Electrical activity within the heart ceases after about thirty seconds, with brain death following shortly thereafter (deathpenaltyinfo.org/descriptions-execution-methods – accessed 8 August 2018) (fivethirtyeight.com/features/is-the-firing-squad-more-humane-than-lethal-injection/ – accessed 8 August 2018).

13 Chidlow, William, *A Second World War Guardsman's True Story* (unpublished, 2001).

47 – Dust to Dust

1 Ramsey, Winston, 'German Spies in Britain', *After the Battle*, Vol. 11, pp.24–25.
2 West, Nigel, *MI5: British Security Operations 1909–1945* (Briarcliff Manor: Stein and Day, 1982) pp.258–59.
3 General Register Office, Stepney Registration District, September 1941, Vol. 1c, p.198, no. 455.
4 Jakobs family documents, 15 August 1941, letter written from Josef Jakobs to his wife and children.
5 KV 4/188, 15 August 1941, Guy Liddell diary entry.
6 Stephens, R.W.G. and Oliver Hoare (ed.), *Camp 020: MI5 and the Nazi Spies* (London: Public Record Office Publications, 2000) p.165.
7 WO 71/1240, 15 August 1941, certificate from DPM to AAG. WO 71/1240, 4 August 1941, Form of Proceedings for General and District Courts Martial.
8 Email (14 March 2014) from David Blake, curator at Museum of Army Chaplaincy, confirms that Griffith was sent to London on 'special duty' from 6 August to 18 August.
9 There are two Catholic cemeteries in London – St Mary's in Kensal Green and St Patrick's in north-east London.

48 – Hounds on the Trail

1 HO 45/25595, no number, 6 August 1941, Procedure to be adopted in issuing announcements to the press – copy of Home Office minutes.
2 'German Spy Shot at the Tower', *The Times*, 16 August 1941, p.9.
3 KV 2/27, no. 47a, 17 August 1941, report from Dixon to Hinchley-Cooke.
4 Ibid.
5 Ibid.
6 Ibid.
7 Ibid.
8 Ibid. This would appear to confirm Dixon's view that the Ministry of Information had told the reporters about Ramsey.
9 KV 2/27, no. 47a, 17 August 1941, report from Dixon to Hinchley-Cooke.
10 Ibid.
11 Ibid
12 KV 2/27, no. 45a, 15 August 1941, *The Star*.
13 HO 45/25595, no number, 17 August 1941, notes on Josef's case.
14 Ibid.
15 KV 2/27, no. 45a, 15 August 1941, *The Star*.
16 CAB 114/17, no. 1a, 15 August 1941, *Evening Standard*.
17 HO 45/25595, no number, 17 August 1941, notes on Josef's case.
18 KV 2/27, no. 45a, 16 August 1941, *Daily Herald*.
19 'Dandy Joseph, Spy in Spats, Caught by H.G.', *Daily Express*, 16 August 1941, p.1.
20 KV 2/27, no. 47a, 17 August 1941, report from Dixon to Hinchley-Cooke, contains witness statements regarding press interest in Josef's case.
21 CAB 114/17, no. 1a, 19 August 1941, letter from Swinton to Petrie.
22 HO 45/25595, no number, 28 August 1941, Home Defence (Security) Executive meeting minutes.
23 CAB 93/7, no number, 28 August 1941, Home Defence (Security) Executive meeting minutes. In 1942, Harker suggested that it would be far more secret and secure if all

neutral and enemy spies could be tried by court martial. He said that all of the cases should be handled as they were in the First World War. Very little information was released to the press after an execution and the enemy was left in the dark as to what had happened to their men. 'In the view of the Security Service, the time has now come when, in the interests of the State, this pandering to public and Press curiosity should terminate.' CAB 114/51, no. 6a, 23 March 1942, letter by Harker.

49 – Czech in the Middle

1 CAB 114/51, no. 1a, 24 May 1941, letter from Brook to Swinton.
2 CAB 114/51, no. 2a, 30 May 1941, letter from Swinton to Petrie.
3 CAB 114/51, no. 1a, 24 May 1941, letter from Brook to Swinton. CAB 114/51, no. 2a, 30 May 1941, letter from Swinton to Petrie. CAB 114/51, no. 3a, 5 June 1941, letter from Swinton to Petrie. CAB 114/51, no. 5a, 7 June 1941, letter from Swinton to Petrie.
4 CAB 114/51, no. 5a, 7 June 1941, letter from Swinton to Petrie.
5 KV 2/31, no. 61a, 23 September 1941, letter from Richter to Short.
6 CRIM 1/1350, 14 October Sessions 1941, Central Criminal Court, p.10.
7 Ibid.
8 KV 2/31 no. 62a, 2 October 1941, letter from Richter to Short.
9 Ibid.
10 KV 2/31, no. 65a, 28 August 1941, letter from Richter to Short.
11 KV 2/32, 23 October 1941, Criminal Court proceedings, Day 3, p.27.
12 Ibid., pp.27–28.
13 Ibid., p.28.
14 Ibid.
15 Ibid., pp.28–29.
16 Ibid., p.29.
17 Ibid., p.30.
18 Ibid., p.30.
19 KV 2/52, 24 January 1944, Criminal Court proceedings, Day 1, pp.2–28.
20 KV 2/32, 23 October 1941, Criminal Court proceedings, Day 3, p.32.
21 Ibid.,
22 KV 2/32, no. 46a, 26 October 1941, report by Grant.
23 CRIM 1/1350, no number, no date, Central Criminal Court note on charge sheet.
24 KV 2/32, no. 46a, 26 October 1941, report by Grant.
25 PCOM 9/909, 27 October 1941, Report of an Attempt at Suicide by Prisoner, Medical Officer's opinion.
26 PCOM 9/909, 28 October 1941, handwritten note by Daly appended to Report of an Attempt at Suicide by Prisoner
27 KV 2/32, no. 67a, 5 November 1941, letter from Richter to DuCann.
28 KV 2/32, no. 65a, 3 November 1941, addition to notice of appeal.
29 KV 2/32, no. 55a, 5 November 1941, report from Robertson to Liddell.
30 KV 2/32, no. 63a, no date, Richter's appeal with proposed redactions marked.
31 KV 2/32, no. 60a, 10 November 1941, note from Tindal Atkinson regarding Richter appeal.
32 HO 144/21576, no number, 27 November 1941, the case of Karel Richter.
33 HO 144/21576, no number, 1 December 1941, untitled report with a scrawled signature.
34 KV 2/32, no. 55a, 5 November 1941, letter from Robertson to Liddell.
35 KV 2/31, minute sheet, 23 November 1941, note from Liddell to Petrie.

36 KV 2/31, no. 70b, 30 November 1941, letter from Stephens to Dick White.

37 KV 2/31, minute sheet, 23 November 1941, note from Liddell to Petrie.

38 KV 2/31, no. 71a, 5 December 1941, note from Liddell to B1a.

39 Ibid.

40 KV 2/31, no. 71a, no date, no author, two-page document simply marked 'Karel Richter'. Likely from Liddell to B1a.

41 KV 2/31, no. 71a, 6 December 1941, note from Liddell to B1a.

42 KV 2/31, no. 71a, 5 December 1941, note from Liddell to B1a. A handwritten comment in the upper margin of this report states, 'Original in PF 63200 Link(?) – German Agent in East Anglia'. I have yet to find such a file reference in the National Archives.

43 Albert Pierrepoint, the hangman at Richter's execution, holds the record for the fastest hanging – 7 seconds. His average was 20 seconds.

44 Pierrepoint, Albert, *Executioner Pierrepoint* (London: George C. Harrap, 1974) pp.140–41.

45 Hayward, James, *Double Agent Snow* (London: Simon & Schuster, 2013) p.252.

50 – The Road to a Successful Prosecution

1 CAB 93/5, 10 September 1940, Security Intelligence Centre, 'Use of Enemy Agents Captured in this Country for counter-Espionage Purposes'.

2 Hinsley, F.H., and C.A.G. Simkins, *British Military Intelligence in the Second World War, Vol. 4, Security and Counter-Intelligence* (New York: Cambridge University Press, 1990) pp.96–97.

3 Stephen, J.F., *A History of the Criminal Law in England, Volume 1* (London: Macmillan & Co., 1883) p.446; Stephen, J.F., *A Digest of the Law of Evidence,* (New York: George Chase, 1885), Part 1, Chapter 4, Article 21, pp.52–53.

4 Stephen, J.F., *A History of the Criminal Law in England, Volume 1* (London: Macmillan & Co., 1883) p.446. Similar phrasing is used in the War Office, *Manual of Military Law, 1929* (London: His Majesty's Stationery Office, 1929 and 1940 addenda), Part I, Chapter VI, Section 75, p.91.

5 Ibid,

6 Ibid.

7 Interesting choice of words, but accurate.

8 KV 2/15, no. 60a, 25 February 1941, memo from Stephens to Dearden.

9 Ibid.

10 Ibid.

11 Ibid.

12 KV 2/15, no. 60a, 25 February 1941, letter from Stephens to Dick White.

13 HO 144/21636, no number, 1 April 1941, opinion by Byrne.

14 CRIM 1/1307, no number, 23 July 1941, report on Druecke and Walti.

15 Ibid.

16 KV 2/15, no. 76a, 16 October 1941, memo from Cussen to Milmo.

17 Kahn, David, *Hitler's Spies* (New York: Macmillan, 1978) p.286.

18 HO 144/21664, no number, no date, Criminal Court proceedings, charge sheet.

19 KV 2/1315, no. 147a, 8 June 1945, Latchmere House liquidation report.

20 KV 2/1315, minute sheet, no. 108, 30 June 1942, note from Milmo to Dick White.

21 KV 2/1315, no. 123a, 13 October 1942, report from Hinchley-Cooke to DPP.

22 KV 2/43, no. 8a, 20 May 1942, RVPS report.

23 KV 2/45, 17 November 1942, Central Criminal Court proceedings, Day 3, p.69.

24 KV 2/1708, no. 40a, no date, note by Sinclair re: *Rex v. Winter*.

25 Ibid.

26 HO 45/25606, 2 December Sessions 1942, Central Criminal Court, charge sheet.

27 KV 2/125, minute sheet, no. 39, 23 January 1943, note from Milmo to Petrie.

28 KV 2/125, no. 57a, 12 February 1943, letter from Milmo to Coles (Home Office).

29 KV 2/125, no. 94a, 15 March 1943, report by MI5.

30 KV 2/125, no number, 16 March 1943, letter from DPP to Hinchley-Cooke.

31 Ibid.

32 KV 2/125, no. 97c, 18 March 1943, letter from Milmo to Maxwell.

33 West, Nigel, *The Guy Liddell Diaries, Volume 2: 1942–1945* (Abingdon: Routledge, 2009), diary entry from 22 March 1943, p.56.

34 KV 2/125, no. 128x, 3 May 1943, report by Stephens.

35 KV 2/125, minute sheet, no. 170, 27 October 1943, note from Milmo.

36 KV 2/1936, no. 80c, 21 November 1943, report by Henderson.

37 Ibid.

38 KV 4/192, 11 October 1943, Guy Liddell diary entry.

39 KV 2/1936, minute sheet, no. 50, 18 October 1943, note from Stamp to Liddell.

40 KV 2/1936, minute sheet, no. 59, 23 October 1943, note from Liddell to Harker.

41 KV 2/1936, minute sheet, no. 60, 25 October 1943, note from Harker to Petrie.

42 KV 2/1936, minute sheet, no. 61, 25 October 1943, note from Harker to Hinchley-Cooke.

43 KV 2/1936, no. 80c, 21 November 1943, report by Stephens.

44 HO 382/74, no number, no date, handwritten note regarding Hansen deportation.

45 KV 2/551, no. 35a, 20 June 1941, report by Sinclair.

46 KV 2/551, no. 43a, 24 June 1944, note from Sinclair to Hinchley-Cooke.

47 KV 2/551, no. 49a, 28 June 1944, report by Sinclair. The ship's captain was in Baltimore.

48 Ibid.

49 Ibid.

50 KV 2/551, no. 45a, 26 June 1944, report by Sampson.

51 Ibid.

52 KV 2/551, no. 49a, 28 June 1944, report by Sinclair.

53 CRIM 1/1604, no. 37, 29 June 1944, *nolle prosequi* order by AG.

54 KV 2/551, no. 51b, 30 June 1944, unsigned request to Maxwell regarding detention of Brodersen.

55 KV 2/551, no. 58b, 3 July 1944, memo by Milmo.

56 Ibid.

57 Ibid.

58 Ibid.

59 Ibid.

51 – Inducements, Threats and Promises

1 KV 2/31, no. 62a, 2 October 1941, letter from Richter to Short.

2 KV 2/24, no. 9a, 2 February 1941, report by Stephens.

3 Ibid.

4 Ibid. He requests that someone [name redacted] be sent to Latchmere House for the purpose of mutual recognition.

5 Ibid.

6 KV 2/31 no. 62a, 2 October 1941, letter from Richter to Short.

7 These were likely obituary notices or newspaper articles of spy executions.

8 KV 2/1315, no. 44a, 1 March 1942, report by Stephens containing interrogation transcripts.

9 KV 2/1315, no. 64k, 10 March 1943, report by Stephens containing interrogation transcripts.

10 KV 2/24, no. 9a, 2 February 1941, report by Stephens.

11 Masterman, J.C., *The Double-Cross System in the War of 1939 to 1945* (New Haven and London: Yale University Press, 1972) p.49.

12 KV 2/27, no. 16a, 17 June 1941, association report between Richter and Josef.

13 KV 2/25, no. 88b, 6 June 1941, memo from Stephens to Dick White. KV 2/25, no. 94b, 16 June 1941, report by Sampson.

14 Stephens, R.W.G., and Oliver Hoare (ed.), *Camp 020: MI5 and the Nazi Spies* (London: Public Record Office Publications, 2000) pp.57–58.

15 KV 2/27, no. 12a, 18 June 1941, memo re: Hinchley-Cooke requesting Josef.

16 Ibid,

17 Castelfranchi, C., and M. Guerini, 'Is it a promise or a threat?', *Pragmatics and Cognition*, Vol. 15 (2), 2007, pp.277–311 (also published in 2006 as ITC-Irst Technical report T06-01-01).

18 KV 2/11, no. 6a, 5 September 1940, interrogation transcript serial no. 188.

19 Ibid.

20 KV 2/107, no. 39a, 5 February 1942, liquidation report on Waldberg, Meier, Pons and Kieboom.

21 Hinsley, F.H., and C.A.G. Simkins, *British Military Intelligence in the Second World War, Vol. 4, Security and Counter-Intelligence* (New York: Cambridge University Press, 1990) p.97.

22 Marcus, Paul, 'It's not just about Miranda: Determining Voluntariness of Confessions in Criminal Prosecutions', *Valparaiso University Law Review*, Vol. 40 (3), p.630.

23 Ibid.

52 – Rule of Law

1 HO 144/21636, 12 June 1941, Central Criminal Court proceedings, Day 1, p.2.

2 Ibid.

3 Ibid., p.4. Crown counsel in this case was the Solicitor General William Jowitt, the deputy to the AG.

4 HO 144/21636, no number, 28 July 1941, unsigned note regarding The Hague Convention.

5 HO 144/21636, no number, 1 August 1941, letter to Blackwell.

6 Ibid.

7 HO 144/21636, no number, 4 August 1941, letter from Whitebrook to Undersecretary of State.

8 KV 2/32, 21 October 1941, Criminal Court proceedings.

9 KV 2/1700, no number, 31 October 1941, memo from Marriott to Stringer. The notebook was apparently found although it was green, not grey.

10 KV 2/26, no number, 25 February 1941, letter from Butler to Ryde.

11 KV 2/32, no. 10a, 14 August 1941, memo from SLB (Hinchley-Cooke's office) to Milmo.

53 – Inefficient Germans

1 KV 4/187, 8 September 1940, Guy Liddell diary entry.

2 Ibid.

3 Ibid.

4 KV 2/15, no. 90a, 26 February 1942, note from Dick White to Petrie.

5 HO 144/21636, 13 June 1941, Central Criminal Court proceedings, Day 2, p.43.

6 KV 2/449, no. 999b, 10 October 1940, report by W2a.

7 KV 2/12, no. 9a, 11 September 1940, summary of conversation between Meier and Waldberg.

8 KV 2/12, no. 12a, 14 September 1940, summary report by Evans.

9 KV 2/449, no. 999b, 10 October 1940, report by Marriott regarding identity cards. I have added the identity card information of Fukken, Josef and Richter to complete the list.

10 KV 4/187, 2 February 1941, Guy Liddell diary entry.

11 Bryden, John, *Fighting to Lose* (Toronto: Dundurn Press, 2014) p.189.

12 CAB 154/105, 1945, report by H.R. Trevor-Roper, 'The German Intelligence Service and the War', pp.9–12.

13 Siedentopf, Monika, *Unternehmen Seelöwe* (München: Deutscher Taschenbuch Verlag, 2014).

14 Ibid., p.50.

15 Ibid., p.80.

16 Ibid., p.82.

17 As quoted in Brown, Anthony Cave, *Bodyguard of Lies* (New York: Bantam Books, 1975) p.207.

18 Siedentopf, Monika, *Unternehmen Seelöwe* (München: Deutscher Taschenbuch Verlag, 2014) p.147.

19 Ibid., p.152.

20 Ibid., p.116.

21 Bryden, John, *Fighting to Lose* (Toronto: Dundurn Press, 2014) p.44.

22 Ibid., p.149.

23 Ibid.

24 Indeed, Druecke and Walti's identity cards were not written in Continental fashion – as seen in KV 2/1705.

25 The identity cards of Fukken, Josef and Richter all had an English '1', whereas those of Druecke and Walti both had a German '1'.

26 Bryden, John, *Fighting to Lose* (Toronto: Dundurn Press, 2014) p.135.

27 Ibid., p.161.

28 Ibid., p.231.

29 Ibid., p.232.

30 Ibid., p.287.

31 Farago, Ladislas, *The Game of the Foxes* (New York: David McKay & Co., 1971) p.272.

54 – Caught in a Web

1 Hayward, James, *Double Agent Snow* (London: Simon & Schuster, 2013) p.216.

2 KV 2/26, no. 121a, 24 January 1946, extract from interrogation of Richter at Bad Oeynhausen. Siedentopf references TNA: KV 2/87 in stating that Josef and Richter were discovered by Emil (Bobby) Bender in 1940. Siedentopf, Monika, *Unternehmen Seelöwe* (München: Deutscher Taschenbuch Verlag, 2014) p.154.

3 KV 2/1964, no. 3b, 4 September 1945, extract from interrogation report of Helmut Oliver.

4 KV 2/1964, no. 2b, 27 February 1946, extract from 1 August 1945 interrogation of Ernst Otto Rodenberg.

5 KV 2/1964, no. 3, 5 January 1950, letter from Intelligence Division (BAOR) to unknown recipient.

6 During his interrogation on 16 April 1941, Josef claimed that he had paid for his training himself and that it had cost him 4,000 RM (equivalent value in 2014 about £13,000). KV 2/25, 65a, 16 April 1941, statement by Josef.

7 Equivalent value in 2014 approximately £640.

8 KV 2/26, no. 96b, 23 June 1941, report by Sampson. Note that folio no. 96b is not complete in the downloadable document from the National Archives. Sampson's interrogation report from 23 June 1941 is missing. The photocopies that I purchased in 2003 include this report.

9 KV 2/25, no.65a, 16 April 1941, statement by Josef.

10 KV 2/25, no. 68a, 25 April 1941, report by Sampson. According to Josef, Boeckel had met Josef's wife and children.

11 KV 4/16, December 1940, German Secret Service, Report No. 2, p.7.

12 West, Nigel, *The Guy Liddell Diaries, Volume 1: 1939–1942* (Abingdon: Routledge, 2005) entry from 25 May 1940, p.83.

13 Simpson, A.W. Brian, *In the Highest Degree Odious* (Oxford: Clarendon Press, 1992) p.409.

14 Ibid., p.410.

15 Masterman, J.C., *The Double-Cross System in the War of 1939 to 1945* (New Haven and London: Yale University Press, 1972) p.54.

16 KV 2/551, no. 58b, 3 July 1944, memo by Milmo.

17 Hinsley, F.H., and C.A.G. Simkins, *British Military Intelligence in the Second World War, Vol. 4, Security and Counter-Intelligence* (New York: Cambridge University Press, 1990) p.97.

Epilogue

1 Grew, Benjamin Dixon, *Prison Governor* (London: Herbert Jenkins Ltd, 1958) p.124.

2 Jakobs family documents, 1941 day planner of Margarete (née Knöffler) Jakobs. '*Heute ist unsere 15th Hochzeitstag und was liegt alles hinter mir leider sehr viel trauriges und wenig schönes. Noch immer ohne jede nachricht. Ob du auch ein wenig an mich denkst? Wo magst du sein?*'

3 Jakobs family documents, 1941 day planner of Margarete (née Knöffler) Jakobs. '*Sechs monate schon kein lebenszeichen. Es ist schrecklich. Und wie lange noch? Es ist manchmal nicht aus zuhalten. Mann ist in vielen so schrecklich allein, da können die Kinder auch nicht immer da sein und können auch nicht helfen. Es bleibt mir wirklich nichts erspart.*'

4 There is some debate as to whether or not the lint circle held at the Guards Museum is actually the one used at Josef's execution. The note accompanying the disc states that it was collected by Guardsman C.V.T. Gordon. Gordon was a guardsman during the First World War. In 1918, he received a commission with the South Staffordshire Regiment. During 1940 and 1941, he was commander of the Infantry Training Centre (Lichfield) of the South Staffordshire Regiment. It is very unlikely that he was present at Josef's execution, nor was he a guardsman in 1941. Gordon's daughter, Collinette Compton, has her father's diaries which state that he was present at the executions of First World War spies. In addition, Bridget Clifford, archivist at the Royal Armouries, states that a relation of the one of the Scots Guards present at Josef's execution has the target and the ropes used to bind Josef to the chair.

Appendix I – Josef's Personal Property

1 KV 2/24, no. 7a, 2 February 1941, property list sent from Robertson to Butler. KV 2/24, no. 20b, no date, list of property compiled by Huntingdonshire Constabulary. KV 2/27, no. 11a, 3 February 1941, report by Mills. Rivett-Carnac letter dated 17 February 1941, as reproduced in Dodman, Dave, and Roy Dudley, *Huntingdon County Police: A Brief History of the Force and Those Who Served with Honour (1857–1965)* (privately published by Dave Dodman, 2003) pp.129–31. KV 2/26, no. 2a, 13 February 1941, report by Humphreys. KV 2/25, no. 82a, 15 May 1941, letter from Stephens to Milmo. KV 2/27, no. 26a, 22 July 1941, letter from Stimson to Cussen. KV 2/27, no number, 22 July 1941, Robertson's list from 2 February 1941 with handwritten comments by Cussen.

2 As identified by Ben Nock of the Military Wireless Museum, based on Humphrey's report and circuit diagrams.

BIBLIOGRAPHY

Primary Sources

The National Archives (TNA)

CAB – Cabinet Office: CAB 114/17, CAB 114/51, CAB 65/10/22, CAB 93/5, CAB 93/6/2, CAB 93/7.

CRIM – Central Criminal Court: CRIM 1/1243, CRIM 1/1307, CRIM 1/1350, CRIM 1/1365, CRIM 1/1454, CRIM 1/1604.

HO – Home Office: HO 144/21471, HO 144/21472, HO 144/21576, HO 144/21636, HO 144/21664, HO 144/22039, HO 382/74, HO 45/19086, HO 45/22382, HO 45/23662, HO 45/25595, HO 45/25606.

J – Supreme Court Judicature: J 77/3611/1933.

KV – Security Service: KV 2/11, KV 2/12, KV 2/13, KV 2/14, KV 2/15, KV 2/16, KV 2/17, KV 2/18, KV 2/19, KV 2/20, KV 2/21, KV 2/22, KV 2/23, KV 2/24, KV 2/25, KV 2/26, KV 2/27, KV 2/30, KV 2/31, KV 2/32, KV 2/33, KV 2/43, KV 2/44, KV 2/45, KV 2/46, KV 2/47, KV 2/48, KV 2/49, KV 2/53, KV 2/54, KV 2/55, KV 2/56, KV 2/60, KV 2/61, KV 2/62, KV 2/85, KV 2/86, KV 2/87, KV 2/88, KV 2/103, KV 2/107, KV 2/114, KV 2/125, KV 2/170, KV 2/449, KV 2/451, KV 2/551, KV 2/1067, KV 2/1068, KV 2/1211, KV 2/1315, KV 2/1316, KV 2/1333, KV 2/1452, KV 2/1699, KV 2/1700, KV 2/1701, KV 2/1702, KV 2/1703, KV 2/1704, KV 2/1705, KV 2/1706, KV 2/1708, KV 2/1936, KV 2/1964, KV 2/2593, KV 2/3319, KV 2/3320, KV 2/3321, KV 3/205, KV 3/206, KV 4/8, KV 4/13, KV 4/14, KV 4/15, KV 4/16, KV 4/19, KV 4/22, KV 4/63, KV 4/80, KV 4/81, KV 4/82, KV 4/115, KV 4/187, KV 4/188, KV 4/189, KV 4/192, KV 4/406, KV 4/407, KV 4/465, KV 4/476.

LCO – Lord Chancellor's Office: LCO 2/1383, LCO 53/54.

MEPO – Metropolitan Police: MEPO 4/127, MEPO 4/189, MEPO 4/338, MEPO 4/350, MEPO 4/351, MEPO 4/358, MEPO 4/359.

PCOM – Prison Commission and Home Office: PCOM 9/890, PCOM 9/909.

PREM – Prime Minister's Office: PREM 3/418/2.

RG – General Register Office: RG 48/1731.

WO – War Office: WO 208/5227, WO 32/18144, WO 32/21943, WO 71/1240, WO 81/170, WO 208/5227.

WORK – Office of Works: WORK 31/813.

London Metropolitan Archives (LMA)

HM Prison Wandsworth Records: Administration: ACC/3444/AD/08/001, ACC/3444/
　　AD/08/003, ACC/3444/AD/07/001.
HM Prison Wandsworth Records: Medical Records: ACC/3444/ME/01/001.
HM Prison Wandsworth Records: Prisoners: ACC/3444/PR/03/002, ACC/3444/
　　PR/02/002, ACC/3444/PR/04/012, ACC/3444/PR/04/019.

Other Archives

Hansard Parliamentary Debate Records
HM Prison Wandsworth Archives
Museum of Army Chaplaincy
Royal Military Police Museum
Royal Armouries Archives
Scots Guards Museum Archives

Private Papers

Chidlow, William, 'A Second World War Guardsman's True Story' (unpublished, 2001).
Jakobs family documents.

Secondary Sources

Andrew, Christopher, *The Defence of the Realm* (Toronto: Penguin Group, 2009).
Bassett, Richard, *Hitler's Spy Chief: The Wilhelm Canaris Mystery* (London: Orion Books,
　　2005), ebook.
Beeby, Dean, *Cargo of Lies: The True Story of a Nazi Double Agent in Canada* (Toronto:
　　University of Toronto Press, 1996).
Bobrick, Benson, *A Passion for Victory* (New York: Alfred A. Knopf, 2012).
Brown, Anthony Cave, *Bodyguard of Lies* (New York: Bantam Books, 1975).
Browne, Douglas G., and E.V. Tullett, *The Scalpel of Scotland Yard: The Life of Sir Bernard
　　Spilsbury* (New York: E.P. Dutton and Company, Inc., 1952).
Bryden, John, *Fighting to Lose* (Toronto: Dundurn Press, 2014).
Cobain, Ian, *Cruel Britannia* (London: Portobello Books, 2012).
Cobain, Ian, *The History Thieves: Secrets, Lies and the Shaping of a Modern Nation* (London:
　　Portobello Books, 2016).
Colvin, Ian, *Master Spy: The Incredible Story of Admiral Wilhelm Canaris, Who, While Hitler's
　　Chief of Intelligence was a Secret Ally of the British* (New York: McGraw-Hill, 1951).
Crowdy, Terry, *Deceiving Hitler: Double Cross and Deception in World War II* (Oxford: Osprey
　　Publishing, 2008), ebook.
Dearden, Harold, *Medicine and Duty* (Kingswood: The Windmill Press, 1928).
Dearden, Harold, *Time and Chance* (London: William Heinemann, 1940).
Dearden, Harold, *Some Cases of Sir Bernard Spilsbury and Others: Death under the Microscope*
　　(London: Hutchison, 1948).
Dodman, Dave, and Roy Dudley, *Huntingdon County Police: A Brief History of the Force and
　　Those Who Served with Honour (1857–1965)* (privately published by Dave Dodman, 2003).
Elliott, Geoffrey, *Gentleman Spymaster* (London: Methuen, 2011).
Farago, Ladislas, *The Game of the Foxes* (New York: David McKay & Co., 1971).
Felstead, Sidney Theodore, *German Spies at Bay* (New York: Bretano's, 1920).

Fry, Helen, *The London Cage: The Secret History of Britain's World War II Interrogation Centre* (New Haven and London: Yale University Press, 2017).

Grew, Benjamin Dixon, *Prison Governor* (London: Herbert Jenkins Ltd, 1958).

Hayward, James, *Double Agent SNOW* (London: Simon & Schuster, 2013).

Hinsley, F.H., and C.A.G. Simkins, *British Military Intelligence in the Second World War, Vol. 4, Security and Counter-Intelligence* (New York: Cambridge University Press, 1990).

Hinsley, F.H., and Michael Howard, *British Military Intelligence in the Second World War, Vol. 5, Strategic Deception* (New York: Cambridge University Press, 1990).

Jackson, Sophie, *British Interrogation Techniques in the Second World War* (Stroud: The History Press, 2012), ebook.

Jonason, Tommy, and Simon Olsson, *Agent TATE* (Stroud: Amberley Publishing, 2011).

Kahn, David, *Hitler's Spies* (New York: Macmillan, 1978).

Kluiters, Frans, De Abwehr in Nederland (1936-1945) (unpublished manuscript, 2006), ebook - available at https://www.nisa-intelligence.nl/contributions.htm

Leimbach, Berthold, *Tondokumente der Kleinkunst und ihre Interpreten 1898–1945* (Göttingen: Leimbach, 1991).

Leverkuehn, Paul, *German Military Intelligence*, trans. R.H. Stevens and Constantine FitzGibbon. (London: Weidenfeld and Nicolson, 1954)

Levine, Joshua, *Operation Fortitude* (London: HarperCollins, 2011).

McCormick, Donald, *Murder by Witchcraft: A Study of the Lower Quinton and Hagley Wood Murders* (London: Arrow Books, 1968).

Macintyre, Ben, *Agent Zigzag* (London: Bloomsbury, 2007).

Macintyre, Ben, *Double Cross: The True Story of the D-Day Spies* (New York: Crown Publishers, 2012), ebook.

McKinstry, Leo, *Operation Sealion: How Britain Crushed the German War Machine's Dreams of Invasion in 1940* (London: John Murray Publishers, 2014), ebook.

Macrakis, Kristie, *Prisoners, Lovers, and Spies: The Story of Invisible Ink from Herodotus to al-Qaeda* (New Haven and London: Yale University Press, 2014), ebook.

Masterman, J.C., *The Double-Cross System in the War of 1939 to 1945* (New Haven and London: Yale University Press, 1972).

Nash, Jay Robert, *Spies: A Narrative Encyclopedia of Dirty Deeds & Double Dealing from Biblical Times to Today* (New York: M. Evans and Company, Inc., 1997).

Ohler, Norman, *Blitzed: Drugs in Nazi Germany* (Penguin Books: London, 2017).

Paine, Lauran, *German Military Intelligence in World War II – The Abwehr* (Briarcliff Manor: Stein and Day, 1984).

Pickett, Carroll (with Carlton Stowers), *Within these Walls: Memoirs of a Death House Chaplain* (New York: St Martin's Press, 2002).

Pierrepoint, Albert, *Executioner Pierrepoint* (London: George C. Harrap, 1974),

Price, Siân, *If You're Reading This … Last Letters from the Front Line* (London: Frontline Books, 2011).

Ritter, K.F., *Aurora* (Bloomington: Xlibris, 2006).

Ritter, Nikolaus, *Deckname Dr Rantzu: Die Aufzeichnungen des Nikolaus Ritter, Offizier im Geheimen Nachrichtendienst* (Hamburg: Hoffmann und Campe Verlag, 1972).

Rose, Andrew, *Lethal Witness: Sir Bernard Spilsbury, Honorary Pathologist* (Kent, OH: Kent State University Press, 2007), ebook.

Scotland, A.P., *The London Cage* (London: Evans Brothers Ltd, 1957).

Searle, Adrian, *The Spy Beside the Sea: The Extraordinary Wartime Story of Dorothy O'Grady* (Stroud: The History Press, 2012), ebook.

Sellers, Leonard, *Shot in the Tower* (London: Leo Cooper, 1997).

Siedentopf, Monika, *Unternehmen Seelöwe* (München: Deutscher Taschenbuch Verlag, 2014).

Simpson, A.W. Brian, *In the Highest Degree Odious* (Oxford: Clarendon Press, 1992).

Stephen, J.F., *A History of the Criminal Law in England, Volume 1* (London: Macmillan & Co., 1883).

Stephen, J.F., *A Digest of the Law of Evidence* (New York: George Chase, 1885).

Stephens, R.W.G., and Oliver Hoare (ed.), *Camp 020: MI5 and the Nazi Spies* (London: Public Record Office Publications, 2000).

War Office, *Manual of Military Law, 1929* (London: His Majesty's Stationery Office, 1929 and 1940 addenda).

War Office, *Provost Training in Peace and War* (London: His Majesty's Publishing Stationery Office, 1950).

Tremain, David, *Rough Justice: The True Story of Agent Dronkers, the Dutch Spy captured by the British* (Stroud: Amberley, 2016).

Webb, Simon, *Execution – A History of Capital Punishment in Britain* (Stroud: The History Press, 2011).

West, Nigel, *The Guy Liddell Diaries, Volume 1: 1939–1942* (Abingdon: Routledge, 2005).

West, Nigel, *The Guy Liddell Diaries, Volume 2: 1942–1945* (Abingdon: Routledge, 2005).

West, Nigel, *MI5: British Security Operations 1909–1945* (Briarcliff Manor: Stein and Day, 1982).

West, Nigel, *Historical Dictionary of World War II Intelligence* (Lanham: Scarecrow Press, 2008).

West, Nigel, *Historical Dictionary of British Intelligence* (Lanham: Scarecrow Press, 2014).

West, Nigel (ed.), *MI5 in the Great War* (London: Biteback Publishing Ltd, 2014), ebook.

West, Nigel, and Madoc Roberts, *SNOW: The Double Life of a World War II Spy* (London: Biteback Publishing Ltd, 2011).

Wighton, Charles, and Günther Peis, *Hitler's Spies and Saboteurs* (New York: Charter Books, 1958).

Witt, Carolinda, *Double Agent CELERY: MI5's Crooked Hero* (Barnsley, Pen & Sword Books Ltd, 2017).

Articles and Websites

Castelfranchi, C., and M. Guerini, 'Is it a promise or a threat?', *Pragmatics and Cognition*, Vol. 15 (2), 2007, pp.277–311 (also published in 2006 as ITC-Irst Technical report T06-01-01).

Daily Express, 'Dandy Joseph, Spy in Spats, Caught by H.G.', 16 August 1941.

Deutsche Verlustlisten 1905. Ausgabe. 21/05/1918. Accessed online via http://www.wbc. poznan.pl/dlibra/publication/182816?tab=1

Marcus, Paul, 'It's not just about Miranda: Determining Voluntariness of Confessions in Criminal Prosecutions', *Valparaiso University Law Review*, Vol. 40 (3), p.630.

Ramsey, Winston, 'German Spies in Britain', *After the Battle*, Vol. 11, pp.1–34.

Seaborne Davies, D., 'The Treachery Act, 1940', *Modern Law Review*, Vol. 4 (3), 1941, p.218.

Simpson, A.W. Brian, 'Trials in camera in security cases', in *Domestic and International Trials, 1700–2000 – The Trial in History, Vol. 2*, R.A. Melikan (ed) (Manchester: Manchester University Press) 2003, Ch. 5, pp.75–106.

Wikipedia – http://de.wikipedia.org/wiki/4._Garde-Regiment_zu_Fu%C3%9F

INDEX